THE WAR AGAINST DOMESTIC VIOLENCE

THE WAR AGAINST DOMESTIC VIOLENCE

EDITED BY **LEE E. ROSS, Ph.D.**

CRC Press
Taylor & Francis Group
Boca Raton London New York

CRC Press is an imprint of the
Taylor & Francis Group, an **informa** business

CRC Press
Taylor & Francis Group
6000 Broken Sound Parkway NW, Suite 300
Boca Raton, FL 33487-2742

© 2010 by Taylor and Francis Group, LLC
CRC Press is an imprint of Taylor & Francis Group, an Informa business

No claim to original U.S. Government works

Printed in the United States of America on acid-free paper
10 9 8 7 6 5 4 3 2 1

International Standard Book Number: 978-1-4398-0048-5 (Hardback)

Library of Congress Cataloging-in-Publication Data

The war against domestic violence / editor, Lee E. Ross.
     p. cm.
   Includes bibliographical references and index.
   ISBN 978-1-4398-0048-5 (alk. paper)
     1. Family violence--Cross-cultural studies. I. Ross, Lee E., 1958-

   HV6626.W35 2010
   362.82'92--dc22   2009043844

Visit the Taylor & Francis Web site at
http://www.taylorandfrancis.com

and the CRC Press Web site at
http://www.crcpress.com

This book is dedicated to

Barbara Pollack, formerly of the Milwaukee Task Force on Family Violence, whose tireless efforts to re-educate those who choose violence, has touched and enriched the lives of so many. She is a mentor, a colleague, and most importantly, a good friend.

All current and former students who espouse a philosophy of nonviolence and who respect themselves and others around them.

Leslie, Christopher, and Alexander: pleasant reminders of God's goodness and grace.

Table of Contents

Acknowledgments

I am indebted to the many people who have generously shared their time and knowledge in the preparation of this collection. The collaborative friendship of my colleagues who contributed the excellent chapters in this book is sincerely appreciated. I wish to extend a special thanks to the staff at CRC Press-Taylor & Francis Group, including Judith Simon (project editor), David Fausel (project coordinator), Andrea Grant (editorial assistant), and Carolyn Spence (acquisitions editor). By far, writing this book was a pleasant and satisfying experience—from submitting a prospectus to witnessing the final product.

The Editor

Dr. Lee E. Ross is associate professor of criminal justice at the University of Central Florida. A graduate of Rutgers University, his research interests span a variety of areas, from his seminal work on religion and social control theory to more recent explorations into unintended consequences of mandatory arrest policies and the dynamics of domestic violence among African Americans. As editor of *African-American Criminologists: 1970–1996, An Annotated Bibliography*, his scholarship can be found in a variety of academic journals, including *Justice Quarterly, Journal of Criminal Justice, Journal of Crime and Justice, Journal of Criminal Justice Education, The Justice Professional, Sociological Spectrum, Sociological Focus,* and *Corrections Today.* Professor Ross also spent several years as a group facilitator to the Milwaukee Domestic Abuse Intervention Program, while teaching graduate and undergraduate courses in the area of domestic violence.

The Contributors

Dr. Julie C. Abril earned her PhD in criminology, law, and society at the University of California, Irvine. She has published widely in the area of Native American Indian crime and justice. She is the author of *Bad Spirits: A Cultural Explanation for Intimate Family Violence: Inside One American Indian Family* (UK: CSP), *Violent Victimization Among One Native American Indian Tribe* (DE: VDM Verlag: Germany), and *Crime and Violence on One Native American Indian Reservation: A Criminological Study of the Southern Ute Indians* (VDM Verlag: Germany).

Dr. Allen Anderson received his PhD in political science, with a specialization in public law and judicial process, from Southern Illinois University in 1984. He has since expanded his study into public health, with a certification from the University of North Carolina–Chapel Hill, and continuing education from both the University of Michigan and Johns Hopkins University. Combining these backgrounds, he has researched HIV/AIDS policies and behaviors in the People's Republic of China since 1990. His research has focused on prisoners, drug abuse, prostitution, internal migration, and general sexual transmission of the AIDS virus. He made his 19th research trip to China in November 2008. Anderson is now working with both the Chinese Foundation for the Prevention of STD and AIDS and the Chinese Ministry of Justice on controlling HIV/AIDS in the mainland prison environment. His domestic research has focused on judicial behavior, plea negotiation, child advocacy, and criminal law.

Dr. Charlene K. Baker is an associate professor of community psychology in the Department of Psychology at the University of Hawai'i at Mānoa. Her research interests include working in collaboration with communities to develop and evaluate culturally appropriate prevention and intervention programs aimed at reducing the prevalence and impact of violence on individuals, families, and communities. Her work also emphasizes the relationship between domestic violence and housing instability, including homelessness, and advocates for policy and programmatic solutions to address these two intersecting social issues.

Dr. Tricia B. Bent-Goodley is professor of social work at Howard University School. A graduate of Columbia University, Dr. Goodley's research has focused on violence against women and girls, HIV prevention, and healthy relationship education. She has developed community and faith-based interventions in domestic violence and relationship education with a focus on strengthening the Black family and the development of culturally competent interventions that build on the strengths of the community. She is the author or co-author of three books in the area of social policy and people of color, is a consulting editor for several scholarly journals, and serves distinctly in a number of local, state, and national elected and appointed leadership positions.

Dr. Christopher W. Blackwell is an assistant professor of graduate affairs within the College of Nursing at the University of Central Florida. His research focus is on health and social disparities experienced by gay, lesbian, bisexual, and transgender persons in American society. His work has been widely published in a variety of scholarly journals and textbooks. In addition to teaching and research, Dr. Blackwell is also a board-certified adult health nurse practitioner and maintains a clinical practice in pulmonary critical care in the Orlando, Florida, area. For more information, visit Dr. Blackwell's professional Web site: http://www.drchristopher.blackwell.com

Dr. Rebecca Bonanno is a New York State-licensed social worker currently working in clinical practice with children and adolescents. She received both her master's in social work and PhD in social welfare at the School of Social Welfare at Stony Brook University in 2003 and 2008, respectively. Dr. Bonanno has conducted research on alternatives to incarceration, including batterer intervention programs, with the Suffolk County Department of Probation on Long Island, New York, and has contributed to studies on parenting and intimate partner abuse. Dr. Bonanno is an adjunct professor at Adelphi University's School of Social Work.

Dr. Leanor Boulin Johnson is professor of African and African American studies in the School of Social Transformation at Arizona State University. A graduate of Purdue University, her main research activities have been in Black family studies, cross-cultural sexuality, and work-family stress. In addition, she is an associate editor of the *Journal of Family Relations*, a consulting editor for the *Journal of Sex Research,* and a reviewer for several other journals. She is also co-author of *Black Families at the Crossroads: Challenges and Prospects.*

Dr. Cynthia Brown is an assistant professor in the Department of Criminal Justice and Legal Studies at the University of Central Florida. A graduate of Mississippi College of Law, she teaches law and the legal environment, law and society, employment discrimination, and contracts. Over the course of the last 15 years, she has provided continuing legal education in the area of domestic violence, while at the same time serving as a Guardian ad Litem. In 2006, she received a doctorate in the administration of criminal justice from the University of Southern Mississippi.

John V. Elmore, Esq. is a practicing criminal defense attorney with offices in Buffalo and Niagara Falls, New York. He is a former New York State trooper, Manhattan assistant district attorney, and New York State assistant attorney general. He has taught criminal justice administration at Buffalo State College and Medaille College. A graduate of Mansfield State University, Attorney Elmore went on to earn a JD from the Syracuse University College of Law. He is also a member of the U.S. Magistrate Selection Committee for the U.S. District Court for the Western District of New York, and a life member of the NAACP. John V. Elmore is the author of *Fighting for Your Life: An African-American Criminal Justice Survival Guide.*

Gina Farrell graduated from the University of Minnesota Duluth with a master's degree in social work in May 2009. She completed a master's research project exploring the child welfare response to co-occurring domestic violence and child maltreatment at a county child protection agency. Ms. Farrell has extensive work experience related to family violence. For the last seven years she has been involved in the domestic violence movement as an advocate, an educator, and program coordinator. She is passionate about working toward equality and justice for all people.

Lynette Feder is a professor in the College of Liberal Arts and Sciences at Portland State University. She has evaluated a wide array of interventions including the police, courts, corrections, and social service agencies. Her recent focus has been to conduct applied research on specific interventions that are methodologically rigorous so as to address both policy questions (evidence-based policy) as well as underlying theoretical issues. In this way, her research attempts to build the knowledge base to aid in the development of future programs and policies while simultaneously answering specific questions about the effectiveness of a particular program. Her two recent experimental studies (The Broward Experiment and the A Test of the Enhanced Nurse Family Partnership), serve as recent examples of this evaluative approach. Dr. Feder has also served as a guest editor for a special issue on domestic violence (*Women and Criminal Justice*) and co-guest editor (with Dr. Robert Boruch) for a special issue on the need for experimental research to guide evidence-based decision-making in criminal justice (*Crime & Delinquency*).

Dr. Shirley Garick has been in the nursing field for 35 years. She has multiple expertise in many areas, including domestic violence, patient safety, drug addiction, and legal consulting. Her primary role as a researcher and professor directs many of her activities within the health care arena. Some of her other activities involve volunteer work for legal aid and help with students' understanding of the priorities of domestic violence and substance abuse within the health care field.

Dr. Debra Heath-Thornton is professor and dean of the Campolo College of Graduate and Professional Studies at Eastern University. A graduate of the University of Rochester, her research interests include comparative justice and restorative justice. She has taught a variety of courses, including restorative justice, social problems, principles of sociology, and comparative criminal justice. One of her areas of expertise is the integration of faith and learning.

Dr. Josephine Kahler is a professor of nursing and founding dean of the College of Health and Behavioral Sciences at Texas A&M University–Texarkana. She earned a doctorate in nursing education administration from the University of South Dakota in 1990 and a master's in nursing from South Dakota State University. She is certified as a clinical nurse specialist in adult mental health nursing and has taught and done clinical practice in this specialty area for many years. Dr. Kahler, originally from New Zealand, lived in many different parts of the world and brings unique perspectives and insight to the behavioral science disciplines.

Dr. Sarah N. Keller has an expertise in public health communication and evaluation. As part of her dissertation at the University of North Carolina–Chapel Hill, she developed and tested a tailored Internet-based health communication intervention to promote adolescent girls' sexual health and a national STD prevention Web site aimed at teenagers. Her research has been published in the *Journal of Health Communication*, the *Journal of Sex Research*, and the international journal *Nursing & Health Science*. In teaching, Dr. Keller is no less committed to public health. She dedicates a class each year to designing and implementing a social marketing campaign.

Dr. Joanne Klevens is an epidemiologist currently at the Division of Violence Prevention, National Center for Injury Prevention and Control, and Centers for Disease Control in Atlanta, Georgia. She works on the development and evaluation of interventions to prevent child maltreatment and intimate partner violence. Dr. Klevens has also done studies on risk factors and preventive interventions for youth violence, adult criminality, and child abuse in Colombia.

Walter Komanski, Esq. is a circuit court judge in Orange County, Florida. For nearly 30 years he has served in various judicial capacities for Orange County, including domestic, circuit, civil, juvenile, and criminal court. A member of the first graduating class of the University of Central Florida, Komanski earned a juris doctor from John Marshall Law School. He is a faculty member of the Florida Judicial Education Committee, an adjunct professor at the University of Central Florida, and a lecturer at Rollins College and Valencia Community College.

Robert T. Magill, Esq. earned his law degree from the Florida A&M University College of Law in the spring of 2009. He has worked in the legal field for over 20 years with his attorney father, Patrick Magill, focusing mainly on commercial litigation and family law. Robert served as a law clerk for Circuit Judge Walter Komanski in the Domestic Relations Division, hearing Domestic violence and high-conflict family law cases in the Ninth Judicial Circuit of the State of Florida. Currently he is teaching at the University of Central Florida.

Dr. Godpower O. Okereke is a professor of sociology and criminal justice at Texas A&M University–Texarkana, where he teaches sociology and criminal justice courses at both the undergraduate and graduate levels. He received his doctorate degree in sociology with concentrations in criminology, social problems/deviance, social psychology, and law enforcement from Oklahoma State University. His research interests and publications cover a broad spectrum of subjects in fields such as sociology, criminal justice, criminology, social psychology, economics, and political economy.

Dr. A. J. Otjen is an assistant professor of marketing and serves as advisor to American Indian Business Leaders. Some of her research endeavors include self-actualization as a test of equality, and gender-specific reactions to a domestic violence campaign. In 2006, her marketing in Domestic and Sexual Violence Campaign was a winner of six Addys Awards.

Dr. Peter Racheotes, a university professor for the past 28 years, is involved in the graduate training of both professional and public school counselors. A graduate of the University of Massachusetts, he has gained expertise in the area of health psychology emphasizing both the prevention of disease and the promotion of health. Currently, Dr. Racheotes works as a therapist and group facilitator in the Batterer's Intervention Program with Domestic Violence Prevention in Texarkana. His research interests are in the area of domestic violence, the judicial system responsibility, and the effects of violence and abuse on children, both cognitively and psychosocially.

Dr. Elizabeth M. Rash is an assistant professor in the College of Nursing at the University of Central Florida and a practicing family nurse practitioner. She has a bachelor's degree in nursing from the University of Central Florida, a master's degree in nursing in the area of family nurse practitioner from the University of Florida, and a doctoral degree in education with a concentration in health care from the University of Central Florida. Her areas of focus have been in wellness and health promotion, with an emphasis on patient empowerment. Her research has included perceptions of sexual offenders in primary health care.

Dr. Melanie Shepard is a professor of social work at the University of Minnesota Duluth. She has conducted and published numerous research studies primarily in the field of domestic violence, and co-edited the book *Coordinating Community Responses to Domestic Violence: Lessons From Duluth and Beyond.* Dr. Shepard has taught primarily graduate-level social work students for the past 25 years and has practiced social work in the fields of mental health, child welfare, and domestic violence.

Dr. Mark A. Winton is an instructor with the Department of Criminal Justice and Legal Studies at the University of Central Florida. He teaches in the graduate program and has developed courses on genocide, family violence, and mental illness and violence. He co-authored a textbook with Dr. Barbara A. Mara on child abuse and neglect. He has a doctorate in sociology from the University of Connecticut and is a licensed mental health counselor in the State of Florida and a national certified counselor.

Dr. Qiang Xu is an assistant professor in the Department of Criminal Justice at Indiana University—South Bend. He received his PhD from Bowling Green State University in 2006, with a major in criminology and deviance and a minor in statistics and quantitative methods. His teaching and research interests include criminological theories, quantitative research methods, comparative perspective of criminal justice systems, gender and race differences in crime, and the applications of geographic information systems (GIS).

Introduction

The War Against Domestic Violence is an edited compilation of chapters concerning various aspects of domestic violence and responses of criminal and social justice systems. Included here are topics rarely found (and discussed) in previous texts. These chapters devote considerable attention toward the experiences and perspectives of criminal and social justice practitioners alongside researchers, child welfare workers, and other renowned scholars across disciplines. In the process, it offers a comprehensive interdisciplinary array of topics bound to stimulate the interest of a diverse audience. One of its major strengths lies in its ability to inform and promote a contemporary understanding of phenomena that are not only dynamic and complex, but also equally difficult to remedy. Overall, the variety in this volume will help readers to appreciate the overwhelming nature of domestic violence and to create strategies to combat its continued rise.

In a society seeking to understand the role of ethnic diversity, pluralism, and differences within and across cultures, nowhere is the need greater than in the area of domestic violence. Like cancer and other diseases that invade and destroy the human body, domestic violence does not discriminate among its victims. Transcending race, ethnicity, gender, culture, age, and social class, it can attack without warning, leaving a path of destruction that claims the lives of mostly women, sometimes men, and far too often innocent children. This reality has led many to conclude that anyone can become a victim of domestic violence. As such, it is incumbent on all of us to help wage a war against domestic violence. But even in doing so, there is disagreement regarding degrees of perceived vulnerability, appreciable harm, and similarity of risk factors among potential victims of different racial and ethnic persuasions. Who is at greater risk for intimate partner homicide? What are some differences in the dynamics of domestic violence between heterosexual, homosexual, lesbian, and transgendered populations? How do rates of domestic violence compare across racial and ethnic groups? Do certain ethnic groups share similar risk factors for domestic violence? What happens to police officers who victimize and physically abuse their partner? Are public defenders complicit in female victimization? Do prosecutors sacrifice and de-prioritize victim safety in the interest of a conviction? These questions occupy many of the chapters in this volume.

In Part I, "Domestic Violence Across and Within Cultures," answers tend to emerge as readers are exposed to a variety of salient issues unique to certain racial/ethnic/cultural groups where they can draw their own conclusions.

In the opening chapter, "An Overview of Intimate Partner Violence Among Latinos," Joanne Klevens suggests that intimate partner violence (IPV) and the likelihood of injury among Latinos are similar to those among others. Unlike some groups, however, much of the driving force behind IPV among Latinos is related to alcohol-drinking patterns and beliefs that approve of IPV. Closely related here is the role of strain, which is inextricably bound to immigration concerns and the process of acculturation. For Klevens, the confluence of language barriers, low levels of education, and income places Latinos at a special disadvantage for accessing and utilizing services. Therefore, strategies to correct and alleviate this problem call for culturally sensitive interventions—especially those that include a Spanish language component.

In Chapter 2 we find that the rate of domestic violence is reportedly higher within the African American community, as Tricia Bent-Goodley focuses on the dynamic interplay between victims and the criminal justice system. In "Domestic Violence in the African American Community: Moving Forward to End Abuse," Bent-Goodley asserts there is still a great deal of resistance, distrust, and fear of reaching out to police for assistance. Past practices suggest that Black women have been stereotyped as too strong, not needing services, too loud, provoking their abusers, having big mouths, or not looking enough like a victim of abuse. Consequently, rather than looking to police for help, more and more victims lean on religious faith and community-based organizations that are, perhaps, better positioned to assist.

In Chapter 3, "Domestic Violence in Asian Cultures," Xu and Anderson report that for various reasons, domestic violence within Asian communities is extremely underreported, which tends to blur our understanding of its complexity. Concerns about close family ties and harmony within the community may discourage Asian victims from disclosing. Explained in part by deeply rooted patriarchy, immigration issues, and communication barriers, the authors claim that Asian women are disproportionately victimized by domestic violence-related homicides. Unexpectedly, victims of such homicides comprise not only the abused but the children and relatives as well.

Chapter 4 segues into Indian country as Julie C. Abril discourses about "Domestic Violence Among Native Americans," where tribal councils and restorative justice are themes reinforced throughout the chapter. Citing a recent report, Abril notes that American Indian and Alaska Native women had higher rates of rape, physical assault, and stalking than any other ethnic group. Individual levels of collective efficacy were significantly associated with reporting violent victimization. Moreover, Abril suggests that Indians who appear more unified in their cultural values are more likely to report violent victimization experiences. Relying on qualitative methodologies—including personal interviews with victims—she reveals a belief in the phenomena of "evil and bad spirits," thought to influence the use of violence within groups. Overall, here research reveals a lack of attachment to culture and substance abuse as primary precipitators of domestic violence among Native Americans.

Part I concludes with a look at domestic violence across continents as Okereke, Racheotes, and Kahler offer Chapter 5, "Domestic Violence in Sub-Saharan Africa." These authors paint a colorful portrait of domestic violence as distinguished from that found in the United States. For instance, the conception of family violence differs, for in the African context, the family is quite inclusive (i.e., extended families, house maids, caregivers, babysitters, or anyone living in the same household). Traditional notions of male patriarchy abound within marital relationships where the subordination of women is underscored by the tradition of "bride price," which reinforces the notion that a husband has purchased his wife, including her labor and sexuality. Five theoretical perspectives are used to explain domestic violence in Sub-Saharan Africa, including weak state status, patriarchy, bias-cultural, economic austerity, and a society in transition.

Having understood and appreciated some of the racial, ethnic, and cultural differences in domestic violence across and within cultures, Part II offers a unique and rarely seen glance into the correlates, causes, and contextual manifestations of domestic violence. Chapter 6 begins the odyssey as Winton and Rash contribute the appropriately titled "Physical Child Abuse, Neglect, and Domestic Violence: A Case Studies Approach." Here, case studies are used to portray connections between physical child abuse, child neglect, and domestic violence. Also included is an assessment of epidemiological research that focuses on the distribution of conditions within a population or society to determine which groups are at greater risk. The authors found that mental disorders and witnessing parental violence were the two biggest risk factors for child abuse, neglect, and domestic violence. In the end, Winton and Rash join others to recommend that additional attention be paid to the role of corporal punishment, sibling abuse, and bullying by non-family members as antecedents to child fatalities (due to abuse or neglect). To that end, they suggest that an integrated perspective that links individual, family, and community approaches can greatly increase our understanding of domestic violence.

If you have ever wondered what happens after child abuse is detected, Chapter 7, "The Response of Child Welfare Agencies to Domestic Violence," authored by Shepard and Farrell, provides invaluable insight. While many of the problems experienced by children in child welfare cases may be related to exposure to domestic violence, the authors suggests that child welfare agencies do not always screen for domestic violence. Therefore, this chapter discusses ways to adequately screen for domestic violence. However, making a determination of child neglect—based on a "failure to protect"—should be done with extreme caution, as it can result in blaming the adult victim, and in some instances strengthen the abuser's coercive control by giving credence to charges that the adult victim is an unfit parent. The authors endorse the Greenbook Project as a model program to promote a collaborative community approach for families experiencing child maltreatment and domestic violence.

Beyond issues of child abuse, neglect, and maltreatment, Chapter 8, "The Connection Between Domestic Violence and Homelessness," reminds readers of the forgotten victims too often caught up in the collateral damage of violence. The evidence not only suggests that these two social problems are correlated, but that domestic violence is among the leading causes of homelessness for women. Charlene Baker cites myriad reasons for this phenomenon, including mental health consequences of repeat victimization, social isolation, failure of formal systems to provide services to help-seeking women, lack of coordination between domestic violence and homeless service systems, lack of affordable housing units, and poverty. The author also encourages a paradigm shift from current practices of compartmentalizing survivors into either women who are victims of domestic violence or those who are homeless. What is required, according to Baker, is the creation of a holistic approach that considers women's simultaneous experiences in order to create a response that supports women as they seek safety and economic stability.

Chapter 9, co-authored by Josephine Kahler, Shirley Garick, and Godpower Okereke, is titled "The Relationship Between Substance Abuse and Domestic Violence." The literature suggests that both victims and offenders turn to commonly used substances, such as alcohol, cocaine, cannabis, and other opiates, to cope with stressful situations. Using the sensitization hypothesis, it is noted that far too often, an occasional use escalates into drug abuse and dependency. While the authors are quick to point out that substance abuse does not cause domestic violence, it is nonetheless a significant correlate that impairs the ability to exercise good judgment. The chapter closes with a case study to portray the intersection between poor mental health and issues of co-dependency. Overall, the message is clear: Once you use it, you will soon abuse it—including loved ones in one's immediate environment.

The final two chapters in Part II look at two very unique victims of domestic violence, both of whom have been relatively neglected by previous researchers. Chapter 10, Christopher Blackwell's contribution, is titled "Domestic Violence in Gay, Lesbian, Bisexual, and Transgender Persons: Populations at Risk." Alluding to the irony of a general lack of scholarly attention shown to domestic violence within the GLBT population, Blackwell asserts that within the general population, up to 10% of individuals identify their sexual orientation as one other than heterosexual. The author suggests that this population is trapped by cultural mythological beliefs and stereotypes that perpetuate misunderstandings. For instance, some individuals believe gay male relationships are less permanent and therefore should be of less concern than heterosexual marriages. This translates into significantly lower levels of empathy toward men in abusive relationships from the general population. Unlike traditional theories and variants of male patriarchy (used to explain heterosexual domestic violence), the author relies on a theory of disempowerment to illustrate and expound upon the dynamics of domestic violence within GLBT populations.

Rounding out this section is another taboo issue in the domestic violence theatre of operations: spouse violence among police officers. In Chapter 11, "Spouse Violence Among Police Officers: Work-Family Linkages," Leanor Boulin Johnson confronts head-on the unpopular topic of police officers who are domestic violence offenders and female officers who—for the most part—are victims of domestic violence. Using the work-family linkage model, the author goes to great lengths to explain these occurrences. Moreover, she finds that police officers violate their partners psychological and physical well-being because of the low cost incurred as the "code of silence" and camaraderie work to protect them from being arrested and, if arrested, they believe that prosecution will be unlikely. As a result, model policies and programs, including the Lautenberg Act, have been developed to address this issue. For this author, however, prevention must begin within the academy and continue throughout the officer's career. Moreover, developing a healthy law enforcement family begins by first recognizing and valuing the work-family linkage.

Part III constitutes the substance of this work: examining how criminal justice systems—through policies, procedures, and operations—respond to domestic violence. Chapter 12, authored by Cynthia Brown and titled "Domestic Violence Policy: Navigating a Path of Obstacles," takes readers on a historical journey to document and highlight the passage of criminal justice legislation in this area. The *laws of chastisement*, adopted during the reign of Romulus in 753 B.C., which accepted and condoned wife abuse, mark the beginning of Brown's documentation. For centuries, according to Brown, authorities have tolerated, if not lauded, a husband's violence against his wife, so long as the "beatings" were a form of chastisement addressing an alleged offense by the wife. Proceeding further, Brown highlights the case of *Bradley v. State* (1924), in which the Supreme Court of Mississippi delivered the first court decision recognizing the husband's right to chastise his wife. The evolution of state and federal legislation concludes with an overview and critique of more recent legislative efforts, including the Violence Against Women's Act, reveling in its strengths while exposing a few of its weaknesses.

In Chapter 13, Robert Magill and Walter Komanski provide an overview of the civil process of obtaining a restraining order in Orange County, Florida. In "Civil Protection Orders Against Domestic Violence: The Fight Against Domestic Violence by Orange County, Florida," readers are given a front-row seat to witness petitioner and respondent concerns with restraining orders. According to the most recent National Violence Against Women Survey, roughly 16% of rape victims, 17% of assault victims, and 37% of stalking victims sought such protection. These orders are a civil remedy, obtained not in criminal court, but instead from a domestic relations judge. In Florida, a victim of domestic violence is afforded four avenues of protection, as injunctions can be obtained to protect a victim from domestic, repeat, dating, and sexual violence. The authors use case studies to illustrate the myriad nuances and pitfalls associated with seeking a restraining order. Chapter 14, "Prosecuting Domestic Violence Cases: Issues and Concerns," also authored by Komanski and Magill, attempts to characterize the discretionary processes and the many considerations a prosecutor goes through when prosecuting cases involving domestic violence. One of the more important considerations is the concept of convictability, operationalized by the authors as a combination of evidence, witness and victim credibility, and the culpability of the perpetrator. Beginning with a journey through the intake and review process, the chapter proceeds on to evidence collection where nondrop policies (i.e., evidence-based prosecution) are discussed at length. From there, the role of plea bargaining is examined as well as trial preparation for victims. There is also considerable discussion regarding what happens when victims abandon their prosecution.

In a truly adversarial fashion—and to even matters out—John Elmore, Esq., opens Chapter 15, "Defending Individuals Charged With Domestic Violence," representing the defendant. As the title implies, Elmore provides an overview of the process in store for defense attorneys. For Elmore, these include steps taken in most criminal cases (such as securing the client's release on bail, conducting investigations, filing discovery and pretrial motions, plea negotiations, and conducting trials). Of equal importance is that defense attorneys must do everything in their power to establish the trust of their client. Interestingly, a defense attorney must appreciate the various theoretical perspectives on the causes of domestic violence. These perspectives not only enable a better understanding of the client, but also provide a glimpse into the behavior and motivations of victims—as each can prove invaluable when defending against domestic violence.

Beyond issues of prosecution and defense, sentencing and punishing batterers—a.k.a. frequent fliers—takes on a whole new dimension altogether. What does it take to rehabilitate—assuming that is the goal—a domestic violence offender? Is court-mandated counseling, combined with other sanctions, an effective strategy? Chapter 16, "Court-Ordered Treatment Programs: An Evaluation of Batterers Anonymous," authored by Rebecca Bonanno, provides answers to these and related questions. As batterer intervention programs (BIPs) have existed for more than three decades, Bonanno reviews the contributions of the women's liberation movement, which helped to establish well-known programs, such as the Duluth model. Like most BIPs, this model includes a psychoeducational component that teaches abusive men about violence, its consequences, and their desire to control females, while encouraging them to take responsibility for their actions. Legitimized and supported by the courts, these programs have expanded to become one of society's first-line weapons in the war against domestic violence. Closely related to this subject is the matter of community supervision as presented in Chapter 17, "Community Supervision of Domestic Violence Offenders: Where We Are and Where We Need to Go." Here Lynette Feder provides a historical overview of developments in this area, including the advent of specialized domestic violence courts. The author is concerned that we do not know whether this recent trend was beneficial or harmful. As such, she remains skeptical of existing efforts—regarded as unscientific—to document the effectiveness of community supervision of batterers. Moreover, Feder suggests that research findings that contradict institutionalized beliefs are often dismissed and leave established practices in place. Moreover, rather than being openly curious about what will work, many in the domestic violence field hold on to beliefs about what they think should work. For Feder, the approach is misguided and demands greater scientific rigor in the measurement and evaluation of program outcomes.

Chapter 18, "Restorative Approaches to Domestic Violence: The Cornerposts in Action," adds yet another dimension to issues of punishing and rehabilitating offenders. Here, Debra Heath-Thornton examines the potential of restorative justice as a theoretical framework to reduce violence among intimates. Rooted in biblical principles and spirituality, a restorative justice approach seeks to address and balance the needs of crime victims, offenders, and communities from where they reside. While restorative justice offers great potential to reduce domestic violence, the author recognizes a need to balance its use with issues of victim safety, maintaining that preservation of the relationship *should not* be a primary goal.

While a restorative justice approach has many redeeming features, few can argue against the age-old adage "an ounce of prevention is worth a pound of cure." To that end, Chapter 19, written by Sarah Keller and A. J. Otjen, outlines and describes a very effective, practical, and proactive approach to raise awareness of and prevent domestic violence. Their chapter, "Creating and Executing an Applied Interdisciplinary Campaign for Domestic Violence Prevention," is the final entry in this volume. Here, the authors describe an interdisciplinary, experiential learning project that combined marketing and communications courses in a domestic violence education campaign to raise awareness and combat common myths surrounding partner violence. The success of this project highlights the potency of interdisciplinary marketing campaigns to educate the public and, in the process, send powerful, visual messages about the reality of domestic violence.

List of Abbreviations

ABA	American Bar Association
ACWF	All-China Women's Federation
AFDC	Aid to Families With Dependent Children
AFSA	Adoption and Safe Families Act
AIDA	Awareness, Interest, Desire, and Action Model
AIDS	Acquired immune deficiency syndrome
AJCJS	*African Journal of Criminology and Justice Studies*
AMC	Applied marketing communication
AMEND	Assisting Mothers to End the Need for Drugs
AWHONN	Association of Women's Health, Obstetric and Neonatal Nurses
BEM	Bilateral electronic monitoring
BIP	Batterer intervention program
BJS	Bureau of Justice Statistics
CAN	Child abuse and neglect
CDC	Centers for Disease Control
CPD	Chicago Police Department
CPS	Child protective services
DAIP	Domestic Abuse Intervention Project
DART	Domestic Violence Assault Team
DOJ	Department of Justice
DSM	*Diagnostic and Statistic Manual of Mental Disorders*
DV	Domestic violence
DVU	Domestic violence (probation) unit
ECOSOC	United Nations Economic and Social Council
ECOWAS	Economic Community for West African States
EM	Electronic monitoring
EMERGE	An abuser education program
FBI	Federal Bureau of Investigation
FGM	Female genital mutilation
GBC	Greater Baltimore Committee
GLBT	Gay, lesbian, bisexual, and transgender
HIV	Human immunodeficiency virus

IACP	International Association of Chiefs of Police
ICPSR	Interuniversity Consortium for Political and Social Research
IGAD	Intergovernmental Authority on Development
IMC	Integrated marketing communication
IMF	International Monetary Fund
IPV	Intimate partner violence
ISP	Intensive supervision on probation
JOD	Judicial Oversight Demonstration
LAPD	Los Angeles Police Department
LGT	Lesbian, gay, and transgender
MADD	Mothers Against Drunk Driving
MECCAS	Means end chain conceptual advertising strategy
NASW	National Association of Social Workers
NCADV	National Coalition Against Domestic Violence
NCJ	National Criminal Justice
NCJRS	National Criminal Justice Reference Service
NCVS	National Crime Victimization Survey
NEM	Negative emotionality
NGO	Nongovernmental organization
NIBRS	National Incident-Based Reporting System
NIDA	National Institute on Drug Abuse
NIMH	National Institute of Mental Health
NIS	National Incidence Study
NVAWS	National Violence Against Women Survey
NYS	New York Statute
OJP	Office of Justice Programs
OPR	Office of Professional Responsibility
PHA	Public housing authority
PRP	Personal and Relationship Profile
PSA	Public Service Announcement
PTSD	Posttraumatic stress disorder
RAVEN	Nonviolence education program
SADC	Southern African Development Community
SAFE	Stress/safety, afraid/abused, friends/family, and emergency plan
SAP	Structural adjustment program
SMC	Social marketing communication
STD	Sexually transmitted disease

SUICSS	Southern Ute Indian Community Safety Survey
TANF	Temporary Aid for Needy Families
UN	United Nations
UNCF	United Negro College Fund
UNPF	United Nations Population Fund
USDOJ	U.S. Department of Justice
VAWA	Violence Against Women Act
VIP	Victim impact panel
VOM	Victim-offender mediation
VORP	Victim-offender reconciliation program
WHO	World Health Organization

An Overview of Intimate Partner Violence Among Latinos[*]

1

JOANNE KLEVENS

Contents

Violence, including intimate partner violence (IPV), is a leading cause of death, disability, and hospitalization in the United States, and as such, it has been targeted for action in the nation's public health plan (U.S. Department of Health and Human Services, 2000). Since 1994, the Centers for Disease Control and Prevention (CDC) has received funding to develop and evaluate programs to prevent violence against women, most of which is attributed to IPV. In addressing health problems such as violence, the CDC utilizes a systematic approach to collect information and translate that information into action (Mercy, Rosenberg, Powell, Broome, & Roper, 1993). This approach involves four interrelated steps:

1. Collect information on the magnitude and severity of the problem to decide if it is, in fact, a priority for intervention.
2. Establish factors associated with the problem to identify populations at risk and potential causes, especially those that are amenable to intervention.

---

[*] This chapter originally appeared in a special issue of *Violence Against Women*, 13(2), pp. 111–122. (2007).

3. Develop and evaluate strategies to modify these factors based on the information generated previously.
4. Disseminate and implement these interventions if they prove to be effective.

Although IPV affects women from all racial and ethnic groups, most research on IPV has been limited to Caucasian women. Many factors would suggest that IPV might be different among other racial and ethnic groups, and thus, the relevance of the extant research on IPV for these other groups is unknown. In the past few years, CDC has promoted research and the development of culturally competent interventions among racial and ethnic minorities. Latinos compose 13.4% of the U.S. population and are currently its largest minority group (U.S. Census Bureau 2004).[1] This chapter gathers findings from studies about Latinos funded by the CDC. These studies include three cross-sectional surveys among rural women in North Carolina (Denham et al., 2007), nonrandomly selected sites across the United States (Ingram, 2007), and teens in Los Angeles (Ocampo, Shelley, & Jaycox, 2007), estimating the magnitude, distribution, and risk factors for IPV; a qualitative study exploring beliefs and perceptions of IPV among Latinos in Oklahoma City (Klevens et al., 2007); and a description of the development and implementation of a culturally appropriate intervention for Latinos in Massachusetts (Whitaker et al., 2007). To put the findings from these five articles into context, this chapter will review the existing literature on IPV among Latinos following the four steps in CDC's public health approach. Comparisons to non-Latinos will be made when possible to identify the differences and similarities.

Magnitude and Severity of IPV Among Latinos

The National Violence Against Women Survey (NVAWS), based on a random sample of the United States, reports a lifetime prevalence rate of exposure to IPV among Latinos of 23.4% (Tjaden & Thoennes, 2000). Denham et al. (2007) report slightly lower lifetime prevalence (19.5%) among rural Latinas. However, based on answers to more specific questions, Ingram (2007) finds that half of the population of Latinos report being exposed to some type of IPV. In all three studies, these rates are similar to or lower than those for non-Latinos from the same communities. Other national and local population-based probability surveys and a statewide surveillance system (Pearlman, Zierler, Gjelsvik, & Verhoek-Oftedahl, 2003) have found higher (Kantor, Jasinski, & Aldorondo, 1994; Sorenson & Telles, 1991; Straus & Smith, 1995), lower (Sorenson, Upchurch, & Shen, 1996), and similar (Kantor, 1997; Rennison & Welchans, 2000) rates of IPV among Latinos compared to non-Latinos. Differences in rates tend to disappear once income, urbanicity, age, drinking (Kantor et al., 1994; Sorenson & Telles, 1991; Straus & Smith, 1995), impulsivity, and family history are controlled for (Caetano, Cunradi, Clark, & Schafer, 2000). Past-year exposure rates of IPV among Latino women vary from 0.7% to 20.0% (Ingram, 2007; Kantor, 1997; Lown & Vega, 2001b; Pearlman et al., 2003; Sorenson et al., 1996; Straus & Smith, 1995), with great variability among Latinos of different origins (Kantor, 1997). Local probability surveys find that rates of female-to-male partner violence among Latinos are just as high (Neff, Holamon, & Schluter, 1995; Sorenson & Telles, 1991) or maybe somewhat higher (Caetano, Cunradi, et al., 2000) as male-to-female partner violence. Rates of mutual partner violence among Latinos are similar to those among non-Latino Whites and much lower than among non-Latino Blacks (Caetano, Ramisetty-Mikler, & Field, 2005). Shelter and clinic studies suggest that multiple forms of mistreatment (psychological, physical, and sexual) appear to be common across different ethnic or racial groups (McFarlane, Wiist, & Watson, 1998; Sorenson, 1996; Krishnan, Hilbert, & VanLeeuwen, 2001). Some studies based on convenience samples report sexual abuse by an intimate partner occurring more frequently for Latinas (Perilla, 1999; Torres, 1991); however, in a population-based survey, it was not more frequent (Sorenson & Telles, 1991). Although the rates and characteristics of victimization may be similar to those of other women, the seriousness of abuse and some of its consequences may be more severe. Suicide ideation may be higher, as reported by a shelter study that found that more than half the Latina participants reported suicidal thoughts or suicide attempts, compared to 35% of other respondents (Krishnan et al., 2001). However, abused Latinas appear equally likely to be injured as Blacks and Whites (Sorenson et al., 1996) and, similar to non-Latinas (Campbell et al., 2002; Coker, Smith, Bethea, King, McKeown, 2000), report poorer physical and mental health (Lown & Vega, 2001b). In sum, various studies consistently show that IPV occurs as frequently among Latinos as among non-Latinos when confounders are controlled for. There is also some preliminary evidence that Latinas experience similar forms of IPV and suffer similar consequences.

Factors Associated With IPV

Despite the equally high rates of IPV among Latinos, there is only a limited amount of research on the factors associated with its occurrence. Latina victims of IPV tend to be younger, less educated, and more economically disadvantaged than non-Latino White victims (Gondolf, Fisher, & McFerron, 1988; West, Kantor, & Jasinski, 1998)—characteristics that reflect the Latino population overall. Similar to non-Latinos (see Schumacher, Feldbau-Kohn, Slep, & Heyman, 2001, for a review), higher IPV rates among Latinos are associated with young age (Ingram, 2007; Lown & Vega, 2001b; Straus & Smith, 1995) urbanicity (Lown & Vega, 2001b; Straus & Smith, 1995), low income (Cunradi, Caetano, & Schafer, 2002; Pearlman et al., 2003; Straus & Smith, 1995; Sugihara & Warner, 2002), witnessing IPV as a child (Perilla, 1999; Rouse, 1988), psychosocial stress (Perilla, Bakeman, & Norris, 1994), mental disorders (Sorenson & Telles, 1991), power, and possessiveness or jealousy (Sugihara & Warner, 2002). The evidence for the importance of beliefs supporting IPV for Latinos is mixed: One national cross-sectional survey found that beliefs that IPV is acceptable were associated with higher IPV rates among Latinos (Kantor et al., 1994), whereas in another, they were not, although they were for non-Latino Whites (Caetano, Nelson, & Cunradi, 2001). In contrast to Whites and Blacks, neighborhood poverty is not a risk factor for IPV among Latinos (Cunradi, Caetano, Clark, & Schafer, 2000). Social support and religiosity appear to be protective factors among Latinos (Denham et al., 2007; Lown & Vega, 2001a). Denham and colleagues also find that Latinas who experienced IPV were more likely than their non-Latina counterparts to have children in the home and to lack health insurance. Although the link between traditional gender role attitudes and IPV is weak (Sugarman & Frankel, 1996), machismo has often been invoked to explain IPV among Latinos (e.g., Campbell, Masaki, & Torres, 1997). However, research shows that male dominance is not that typical among Latinos who tend to be more egalitarian in domestic decision making (Baca-Zinn, 1982; Sugihara & Warner, 2002), and in fact, attitudes toward gender roles have not been associated with IPV among Latinos (Neff et al., 1995; Perilla et al., 1994). Nonetheless, battered Latinas are almost twice as likely to be living in a male-dominated relationship than battered non-Latino White women (West et al., 1998). Moreover, Latinas who earn more than their partners appear to be at greater risk of abuse (Perilla et al., 1994), a finding that raises another issue. The results from the focus group interviews presented in Klevens et al. (2007) suggest that IPV might result when roles change. In Morash, Bui, and Santiago's (2000) qualitative study, role change was a characteristic of families experiencing physical and emotional abuse and was explained by women feeling disappointed that their husbands were not performing the expected role of family provider. More research is needed to clarify the importance of male dominance and role strain as risk factors of IPV for Latinos.

As in other population groups, alcohol use is associated with increased risk for IPV among Latinos (Kantor, 1997; Neff et al., 1995; Perilla et al., 1994; West et al., 1998). Male drinking during an IPV incident is equally common among non-Latino Whites and Latinos (29%; Caetano, Schafer, Clark, Cunradi, & Raspberry, 2000) and much lower than among Blacks. IPV increases with the frequency of alcohol use among Whites, but among Latinos, abstainers and frequent drinkers have the highest rates (Caetano,

Cunradi, et al., 2000). Binge drinking is also associated with IPV, but not as strongly for Latinos and Whites as for Blacks (Caetano, Schafer, et al., 2000).

Although reporting social problems as a consequence of alcohol use and alcohol dependence-related symptoms are associated with IPV among Whites and Blacks, respectively, neither is associated with IPV among Latinos (Caetano et al., 2001). Taken together, these findings suggest that alcohol-drinking patterns and their subsequent consequences may have less explanatory value for the occurrence of IPV among Latinos than among other groups.

IPV appears to begin early during a relationship in both non-Latino White and Latino couples, either during dating or in the first year of cohabitation (Krishnan, Hilbert, VanLeeuwen, & Kolia, 1997). Studies on persistence and desistence of IPV are scarce, and even more so studies that compare different ethnic or racial groups. A notable exception is Jasinski's (2001) analysis based on two waves of the National Survey of Families and Households. In her analysis, young age was the only predictor of persistence among non-Latino Whites and Blacks, whereas longer length of employment and cohabitation (vs. married) were the two factors that predicted persistence of IPV among Latinos. Cessation of IPV was predicted by young age among non-Latino Whites and lower levels of employment among Blacks. None of the risk factors explored predicted cessation among Latinos.

The main triggers for IPV incidents (jealousy and husband's drinking) appear to be similar across ethnic and racial groups, but conflicts over housekeeping money, wife's going out, and wife's pregnancy may be more frequent among Latinos (Torres, 1991). Torres (1991) also found that battering most often occurred on Friday and Saturday evenings and nights for both Latinas and non-Latino White women, in the presence of children. However, when other adults were present, they were more likely to be family members in the case of Latinas.

Immigration is a common experience for many Latinos. Of Latinos in the United States, 40% were born in other countries (Ramirez & De La Cruz, 2003). More than half entered the United States between 1990 and 2002. Immigration often implies acculturation, that is, adapting to new cultural norms and practices, which can have special implications for IPV. The impact of acculturation on IPV has been explored in various studies. Ingram (2007) found that rates of IPV among Latinos increased the longer they lived in the United States. Other studies using different indicators for acculturation also show that more acculturated Latinos have higher rates of IPV than the less acculturated (Caetano, Schafer, Clark, & Cunradi, 1998; Kantor et al., 1994; Lown & Vega, 2001b; Sanderson, Coker, Roberts, Tortolero, & Reininger, 2004; Sorenson & Telles, 1991), although the highest levels of IPV tend to occur among those at medium levels of acculturation (Caetano, Ramisetty-Mikler, & McGrath, 2004; Caetano, Schafer, et al., 2000). However, Kantor

and colleagues (1994) found no differences in IPV rates by levels of acculturation once socioeconomic factors were controlled for. In sum, Latinos share
many of the same risk factors as those observed among non-Latinos, except
that beliefs approving IPV and alcohol-drinking patterns may not have much
explanatory value for the occurrence of IPV among Latinos. Role strain,
especially as a result of immigration and acculturation, might be unique to
Latinos, and its importance and the importance of male dominance among
Latinas experiencing IPV deserve more research.

Developing and Evaluating Interventions

Published papers on interventions that include Latinos are scant. A randomized controlled trial among women recruited from a family violence unit in an
urban district attorney's office in which 41% were Spanish-speaking women
compared standard services offered by the district attorney's office to standard services plus six telephone sessions on safety behaviors (McFarlane et
al., 2004). This trial found that these additional telephone sessions improved
safety behavior compared with standard treatment at 3, 6, 12, and 18 months.
A controlled trial among Latinas comparing unlimited counseling plus a
mentor (who might be considered to have acted as an advocate) to unlimited counseling only and to a wallet-sized resource card found a decrease in
levels of violence and threats of violence at follow-up 2 months postpartum
in all three groups, which was sustained through follow-ups at 6, 12, and
18 months (McFarlane, Soeken, & Wiist, 2000). This trial found no significant difference in severity of violence among either type of counseling group
and the resource card intervention. Physical violence and threats of violence
scores remained consistently lower at each follow-up for the counseling plus
mentor group (but not reaching statistical significance), whereas scores for
women in the counseling-only group were consistently higher than those in
the resource card group.

Both of the previous interventions are similar to efforts being implemented among non-Latinos and, except for bilingual counselors, were
not otherwise adapted for Latinos. Interventions that have been especially
developed for Latinos are less common. In this issue, Whitaker et al. (2007)
describe how networking among agencies may provide a more culturally
appropriate intervention for two Latino communities in Massachusetts.
The agencies in the network share expertise on cultural competence and are
able to utilize the linguistic capacity of other organizations to communicate
with non-English-speaking clients and thus provide better services for the
Latino community. In the De Madres a Madres program (McFarlane, Kelly,
Rodriguez, & Ferry, 1993), community leaders identified female volunteers
who were then trained to reach out to pregnant women in their communities

and provide support and community resource information. Some have used Brazilian educator Paulo Freire's problem-posing methods to ensure respect for Latinos' beliefs and values (Carrillo & Goubaud-Reyna, 1998; Perilla & Perez, 2001). Problem-posing techniques are based on the assumption that participants have a wealth of knowledge and practical experience about issues and that they are thinking and creative people. In this approach, the educator utilizes a picture, poem, song, skit, or story to present a problem and then facilitates a group discussion on what, who, and why, and what to do about the problem.

Others have used an extension of Freire's approach, participatory research, to develop their programs for Latinas (Maciak, Guzman, Santiago, Villalobos, & Israel, 1999; Rodriguez, 1999). Participatory research is a combination of research, education, and social action. It involves a cyclical problem-solving process that may use any qualitative and quantitative research methods, problem posing, and other educational techniques. In participatory research, those affected by the problem participate in every phase of the research and action process along with the professional or researcher in a collaborative way, in which both have needs and expertise to contribute. Through their participation, participatory research becomes a learning process for those involved. The process begins with people's concrete experiences and shared problems and moves to critical analysis of the problem and its underlying causes by collecting relevant information, drawing on people's experiences and knowledge, and participating in collective discussions that should lead to collective decisions on the course of action. Through participation in this process, participants are expected to gain problem-solving skills, transform their understanding about the nature of the problem, raise their critical awareness of the context and underlying causes, increase their feelings of self-efficacy and control, and thus feel empowered to take action for the purpose of change.

Barriers to Intervention

Battered Latinas return to their abusers more often than non-Latino White women (Torres, 1991) and often prefer to stay with their abuser (Dutton, Orloff, & Hass, 2000). Economic dependence, fear of losing custody of their children, not wanting to separate the children from their father, believing that their partner will ultimately change, and love are reasons Latinas provide for not leaving their abusive partner (Dutton et al., 2000). Based on Latinas' wishes to stay with their partners, Perilla and Perez (2001) developed an intervention with components for both partners and their children.

Latinos may also be at a special disadvantage for accessing and utilizing services. In addition to the language barriers, low levels of education and

income, and poor knowledge of existing services, many Latinos are undocumented, which may add real or perceived barriers to utilizing services.
Culture and immigration experiences might affect beliefs and make the
experience of IPV different for Latinos (Kasturirangan & Williams, 2003).
Many immigrant women may fear seeking help from authorities because of
negative experiences in their home countries or fear of deportation (Bauer,
Rodriguez, Quiroga, & Flores-Ortiz, 2000; McFarlane, Wiist, & Soeken,
1999).

Battered Latinas have been found to seek help less often from both informal and formal sources (West et al., 1998), and shelter sample studies suggest
they tend to stay longer in an abusive relationship before seeking assistance
(Gondolf et al., 1988; Torres, 1991). The level of acculturation increases the
odds of help seeking among Latinas (West et al., 1998). Although victims of
IPV from different ethnic or racial groups tend to initially share their experiences with family and friends (Dutton et al., 2000; Horton & Johnson, 1993;
Ingram, 2007; Krishnan, et al., 1997; West et al., 1998), West et al. (1998)
found that Latinas were half as likely to consult family and friends, and in
one study based on a shelter sample, Latinas reported receiving less help from
family and friends compared to non-Latino White women (O'Keefe, 1994).
Ocampo et al. (2007) show that Latino teens are more likely to seek help from
friends when in a situation of dating violence than turn to adults or seek
formal help (e.g., health professionals), although the quality of help offered
by teens related to dating violence is perceived as being limited. A national
probability sample and two shelter sample studies found that Latinas were
more likely to contact police (Gondolf et al., 1988; Torres, 1991; West et al.,
1998). However, another study among women in shelters found that Latinas
may be less likely to report incidents to law enforcement or seek medical
attention (Krishnan et al., 1997), whereas another found them to be equally
likely (Krishnan et al., 2001). Ingram (2007) found that Latinos went to shelters significantly less often than did non-Latinos. Latinas may also be less
likely to seek help from mental health services (West et al., 1998) or clergy or
social services (Gondolf et al., 1991; Torres, 1991), although they tend to go
to clergy before going to a shelter more often than non-Latino White women
(Torres, 1987). Interestingly, clergy (and police) are described as reticent to
intervene in cases of IPV across all ethnic/racial groups (Sorenson, 1996).

Based on in-depth interviews, the main factor influencing Latinas' decisions about seeking help or leaving or staying with the abuser appears to be
the welfare of their children (Acevedo, 2000; Bauer et al., 2000; Torres, 1991).
Barriers to seeking help include lack of financial means; fear of deportation,
of losing custody of their children, or of their situation worsening; beliefs
that abuse must be tolerated or that police, health care providers, and other
institutions are oblivious to IPV or will discriminate against them; being
unaware of available services; language difficulties; preferences for an intact

family; and lack of transportation (Acevedo, 2000; Bauer et al., 2000; Dutton et al., 2000). In one study, the services most used by battered Latinas were Medicaid, food stamps, immigration assistance, and maternal and child health care (Dutton et al., 2000). However, few Latinas qualifying for these government benefits sought them.

Dissemination and Implementation

As noted in the previous section, there are few interventions developed and evaluated among Latinos. Indeed, except for isolated trials testing the effectiveness of advocacy and safety planning (see Klevens & Sadowski, 2004, for a review), the field of IPV lacks rigorous evaluation of interventions that can be disseminated.

Conclusions

Many of the studies reviewed here were based on convenience samples or random samples of selected locations, and thus the findings may not be representative of Latinos in the United States. However, taken together, this review suggests, first, that IPV affects Latinos about as much as non-Latinos and is similar in its manifestations and consequences. Many of the risk factors associated with its occurrence are the same as those observed among non-Latinos, except that beliefs approving IPV and alcohol-drinking patterns may not have much explanatory value for the occurrence of IPV among Latinos. Role strain, especially as a result of immigration and acculturation, might be unique to Latinos, and its significance and the importance of male dominance among Latinas experiencing IPV deserve more research. Efforts to develop and evaluate interventions among Latinos are incipient, as they are in the field of IPV, and resources should be allocated to stimulate these endeavors.

However, in the development of these interventions, the factors that often lead Latinas to delay seeking help need to be considered. In conclusion, this overview and the articles in this special issue support findings from others that suggest there are more similarities than differences between Latinos' and non-Latinos' experiences with IPV. Various crossnational, shelter, and focus group studies (e.g., Count, Brown, & Campbell, 1992; Levinson, 1989; Sorenson, 1996; Torres, 1991) suggest that there is a common thread in women's experiences of IPV across different cultures. Nevertheless, although the core experience may be similar, intimate partner relationships must be understood within the context of a group's situation in our society. For many Latinos in the United States, IPV is often colored by experiences of immigration (frequently illegal), acculturation, and socioeconomic disadvantage. Although it is plausible for interventions developed for other ethnic groups to work for Latinos, these efforts should be accompanied by activities to address these additional issues. Moreover, Latinos are a very heterogeneous group. More research is needed to establish potential differences in the experiences of IPV among subgroups of the Latino population.

Endnote

1. The term *Latino* is used in this article to refer to individuals born in or with ancestry from Mexico, Central America, and Spanish-speaking countries in the Caribbean and South America.

References

Acevedo, M. J. (2000). Battered immigrant Mexican women's perspectives regarding abuse and help seeking. *Journal of Multicultural Social Work, 8*, 243–282.

Baca-Zinn, M. (1982). Chicano men and masculinity. *Journal of Ethnic Studies, 10,* 29–44.

Bauer, H. M., Rodriguez, M. A., Quiroga, S. S., & Flores-Ortiz, Y. G. (2000). Barriers to health care for abused Latina and Asian immigrant women. *Journal of Health Care for the Poor & Underserved, 11*, 33–44.

Caetano, R., Cunradi, C. B., Clark, C. L., & Schafer, J. (2000). IPV and drinking patterns among White, Black, and Latino couples in the U.S. *Journal of Substance Abuse, 11*, 123–138.

Caetano, R., Nelson, S., & Cunradi, C. (2001). Intimate partner violence, dependence symptoms and social consequences from drinking among White, Black, and Latino couples in the United States. *American Journal of Addictions, 10*, 60–69.

Caetano, R., Ramisetty-Mikler, S., & Field, C. A. (2005). Unidirectional and bidirectional intimate partner violence among White, Black, and Latino couples in the United States. *Violence and Victims, 20*, 393–405.

Caetano, R., Ramisetty-Mikler, S., & McGrath, C. (2004). Acculturation, drinking, and intimate partner violence among Latino couples in the United States: A longitudinal study. *Hispanic Journal of Behavioral Sciences, 26*, 60–78.

Caetano, R., Schafer, J., Clark, C. L., & Cunradi, C. B. (1998). Intimate partner violence, acculturation and alcohol consumption among Latino couples in the U.S. Cited in Caetano, R., Ramisetty-Mikler, S., & McGrath, C. (2004). Acculturation, drinking, and intimate partner violence among Latino couples in the United States: A longitudinal study. *Hispanic Journal of Behavioral Sciences, 26*, 60–78.

Caetano, R., Schafer, J., Clark, C. L., Cunradi, C. B., & Raspberry, K. (2000). IPV, acculturation, and alcohol consumption among Latino couples in the United States. *Journal of Interpersonal Violence, 15*, 2–45.

Campbell, D. W., Masaki, B., & Torres, S. (1997). "Water on rock": Changing domestic violence perceptions in the African American, Asian American, and Latino communities. In E. Klein, J. Campbell, E. Soler, & M. Ghez (Eds.), *Ending domestic violence: Changing public perceptions/halting the epidemic* (pp. 64–87). Thousand Oaks, CA: Sage.

Campbell, J., Jones, A. S., Dienemann, J., Kub, J., Schollenberger, J., O'Campo, P., et al. (2002). Intimate partner violence and physical health consequences. *Archives of Internal Medicine, 162,* 1157–1163.

Carrillo, R., & Goubaud-Reyna, R. (1998). Clinical treatment of Latino domestic violence offenders. In R. Carrillo & J. Tello (Eds.), *Family violence and men of color: Healing the wounded male spirit* (pp. 53–73). New York: Springer.

Coker, A. L., Smith, P. H., Bethea, L., King, M. R., & McKeown, R. E. (2000). Physical health consequences of physical and psychological intimate partner violence. *Archives of Family Medicine, 9,* 451–457.

Count, D. A., Brown, J. K., & Campbell, J. C. (1992). *Sanctions and sanctuary: Cultural perspectives on the beating of wives.* San Francisco: Westview.

Cunradi, C. B., Caetano, R., Clark, C. L., & Schafer, J. (2000). Neighborhood poverty as a predictor of intimate partner violence among White, Black, and Latino couples in the United States. *Annals of Epidemiology, 10,* 297–308.

Cunradi, C. B., Caetano, R., & Schafer, J. (2002). Socioeconomic predictors of intimate partner violence among White, Black, and Latino couples in the United States. *Journal of Family Violence, 17,* 377–389.

Denham, A. C., Frasier, P. Y., Hooten, E. G., Belton, L., Newton, W., Gonzalez, P., et al. (2007). Intimate partner violence among Latinas in eastern North Carolina. *Violence Against Women, 13,* 123–140.

Dutton, M. A., Orloff, L. E., & Hass, G. A. (2000). Characteristics of help-seeking behaviors, resources and service needs of battered immigrant Latinas: Legal and policy implications. *Georgetown Journal on Poverty Law & Policy, 7,* 245–305.

Gondolf, E. W., Fisher, E., & McFerron, R. (1988). Racial differences among shelter residents: A comparison of non-Latino White, Black, and Latino battered women. In R. L. Hampton (Ed.), *Black family violence: Current research and theory* (pp. 103–113). Lexington, MA: Lexington Books.

Horton, R. L., & Johnson, B. L. (1993). Profile and strategies of women who have ended abuse. *Families in Society, 74,* 481–491.

Ingram, E. M. (2007). A comparison of help seeking between Latino and non-Latino victims of intimate partner violence. *Violence Against Women, 13,* 159–171.

Jasinski, J. L. (2001). Physical violence among non-Latino White, African American, and Latino couples: Ethnic differences in persistence and cessation. *Violence and Victims, 16,* 479–490.

Kantor, G. K. (1997). Alcohol and spouse abuse: Ethnic differences. *Recent Developments in Alcoholism, 13,* 57–79.

Kantor, G. K., Jasinski, J. L., & Aldorondo, E. (1994). Sociocultural status and incidents of marital violence in Latino families. *Violence and Victims, 9,* 207–222.

Kasturirangan, A., & Williams, E. N. (2003). Counseling Latina battered women: A qualitative study of the Latina perspective. *Journal of Multicultural Counseling and Development, 31,* 162–178.

Klevens, J., Shelley, G., Clavel-Arcas, C., Barney, D. D., Tobar, C., Duran, E. S., et al. (2007). Latinos' perspectives and experiences with intimate partner violence. *Violence Against Women, 13*, 141–158.

Krishnan, S., Hilbert, J. C., & VanLeeuwen, D. (2001). Domestic violence and help-seeking behaviors among rural women: Results from a shelter-based study. *Family and Community Health, 24*, 28–38.

Krishnan, S. P., Hilbert, J. C., VanLeeuwen, D., & Kolia, R. (1997). Documenting domestic violence among ethnically diverse populations: Results from a preliminary study. *Family and Community Health, 20*, 32–48.

Levinson, D. (1989). *Family violence in cross-cultural perspective.* Newbury Park, CA: Sage.

Lown, E. A., & Vega, W. (2001a). Intimate partner violence and health: Self-assured health, chronic health, and somatic symptoms among Mexican-American women. *Psychosomatic Medicine, 63*, 352–360.

Lown, E. A., & Vega, W. (2001b). Prevalence and predictors of physical partner abuse among Mexican American women. *American Journal of Public Health, 91*, 441–445.

Maciak, B. J., Guzman, R., Santiago, A., Villalobos, G., & Israel, B.A. (1999). Establishing LA VIDA: A community-based partnership to prevent intimate violence against Latina women. *Health Education & Behavior, 26*, 821–840.

McFarlane, J., Kelly, E., Rodriguez, R., & Ferry, J. (1993). *De madres a madres*: Women building community coalitions for health. *Health Care for Women International, 15*, 465–476.

McFarlane, J., Malecha, A., Gist, J., Watson, K., Batten, E., Hall, I., et al. (2004). Increasing the safety promoting behaviors of abused women. *American Journal of Nursing, 104*, 40–50.

McFarlane, J., Soeken, K., & Wiist, W. (2000). An evaluation of interventions to decrease IPV to pregnant women. *Public Health Nursing, 17*, 443–451.

McFarlane, J. M., Wiist, W., & Soeken, K. (1999). Use of counseling by abused Latino women. *Journal of Women's Health & Gender-Based Medicine, 8*, 541–546.

McFarlane, J. M., Wiist, W., & Watson, M. (1998). Predicting physical abuse against pregnant Latino women. *American Journal of Preventive Medicine, 15*, 134–138.

Mercy, J. M., Rosenberg, M. L., Powell, K. E., Broome, C. V., & Roper, W. L. (1993). Public health policy for preventing violence. *Health Affairs, 12*, 7–29.

Morash, M., Bui, H. N., & Santiago, A. M. (2000). Cultural-specific gender ideology and wife abuse in Mexican-descent families. *International Journal of Victimology, 7*, 67–91.

Neff, J. A., Holamon, B., & Schluter, T. D. (1995). Spousal violence among non-Latino Whites, Blacks, and Mexican Americans: The role of demographic variables, psychosocial predictors, and alcohol consumption. *Journal of Family Violence, 10*, 1–21.

Ocampo, B. W., Shelley, G., & Jaycox, L. (2007). Latino teens talk about help seeking and help giving in relation to dating violence. *Violence Against Women, 13*, 172–189.

O'Keefe, M. (1994). Racial/ethnic differences among battered women and their children. *Journal of Child and Family Studies, 3*, 283–305.

Pearlman, D. N., Zierler, S., Gjelsvik, A., & Verhoek-Oftedahl, W. (2003). Neighborhood environment, racial position, and risk of police reported domestic violence: A contextual analysis. *Public Health Reports, 118*, 44–58.

Perilla, J. L. (1999). Domestic violence as a human rights issue: The case of immigrant Latinos. *Latino Journal of Behavioral Sciences, 21*, 107–133.

Perilla, J. L., Bakeman, R., & Norris, F. H. (1994). Culture and domestic violence: The ecology of abused Latinas. *Violence and Victims, 9*, 325–339.

Perilla, J. L., & Perez, F. (2001). A program for immigrant Latino men who batter within the context of a comprehensive family intervention. In E. Aldarondo & F. Mederos (Eds.), *Working with men who batter: Intervention and prevention strategies for a diverse society* (pp. 11.1–11.31). New York: Civic Research Institute.

Ramirez, R. R., & De La Cruz, G. P. (2003). *The Latino population in the United States. March 2002. Current population reports P20-545*. Retrieved October 22, 2004, from http://www.census.gov/prod/2003pubs/p20-545.pdf

Rennison, C. M., & Welchans, S. (2000). *Intimate partner violence* (Special Report NCJ 178247). Washington, DC: U.S. Bureau of Justice Statistics, National Institute of Justice.

Rodriguez, R. (1999). The power of the collective: Battered migrant farmworker women creating safe spaces. *Health Care for Women International, 20*, 417–426.

Rouse, L. P. (1988). Abuse in dating relationships: A comparison of Blacks, Whites, and Latinos. *Journal of College Student Development, 29*, 312–319.

Sanderson, M., Coker, A. L., Roberts, R. E., Tortolero, S. R., & Reininger, B. M. (2004). Acculturation, ethnic identity, and dating violence among Latino ninth-grade students. *Preventive Medicine, 39*, 373–383.

Schumacher, J. A., Feldbau-Kohn, S., Slep, A. M. S., & Heyman, R. E. (2001). Risk factors for male-to-female partner physical abuse. *Aggression and Violent Behavior, 6*, 281–352.

Sorenson, S. B. (1996). Violence against women: Examining ethnic differences and commonalities. *Evaluation Review, 20*, 123–145.

Sorenson, S. B., & Telles, C. A. (1991). Self-reports of spousal violence in a Mexican-American and non-Latino White population. *Violence and Victims, 6*, 3–15.

Sorenson, S. B., Upchurch, D. M., & Shen, H. (1996). Violence and injury in marital arguments: Risk patterns and gender differences. *American Journal of Public Health, 86*, 35–40.

Straus, M. A., & Smith, C. (1995). Violence in Latino families in the United States: Incidence rates and structural interpretations. In M. A. Straus & R. J. Gelles (Eds.), *Physical violence in American families: Risk factors and adaptations to violence in 8,145 families* (pp. 241–367). New Brunswick, NJ: Transaction.

Sugarman, D. B., & Frankel, S. L. (1996). Patriarchal ideology and wife-assault: A meta-analytic review. *Journal of Family Violence, 11*, 13–40.

Sugihara, Y., & Warner, J. A. (2002). Dominance and domestic abuse among Mexican Americans: Gender differences in the etiology of violence in intimate relationships. *Journal of Family Violence, 17*, 315–340.

Tjaden, P., & Thoennes, N. (2000). *Extent, nature, and consequences of IPV: Findings from the National Violence Against Women Survey*. Washington, DC: National Institute of Justice.

Torres, S. (1987). Latino-American battered women: Why consider cultural differences? *Response, 10*, 20–21.

Torres, S. (1991). A comparison of wife abuse between two cultures: Perceptions, atti-
    tudes, nature, and extent. *Issues in Mental Health Nursing, 12,* 113–131.
U.S. Census Bureau. (2004, September 8). *Facts for features: Hispanic heritage month,
    2004.* Retrieved October 22, 2004, from http://www.census.gov/Press-Release/
    www/releases/archives/facts_for_features_special_editions/007173.html
U.S. Department of Health and Human Services. (2000). *Healthy people 2010:
    Understanding and improving health and objectives for improving health* (2nd
    ed., Vols. 1 & 2). Washington, DC: Government Printing Office.
West, C. M., Kantor, G. K., & Jasinski, J. L. (1998). Sociodemographic predictors and
    cultural barriers to help-seeking behavior by Latina and non-Latino White
    American battered women. *Violence and Victims, 13,* 361–375.
Whitaker, D. J., Baker, C. K., Pratt, C., Silverman, J., Reed, E., Suri, S., et al.
    (2007). A network model for providing culturally competent services for
    intimate partner violence and sexual violence. *Violence Against Women, 13,*
    190–209.

Domestic Violence in the African American Community

Moving Forward to End Abuse

2

TRICIA B. BENT-GOODLEY

Contents

Domestic violence poses many threats and challenges within the African American community. The Black Women's Health Imperative actually designated domestic violence as the number one public health issue impacting African American women in 1997 (Joseph, 1997). Largely hidden from public view, domestic violence often takes place secretly in homes, with women questioning how to respond, when to leave, and what to do. Social, health, and criminal justice systems have also been faced with the same questions: how to respond, when women should leave, and what should be done to address the violence. Domestic violence is a major issue that impacts all persons regardless of race, ethnicity, age, socioeconomic status, religion, or sexual orientation. Domestic violence is defined as "a pattern of assaultive and coercive behaviors including physical, sexual, and psychological attacks, as well as economic coercion that adults or adolescents use against their intimate partners" (Schechter & Ganley, 1995, p. 10). While there has been an increasing focus on male victims and female perpetrators, women are consistently more often victims with male perpetrators. Overall, 5 million people reportedly experience domestic violence in this country each year (National Center for Injury Prevention and Control, 2003), and women continue to be the victims of abuse by their male partners over 90% of the time (Rennison & Welchans, 2000). In 2007, it was reported that domestic violence rates were declining for the general population; yet, the rates remained constant for African American women (Catalano, 2007). While the decrease in overall rates is still being disputed in the field, the questions as to how and why African American women are at, what appears to be, an increased risk of experiencing domestic violence still persist. This chapter will examine statistics related to domestic violence in the African American community, discuss some of the challenges and barriers experienced by the African American community to stop domestic violence, and end with recommendations as to how to move forward to eradicate domestic violence in the African American community.

Prevalence of Domestic Violence in the African American Community

The rate of domestic violence has reportedly been higher in the African American community (Catalano, 2007; Rennison & Welchans, 2000; Tjaden & Thoennes, 2000). African American women and men have experienced domestic violence at 35% and 62% higher rates than have White women and men, respectively. Compared with other groups of color, African American women and men have experienced domestic violence at a rate of 22% higher than women and men of other races/ethnicities. These numbers are largely attributed to age and socioeconomic status. African American women between the ages of 20 and 24 report a significantly higher rate of abuse than White women in the same age group (Rennison, 2001). A recent study found, however, that there was a similar rate of nonfatal intimate partner victimization between African American and White females over the age of 12 between 2001 and 2005 (Catalano, 2007). Persons in lower-income households consistently report a higher rate of violence than those from middle- and upper-income households (citations). While the number of murders resulting from intimate partner violence has dropped for all racial groups, African Americans still have a rate four times that of White Americans (Greenfeld et al., 1998). Women have the highest overall rate of being killed by an intimate partner, and the rate is highest for African American women that are in nonmarried relationships (Fox & Zawitz, 2007).

These statistics raise important questions. They speak to a high rate of violence among young African Americans that are poor and in nonmarried relationships. However, there are important methodological issues that raise concern as well (Campbell, 1993; Hampton, Carrillo, & Kim, 1998; Hampton & Yung, 1996; Lockhart, 1985). Low sample sizes of African Americans in studies have been the subject of doubt of research findings (Hampton & Yung, 1996; Lockhart, 1985; Bent-Goodley, 2005a). In addition, the cultural acceptability of the questions and research methodology has caused concern. For example, the language often used in the field has been found to not have the same meaning in the African American community, bringing to question if the participants in research actually interpreted the questions as intended, and whether the participants felt comfortable enough with the researcher to answer questions authentically (Bent-Goodley, 2004; Bent-Goodley, 2005b; Bent-Goodley & Williams, 2005). An additional challenge to these research findings is that police reports often do not specify intimate partner-related crimes; therefore, it is possible that the crime-related data do not include assaults, homicides, and other crimes that are actually attributable to domestic violence. Also, there is a greater law enforcement presence in communities of color and poor communities, which may account for the larger numbers of reported crimes to law enforcement. Finally, many communities of color lack health insurance, which impacts being able to utilize other professionals, such as doctors, clinical social workers, psychologists, and psychiatrists, that are often sought after in White and middle-class communities to help deal with domestic violence. So, there are justifiable questions regarding the stated prevalence of domestic violence in the African American community.

While the research suggests that domestic violence is higher in Black and in Native American communities (Rennison & Welchans, 2000; Tjaden & Thoennes, 2000), there are also important methodological and structural concerns to consider when examining the research. This assertion does not mean that domestic violence is not a serious issue in the Black community. Nor does it circumvent the notion that this issue is pervasive in the Black community. What it does say is that it is important to understand the full context and limitations of research before one ascribes perceptions of populations of people. Accepting that domestic violence is a serious issue in its community, the African American community faces and must address unique barriers and challenges to obtaining supports and services.

Barriers and Challenges to Receiving Services

African Americans experience multiple barriers when attempting to access services. Coupled with systemic discriminatory treatment are multiple barriers that make it difficult to obtain help, including limited culturally competent services that are geographically available, the historical context of abuse, and messages of racial loyalty that make it difficult to seek help.

Systemic Discriminatory Treatment

The criminal justice system has increasingly become the mechanism most often used to respond to domestic violence (Fagan, 1996). While many African American women turn to the law enforcement system to help stop abuse, there is still great resistance, distrust, and fear of reaching out to police for assistance (Bent-Goodley & Williams, 2008; Gondolf & Williams, 2001; Joseph, 1997; Richie, 1996; West, 1999; Williams, 1999). Typically, when an African American reaches out to the police for domestic violence, the person feels that there is no other resource available, is reaching out for someone in an abusive situation and does not know what to do, or wants the abuse at that moment to stop (West, 1999, 2003). Law enforcement officers are not viewed as a friendly resource but a last option when other options have failed, are unknown, or nonexistent. When interacting with the criminal justice system for domestic violence, there is a similar parallel to other areas of crime and justice. That is, African Americans are disproportionately more likely to be arrested, prosecuted, jailed, and imprisoned than other racial and ethnic groups due to domestic violence (Mills, 1998; Richie, 1996; Roberts, 1994). This disproportionate response is relevant not just for the perpetrators, but also for African American survivors of abuse. In addition to criminal justice responses, African Americans have also been victims of discriminatory treatment when reaching out for social service supports. For instance, African American women have been stereotyped as too strong, not needing services, physically capable of taking care of themselves, too loud, bringing on the abuse, or not looking enough like a victim of abuse (Richie, 1996; West, 1999). Reports of domestic violence shelters and providers turning African American women away due to these stereotypic images of African American womanhood are frightening considering the significant amount of courage and risk taken when a woman seeks help for domestic violence. This startling disparate treatment serves to reinforce the perception in the community that formal providers and systems cannot be trusted and that discriminatory treatment is always a consideration when interacting with outside systems.

Limited Culturally Competent Services
That Are Geographically Available

These perceptions of formal systems and providers are then reinforced when services are geographically inaccessible or not culturally competent. Many providers still feel that domestic violence is the same for every person and does not require a culturally competent response. Some providers still relegate cultural competence to having a staff person that looks like the person as meeting a culturally competent response. These incorrect and limited assumptions of culture are profoundly charged and can be even more harmful for the very people that providers want to serve. Locating services outside of the community can effectively eliminate people from obtaining services they need due to the inability to travel to different locations due to transportation costs, poor transportation systems, or logistical prohibitions of traveling with children. When African American women are able to access these services, they often find that they are not culturally relevant to them and are sometimes, consequently, isolating and further damaging (Bent-Goodley, 2005a; Williams, 2007). Service providers may not acknowledge the nuances of their language (Bent-Goodley, 2005b). Often, the women may feel that the provider does not understand them based on their race or their presumed class status. The program may miss gathering sensitive information in assessment because it does not understand the cultural context of defining domestic violence or may not know how to interpret communication messages or tones of speech (Bent-Goodley, 2005b). Familial patterns and communal foci are also important from a cultural standpoint (Bent-Goodley, 2005b; Boyd-Franklin, 2006; Hill, 1997). The family is viewed not just as biological relatives, but also those that are part of the extended family and fictive kin that play critical roles to the family. Not understanding the value and importance of the extended family can also impede a provider's ability to work with African American women. The family is not just an outside entity to the woman, but often central to her thinking about herself, her role, and her position. Thus, the family and its role for African American women are important to understand. Next, the focus on community is an important cultural factor. The communal focus has also been regarded as a strength in the African American community (Hill, 1997). The community provides official and unofficial sanctioning of behavior. African American women are deeply engaged in the community, from being involved in their faith-based groups to actively participating in sororities and neighborhood block associations (Carlton-Laney, 2001). Consequently, it is important to understand how the community impacts the woman from a cultural context. Being unfamiliar with the faith-based community or the significance of religion and spirituality for coping and assistance may also further divide the practitioner, agency, and the person seeking services. Religion and spirituality play a particularly important role in coping for African American women (Bell & Mattis, 2000; Bent-Goodley & Fowler, 2006; Nason-Clark, 2004; Hassouneh-Phillips, 2003; Musgrave, Allen, & Allen, 2002). They provide a means of dealing with sensitive issues and a place for healing and support. While faith-based communities have struggled with adequately and competently providing such supports and services to survivors of domestic violence, they are nevertheless one of the first places that survivors turn to for support and assistance.

The Historical Context of Abuse

The historical context of abuse continues to be identified in studies on perceptions of African Americans toward domestic violence (Bent-Goodley, 2004; Bent-Goodley & Williams, 2005, 2008; Hampton & Gullotta, 2006). Issues from the enslavement of African people to postslavery treatment and the Jim Crow era have all been identified as having left lasting impressions on how African American males and females relate to each other (Hill, 1997; Martin & Martin, 1995). The inability to marry and form lasting, loving partnerships is among the major consequences of slavery. Creating structures sanctioning African American men as the head of the household and owner of African American women's labor created tension and friction in the home post-legalized slavery (Franklin, 2000). Further challenges imposed by forcing men out of the household to receive public welfare benefits has also been identified as systemically diminishing African American male relationships (Martin & Martin, 1995). These and other historical challenges have taken place amidst systemic patterns of racism and discrimination that have made it difficult for African Americans to seek help outside of the community and formulate healthy bonds and relationships. These challenges have also made it difficult to pass on healthy messages about gender socialization to teach healthy forms of masculinity, femininity, and relationships. Thus, domestic violence takes place within this larger issue of a persistent historical context that is repeatedly identified as troubling and problematic as it relates to domestic violence in the African American community.

Messages of Racial Loyalty

Racial loyalty has been defined as when "the African American woman may withstand abuse and make a conscious self-sacrifice for what she perceives as the greater good of the community but to her own physical, psychological, and spiritual detriment" (Bent-Goodley, 2001, p. 323). Racial loyalty is an important construct to understand because it informs delayed help seeking and, often, a lack of willingness to reach out for supports and services even when it is known by the survivor to be needed. African American women often make a conscious effort not to reach out to formal providers to avoid bringing shame to the community or reinforcing negative stereotypes of African Americans, in general, and African American relationships more specifically (Richie, 1996; West, 1999). Talking about the violence being experienced has been viewed as breaking secrecy and being more harmful than helpful to the family and community. It has been viewed as a violation of trust and even a lack of recognition of what is needed to sustain a relationship. These kinds of issues make it that more challenging to address this already complex issue.

Implications

There are many implications for how to address domestic violence in the African American community based on the statistics and barriers identified. What is emphasized is that finding the solutions to address domestic violence requires a true partnership between the community and professional providers. One group cannot do it alone. It is necessary to work together to create sustainable solutions that recognize the unique circumstances and great diversity within the African American community. First, there needs to be a significant investment in healthy relationship education in the African American community. Second, there must be a promotion of developing community and faith-based responses to domestic violence. Third, more money needs to be invested in primary prevention efforts to stop abuse from occurring, and finally, increasing our knowledge of culturally targeted interventions for African Americans struggling with this issue is important.

Invest in Healthy Relationship Education

Investing in healthy relationship education is key to finding lasting solutions to address domestic violence in the African American community. First, it is of critical importance to include men as partners in eradicating abuse. While there are significant amounts of abuse taking place within the African American community, there are far more relationships that are healthy with African American men that are positive and capable of serving as models of character and Black masculinity. These men are needed to help disentangle violence from relationships and help other men find healthy and violence-free ways of addressing domestic violence. Second, African American women also need support to enrich their understanding of how to address the intersectional oppression they encounter as women of color. At the same time, greater support is needed to develop culturally based healthy relationship education programs that recognize the intersectional dynamics of abuse and the historical context in which it takes place. Without an interlocking focus, such programs will not be as effective or as lasting among African Americans.

Promote More Community and Faith-Based Responses

There is a distinct and important role for community and faith-based organizations to play in responding to domestic violence. While the provider community offers critical knowledge and skills to addressing domestic violence, community and faith-based providers offer credibility, trust, a long-term history within the community, and are available when formal service providers are often unavailable. Thus, these organizations should be an active contributor to creating sustainable efforts to respond to abuse. Often these organizations are accessed during focus groups or when grants are being formulated. Rarely are they sought afterwards for their advice, guidance, and counsel on larger systemic issues related to domestic violence, critiquing interventions, assisting with staffing challenges, or promoting positive messages. Community and faith-based organizations are often the first place women of color turn to for support around domestic violence issues. Therefore, they can offer unique supports in facilitating help seeking, enhancing coping mechanisms, and having a sense of additional supports available. It makes sense that they both be better prepared to address domestic violence and more engaged in finding lasting solutions and strategies to assist among formal provider systems. Community and faith-based providers can also be organized to question charges of discriminatory treatment and stereotyping in formal systems. They can serve as a venue for achieving social justice and countering discrimination that is experienced. Thus, community and faith-based groups offer multiple opportunities to address domestic violence.

Invest in Primary Prevention Efforts

Domestic violence is increasing among our teen population. Dating violence is on the rise, with one in four adolescent girls experiencing violence at the hands of an intimate partner. This rise is a reflection of the limited number of primary prevention strategies that are available to stop domestic violence. Primary prevention must receive additional funding that is reflective of diverse communities' needs, must be culturally targeted and specific, and available for a long enough period of time that it can be sufficiently evaluated.

Often, monies are provided for interventions because of the need to keep people safe and respond to crises and potential lethality. Yet, little is done to prevent more people from becoming victims or perpetrators of abuse. Little is done to test wide and varied primary prevention efforts that are culturally specific and can be available to diverse communities. Primary prevention must include an intergenerational approach that targets children, adolescents, and adults across the life course. Recognizing that anyone can be a victim or perpetrator of abuse, primary prevention needs to be focused among all populations, including those that are viewed as not needing economic or social supports.

Increase and Fund Culturally Competent Responses and Programs

Greater attention needs to be given to increasing the number of culturally competent responses and programs available to African Americans trying to deal with this issue. It should not be acceptable to give funding to organizations that do not reflect the cultural needs of the population they serve. Organizations should be required to evidence cultural competence, or they should not be allowed to receive public funding to provide services. While this may seem harsh, it is critical that services are provided to meet the needs of the woman or man that needs them. If service provision is truly about the client, then the services must be designed, administered, and evaluated in ways that speak to the client, not the provider. In addition to increased opportunities for training in cultural competence, more attention needs to be given to ensuring that the worker can evidence culturally competent strategies and approaches, and that organizations can produce policies, programs, and staffing patterns that are reflective proportionately of the population being served. Cultural competence should not be relegated to some separate requirement that has to be met, but as a way of more efficiently and more effectively meeting the needs of people seeking help. The cultural context also needs to be further researched to really begin to strengthen understandings of how culture and intersections of culture impact domestic violence.

Conclusion

While domestic violence is a complex issue in the African American community, there is also hope for change. The criminal justice system is not the only way to respond to domestic violence in the African American community. There continue to be African American couples that are in healthy relationships that are violence-free, respectful, and flourishing. These couples can become resources to generating new solutions to end abuse. Our community and faith-based organizations are unique entities situated to assist in finding solutions to end abuse and to provide emergency and other types of assistance to both victims and perpetrators of abuse. Creating culturally competent responses of formal providers and advancing primary prevention efforts in this area are necessary to stem the tide of abuse. Finding ways of addressing the cultural and historical contexts of abuse are necessary to bring about the changes sought to stop abuse. Working together, we can diminish and advance the eradication of domestic violence in the African American community.

References

Bell, C., & Mattis, J. (2000). The importance of cultural competence in ministering to African American victims of domestic violence. *Violence Against Women, 6,* 515–532.

Bent-Goodley, T. B. (2001). Eradicating domestic violence in the African American community: A literature review and action agenda. *Trauma, Violence and Abuse, 2,* 316–330.

Bent-Goodley, T. B. (2004). Perceptions of domestic violence: A dialogue with African American women. *Health and Social Work, 29,* 307–316.

Bent-Goodley, T. B. (2005a). Culture and domestic violence: Transforming knowledge development. *Journal of Interpersonal Violence, 20,* 195–203.

Bent-Goodley, T. B. (2005b). An African-centered approach to domestic violence. *Families in Society, 86,* 264–283.

Bent-Goodley, T. B., & Fowler, D. (2006). Spiritual and religious abuse: Expanding what is known about domestic violence. *Affilia, 21,* 282–295.

Bent-Goodley, T. B., & Williams, O. (2005). *Community insights on domestic violence among African Americans: Conversations about domestic violence and other issues affecting their community—Seattle, Washington.* Minneapolis: Institute on Domestic Violence in the African American Community.

Bent-Goodley, T. B., & Williams, O. (2008). *Community insights on domestic violence among African Americans: Conversations about domestic violence and other issues affecting their community—Detroit, Michigan.* Minneapolis: Institute on Domestic Violence in the African American Community.

Boyd-Franklin, N. (2006). *Black families in therapy: A multisystems approach* (2nd ed.). New York: Guilford.

Campbell, D. (1993). Nursing care of African American battered women: Afrocentric perspectives. *AWHONN's Clinical Issues, 4,* 407–415.

Carlton-Laney, I. (Ed.). (2001). *African American leadership: An empowerment tradition in social welfare history.* Washington, DC: NASW Press.

Catalano, S. (2007). *Intimate partner violence in the United States.* Washington, DC: Office of Justice Programs.

Fagan, J. (1996). *The criminalization of domestic violence: Promises and limitations.* Washington, DC: U.S. Department of Justice, Office of Justice Programs.

Fox, J., & Zawitz, M. (2007). *Homicide trends in the United States.* Washington, DC: U.S. Department of Justice.

Franklin, D. (2000). *What's love got to do with it? Understanding and healing the rift between Black men and women.* New York: Simon & Schuster.

Gondolf, E., & Williams, O. (2001). Culturally focused batterer counseling for African American men. *Trauma, Violence & Abuse, 2,* 283–295.

Greenfeld, L., Rand, M., Craven, D., Klaus, P., Perkins, C., Ringel, C., et al. (1998). *Violence by intimates: Analysis of data on crimes by current or former spouses, boyfriends, and girlfriends* (NCJ 167237). Washington, DC: U.S. Department of Justice, Office of Justice Programs.

Hampton, R., Carrillo, R., & Kim, J. (1998). Violence in communities of color. In R. Carrillo & J. Tello (Eds.), *Family violence and men of color: Healing the wounded male spirit* (pp. 1–30). New York: Springer.

Hampton, R., & Gullotta, T. (Eds.). (2006). *Interpersonal violence in the African American community: Evidence based prevention and treatment practices.* New York: Springer.

Hampton, R., & Yung, B. (1996). Violence in communities of color: Where we were, where we are, and where we need to be. In R. Hampton, P. Jenkins, & T. Gullotta (Eds.), *Preventing violence in America* (pp. 53–86). Thousand Oaks, CA: Sage Publications.

Hassouneh-Phillips, D. (2003). Strength and vulnerability: Spirituality in abused American Muslim women's lives. *Issues in Mental Health Nursing, 24,* 681–694.

Hill, R. (1997). *The strengths of African American families: Twenty-five years later.* Washington, DC: R & B Publishers.

Joseph, J. (1997). Woman battering: A comparative analysis of Black and White women. In G. Kantor & J. Jasinski (Eds.), *Out of darkness: Contemporary perspectives on family violence* (pp. 161–169). Thousand Oaks, CA: Sage Publications.

Lockhart, L. (1985). Methodological issues in comparative racial analyses: The case of wife abuse. *Research and Abstracts, 13,* 35–41.

Martin, E., & Martin, J. (1995). *Social work and the Black experience.* Washington, DC: NASW Press.

Mills, L. (1998). Mandatory arrest and prosecution policies for domestic violence: A critical literature review and the case for more research to test victim empowerment approaches. *Criminal Justice and Behavior, 25,* 306–318.

Nason-Clark, N. (2004). When terror strikes at home: The interface between religion and domestic violence. *Journal for the Scientific Study of Religion, 43,* 303–310.

National Center for Injury Prevention and Control. (2003). *Costs of intimate partner violence against women in the United States.* Atlanta, GA: Centers for Disease Control and Prevention.

Rennison, C., & Welchans, S. (2000). *Intimate partner violence* (NCJ 178247). Washington, DC: U.S. Department of Justice, Office of Justice Programs.

Richie, B. E. (1996). *Compelled to crime: The gender entrapment of battered Black women.* New York: Routledge.

Roberts, T. (1994). When violence hits home. *Health Quest, 5,* 50–53.

Schechter, S., & Ganley, A. (1995). *Domestic violence: A national curriculum for family preservation practitioners.* San Francisco: Family Violence Prevention Fund.

Tjaden, P., & Thoennes, N. (2000). *Extent, nature and consequences of intimate partner violence: Findings from the National Violence Against Women Survey* (NCJ 181867). Washington, DC: U.S. Department of Justice, Office of Justice Programs.

West, C. (2003). *Violence in the lives of Black women: Battered, black and blue.* New York: Routledge.

West, T. (1999). *Wounds of the spirit: Black women, violence and resistance ethics.* New York: New York University Press.

Williams, O. (1999). Working in groups with African American men who batter. In L. E. Davis (Ed.), *Working with African American males: A guide to practice* (pp. 229–242). Thousand Oaks, CA: Sage Publications.

Williams, O. (2007). *Concepts in creating culturally responsive services for supervised visitation centers.* Minneapolis: Institute on Domestic Violence in the African American Community.

Domestic Violence in Asian Cultures

3

QIANG XU
ALLEN ANDERSON

Contents

Scope of the Problem

According to the U.S. Census 2000, there are about 11.9 million Asians in the United States, which represent 4.2% of the total U.S. population. For various reasons, domestic violence within Asian communities tends to shy away from the view of the mainstream society. Nevertheless, as in many cultures, domestic violence is not uncommon within Asian cultures. Thousands of women within Asian American communities have been adversely impacted as victims of domestic violence in their lives and development. Since the rise of the feminist approach in criminological research in the 1970s, awareness and concerns of domestic violence have been growing within the Asian communities, as in other ethnic communities. Due to limitations of data on other types of domestic violence within Asian communities, such as child abuse, the discussion of domestic violence in the present chapter will be centered on violence between intimate partners.

Although data collection and research on domestic violence within Asian communities in the United States has a brief history of about two decades, research based on national representative samples and local focus groups has substantiated and documented the extent of the problem of domestic violence within Asian communities. One study based on a national representative sample found that 12.8% of Asian American women had experienced at least one physical assault by an intimate partner, and 3.8% of Asian American women were victims of rape by an intimate partner (Tjaden &

Thoennes, 2000). Findings from this research showed that the rate of physical assault within Asian communities was lower than those reported by Whites (21.3%); African Americans (26.3%); Hispanics, of any race (21.2%); mixed race (27.0%); and American Indians and Alaskan Natives (30.7%). The lower rate of domestic violence within Asian communities, however, has to be interpreted with caution due to the problem of underreporting and measurement of domestic violence. Nonetheless, several community-based research projects suggested the pervasiveness of domestic violence within Asian communities. One study based on Korean women living in Chicago (Song-Kim, 1992) found that 60% of the respondents reported physical violence by an intimate partner in their lifetime. A similar study on domestic violence in the Korean American community in San Francisco (Shimtuh, 2000) adopted an indirect measure of physical violence and found a 42% prevalence rate within the Korean communities in the San Francisco Bay Area. Another research project based on a sample of South Asian women in Boston (Raj & Silverman, 2002) found that 41% of the respondents reported being victimized by physical or sexual abuse, or both, during their lifetime.

Research conducted in other Asian ethnic communities, including the Chinese, Cambodian, and Vietnamese communities (Yick, 2000; Yoshioka, Dang, Shewmangal, Vhan, & Tan, 2000), has shown a similar prevalence rate of domestic violence. With the growing awareness of domestic violence within Asian communities, more recent research not only measured physical abuse and sexual abuse but also incorporated a substantive measurement of other types of abuse by intimate partners. It can be argued that for many victims of domestic violence, the pain and suffering of emotional abuse is more detrimental than physical abuse, and many victims of emotional abuse are less likely to report this type of abuse due to lack of physical evidence. Among other factors, one study based on a random sample of Japanese American women in Los Angeles (Yoshihama, 1999) suggested that the prevalence of domestic violence was about 61% among the respondents. In this project, the measurement of domestic violence comprised physical, emotional, and sexual violence. Nevertheless, physical abuse is most reported in this study. In a subsequent study, 52% of the respondents reported having experienced physical violence in their lifetime (Yoshihama & Gillespie, 2002). Another study measured different forms of abuse by intimate partners, including domination, controlling, physical, psychological, and sexual abuse (McDonnell & Abdulla, 2001). The findings suggested that 67% of the respondents experienced some forms of domination and controlling, and 48% reported frequent psychological abuse by intimate partners. Despite these studies, it is unknown to what extent emotional abuse, together with other types of abuse, was underreported in many Asian ethnic communities.

The problem of domestic violence within Asian American communities is also reflected in the reports of domestic violence-related homicides.

Several studies on domestic violence suggested that Asian women were disproportionately victimized in domestic violence-related homicides, typically involving a long history of being abused and attempts to escape from an abusive relationship. Victims of such homicide comprised the abused women, their relatives, and children (Tong, 1992). According to a death review report compiled by Santa Clara County in California (Death Review Subcommittee of the Domestic Violence Council, 1997), 31% of the women killed in domestic violence-related homicides from 1993 to 1997 were Asians. The ratio is almost twice that of Asians living in Santa Clara County. Similar disproportionate patterns were observed in Boston in 1991, where Asians represented a mere 2.4% of the population, but 13% of women and children victims of domestic violence-related homicides were Asians (Tong, 1992).

It should be pointed out that contemporary data and research on domestic violence within Asian communities may not reflect all aspects of the problem due to various reasons. Underreporting is one of the most problematic issues. Tjaden and Thoennes (2000) suggested that our knowledge about domestic violence in Asian communities is limited, and it is difficult to explain why Asians reported less domestic violence than other ethnic groups in the United States. One factor that contributes to the underreporting problem is the culture values in Asian communities. Concerns about close family ties and harmony within the community may discourage victims in the Asian community to disclose domestic violence (Warrier, 2004). Sometimes, victims feel ashamed to ask for help or even talk about it in their defense. Therefore, contemporary data on domestic violence within Asian communities may only capture the most serious cases of domestic violence, while many less serious incidents go unreported and undetected. Other factors that blur our understanding of domestic violence within Asian communities are the complexity of the cultural backgrounds of the Asian communities and the general tendency to study all Asian communities as a whole. Asian American communities comprise members from different parts of Asia, bearing different languages, religions, and cultural heritages. For instance, immigrants from Northeast Asia, such as Chinese, Korean and Japanese, can have totally different attitudes toward domestic violence than people from Southeast Asia, such as Cambodians and Vietnamese. Among immigrants from various Asian cultures, there are variations in people's attitudes toward domestic violence (Malley-Morrison & Hines, 2005). Therefore, more specific research, based on individual Asian ethnic groups, is necessary to have a better understanding of the scope of domestic violence.

Although there is limited information about individual Asian ethnic groups based on large samples in the United States, a general survey of the situation of domestic violence in their home countries will help to understand the problem within their historical and cultural contexts.

According to the U.S Census 2000, immigrants from China represent the largest Asian community in the United States, and every year more than 5,000 Chinese become permanent residents of the United States. In China, however, there were no official statistics of domestic violence before the 1990s. In a survey conducted by China's All-China Women's Federation (ACWF, 1990), the authority of women's rights in China, 30% of the respondents reported having been beaten by their husbands at least once. That suggested a total of 56.2 million women who had been victims of physical violence at least once in their lifetime. A more recent survey by the ACWF (2004) suggested that there were more incidents of domestic violence in rural areas of China, in young families, and in households with lower educational levels. East Indians are the second largest Asian communities in the United States. According to the estimate of the Human Rights Watch (2005), domestic violence in India was as prevalent as in many other South Asian countries. It was estimated that (on average) there was one case of cruelty by husband or relatives against women every nine minutes in India. In other parts of Asia, domestic violence is also pervasive. A research project founded by the Soros Foundation (2003) suggested that domestic violence against women comprised about 57.4% of all the criminal cases in Mongolia. Domestic violence against women is even worse in West Asia. In many West Asian countries, including Iran, Saudi Arabia, and other countries with Islamic traditions, women had the highest rate of victimization for all types of physical violence, including physical punishment by intimate partners and relatives. Although awareness of domestic violence has been growing in many Asian nations and among many new immigrants from Asia, today there are still many incidents of domestic violence in Asian nations and among Asian American communities.

Causes of Domestic Violence in Asian Communities

There are several causes of domestic violence in Asian communities. Deep-rooted patriarchy in Asian cultures and its penetrating influence on Asian communities in the United States is one of the most important causes of domestic violence. Patriarchy is not only belief in male chauvinism but also involves mechanism to maintain male supremacy in all facets of life. One study based on a national focus group of Asian Americans (Warrier, 2004) suggested that the majority of the respondents believe that patriarchy and sexism are major causes of domestic violence in their lives. In many Asian cultures, women were socialized to strictly abide by the gender role and accept violence as a normal part of their lives. In contrast, males are socialized to believe that physical violence against women is an effective means to express male dominance and maintain the power and control in a relationship.

Although patriarchy is not a unique cause of domestic violence in Asian cultures, the impact of patriarchy in Asian cultures tends to be amplified by inadequate responses from the criminal justice system in most Asian nations. In many Asian languages, there is no such phrase called "domestic violence." In Chinese, for example, incidents of domestic violence are named *Da Lao Po*, which means "wife beating." In traditional Chinese values, wife beating is regarded as a private affair within a family, which should not be intervened in. For years in China there was no specific legal code to control domestic violence. A Chinese proverb, "Qing Guan Nan Duan Jia Wu Shi," meaning "Even the wisest judge cannot rule on family matters," demonstrates why historically there was limited legal response to domestic violence in China. Similar to the American experience, cases of domestic violence in China used to be handled as family disputes and police generally were reluctant to handle such cases. Not until 2007 did the Ministry of Public Security of China officially confirm that police would handle cases of domestic violence differently than a regular family dispute. Within this macro sociocultural background, many Chinese men who were perpetrators of domestic violence did not need any cause or excuse for beating their wives because it was taken for granted in the culture and could sometimes be worth boasting about.

In some remote rural areas of China, bride trafficking is still practiced and well received in some local communities. In recent years, with the rapid increase of domestic violence cases and the work of All-China Women's Federation (ACWF), a series of legislation has been enacted, including revision of the marriage law and providing protection of the rights of women in legal procedures. In other Asian nations, patriarchy and male dominance were also well entrenched. According to the National Crime Records Bureau of India (2005), a crime against women was committed every three minutes. Despite the high volume of domestic violence, there was no specific legislation to deal with all types of domestic violence in India. It is the same case with many other South Asian and West Asian nations. The extreme form of patriarchy in Asian culture was well exemplified in the so-called Hudood law. Under this law, if a woman makes a rape allegation, she must provide four pious male witnesses or face a charge of adultery herself. This law was commonly applied in Pakistan and many West Asian Islamic nations. Given this deep-rooted cultural legacy of patriarchy and male dominance in many Asian cultures and the fact that most Asian Americans were foreign born, it is reasonable to believe that patriarchy is a major cause of domestic violence within Asian communities in the United States.

Suspicion about extramarital affairs is another cause, and sometimes a "justifiable" reason, of domestic violence within Asian communities. One study (Yick & Agbayani-Siewert, 1997) found about 50% of the Chinese American respondents believed that wife beating was justifiable in cases of defense of self and defense of a child. The older Chinese Americans in the sample had tolerance of intimate violence committed in response to a wife's extramarital affair. Influenced by belief in patriarchy, many Asian American men believe they should have total control of their wives. Consequently, any aberrant behaviors such as returning home late from work or other suspected behaviors of infidelity are subject to verbal or physical abuse. In our current study based on a focus group of Asian American respondents in a Midwest state, it is found that half of the respondents reported suspicion about extramarital affairs as a major cause for verbal abuse and physical abuse by intimate partners.

Stress in life, including but not limited to concerns about employment, child care, and care of parents, is also an important cause of domestic violence in Asian communities. In our focus group, more than 60% of the respondents suggested that perceived stress in life is another important cause for all kinds of family disputes, including physical abuse by an intimate partner. Certainly stress should not be used as an excuse for perpetrators of domestic violence. The point is that many reported cases of domestic violence, including cases of murder-suicide, within Asian communities can be traced back to excessive stressful life events not generally known to the mainstream culture. The triggers of stress can vary across different Asian ethnic groups. In some South Asian communities, for instance, the payment or nonpayment of dowry and its variants in the United States, can cause serious forms of domestic violence (Warriers, 2004). Therefore, it seems that causes of domestic violence within Asian communities are not dramatically different from those in other cultures. However, a long tradition of patriarchy and contemporary practice of male dominance in Asian cultures tends to fortify and perpetuate the problem of domestic violence.

Dynamics of Domestic Violence Within Asian Communities

As mentioned above, even within the Asian communities, there are various ethnic groups that are different in religion, cultural heritage, and aspects of socioeconomic development. While it is difficult to present a general picture that covers all the characteristics of domestic violence within Asian communities, it is important to highlight some of its unique aspects within Asian communities.

One of the unique aspects of domestic violence within Asian American communities is the problem of underreporting. On one hand, most Eastern cultural beliefs make a woman victim less likely to report domestic violence in public because of fear of shame to her family members and community, and also because of the general tolerance of domestic violence with the Asian cultures. Consequently, many incidents are not known and perpetuators are not disclosed. On the other hand, due to this underreporting problem, mainstream culture may underestimate the real situation of domestic violence in Asian communities; hence, little assistance will be available to the victims. One respondent from our focus group told her story about tolerating her abusive husband for more than 20 years without asking for any help from relatives. The only time the abusive husband was put into jail was when her daughter called the police and reported one incident as a witness. When she finally decided to divorce the abusive husband, she found herself a target of increased harassment at her work and had to eventually move out of her house. Even in that situation, she never thought of filing a protection order with the court. For many Asian women victims, they still treat domestic violence as a private affair within a family. In a recent survey conducted by the International Institute for Population Studies (2006) in India, 56% of Indian women believed that wife beating would be justified under certain circumstances. Those circumstances range from going out without the husband's permission to cooking a bad meal.

The other important factor that helps to understand domestic violence is the unique immigrant experiences of the Asian communities. For many women who do not have permanent residence in the United States, they often have to pay the high price of tolerating their abusive husbands and stay in the marriage in order to maintain legal status. In 2007, some amendments were added to the immigration laws to assist victims of domestic violence as an aftermath of a Chinese woman beaten to death by her abusive husband after long suffering from physical violence. For many Asian communities, language barriers and lack of knowledge of the criminal justice system in the United States create tremendous problems in times of victimization by an abusive spouse. Unfortunately, victims within Asian communities have to deal with constraints of their own contexts as well as isolation from the assistance of the mainstream society.

In a study by Asian and Pacific Islander Institute (2005), it is suggested that there are two distinguishing dynamics of domestic violence in Asian communities. One is that there are multiple batterers in the home. Male and female in-laws are more likely to be involved as perpetrators of domestic violence. This is partly due to the fact that in many Asian communities, children and parents often share the same home and live together even after the children get married. The other distinguishing dynamics is that women victims of domestic violence are more likely to be pushed out of the relationship or out of the family home. This point is corroborated by respondents in our study based on a focus group in a Midwestern state, and it was particularly true when the abusive partner was involved in extramarital affairs. Understanding these dynamics of domestic violence within Asian communities will help provide relevant policy implications to address the needs of the victims.

Theoretical Explanation

Considering the scope of domestic violence and the unique dynamics of the problem, power control theory (Hagan, Gillis, & Simpson, 1987) and feminist theories (Chesney-Lind, 1989) seem to be more applicable to explain domestic violence within Asian communities. In many traditional Asian cultures, wives and daughters were regarded as private property of fathers and husbands. Although women are gaining more independence in contemporary society, the belief of male chauvinism persists in all facets of Asian communities. For instance, a typical Chinese couple is comprised of a husband with a higher educational background, higher salary, and higher political ranking. If the pattern does not hold, there can be problems that herald domestic violence. For many Chinese, a couple composed of a husband with a master's degree and a wife with a doctoral degree appears to be odd and unconventional. The situation becomes worse when a wife works in a high-paying job and a husband is unemployed. More often than not, domestic violence is used as a convenient means to express male dominance and authority in the household. In a patriarchal social system, domestic violence is only one form of gender inequality, which may be traced to other forms of social inequality, such as inequality in social economic status. In some Asian cultures, such as Japanese, Korean, and even Taiwanese, women usually stay at home taking care of the family and children and men work outside. Without independent economic resources, women in those cultures can have a hard time coping with domestic violence. Hence, without gender equality in other spheres of life, such as equality in education and employment, domestic violence in Asian communities may not be addressed appropriately.

Response to Domestic Violence in Asian Cultures

Although domestic violence is pervasive in Asian cultures, there have not been serious criminal justice responses to domestic violence until about two decades ago. In many Asian nations, legal codes dealing with domestic violence are a totally new sphere. In China, the belief that domestic violence is a family dispute dominated for decades. Public awareness of domestic violence began in the 1990s and grew rapidly after the Fourth World Conference on Women in 1995. Significant legislative effort to address domestic violence took place in 2001 with the revision of the marriage law. For the first time, provisions of domestic violence were written into policies and laws in China. The ACWF has also made great efforts to coordinate victim assistance programs, development of professional organizations, and policy-making processes related to domestic violence in China. A woman victim of domestic violence in China has the option of going to a local women's federation or to the ACWF for help. If the initial mediation does not work, the case will be referred to the courts. A perpetrator found guilty will then be punished according to the criminal law or local regulations of domestic violence.

Other Asian nations have witnessed a similar growth in the awareness of domestic violence over time. Nevertheless, efforts from the legislature developed slowly, especially in South and West Asian nations. In India, a landmark new law to tackle domestic violence was enacted in 2006 that banned harassment by way of dowry demands and gave sweeping powers to a magistrate to issue protection orders where needed. This new law also provided a comprehensive definition of domestic violence that differentiated actual and threat of abuse and defined physical, emotional, sexual, and economic abuse. In Pakistan, where awareness of domestic violence is low and the problem is extensive, the government tried to reform its Hudood law in 2006, though the actual effects of the reform are questionable. In most Western Asian nations, there were virtually no legislative changes to address the problem of domestic violence. The situations of women in those nations remain as difficult as decades ago.

Changes in policies and laws in Asian nations and the growing awareness of domestic violence among the Asian American communities jointly affect their attitude toward domestic violence. Nevertheless, Asian communities maintain a higher level of tolerance of domestic violence than other ethnic groups. A national telephone survey based on probability sample found that Asian women were less likely to treat various interactions as domestic violence than women of other ethnic groups, which suggested a high tolerance of domestic violence among Asian women (Klein, Campbell, Soler, & Ghez, 1997). Another study, based on Japanese Americans living in Los Angeles, suggested that belief in traditional values of Asian culture, such as conflict avoidance, submission to male domination, value of collective family welfare, and an aversion to seeking help, significantly affect how they respond to domestic violence (Yoshihama & Gillespie, 2002).

It can be argued that the responsiveness of the criminal justice system to domestic violence largely depends on how likely it is the victims will report the problems. Presently there is limited information about the rate of reporting domestic violence and the rate of utilization of the victim assistance facilities. Nevertheless, several studies suggested that among Asian communities, there were some variations in the attitude to seeking help from friends or intervention from an agency. One study (McDonnell & Abdulla, 2001) found that only 16% of the domestic violence victims tried to call the police and 9% of the victims actually received help from an assistance agency. In the same study 66% of the victims sought help from either family or friends. Another study (Yoshioka & Dang, 2000) suggested that among a sample of Asian ethnic groups, South Asians were most likely to endorse seeking help from either a friend or the police. Raj and Silverman (2002) found that among the sample of South Asians, only 11% of the victims actually received counseling services for domestic violence, while only 3.1% of the victims actually got a restraining order against an abusive partner. These findings suggested that seeking assistance from formal agencies and the police is not common for all Asian communities. South Asians are more likely to seek help from formal agencies or the police than other Asian ethnic groups.

There are many reasons why Asian victims of domestic violence are less likely to seek help from formal support agencies and the police. One study (Warrier, 2004), based on a national focus group of Asian Americans, suggested that there were several barriers Asian victims had to deal with while seeking help from formal agencies. Fear of racism and worries about no action from the police were the major concerns that kept the respondents from asking for help from the police. For many female victims, concerns about cultural identity and discrimination by the mainstream society put them in a dilemma when they were victimized and seeking help.

In many Asian ethnic communities in the United States, many residents do not speak English and rarely have contact with the criminal justice system. Once being victimized, they are less likely to call for help from the criminal justice system primarily because of language barriers and lack of knowledge of the criminal justice system. Communication barriers between the victims and operators of the help hotline also reduce the likelihood of calling the hotline for help. Those communication barriers present challenges for the criminal justice professionals as well. For instance, if the police cannot quite understand the victim's description of the problem, they may not be able to evaluate the problem and make appropriate decisions in time. Many respondents from our focus group expressed their concern about the mishandling of some cases of domestic violence among their communities. In one extreme case, a husband was falsely charged with domestic violence because his wife gave false information and pretended that she could not speak English.

Tentative Solutions to Domestic Violence in Asian Communities

Domestic violence in Asian communities has been complicated by a number of factors unique to many Asians, including—but not limited to—a long tradition of patriarchy and high tolerance of domestic violence, concerns about publicizing domestic violence due to pressure within the community and belief in family harmony, unique immigration experiences, and communication barriers with the criminal justice system. In order to deal with domestic violence within the Asian communities effectively, it is necessary to keep in mind those unique characteristics. To eliminate the deep-rooted tradition of patriarchy, an educational campaign should be focused on enhancing awareness of domestic violence and gender equality among not only adults but also children in the Asian communities. If children were socialized into a culture that has a high tolerance of domestic violence, it would cause subsequent problems not only within the families and communities but also for the rest of the society. More importantly, the cycle of domestic violence will not stop without a prospective strategy. Given the fact that the majority of Asians in the United States are foreign born, efforts to educate the younger Asian population are necessary to break the cycle of domestic violence within Asian communities.

In addition to early education among children, raising awareness of domestic violence and available resources among the entire Asian community is also necessary to reduce domestic violence. In Yoshihama and Gillespie's study (2002), based on a sample of Japanese respondents, U.S.-born respondents were significantly more likely to effectively protect themselves than their Japan-born counterparts. This finding suggested that U.S.-born respondents had more knowledge about domestic violence and available resources to deal with it than their Japan-born counterparts. If the victims of domestic violence are encouraged to speak out and also know where they can get help, it will gradually change the overall community attitude from passively tolerating domestic violence to actively dealing with and preventing it. Thus, cases of domestic violence in Asian communities will attract more attention from the rest of society and victims will receive more support and help.

Improving the effectiveness of services and responses from formal agencies is another important domain to focus on in order to reduce domestic violence within Asian communities. To achieve this goal, a thorough understanding of the victim's background, which seems to be challenging to many service providers and criminal justice professionals, is crucial to deal with the problem appropriately. For instance, Warrier (2004) suggested that failure to understand the unique issues facing immigrant and refugee women victims would not adequately address their problems. Many service providers and police officers have limited knowledge about immigration laws and the critical situation of immigrant women, especially in cases where the legal immigration status may be impacted due to the disposition of a perpetrator. Sometimes pressure to prosecute the perpetrator causes serious concerns for a woman victim whose legal immigrant status depends on the perpetrator. Furthermore, a woman victim whose immigration status is questionable can be denied service by shelters or may have limited access to those shelters (Warrier, 2004).

Some legal responses, such as mandatory arrest of domestic violence perpetrators, turned out to be no more effective in reducing recidivism in Asian communities than in other ethnic communities in the United States (Maxwell, Garner, & Fagan, 2001). Other common concerns among Asian victims of domestic violence, such as incapable interpreters and inconsistent services, are still to be addressed in order to improve the effectiveness of responses to domestic violence. Therefore, enhancing awareness of domestic violence within Asian communities is a task for service providers and criminal justice professionals as well. With the contemporary orientation of community-based policing, problems of domestic violence within Asian communities can be addressed more effectively by developing a close relationship with Asian communities and by recruiting more qualified members from Asian communities to work for the criminal justice system and various victim assistance providers.

While reforms in legal responses to domestic violence based on empirical research have been going on for decades, some important aspects of research on Asian communities should be given due attention. As mentioned previously in this chapter, the notion of Asian communities comprises a variety of Asian ethnic groups and cultures. As most of the previous studies on domestic violence within Asian communities were based on samples of heterogeneous Asian ethnic groups, results and generalizations should be interpreted with caution. Many factors in their home countries, such as religious belief, historical tradition, political ideology, alongside educational and economic development, contribute to contemporary patterns and characteristics of domestic violence within different Asian ethnic groups in the United States. Hence, future research within Asian communities should be based on individual Asian ethnic groups rather than a comprehensive Asian sample.

Second, an idiographic and qualitative research design based on samples from a local setting, and with detailed information from each individual respondent, will be more appropriate to study domestic violence within Asian communities. Quantitative research designs, based on probability sampling, are not always effective due to the small sample size and different geographic distribution of Asian communities in the United States. For instance, research based on Asian communities from California, New York, and Hawaii, where collectively more than 51% of the Asian population in the United States lives (Census 2000), may provide different findings of domestic violence from those conducted in other areas, such as in some Midwestern states. Unique social contexts in local settings, such as population density, history of immigration, political environment, and dynamics of local economy, play a part in shaping patterns of domestic violence within Asian communities. Thus, although people within individual Asian ethnic groups share a similar culture and attitude toward domestic violence, their particular experiences of domestic violence typically reported in empirical research are more applicable to the local Asian communities than to Asian communities living in different localities in the United States.

References

ACWF. All-China Women's Federation's Report (1990). Bejing, Author.

ACWF. All-China Women's Federation's Report (2004). Bejing, Author.

Asian and Pacific Islander Institute. http://apirhf.org/ Data last retrieved October 2008.

Barnes, J. S., & Bennett, C. E. (2002). *The Asian population: 2000.* U.S. Census Bureau.

Chesney-Lind, M. (1989). Girl's crime and woman's place: Toward a feminist model of female delinquency. *Crime and Delinquency, 35,* 5–29.

Hagan, J., Gillis, A. R., & Simpson, J. (1987). Class in the household: A power-control theory of gender and delinquency. *American Journal of Sociology, 92,* 788–816.

Human Rights Watch. http://www.hrw.org/ Data last retrieved October 2008.

Klein, E., Campbell, J., Soler, E., & Ghez, M. (Eds.). (1997). *Ending domestic violence: Changing public perceptions/halting the epidemic.* Thousand Oaks, CA: Sage.

Malley-Morrison, K., & Hines, D. A. (2005). *Family violence in a cultural perspective: Defining, understanding, and combating abuse.* Thousand Oaks, CA: Sage Publications.

Malone H. (1999, September 25). Asian task force encouraged by drop in domestic abuse deaths, group will hold its sixth annual fund-raiser today. *Boston Globe,* p. B3.

Maxwell, C. D., Garner, J. H., & Fagan, J. A. (2001). *The effects of arrest on intimate partner violence: New evidence from the Spouse Assault Replication Program* (NCJ 188199). Washington, DC: Department of Justice.

McDonnell, K. A., & Abdulla, S. E. (2001). *Project AWARE: Research project.* Washington, DC: Asian/Pacific Islander Domestic Violence Resource Project.

National Crime Records Bureau (2005). *Crime in India.* Ministry of Home Affairs.

Raj, A., & Silverman, J. (2002). Intimate partner violence against South-Asian women in Greater Boston. *Journal of the American Medical Women's Association, 57,* 111–114.

Santa Clara County Death Review Subcommittee of the Domestic Violence Council. (1997). *Death Review Committee final report.* San Jose: Author.

Song-Kim, Y. I. (1992). Battered Korean women in urban United States. In S. M. Furuto, B. Renuka, D. K. Chung, K. Murase, & F. Ross-Sheriff (Eds.), *Social work practice with Asian Americans: Sage sourcebooks for the human services series* (Vol. 20, pp. 213–226). Newbury Park, CA: Sage.

Tjaden, P., & Thoennes, N. (2000). *Extent, nature, and consequences of intimate partner violence: Research report.* Washington, DC: National Institute of Justice and the Centers for Disease Control and Prevention.

Tong, B. Q. M. (1992, November 9). A haven without barriers: Task force is seeking a refuge for battered Asian women. *Boston Globe,* p. 17.

Warrier, S. (2004). *(Un)heard voices: Domestic violence in the Asian American community.* U.S. Department of Justice, Office on Violence Against Women Grants Office.

Yick, A. G. (2000). Predictors of physical spousal/intimate violence in Chinese American families. *Journal of Family Violence, 15,* 249–267.

Yoshihama, M. (1999). Domestic violence against women of Japanese descent in Los Angeles: Two methods of estimating prevalence. *Violence Against Women, 5,* 869–897.

Yoshihama, M. (2000). Reinterpreting strength and safety in a socio-cultural context: Dynamics of domestic violence and experiences of women of Japanese descent. *Children Youth Services Review, 22*, 207–229.

Yoshihama, M., & Gillespie, B. (2002). Age adjustment and recall bias in the analysis of domestic violence data: Methodological improvement through the application of survival analysis methods. *Journal of Family Violence, 17*, 199–221.

Yoshioka, M. R., & Dang, Q. (2000). *Asian Family Violence Report: A study of the Cambodian, Chinese, Korean, South Asian, and Vietnamese communities in Massachusetts*. Boston: Asian Task Force Against Domestic Violence.

Yoshioka, M., Dang, Q., Shewmangal, N., Vhan, & Tan, C. I. (2000). *Asian Family Violence Report: A study of the Cambodian, Chinese, Korean, South Asian and Vietnamese*. Asian Task Force Against Domestic Violence.

Domestic Violence Among Native Americans

4

JULIE C. ABRIL

Contents

Introduction

The purpose of this chapter is to discuss domestic violence among Native Americans (hereafter, Indians). It will also touch on the prevalence, potential causes, official and cultural responses, and how the problem is conceptualized in tribal communities. At the end of this chapter, readers will be able to determine if the problem of domestic violence is any more or less significant in tribal communities than it is among other, non-Indian groups.

Extent and Prevalence

There is contention regarding the extent and prevalence of domestic violence occurring among Indians. The vast majority of studies done to determine the rate of domestic violence among Native Americans indicate a higher prevalence than among other races/ethnicities. But these studies are fraught with many flaws, such that the resulting data must be viewed with extreme caution. Most are limited to individual site studies; all have negative validity issues associated with them, such as a low number of participants, multiple recounting of incidents, data that are only taken from domestic violence shelters and their clients when it is well known that most victims do not use these services, and other methodological issues. The federal statistics on this matter are not much better.

The Bureau of Justice Statistics published *American Indians and Crime* (Greenfeld & Smith, 1999) in response to pressure from victim advocates and researchers searching for data on violence occurring among Indians. This was the first comprehensive statistical report on crime and violent victimization among Indians issued by the U.S. Department of Justice. It was reported that while Indians account for less than 1% of the U.S. population, they experience violent victimization at a rate of 124 incidents per 1,000 persons over age 12, whereas all races have a violent victimization rate of 50 incidents per 1,000 persons over age 12. According to these federal statistics, this means that Indians experience violent victimization at more than twice the national average. Other sources of data, such as the National Incident-Based Reporting System (NIBRS), are too new and underutilized to be of assistance. Also, lower-level misdemeanor acts of domestic violence tried on tribal lands are often not reported. The Uniform Crime Report, too, does not capture domestic violence among Indians.

In 2004, the Bureau of Justice Statistics again reported that Indians experience more than twice the rate of violence than the rest of the nation (Perry, 2004). It was reported that Indians experience an estimated one violent crime for every 10 residents aged 12 years or older. While the rate of violent victimization for all races is 41 incidents per 1,000 residents, for Indians, it is 101 incidents per 1,000 residents. These data come from the National Crime Victimization Survey (NCVS), a survey of victimization with known methodological weaknesses related to capturing reports of violent victimization occurring among Indians who live on reservations (Interuniversity Consortium for Political and Social Research [ICPSR], 2006). The NCVS is used because it is the only semicomprehensive data source for national rates of violent victimization among Indians. What little is known about violent victimization among Indians is that it is predominantly a result of domestic violence.

The National Violence Against Women Survey (NVAWS) (Tjaden & Thoennes, 2006) found that American Indian and Alaskan Native women had significantly higher rates of rape (34.1% higher), stalking (17% higher), and physical assault (61.4% higher) than any other ethnic group in the study. One of the known problems with the NVAWS is that the various unique cultural characteristics of the numerous tribal nations are hidden because all Indians and Alaskan Natives were grouped as one. Abril's (2005) study of the Southern Ute Indian tribe, however, found that poor, young Ute women were more likely to report violent victimization than any others in her study. In 2007, Abril (2007b) further found that those who most identified as Native American Indian were approximately three times more likely than non-Indians to report violent victimization than those people who live within the same community.

What is known about family violence among Native American Indians? There is little scientifically sound social science research available on family violence occurring within Native American Indian communities in general and within the families in particular. Yuan, Koss, Polacca, and Goldman (2006), however, conducted a recent study of the risk factors for victimization among American Indian women and men. They concluded that Indian women who exhibited the following characteristics were more likely to be at risk for physical assault: marital status, having an alcoholic parent, childhood maltreatment, and lifetime alcohol dependence. Male Indians who experienced lifetime alcohol dependence and child maltreatment were at risk for physical assault. For rape and sexual assault among Indian women, wrote Yuan et al. (2006), marital status, childhood maltreatment, and lifetime alcohol dependence were also risk factors. In addition to these findings, Evans-Campbell, Lindhorst, Huang, and Walters (2006) cited multiple victimization experiences as another risk factor for assault.

Early research on factors associated with reporting violent victimization focused on mainstream majority victims. Current research is focused on other minority group members (Wyatt, Axelrod, Chin, Carmona & Loeb, 2000; Lee, Thompson-Sanders, & Mechanic, 2002). Other research on the predictors of violent victimization among Indians appears in the psychological and medical literatures (Yuan et al., 2006). Research on victimization among Indians is scarce in the sociological and criminological literatures. Abril (2007b) reported that of those 85 Indian interview subjects, a majority (n = 47, or 55.2%) reported being a victim of domestic violence within the previous five years.

Individual levels of collective efficacy (a combination of informal social control and social cohesion) were significantly associated with reporting violent victimization (Abril, 2005). That is, those who scored higher on an individual-level collective efficacy scale were more likely to report violent victimization than those who scored lower. Involved and cohesive community members reported more incidents of violent victimization. This might be an artifact of the collective conscience and personal beliefs that authorities should be advised of community violence in an effort to respond effectively to such. The perceived safety of the victim(s) (Bachman, 1998), options for leaving the location of victimization that play into a victim's decision to move and financial considerations (Dugan, 1999), and the perception that one's report to the police or researcher would actually result in a positive outcome for the victim (Bachman, 1998) are only a few of the variables that may also influence a decision to report violent victimization.

While Abril's (2005) study also found that poor, young Indians were more likely than others to report violent victimization, this may be because they experience more violent victimization. Past empirical studies have shown that poor, young minorities experience more violent victimization because they tend to associate with other young people who may be violent and who may also live in the more disadvantaged communities (Vigil, 2002). These findings suggest culture and ethnic identity may be important variables to consider when comparing reports of violent victimization between groups (Abril, 2007b). Thus, it might be inadvisable to make broad statements about differences in rates of reports of violent victimization between different social groups without consideration of the effects of culture and identity. Future victimization studies should include individual level measures of culture, identity, and community values in order to develop better policy responses to victimization.

It could therefore be concluded that based on current data that do exist, there are no differences in the rates and prevalence of domestic violence and violent victimization than what occurs in any other similarly situated non-Indian community.

Contextual Versus "Traditional" Causes

In the Southern Ute Indian Community Safety Survey (SUICSS) (Abril, 2005), many Indians not only reported their own victimization and those of others, but also reported their perception that evil spirits or negative spiritual entities were involved in the violence they experienced.

In Abril's (2007b) study of Indian identity and reporting violent victim-ization differences between the Indians and the non-Indians, all relevant variables were significant. There were significant differences between the Indians and non-Indians on the Indian cultural values scale. The Indians reported higher scores (indicating a stronger cultural identity) and appeared to be more unified in their overall cultural values than non-Indians. Table 4.1 presents the mean scores on the Indian cultural values scale for Indians and non-Indians who live within the same community.

Table 4.1   Indian Cultural Values (Mean Scores)

	Indian	Non-Indian	Significance
Cultural values	41.18 (SD 8.714)	34.31 (SD 9.628)	.000

Source: Abril, J. C. (2007b). Native American Indian identity and violent victimization. *International Perspectives in Victimology*, 3, 22–28.

In another analysis, significant differences were found between the Indians and non-Indians on violent victimization when controlling for ethnicity (Abril, 2007b). Indians were more than three times as likely to report violent victimization as were non-Indians. While there were less significant differences between the groups when controlling for culture, Indians were still 1.161 times more likely to report violent victimization than were non-Indians. While statistical significance was lacking in a cultural regression analysis, those Indian subjects reporting higher scores on the Indian cultural values scale reported more violent victimization. This may be because community perceptions of the seriousness of street and cultural crime and the view that police should respond to neighborhood problems are thought to be associated with reporting crime (Abril, 2005).

When Abril (2008) asked Southern Ute Indians if they thought evil spirits were involved in violence perpetration, many interviewees reported this to be so. Below is an excerpt from one such interview.

Are evil spirits involved in violence and conflict?

Yes. When my oldest daughter, when I was pregnant with her. Her dad, that was 21 years ago, 22 years ago; when I was pregnant with her. I didn't know he had a loaded rifle, he had been drinking. He came home—he was really mad about something or other. When you're a wife you know … you have that fear, you know that feeling. You know something's gonna happen but you don't know what. You got that fight or flight instinct in you and you try to be the peacemaker or whatever. I just happened to get up and I was coming to our bedroom and I heard a shot and … if I hadn't turned, he would have killed both me and my daughter. He missed me. He was having a hard time repositioning that rifle. I thought this was something I'm really gonna have to know how to talk to him about. It wasn't only that. He was … we lived over at Ute Mountain. The place we lived at was kind of possessed. The house was possessed. I saw it in his face. His eyes were yellow. His lips curled back and you can't tell me a natural human being can do that. His voice changed. It got really low. It reminded me of something I saw in a movie. But he had been drinking. He called me a bitch, a whore. He used to hit me with his hands too. I defended myself with my hands being raised in front of my face. And I ran even when I was pregnant. He hit me with the rifle butt on my ankle and I got a scar there. I never had broken a bone or anything like that. I used to talk to a counselor and I used to go see some of my friends who were counselors. I think it was just a matter of talking about the situation. Clearing your head is really important because if your spirit holds all that in you then your spirit gets sick. To me that's the way cancer is too. People have a lot of anger or a lot of hatred and I think that's what causes cancer to spread. Also, I've taken courses on domestic violence. My daughter is aware, too. The police were never involved. When I was pregnant with my second daughter and her father, he used to come home drunk and we'd fight. I used to tell my daughter to call the police if things get really bad. There were a couple times the police came and one time he was in jail because he was mumbling something. I didn't have to sign anything. It was fine. He was in jail for 3 or 4 months. One time he jumped on my car and my daughter thought I ran over him. I said, "No, I didn't." I had access to a working telephone but he never prevented me from reporting him to the police. I never used the Crime Victim's Services. He's dead. No contact in 16 or 17 years.

Do you think there are bad spirits involved in domestic violence?

You know, some people say there is but I don't think so. I think that you as a human being should be aware of what kinds of situations you put yourself in. I understand that drinking and drugs ... if you're strong. You need to be a strong person. It took me a long time to understand what it meant. Once you have kids and your own home, then you understand what being strong is. When these Indian men say they are possessed and they run off to see a Medicine Man.

Many other interviewees reported they believe some sort of bad spiritual influences are at least partly responsible for violence within the group. While many reported that "bad people," those who "drink and drug" or are "possessive and jealous," are responsible for their behavior, many more felt that the behavior was caused by "bad medicine." *Bad medicine* is the term for witchcraft and sorcery. Reports of using bad medicine were common. People told stories of personal encounters with bad medicine and how they were related to conflict in the home and with others. Such stories include the following: "I feel like bad medicine is being used. It's just overwhelming. People say they can see the devil downtown in the bars and at the casino"; "I've seen the devil in the boy's dorm. He had horns, I just seen the silhouette of him and I could feel evil"; or "Witchcraft I believe in that, I know it's true. I've been to a medicine man ... I believe because it's my tradition." One woman reported the following: "We found out we were being witched. They (the spirits) wanted us to split ... can't say who was witching us, it was just a feeling in the house, it was scary so I saw a medicine man and he helped us out. He took a lot of stuff that was buried right in our house." Another woman reported that she too sought the services of a medicine man when she felt witched: "When we first started having troubles, we went to see a medicine man. The medicine man told us things that had occurred, where he had picked up the bad medicine. When he [my husband] was out drink'n' somebody stole something of his, hair maybe." Finally, one older woman told me the story of her recent experience with witchcraft: "We went to a medicine man to find out why my son was acting the way he did, why he hit his sister. We found out that people were jealous of my little family and they wanted us to fight each other. The medicine man really didn't go into detail. I can read things from charcoals, I saw things for myself. I saw images. I saw persons doing that."

Some social scientists and philosophers argue that social disorganization, marginalization, and colonialism are causes of domestic violence among Indians. Yet the literature indicates that lack of attachment to culture and substance abuse are primarily the precipitators to domestic violence among Native Americans. Traditional cultural beliefs such as the use of witchcraft and sorcery are also thought to be responsible for domestic violence (Abril, 2008).

Law Enforcement Responses

Violent Victimization in Indian Country

Rhetoric surrounding Indian country often includes the notion that much violence occurs within reservation communities. Indeed, domestic violence, fighting while intoxicated, and other types of combat were found to occur on the Southern Ute reservation. While the reports of violent victimization were significant, the actual prevalence was not dissimilar to those found in other non-Indian communities. As violence does occur and is often taken to extreme levels, tribes take steps to prevent it and restore order and give the victim a sense of justice.

Tribal Responses to Violent Victimization

Victims

It has also been reported that those who are not into the stereotypical "drink'n' and drug'n'" scene are often targeted by youth for victimization (Abril, 2007b). Victims of violence are provided the services of the Crime Victim's Services within the police department. The services are similar to those found in non-Indian communities. Victims of crime are also encouraged to participate in cultural and spiritual activities in an effort to restore their spirit, which is likely to have been harmed by the violence. As is the case with violent victimization in other communities, substance abuse may have played a role in the event. If this was the situation, the victim is also offered substance abuse treatment to prevent further incidents. Informal counseling while engaging in cultural practices such as pottery making, basket weaving, and beading is a common form of social comfort offered to female victims. Victims of crime are also given the opportunity to participate in the legal proceedings against the offender. Other studies have shown this to have somewhat of a healing or justice effect on the psychological well-being of the victims and their families.

Offenders

Violent offenders are usually incarcerated and, depending on the severity of the offense, face trial in either the tribal or federal court, or both. Because substance abuse in this community is significantly associated with violent offending, offenders are often court ordered to attend the drug and alcohol treatment program called Peaceful Spirits. Because it is widely believed in the tribal community that those who engage in violent behavior are also those who are more distant from the cultural values, a culturally based rehabilitative program was instituted in the tribal jail. However, other research has shown that those most involved with the Indian culture and having a strong Indian identity are often victimized more because of it (Abril, 2007b). Thus, it is unclear if these culturally based rehabilitation programs are beneficial to an offender or not. However, the community and the offenders themselves believe them to be beneficial, and in the end, the perception that they are helpful in ending the violence is what matters most.

Elder Abuse in Indian Country

In Carson's (1995) review of the literature on elder abuse in Indian country, he deduced several factors that might put elders at risk for abuse and may protect them from such. Carson cited a study by Wolf and Pillemar (1989, p. 18) that describes the types of abuse elders suffer, such as (1) physical violence; (2) psychological abuse; (3) material abuse, misappropriation of personal items; (4) active neglect; and (5) passive neglect. Sexual abuse is often cited by researchers as a form of abuse that is directed toward elders (Steinmetz, 1990). This is no different in the study of the Southern Ute Indian group.

Carson (1995, p. 29) reported that certain risk factors exist. These include poverty, changes in kinship systems, acculturation stress, and other factors that include financial dependency, poor health status of many elders, negative effects of technology, changes in values, a lack of interest in the elderly by the young, and the fact that many young people are leading the tribe as opposed to the elders. Protective factors included teaching children to respect the elders, a culture of mutual dependence and respect, strong extended families, deep tribal cultural customs, and optimism and contentment that are derived from a "cosmic identity," deep sense of spirituality, and ritualistic and religious practices. Finally, Abril's (2003, 2007a) study of violations of Indian cultural values by Indians found that Indians viewed disrespect of elders as a very serious matter.

Tribal Responses to Elder Abuse

Victims

Victims of elder abuse are cared for with great sensitivity and concern by tribes. The use of court-appointed conservatorships and placing the elder in the tribally run nursing home where he or she is going to be cared for are a few of the methods employed to bring feelings of justice to the victim as well as to protect him or her from future harm. Also, the council of elders regularly visits with the abused elder to keep him or her informed on tribal matters.

Offenders

As it is widely believed and the data show that much of the financial abuse stems from the offender's substance abuse problems, additional steps in addressing the offender are used. Restitution, participation in Peaceful Spirits, jail, prison, and temporary restraining orders are often used. In extreme cases, the tribal council will enforce the Removal and Exclusion Act (Southern Ute Indian Tribe, 1941) to permanently remove the offender from the reservation community—the modern form of banishment.

Effectiveness of Response Systems

Responses to domestic violence are only as effective as there are (1) numbers of police to respond to incidents, (2) number and extent of resources to care for the victim and remove the offender from the situation, and (3) interest by the victim to remove himself or herself from both the situation and the negative relationship where the violence is occurring.

Philosophical Differences and Solutions

As indicated above, many Native Americans see domestic violence as a result of lack of attachment to their specific culture, witchcraft and sorcery, and abuse of drugs and alcohol. Many Indians indicated that if people were more involved in their culture, stayed away from those who practice "bad medicine," and ceased "drink'n' and drug'n,'" there would be less opportunity for violence to permeate their relationships (Abril, 2008).

Restorative Justice

Various models of restorative justice are derivatives from cultures such as the Australian Aborigines, Canadian Aboriginals, New Zealand Maoris, and various other indigenous cultures from around the globe. Some models reference those once thought to be used by Native American Indians and those currently used by Alaskan Natives. No scientifically sound data exist, however, that support traditional restorative justice methods as being effective in reducing domestic violence among Native Americans. Both victims and perpetrators report that once substance abuse issues are resolved, violence lessens. Moreover, as the perpetrators age, they reported, they tend to reduce their violent behaviors. Also, restorative justice methods are not used in all tribal communities, so it is unclear if they work when they are used, if they are used at all.

Perception of the Problem and a Possible Solution

Currently, the data are so flawed that it is difficult to determine the extent of the problem. As with many criminological issues (e.g., gang violence), the issue of domestic violence is often sensationalized with anecdotal data providing the basis for the current rhetoric surrounding the issue. Potential solutions that are most likely to be effective in treating domestic violence are already in use in a variety of non-Indian communities. Using the same best practices used in non-Indian communities (such as substance abuse treatment, relocation and housing of victims, etc.) in conjunction with cultural and spiritual immersion and identity solidification appears to be the best option for treating domestic violence among Native Americans.

Understanding Domestic Violence Among Native Americans

More research is needed to understand the characteristics and prevalence of domestic violence and victimization among Native Americans. The U.S. Department of Justice Office of Violence Against Women is working diligently to support research in this area. Yet, with lack of interest in this area by qualified and competent research scientists, the data that are eventually produced may be just as flawed as the data that currently exist.

References

Abril, J. C. (2003, November). Final project report: Findings from the Southern Ute Indian Community Safety Survey: A report to the United States Department of Justice, Bureau of Justice Statistics. Summarized in Perry, S. W. (2005).

American Indians and crime: 1992–2001. Department of Justice/Bureau of Justice Statistics. Retrieved October 11, 2009, from http://www.ojp.usdoj.gov/bjs/pub/pdf/aic02.pdf

Abril, J. C. (2005). *The relevance of culture, ethnic identity, and collective efficacy to violent victimization in one Native American Indian tribal community.* PhD dissertation, University of California, Irvine.

Abril, J. C. (2007a). Perceptions of crime seriousness, cultural values, and collective efficacy between Native American Indians and non-Indians who live within the same reservation community. *Applied Psychology in Criminal Justice, 3,* 172–196.

Abril, J. C. (2007b). Native American Indian identity and violent victimization. *International Perspectives in Victimology, 3,* 22–28.

Abril, J. C. (2008). *Bad spirits: A cultural explanation for intimate family violence: Inside one American Indian family.* Cambridge, UK: Cambridge Scholars Publishing.

Bachman, R. (1998). The factors related to rape reporting behavior and arrest: New evidence from the National Crime Victimization Survey. *Criminal Justice and Behavior, 25,* 8–29.

Carson, D. K. (1995). American Indian elder abuse: Risk and protective factors amongst the oldest Americans. *Journal of Elder Abuse and Neglect, 7,* 17–39.

Dugan, L. (1999). Effect of criminal victimization on a household's moving decision. *Criminology, 37,* 903–930.

Evans-Campbell, T., Lindhorst, T., Huang, B. & Walters, K. L. (2006). Interpersonal violence in the lives of urban American Indian and Alaskan Native women: Implications for health, mental health, and help-seeking. *American Journal of Public Health, 96,* 1416–1422.

Greenfeld, L. A., & Smith, S. K. (1999, February). *American Indians and crime* (NCJ 173386). Washington, DC: USDOJ/OJP/BJS.

Interuniversity Consortium for Political and Social Research (ICPSR). (2006). *Summer seminar in quantitative analysis in crime and criminal justice* (USDOJ/NIJ/BJS). Ann Arbor: University of Michigan.

Lee, R. K., Thompson-Sanders, V. L., & Mechanic, M. B. (2002). Intimate partner violence and women of color: A call for innovations. *American Journal of Public Health, 92,* 530–534.

Perry, S.W. (2004). *A BJS statistical profile, 1992–2002: American Indians and crime* (NCJ 203097). Washington, DC: USDOJ/OJP/BJS.

Southern Ute Indian Tribe. (1941). *Southern Ute Indian tribal code.* Ignacio, CO.

Steinmetz, M. (1990). Elder abuse: Myth or reality. In T. H. Brubaker (Ed.), *Family relationships in later life.* Thousand Oaks, CA: Sage Publications.

Tjaden, P., & Thoennes, N. (2006). *Extent, nature, and consequences of rape victimization: Findings from the National Violence Against Women Survey* (NCJ 210346). Washington, DC: USDOJ/OJP/BJS.

Vigil, J. D. (2002). A *rainbow of gangs: Street cultures in the mega-city.* University of Texas Press.

Wolf, R. S., & Pillemar, K. A. (1989). *Helping elderly victims: The reality of elder abuse.* New York: Columbia University Press.

Wyatt, G. E., Axelrod, J., Chin, D., Carmona, J., & Loeb, T.B. (2000). Examining patterns of vulnerability to domestic violence among African American women. *Violence Against Women, 6,* 495–514.

Yuan, N., Koss, M. P., Polacca, M., & Goldman, D. (2006). Risk factors for physical assault and rape among six Native American tribes. *Journal of Interpersonal Violence, 21,* 1566–1590.

Domestic Violence in Sub-Saharan Africa

5

GODPOWER O. OKEREKE
PETER RACHEOTES
JOSEPHINE KAHLER

Contents

Introduction

According to the New York State Commission on Domestic Violence Fatalities, "Domestic violence refers to a pattern of behaviors involving physical, sexual, economic, and emotional abuse, alone or in combination, by an intimate partner often for the purpose of establishing and maintaining power and control over the other partner" (Pirro, 1997). This gender-neutral definition recognizes that men can also be victims of domestic violence. But, for the purposes of this chapter, domestic violence refers to acts of violence primarily committed by men (husbands, ex-husbands, boyfriends, ex-boyfriends, fathers, fathers-in-law, ex-fathers-in-law, stepfathers, brothers-in-law, ex-brothers-in-law, brothers, and other male family members) against women (wives, ex-wives, co-wives, girlfriends, ex-girlfriends, daughters-in-law, ex-daughters-in-law, sisters-in-law, and ex-sisters-in-law), girls (daughters, stepdaughters, granddaughters), and other female members of the household (sisters-in-law, house maids, female caregivers, and female baby sitters). This does not mean that men in Sub-Saharan Africa do not become victims of domestic violence. Rather, it stresses the point that relative to the social

53

organization and patriarchal nature of African societies and families, the overwhelming majority of the victims of domestic violence in Sub-Saharan Africa are women and girls (Okereke, 2006). It also stresses the point that the "family" in the traditional African context often includes members of the extended families of the couple as well as other females who serve as house maids, caregivers, or babysitters, all living in the same household.

In addition, the customary system of law, which governs the daily life of most women in Sub-Saharan Africa, and which defines the responsibilities, duties, obligations, and rights of men and women within the society in general, and the family in particular, subordinates women to the overall authority of male members of the household (Okereke, 2006). In a marital relationship, this subordination of women is underscored by the tradition of "bride price," which reinforces the notion that a husband has purchased his wife, including her labor and sexuality (Von Struensee, 2005). Therefore, the problem of domestic violence in Sub-Saharan Africa is first, a gender issue (primarily affects women), and second, a human rights issue (women are subjugated to the authority of male members of the family and denied the right to decide for themselves). Given these realities, a discussion of the problem of domestic violence in the African context cannot be gender-neutral, nor can it be limited to violence between intimates. Such discussion must include all of those who exercise or are likely to exercise control over all female members of the household (Okereke, 2006).

Prevalence of Domestic Violence in Sub-Saharan Africa

The United Nations' report *The State of the World Population* (2000) noted that gender-based violence (perpetrated against women and girls for the mere fact that they are women and girls) was a major public health concern and a serious violation of basic human rights. This report noted that this type of violence was rampant in Africa (United Nations, 2000). In a similar report, *The State of the World Population 2005*, the international organization further observed that domestic violence is by far the most common form of gender-based violence, affecting as many as 69% of women in some countries (United Nations, 2005). A multicountry study (including three in Sub-Saharan Africa—Tanzania, Namibia, and Ethiopia) on women's health and domestic violence against women by the World Health Organization (WHO) notes that the problem of domestic violence against women and girls in Africa by an intimate partner has contributed tremendously to the spread of HIV/AIDS within the subregion. The WHO study reported that whereas 48.5% of the 3,270 participants between the ages of 15 and 49 from Tanzania reported physical abuse (with 21% reporting severe injuries), 27% reported being sexually abused. Thirty-six of the 1,500 participants from Namibia reported being physically or sexually abused, and 20% of them were victimized within the last year. Of the 3,016 participants from Ethiopia, 49% reported being physically abused at some point in their lives, and 29% reported being physically abused within the year prior to the study. The Ethiopian team also found that 59% of the participants had experienced sexual violence at some point in their lives, and 44% reported that they had experienced sexual violence within the preceding 12 months. Combining the data for physical and sexual violence, 71% of ever-partnered women reported experiencing either physical or sexual violence, or both, over their lifetime, and 35% reported having experienced at least one severe form of physical violence (World Health Organization, 2005).

Further, a cross-sectional study of 144 Sierra Leonean women surveyed in a study of AIDS knowledge, attitudes, and behavior in 1998 found that 66.7% of the women reported being physically abused, 50.7% reported having been forced to have sexual intercourse, and 76.6% reported either forced sex or physical violence by an intimate partner (Coker & Richter, 1998). In a survey of 5,109 women of reproductive age in the Rakai District of Uganda carried out in 1998 and 1999, 30% of the women reported they had experienced physical violence from their current partner—20% during the year prior to the survey, while 60% of the abused women experienced three or more incidents during the last year (Koenig et al., 2003). Also, according to Global Business Coalition on HIV/AIDS, Tuberculosis and Malaria (2007), research in Sub-Saharan Africa showed that 30% of girls stated that their first intercourse was forced, and 71% reported being victims of forced sexual intercourse. Furthermore, in an article entitled "Entrenched Epidemic: Wife-Beating in Africa," Sharon LaFraniere points out that nowhere in the world is the physical abuse of women more entrenched and accepted as a way of life than in Sub-Saharan Africa. According to her, one in three Nigerian women report being physically abused by a male partner. She also says that the wife of a deputy governor of a northern state told reporters in 2004 that her husband beat her incessantly, in part because she watched movies on television. She further points out that one of President Olusegun Obasanjo's appointees to a national anticorruption commission in 2000 was allegedly killed by her husband two days after she asked the state police commissioner to protect her (LaFraniere, 2005). According to her, almost 50% of women surveyed in Zambia in a 2004 study financed by the United States stated that they have been physically abused by an intimate partner. She reiterates that researchers for the Medical Research Council in 2004 estimated that a male partner kills a girlfriend or spouse in South Africa every six hours—the highest mortality rate from domestic violence ever reported—and that domestic violence accounts for 6 in 10 murder cases in court in Zimbabwe (LaFraniere, 2005).

Furthermore, a cross-sectional study of 1,368 randomly selected South African men on sexual violence against their intimate partners revealed that 15.3% of the men admitted having perpetrated sexual violence against their partners (Abrahams, Jewkes, Hoffman, & Laubsher, 2004). A similar study of 1,370 rural young South African men between the ages of 15 and 26 in 2006 found 16.3% of the men admitting raping a nonpartner, whereas 8.4% of them admitted being sexually violent toward their intimate partners. This study also found that 44.3% of those who admitted raping an intimate partner also admitted raping a nonpartner (Jewkes et al., 2006). In a cross-sectional household survey of 20,639 adults between the ages of 16 and 60 from eight countries in southern Africa (Botswana, Lesotho, Malawi, Mozambique, Namibia, Swaziland, Zambia, and Zimbabwe) researchers found that 18% of the female participants had been physically abused by their intimate partner within the last 12 months (Anderson, Ho-Foster, Mitchell, Scheepers, & Goldstein, 2007). In another study of intimate partner violence against women in Eastern Uganda, researchers found that 54% of the 553 participants had experienced intimate partner violence, 14% of them within the last year (Karamagi, Tumwine, Tyileskar, & Heggenhougen, 2006).

According to Charlotte Watts and Susannah Mayhew, cross-sectional household surveys in Zimbabwe and Ethiopia found that 26% and 59%, respectively, of ever-partnered women have been forced by their partner to have sex, with 20% and 40% reporting unwanted sexual intercourse in the year before the surveys. Also according to them, 77% of pregnant Ethiopian women report being beaten by their intimate partner during pregnancy, and 28% of these women report being punched or kicked in the stomach by the father of the child. Consequently, they say, 57% of women living in Eastern Cape in South Africa believe that they cannot refuse sex with their partner (Watts & Mayhew, 2004). A recent study of young women between the ages of 12 and 24 in Kenya revealed that 21% of them had been coerced into sexual intercourse. In a similar study in Ghana, 25% of young women within the same age group reported that their first sexual intercourse had been forced (Erulkar, 2004). As is evident from the foregoing, domestic violence is a major problem in Sub-Saharan Africa. Relative to the above, it is evident that domestic violence and violence against women and girls are major public health issues in Sub-Saharan Africa.

Forms of Domestic Violence in Sub-Saharan Africa

The United Nations Special Rapporteur on Violence Against Women recommends not only that national governments pass laws that prohibit violence against women both in the family and within interpersonal relationships, but also that the language of such laws should be clear and unambiguous in protecting female victims from gender-specific violence within the family and intimate relationships. According to this document, the following types of domestic violence occur in Sub-Saharan Africa:

Physical abuse: Domestic physical abuse that occurs in Sub-Saharan Africa includes slapping, punching, hitting, kicking, shoving, holding, restraining, confining, scratching, biting, throwing things at the person, threatening or attacking the person with a weapon, locking the person in or out of the house or abandoning the person in a dangerous place, refusing to provide assistance when the person is injured, sick, or pregnant, breaking bones, burning, and murder.

Sexual abuse: Sexual abuse includes raping or threatening to rape a woman or girl; forcing the woman or girl to have sex when she does not want to; forcing the woman or girl to perform sexual acts she does not like; and forcing the woman or girl to wear clothes or do sexual things that make the victim uncomfortable.

Emotional abuse: Domestic emotional abuse that is common in Sub-Saharan Africa includes raining insults on the woman, calling her names, ridiculing the woman, ignoring the woman, engaging in intimidating and controlling behaviors, leveling false accusations against the woman, issuing threats against the woman or her family, or both, belittling the woman, yelling or screaming at the woman without justification, constant harassment, embarrassing the woman in public, making fun of or mocking the woman, criticizing everything the woman does, not trusting the woman's decision making, blaming the woman for anything that goes wrong, and making the woman stay in the house after a fight.

Financial or material abuse: Financial or material abuse occurs when a husband or a man prevents his wife or the female from getting a job, takes and spends her money, takes or destroys her possessions, spends most of the family money on himself alone, expects the woman to account for every penny, and hides financial information from the woman.

Spiritual abuse: Spiritual abuse includes using the woman's religious beliefs to manipulate her, preventing her from practicing her religious or spiritual beliefs, ridiculing the woman's religious or spiritual beliefs, or forcing the children to be reared in a faith that the woman does not agree to.

Causes of Domestic Violence in Sub-Saharan Africa

In an exploratory study of the status of women and girl children and the problem of violence against women and young girls in Africa in 2006, Okereke
identified some of the reasons why the incidence of various forms of violence is high in Africa. Among the reasons identified is nonenforcement of
existing legislations that prohibit violence against women. According to him,
many countries in Sub-Saharan Africa (Burkina Faso, Cameroon, Ghana,
Ethiopia, Kenya, Mauritius, Mozambique, Namibia, Nigeria, Republic of
Benin, Republic of Congo, Senegal, Sierra Leone, Swaziland, Tanzania, Togo,
Uganda, and Zambia) have legislations that in one way or another prohibit
violence against women and girls, but such laws are not being enforced.
He also pointed out that many countries have yet to pass laws prohibiting
domestic violence, spousal rape, and wife beating. Also according to him,
many aspects of statutory law, civil law, general law, customary law, and religious law in many countries in Sub-Saharan Africa still discriminate against
women and young girls and, in so doing, make them vulnerable to gender-
based violence, particularly within the home (Okereke, 2006).

Violence against women within the home in Sub-Saharan Africa also
results from harmful or prejudicial traditions, customs, beliefs, and practices to which African peoples still subscribe. Among these are the following
(Okereke, 2006):

- Female genital mutilation (FGM)
- Customs that prohibit women from inheriting property from fami-
  lies of origin or from marital families
- Customs that view widows as part of their husband's inheritance
  property
- Customs that still provide for the payment of bride price or dowry as
  part of the marriage process
- Customs that support gender-specific socialization
- Differential expectations of boys and girls and men and women
  within the family and husbands and wives
- Belief in the inherent superiority of males
- The view that a husband has the right to use some amount of force to
  "correct" all members of his family, including his wife
- The observance of widowhood rites
- The practice of condoning abduction and rape of young girls if
  the kidnapper and abuser agrees to marry the young girl (mar-
  riage by abduction)
- The practice of betrothing very young girls to men old enough to be
  their fathers (child marriages)

- Customs that support early marriages of very young boys and girls (arranged marriages)
- Customs that support "shotgun weddings" (forcing a man to marry a girl due to unplanned pregnancy)
- Customs that give men and husbands guardianship authority over all females within the household
- Values that give men proprietary rights over women and girls
- Customs that allow men to have multiple wives simultaneously
- Customs that blame wives for not bearing children or having only female children for their husbands
- Beliefs and practices against wives who have too many (five or more) children for their husbands

Other causes of domestic violence against women in Sub-Saharan Africa include economic crises (increased unemployment, economic discrimination, and feminization of absolute poverty). These resulted from the implementation of the structural adjustment programs (SAPs) required by the International Monetary Fund (IMF) and World Bank as part of their loan conditionalities across countries in Sub-Saharan Africa. Some believe that the implementation of those conditionalities to some degree exacerbated the problem of domestic violence against women within the region (Osirim, 2001). Also contributing to domestic violence in Sub-Saharan Africa are the following (United Nations Children's Fund [UNCF], 2000):

- Women's economic dependence on men
- Limited access to cash and credit
- Nonprovision for child support or wife maintenance after divorce
- Limited access to employment in both the formal and informal sectors of the economy
- Limited access to education and training for women
- Inadequate laws addressing divorce, child custody, and maintenance issues
- Ambiguous legal definitions of rape and domestic abuse
- Insensitive treatment of women and girls by the police and the judiciary
- Underrepresentation of women in politics, in positions of power, and in the legal and medical professions
- The view that the family is a private domain and therefore should be beyond the control of the state

Consequences of Domestic Violence
Across Sub-Saharan Africa

One of the consequences of domestic violence in Sub-Saharan Africa is high incidence of maternal mortality. This problem is worse in countries such as Ethiopia, where child marriages, forced marriages, shotgun weddings, and marriage following abduction and rape of young girls are common practices. As a result of these practices, the median age of marriage in Ethiopia is said to be below 15 years of age. According to a recent publication by the United Nations, such early marriages cause more than 25,000 Ethiopian women to die each year during childbirth, and another 50,000 are disabled after giving birth because young girls are getting pregnant and having babies when their pelvises are not mature enough to deliver them. According to the United Nations report, early marriages, pregnancies, births, and lack of a medical attendant (barely 10% of pregnant women in Ethiopia deliver with the help of a skilled birth attendant) expose Ethiopian women to high maternal death rates and maternal morbidities (Majtenyi, 2005).

Another consequence of domestic violence in Sub-Saharan Africa is the high prevalence of sexually transmitted diseases among young women and girls. A local organization in Zaria, Nigeria, found in 1990 that 16% of hospital patients with sexually transmitted diseases (STDs) were girls under the age of 5. Also in 1990, the Genito-Urinary Center in Harare, Zimbabwe, treated more than 900 girls under the age of 12 for STDs (Kimani, 2007). More importantly, domestic violence and abuse of women has led to what some have called the feminization of HIV/AIDS in Sub-Saharan Africa, where heterosexual sex is said to be the dominant mode of the transmission of the disease. Domestic violence and abuse of young girls is said to have led to a situation where women and young girls bear the burden of the HIV/AIDS epidemic within the region. This region is said to have the highest rates of people living with HIV/AIDS and contains 77% of all women worldwide living with the disease. Among all young people living with HIV/AIDS within Sub-Saharan Africa, 62% of them are women. This situation is worse in some countries within the region. For example, in South Africa, the ratio of HIV positive females to males is said to be 24:10, whereas in countries such as Kenya and Mali the ratio is as high as 45:10 (Global Business Coalition on HIV/AIDS, Tuberculosis and Malaria, 2007).

According to the United Nations Population Fund's (UNPF) *State of the World Population 2005*, survivors of domestic and gender-based violence suffer lifelong emotional distress, mental health problems, and poor reproductive health. UNPF maintains that abused women are at a higher risk of miscarriages and stillbirths, experience infant deaths, and are more likely to give birth to low-birth-weight children (a risk factor for neonatal and infant deaths). It also states that children of abused women are more likely to be malnourished, sick often, and less likely to have been immunized against childhood diseases. The international organization also states that domestic violence can severely impair a woman's ability to nurture the development of her children, and that mothers who are abused are more likely to be depressed and have feelings of hopelessness (UNPF, 2005). Another consequence of domestic violence and abuse of women and girls in Sub-Saharan Africa is the feminization of poverty. Whereas the term *feminization of poverty* in the United States refers to the increasing number of single-female-headed households, in Sub-Saharan Africa poverty among women is caused by general disenfranchisement of women by discriminatory civil and customary laws, gender-bias cultural beliefs and practices, traditions that place higher value on men, denial of property rights, denial of access to education, denial of right to own and operate businesses, and denial of right to make decisions concerning their bodies (Okereke, 2006).

Theories of Domestic Violence in Sub-Saharan Africa

Five general theoretical explanations can be applied to the problem of domestic violence in Sub-Saharan Africa. One of those theories is the weak state apparatus theory, which hinges on the idea that domestic violence results from the inability or the unwillingness of the state to protect the human rights of women. Supporting this theory is the argument that since most African states have ratified numerous international and regional conventions and covenants that either explicitly or implicitly define domestic violence as a violation of women's human rights, it is therefore a crime. Furthermore, since most African constitutions prohibit gender-based discrimination, domestic violence therefore results from the inability or unwillingness of the state to enforce the law and the tenets of its constitution.

The second explanation of domestic violence in the Sub-Saharan Africa context is what we would refer to as the patriarchy theory. This theory sees domestic violence as resulting from the patriarchal nature of African societies. Because traditional African societies are highly patriarchal and a woman's place within this scheme is decidedly subordinate, gender inequality is institutionalized. For example, under most African systems of customary law, women have no right to inherit from either families of origin or marital families, are regarded as part of their husband's inheritance property, are excluded from ownership of communal land, and are almost without remedy upon divorce. According to this view, the institutionalization of gender inequality gives rise to domestic violence.

The third theoretical explanation of domestic violence in Sub-Saharan Africa is the bias-cultural theory, which emphasizes the power of tradition and norms within African societies and how those contribute to the wide-spread incidence of domestic violence. African culture, by its very nature, tenets, norms and values, is biased toward women and girls. Sometimes the connection between domestic violence and such biased culture, norms, and values is direct, as is the case with wife beating, which is regarded as normal among various ethnic groups in Sub-Saharan Africa. At other times, the impact of African culture, norms, and values on the incidence of domestic violence is indirect. Examples include the uneven distribution of power within traditional African marriages, the acceptance of polygamy, the acceptance of male promiscuity, the power of the extended family over married couples, and the requirement of dowry payment as part of the marriage process. The payment of bride price to the family of the wife prior to the marriage makes it difficult for women to leave abusive husbands unless their families are willing to return the amount paid.

Incidence of domestic violence in Sub-Saharan could also be explained with what can be referred to as the economic austerity theory. Decades of poor economic growth and high debt burdens in many African countries caused the International Monetary Fund (IMF), the World Bank, the World Trade Organization, and the industrialized countries of today to force countries in Sub-Saharan Africa to reduce public spending in education and in welfare programs, eliminate social programs for the poor, privatize public institutions, and open up their economies to unrestricted world trade (Okereke, 2009). These measures, commonly referred to as structural adjustment programs (SAPs), led to the sale of public enterprises for a fraction of what they are worth, and resulted in mass layoffs, high unemployment, and high incidence of absolute poverty. The resulting economic austerity made it difficult or even impossible for many men to provide for their families. This situation has increased the incidence of all forms of violence against women and girls (Okereke, 2006).

The fifth and final theory that could be used to explain the incidence of domestic violence in Sub-Saharan Africa is what has been referred to as society in transition theory. According to this theory, incidence of domestic violence is high in Sub-Saharan Africa due to the fact that the society is in transition from traditional cultures to a modern, urbanized society. With increasing urbanization, the theory holds, couples may live far from their families of origin, who traditionally mediated disputes concerning domestic situations and were able to moderate the severity of wife abuse. According to this theory, the influence of the family over its members is also weakening as more family members enter the cash economy and are thus not as interdependent economically as they were previously. Women's growing independence as they enter the cash economy and have more opportunities to interact with each other and with other men have made it difficult for them to perform traditionally expected household chores. This situation increases their vulnerability to domestic violence. Also adding to the problem of domestic violence in the modernizing Sub-Saharan Africa is the fact that the modern economy does not lend itself to the institution of polygamy. Many times, the man leaves his wife or wives and their children in the village to live alone in the city. While in the city, he gets a "city wife" and sooner or later has children with her. Whereas his limited income can barely support his city family, his wives and children in the village and members of his extended family continue to request support from him. The inability of men to meet these obligations increases women's vulnerability to domestic violence.

The Criminal Justice System and the Problem of Domestic Violence in Sub-Saharan Africa

The way the criminal justice system in Sub-Saharan Africa handles the problem of domestic violence can be gleaned from comments made by criminal justice officials in Uganda following the death of a pregnant woman while she was supposedly having sex voluntarily with her abusive husband. Reacting to pressure from the media that the death be carefully investigated, the director of public prosecution (as in Kulubya, 2002, p. 3) said:

> According to Ugandan law, a spouse is entitled to sex regardless of their partner's consent. If you are married, it can't be rape because you are fulfilling your marital obligations. Marital rape is a concept for people in Western countries.

If the person who, by virtue of his office, is supposed to prosecute the perpetrator has this attitude about rape, victims would be reluctant to go to the police. Compounding this problem is the fact that in Uganda (as is the case in many parts of Sub-Saharan African), women who speak of rape at the hands of their husbands are stigmatized and ostracized by the entire community because it is taboo to discuss domestic violence. Consequently, women and girls who are victims of rape (marital or otherwise) are reluctant to speak to the authorities or anyone about their ordeal. Those who do find neither sympathy nor justice because victims of rape (marital rape, especially) can only press charges for assault, which carries a short jail term. Furthermore, the police in Sub-Saharan Africa are ill-equipped to investigate and collect scientific evidence necessary for successful prosecutions of rape cases; the police do not have the technology that is required for a successful scientific investigation and prosecution of criminal cases. Alluding to this handicap, a police officer referring to the above case said: "Even if there was a law on marital rape in the statutes, it would be difficult to collect evidence and cases would boil down to the word of one spouse against the other" (Kulubya, 2002, p. 3).

Given the fact that women and girls are the primary victims of domestic violence in Sub-Saharan Africa and the vast majority of criminal justice officials are men, the victims of abuse who go to the police are taunted, ridiculed, and sometimes threatened with jail time if they do not go away to settle their problem at home. Those whose cases go to court are often persuaded by judges not to drag their husband to court because they are married and have children, as was the case with a woman who was nearly raped to death by her drunk husband. Even in countries that have passed laws against domestic violence, it is still an uphill battle for abused women to get justice due to loopholes in the legal system and nonsupportive attitudes of criminal justice officials. For example, a 1995 study of five southern African countries by *Women in Law and Development* showed that most men who kill their wives in the course of domestic disputes are charged with lesser offenses and judges give them lighter sentences. In one such case, the judge suspended a three-year sentence because he felt the defendant was provoked by the victim. The judge declared: "The provocation offered by your wife was such that any self-respecting person would lose control. The facts reveal that you did not use a lethal weapon; you only used your fists. I feel this case calls for maximum leniency" (Ndlovu, 2002, p. 6)

In another case, a man who beat his wife to death was given 18 months for manslaughter and was told by the judge to refrain from violence the next time he marries (Ndlovu, 2002). When women in Sub-Saharan Africa are doubly victimized in this way, they really have nowhere to go because other government officials and the general public share similar viewpoints. For example, when Ugandan Vice President Specioza Kazibwe revealed that her husband had been battering her and cited this as the reason for the breakup of their marriage in 2002, she was heavily criticized by both men and women, for setting a bad example. Reacting to this revelation, Minister for Agriculture Kibirige Ssebunnya advised women to keep their family problems (including domestic violence) to themselves. Other men accused the vice president of inciting women to abandon their marriages for "petty things like a few slaps here and there" (Nankinga, 2002, p. 7). As a result of this attitude on the part of top government officials, criminal justice officials, and the general public, victims of the most brutal forms of domestic violence suffer in silence.

State Efforts at Controlling Domestic Violence in Sub-Saharan Africa

Whereas all countries in Sub-Saharan Africa can be said to have recognized the need to protect women and young girls from gender-based violence and have taken various steps designed to protect them, there tends to be less agreement concerning the criminalization of domestic or intimate partner violence. The most contested issue in this regard is the criminalization of marital rape. Most men in Sub-Saharan Africa believe that marriage gives them unlimited access to their wives and entitles them to sex anytime they want it. The payment of bride price as part of the marriage process complicates this problem, as some men believe that such payment entitles the husband—the buyer—to full ownership rights over his wife (Okereke, 2006). Another reason criminalization of domestic violence is a contested issue is the fact that such abuse is rooted in age-long traditions, beliefs, and practices that have been handed down from one generation to another. The other major question facing reformers in this regard is whether to criminalize wife battery. Advocates of the criminal justice approach to both marital rape and wife battery point to the symbolic power of the law and argue that arrest, prosecution, conviction, and punishment of perpetrators of both marital rape and wife beating are a process that carries the clear condemnation of society for the conduct of the abuser and acknowledges his personal responsibility for the behavior.

State governments in Sub-Saharan Africa have also engaged in various legislative actions in an effort to control domestic violence. Although this approach to the problem of domestic violence in Sub-Saharan Africa is new, there tends to be an increasing belief that special laws need to be passed to protect women and young girls from violence. In some of the countries, for example, South Africa, the police are under legal obligation to move a domestic violence case forward even when the victim, under social pressure, does not want to press charges. Under the South African domestic violence law, the police are required to explain to the victims that they are there to assist them in any way possible, including helping them find shelter, obtain medical treatment, issue an order of protection, as well as bring criminal charges against the abuser (Vetten, 2005). In those countries in Sub-Saharan Africa where laws against domestic violence have been passed, efforts are being made to sensitize law enforcement officers, medical practitioners, legal professionals, school teachers, and community leaders to the problem and costs of domestic violence not only for the individual victim but also for the society at large. Even in those countries where laws prohibiting domestic violence have not been passed, government agencies are taking steps to educate the public about the dangers of domestic violence, whereas civil society organizations and local and international nongovernmental organizations (NGOs) are providing needed services to victims, including legal services at little or no cost to the victims (Okereke, 2006).

Another area where there are noticeable strides taken by states in Sub-Saharan Africa to stem the tide of domestic violence within the region is government's efforts to strengthen the policy framework at the intergovernmental levels. An example of such efforts is the African Union's

Additional Protocol to the African Charter on Human and Peoples' Rights in Africa, which amplifies the human rights of women as guaranteed by the African Charter. This document obliges state governments to take legislative actions to ensure that the rights of women are protected. The Inter-Governmental Authority on Development (IGAD) formed by countries in East Africa and the Horn of Africa (Djibouti, Ethiopia, Eritrea, Kenya, Somalia, Sudan, and Uganda) is leading the campaign against all forms of violence against women within the subregion. Furthermore, the East African Community made up of Burundi, Kenya, Tanzania, Rwanda, and Uganda has also launched a campaign against violence against women and girls to educate the public about the ills of domestic violence and to promote gender equality. The Southern African Development Community (SADC) made up of Angola, Botswana, Lesotho, Malawi, Mozambique, Swaziland, Tanzania, Zambia, Zimbabwe, Namibia, South Africa, Mauritius, Democratic Republic of Congo, and Madagascar also lists violence against women and young girls as one of the issues that need their collective attention within the subregion. The Economic Community for West African States (ECOWAS), under the ECOWAS Revised Treaty of 1993, declared its commitment to fight violence against women and children through the enhancement of the economic, social, and cultural conditions of women (Okereke, 2006).

Conclusion

Although domestic violence is a worldwide problem, it is particularly problematic in Sub-Saharan Africa as a result of the many traditions, customs, values, beliefs, and practices that are highly prejudicial and discriminatory toward women and young girls. Especially troubling are customs dealing with inheritance of property, wife inheritance, payment of dowries as part of the marriage process, marriage by abduction, forced marriages, early marriages, shotgun weddings, the practice of widowhood rites, the acceptance of polygyny, the differential expectations of men and women in marital relationships, attitudes concerning wife beating, and the socializing process of boys and girls, which is constructed to instill a feeling of inferiority and fear in girls and teach women that violence is an inevitable part of both family and marriage relationships (Watts, Keogh, Ndiovu, & Kwaramba, 1998). In response, quite a few African states have passed laws banning various forms of gender-based violence. Because abuse of women and young girls is so deeply embedded in African culture, traditions, values, beliefs, and practices, merely passing gender-sensitive laws and anti-domestic violence legislations, though commendable, will have limited effects. It is therefore imperative that such legislations detail the responsibilities of individuals and agencies who, by virtue of their social positions, will come in contact with the victims of domestic violence. Such legislations should also include the consequences of noncompliance with the requirements of the law, because without such clauses, the law will have little or no effect.

Further, research on violence against women and young girls in Africa shows that many pieces of statutory, general, civil, customary, and religious laws or sections thereof still discriminate against women and young girls (Okereke, 2006). Not only do such discriminatory laws need to be revised, but the governments of African states need to embark on extensive public enlightenment campaigns to educate both men and women about the ills and effects of those age-long traditions, customs, values, beliefs, and practices. Such campaigns should include but not be limited to parents and other family members, criminal justice officials, social workers, health providers, school teachers, faith community leaders, counselors, local chiefs, local government officials, and the general public. The campaigns should also emphasize the connection between forced sex and the spread of HIV/AIDS and other STDs; the connection between early marriages and the high incidence of maternal deaths, stillbirths, low birth weights, and infant mortality rates, as well as poor reproductive health and the effects of domestic violence on children who witness such violence; and the connection between discriminatory customs, traditions, beliefs, and practices and the increase in absolute poverty within the continent. To be successful in this respect, state governments should criminalize all forms of violence against women and young girls and devote a portion of the national budget to programs designed to prevent and respond to such violence. State governments should also mandate special training for police and judicial officials to sensitize them to the causes and effects of all forms of violence against women, and health care workers should be trained to recognize signs of abuse and to respond to such violence. The authors believe that over time, people will begin to see why certain customs, traditions, values, beliefs, and practices should be abandoned.

References

Abrahams, N., Jewkes R., Hoffman, M., & Laubsher, R. (2004). Sexual violence against intimate partners in Cape Town: Prevalence and risk factors reported by men. *Bulletin of World Health Organization, 82*(5). Retrieved September 12, 2008, from http://www.ncbi.nlm.nih.gov/pubmed/15298223

Anderson, N., Ho-Foster, A., Mitchell, S., Scheepers, E., & Goldstein, S. (2007, July 11). Risk factors for domestic physical violence: National cross-sectional household surveys in eight Southern African countries. *BioMed Central Women's Health*. Retrieved September 15, 2008, from http://www.pubmedcentral.nih/gov/articlerender.fcgi?artid=2042491

Coker, A. L., & Richter, D. L. (1998, April). Violence against women in Sierra Leone: Frequency and correlates of intimate partner violence and forced sexual intercourse. *African Journal of Reproductive Health, 2*(1). Retrieved September 2, 2008, from http://www.ncbi.nlm.nih.gov/pubmed/10214430

Erulkar, A. (2004, December). The experience of sexual coercion among young people in Kenya. *International Family Planning Perspectives, 30*(4). Retrieved August 31, 2008, from http://www.guttmacher.org/pubs/journals/3018204.html

Global Business Coalition on HIV/AIDS, Tuberculosis and Malaria. (2007, June). *Overview of the feminization of HIV/AIDS in Sub-Saharan Africa.* Author. Retrieved September 3, 2008, from http://www.businessfightaids.org/hwhe

Jewkes, R, Dunkle, K., Koss, M. P., Levin, J. B., Nduna, M., Jama, N., et al. (2006, September). Rape perpetrated by young rural South African men: Prevalence, patterns, and risk factors. *Social Science & Medicine, 63*(11).

Karamagi, C., Tumwine, J. K., Tyileskar, T., & Heggenhougen, K. (2006, November 20). Intimate partner violence against women in Eastern Uganda: Implications for HIV prevention. *BioMed Central Public Health.* Retrieved August 31, 2008, from http://www.ncbi.nlm.nih.gov/pubmed/17116252

Kimani, M. (2007, July). Taking on violence against women in Africa: International norms, local activism start to alter laws, attitudes. *African Renewal, 21*(2). Retrieved August 26, 2008, from http://www.un.org/ecosocdev/geninfo/afrec/vol21no2212-violence-against-women.html

Koenig, M. A., Lutalo, T., Zhao, F., Nalugoda, F., Wabwire-Mangen, F., Kiwanuka, N., et al. (2003). Domestic violence in rural Uganda: Evidence from a community-based study. *Bulletin of the World Health Organization,* No. 81.

Kulubya, S. (2002, November). Marriages straight out of hell. *African Women: Special Report on Domestic Violence,* Issue 7. Retrieved August 20, 2008, from www.africawoman.net

LaFraniere, S. (2005). Entrenched epidemic: Wife-beating in Africa. *New York Times,* August 11. Retrieved September 24, 2008, from http://www.nytimes.com/2005/08/11/international/africa/11women.html

Majtenyi, C. (2005, October 13). *UN: Domestic violence rampant in Ethiopia.* Retrieved August 28, 2008, from http://www.voanews.com/english/archive/2005-10/2005-10-13-voa47.cfm

Nankinga, M. (2002, November). Hide in the kitchen if your man beats you. *African Women: Special Report on Domestic Violence,* Issue 7, 2002. Retrieved August 20, 2008, from www.africawoman.net

Ndlovu, S. (2002, November). Can there be justice for these victims? *African Women: Special Report on Domestic Violence,* Issue 7. Retrieved August 20, 2008, from www.africawoman.net.

Okereke, G. (2006, June). Violence against women in Africa. *African Journal of Criminology & Justice Studies, 2*(1).

Okereke, G. (2009). Some reflections on the road to economic development. *International Journal of Business and Econmics Perspectives, 4*(1).

Osirim, M. J. (2001). Crisis in the state and the family: Violence against women in Zimbabwe. *African Studies Quarterly: The Online Journal for African Studies.* Retrieved September 18, 2008, from http://web.africa.ufl.edu/asq/v7/v7i2a8.htm

Pirro, J. F. (1997). *Commission on domestic violence fatalities: Report to the governor.* Retrieved September 17, 2008, from http://www.opdv.state.ny.us/publications/fatality/index.html

United Nations. (2000). *The State of the World Population 2000.* United Nations General Assembly, Fifty-fifth Session, United Nations Population Fund.

United Nations. (2005). *The State of the World Population 2005.* United Nations Population Fund. Retrieved August 23, 2008, from http://www.unfpa/org/swp/2005/english/ch7/index.htm

United Nations Children's Fund. (2000). *Domestic Biolence Against Women and Girls.* Florence, Italy: United Nations Children's Fund Innocenti Research Center.

United Nations Population Fund. (2005). *The State of the World Population 2005.* Retrieved October 6, 2008, from http://www.unfpa.org/swp/2005/english/ch7/index.htm

Vetten, L. (2005). *Violence against women: Good practices in combating and eliminating violence against women.* Vienna, Austria: United Nations Division for the Advancement of Women.

Von Struensee, V. (2005). *The Domestic Relations Bill in Uganda: Potential for addressing polygamy, bride price, cohabitation, marital rape, widow inheritance, and female genital mutilation.* Retrieved August 10, 2008, from http://www.prevent-gbvafrica.org/downloads/drb

Watts, C., Keogh, E., Ndiovu, M., & Kwaramba, R. (1998). Withholding of sex and forced sex: Dimensions of violence against Zimbabwean women. *Reproductive Health Matters, 6,* 57–65.

Watts, C., & Mayhew, S. (2004, December). Reproductive health services and intimate partner violence: Shaping a pragmatic response in Sub-Saharan Africa. *International Family Planning Perspectives, 30*(4).

World Health Organization. (2005). *WHO multi-country study on women's health and domestic violence against women.* Author. Retrieved September 14, 2008, from http://www.who.int/gender/violence/who_multicountry_study/en/

Physical Child Abuse, Neglect, and Domestic Violence

A Case Studies Approach

6

MARK A. WINTON
ELIZABETH M. RASH

Contents

Introduction

The goal of this chapter is to examine the connections between physical child abuse, child neglect, and domestic violence, also known as intimate partner violence (IPV). This will include a discussion of the definitions of child abuse and neglect (CAN) and IPV, the epidemiology and risk factors for CAN and IPV, the types of perpetrators, and various assessment tools, as well as explication of the mental illness, feminist, and intergenerational transmission of violence theories.

Historically, CAN and IPV have been studied separately, but recent research indicates that an integrated approach is warranted, as CAN and IPV often co-occur within the same family (Appel & Holden, 1998; Bevan & Higgins, 2002; Gewirtz & Edleson, 2007; Winton & Mara, 2001). Consequently, failing to screen for both CAN and IPV may provide a limited understanding of the family dynamics and result in inappropriate interventions.

Based on a composite of several families from the authors' clinical work, a case study will be presented in selected sections of the chapter to illustrate the connections between research and practice.

Case Summary: Part 1

The Jones family sought out counseling after several family stressors led to increased conflict. The family consists of Mr. Jones, age 35, Mrs. Jones, age 33, Lisa, age 9, and 6-year-old Ben. Mr. and Mrs. Jones were both employed in management positions until three weeks ago, when Mr. Jones was laid off.

Mr. and Mrs. Jones are college educated and live in a middle-class neighborhood where "people just mind their own business." The family identifies themselves as Christian, and they attend church at least once a week. Religion is an important part of their life. Their daughter attends public school and their son attends a school at their church. Mr. Jones states, "I am worried I might not be able to find a job and then we might have to move." Mrs. Jones indicates that they have been fighting more frequently. She describes this as yelling, pushing and shoving, and storming out of the room. Mrs. Jones reports that she has thrown drinking glasses on the floor on several occasions, resulting in a piece of glass cutting Mr. Jones's arm. They affirm that "the children have not seen us pushing each other but certainly have heard our arguments."

Mrs. Jones has Lisa babysit her brother when they go to evening church events. She and Mr. Jones use disciplinary spankings with a paddle or belt. Mrs. Jones reports that Ben has recently been wetting his bed two or three times a week. Ben's asthma has also been worse, which she believes is probably due to Mr. Jones's cigarette smoking. Additionally, Ben has been hitting his sister when he gets frustrated and gave her a bloody nose on one occasion. Mr. and Mrs. Jones think that he is "probably just anxious with all the problems going on."

Definitions

The following definitions of CAN and IPV are used by researchers and clinicians. Interestingly, one of the definitions of emotional neglect includes a child observing IPV. This suggests that if IPV is present, then child neglect may be coexisting.

Child physical abuse: Physical abuse is defined in the Third National Incidence Study of Child Abuse and Neglect (NIS-3) (Sedlak & Broadhurst, 1996) as acts including "hitting with a hand, stick, strap, or other object; punching; kicking; shaking; throwing; burning; stabbing; or choking a child" (p. 2-10).

Child neglect: The following definitions of neglect are also from NIS-3 (Sedlak & Broadhurst, 1996, pp. 2-16–2-19).

Physical neglect includes:

Refusal of health care: Failure to provide or allow needed care in accord with recommendations of a competent health care professional for a physical injury, illness, medical condition, or impairment.

Delay in health care: Failure to seek timely and appropriate medical care for a serious health problem that any reasonable layperson would have recognized as needing professional medical attention.

Abandonment: Desertion of a child without arranging for reasonable care and supervision.

Expulsion: Other blatant refusals of custody, such as permanent or indefinite expulsion of a child from the home without adequate arrangement for care by others or refusal to accept custody of a returned runaway.

Other custody issues: Custody-related forms of inattention to the child's needs other than those covered by abandonment or expulsion.

Inadequate supervision: Child left unsupervised or inadequately supervised for extended periods of time or allowed to remain away from home overnight without the parent/substitute knowing (or attempting to determine) the child's whereabouts.

Other physical neglect: Conspicuous inattention to avoidable hazards in the home; inadequate nutrition, clothing, or hygiene; and other forms of reckless disregard of the child's safety and welfare, such as driving with the child while intoxicated, leaving a young child unattended in a motor vehicle, and so forth.

Educational neglect includes:

Permitted chronic truancy: Habitual truancy averaging at least five days a month was classifiable under this form of maltreatment if the parent/guardian had been informed of the problem and had not attempted to intervene.

Failure to enroll/other truancy: Failure to register or enroll a child of mandatory school age, causing the child to miss at least one month of school; or a pattern of keeping a school-age child home for nonlegitimate reasons (e.g., to work, to care for siblings, etc.) an average of at least three days a month.

Inattention to special education needs: Refusal to allow or failure to obtain recommended remedial education services, or neglect in obtaining or following through with treatment for a child's diagnosed learning disorder or other special education need without reasonable cause.

Emotional neglect consists of:

Inadequate nurturance/affection: Marked inattention to the child's needs for affection, emotional support, attention, or competence.

Chronic/extreme spouse abuse: Chronic or extreme spouse abuse or other domestic violence in the child's presence.

Permitted drug/alcohol abuse: Encouraging or permitting of drug or alcohol use by the child; cases of the child's drug/alcohol use were included in this category if it appeared that the parent/guardian had been informed about the problem and had not attempted to intervene.

Permitted other maladaptive behavior: Encouragement or permitting of other maladaptive behavior (e.g., severe assaultiveness, chronic delinquency) under circumstances where the parent/guardian had reason to be aware of the existence and seriousness of the problem but did not attempt to intervene.

Refusal of psychological care: Refusal to allow needed and available treatment for a child's emotional or behavioral impairment or problem in accord with competent professional recommendation.

Delay in psychological care: Failure to seek or provide needed treatment for a child's emotional or behavioral impairment or problem that any reasonable layperson would have recognized as needing professional psychological attention (e.g., severe depression, suicide attempt).

Other emotional neglect: Other inattention to the child's developmental/emotional needs not classifiable under any of the above forms of emotional neglect (e.g., markedly overprotective restrictions that foster immaturity or emotional overdependence, chronically applying expectations clearly inappropriate in relation to the child's age or level of development, etc.).

Intimate Partner Violence (IPV)

The Centers for Disease Control and Prevention defines IPV as "actual or threatened physical, sexual, psychological, or stalking violence by current or former intimate partners" (Thompson, Basile, Hertz, & Sitterle, 2006, p. 1).

Epidemiology and Risk Factors of IPV and CAN

Epidemiological studies focus on the distribution of conditions within a population or society and provide us with information regarding which groups are at greater risk. Based on child protective official reports, during 2006:

> 64.1 percent of victims experienced neglect, 16.0 percent were physically abused, 8.8 percent were sexually abused, 6.6 percent were psychologically maltreated, and 2.2 were medically neglected. In addition, 15.1 percent of victims experienced such "other" types of maltreatment as "abandonment," "threats of harm to the child," or "congenital drug addiction." (U.S. Department of Health and Human Services, 2008, p. 27)

According to Sedlak and Broadhurst (1996), male and female caretakers both engage in child maltreatment, but female caretakers are more likely to be reported for physical abuse, emotional maltreatment, and neglect, and male caretakers are more likely to be reported for sexual abuse. The higher rate of CAN by females is most likely due to the greater number of hours that females spend with children in caretaker roles (Winton & Mara, 2001).

Some of the risk factors suggested for CAN include single-parent household, young age of parent, living below the poverty level, low education, unemployment, lack of social support, and drug use (Sedlak & Broadhurst, 1996; Winton & Mara, 2001; Wolfner & Gelles, 1993). Children whose parents use drugs and alcohol are at increased risk for physical abuse and neglect, and the parents themselves are also at greater risk for IPV (Winton & Mara, 2001). In addition, pregnant women who use drugs or alcohol may be charged with neglect.

In their groundbreaking National Family Violence Surveys, Straus and Gelles (1986) reported that husband-to-wife overall violence (husbands engaging in violence toward wives) in 1975 was 121 per 1,000 couples and in 1985 had declined to 113 per 1,000 couples. The rate for severe violence for husband-to-wife violence was 38 per 1,000 couples in 1975 and declined to 30 per 1,000 couples in 1985. The rate for wife-to-husband overall violence was 116 per 1,000 couples in 1975 and 121 per 1,000 couples in 1985, and for severe violence was 46 per 1,000 couples in 1975 and 44 per 1,000 couples in 1985. These studies showed that men and women have similar rates of violence toward each other, although women were more likely to report injuries. The decrease in violence may be related to study design or improved interventions and is still being debated.

In another study, Tjaden and Thoennes (1998) found that 52% of the women and 66% of the men reported child physical abuse or adult victimization. They also established that women were significantly more likely to report being assaulted by an intimate partner.

Whitaker, Haileyesus, Swahn, and Saltzman (2007) suggested that reciprocal or mutual intimate partner violence occurred frequently and was more likely to result in an injury. These results challenge the current paradigm of asymmetrical or unbalanced violence and lead to new ways of conceptualizing treatment programs that have traditionally focused on nonreciprocal violence.

Divorcing couples may be at higher risk for IPV and their children for CAN (Adelman, 2000; Pagelow, 1993; Rennison & Welchans, 2000). In fact, IPV may be the primary reason for the divorce (Kurtz, 1996). In many states, laws have been enacted mandating that divorcing parents attend a seminar on minimizing the effects of divorce on children. These seminars include discussions of the negative impact of conflict and IPV on children.

There are inconsistencies within the epidemiological and risk-based studies. Problems exist when attempting to compare different studies due to different sampling frames (community or clinical), type of sampling (probability or nonprobability), research design (cross-sectional or longitudinal), definitions of violence, types of violence, time frame (past year or lifetime), and data analysis techniques (Tolan, Gorman-Smith, & Henry, 2006). For example, the statistics from child protective services reflect only those cases that are actually reported, leading to an underestimation of the true prevalence of child maltreatment.

Types of Abusers

Many typologies of CAN and IPV perpetrators have been described. For example, high-risk, moderate-risk, and low-risk batterers were described by Cavanaugh and Gelles (2005). By using cluster analysis, Chiffriller, Hennessy, and Zappone (2006) found five profiles of male batterers: pathological, sexually violent, generally violent, psychologically violent, and family only.

Ehrensaft, Moffitt, and Caspi (2004) contrasted the common couples abuser, who engages in less frequent and less severe abuse, with the clinically abusive perpetrator, who engages in more frequent and severe abuse, is more likely to cause medical injury to the partner, uses more drugs and alcohol, has higher rates of psychopathology, and is more likely to be convicted.

Jacobson and Gottman (1998) identified two types of men who batter: cobras and pit bulls. The cobras were more likely to be belligerent, defensive, emotionally abusive, have higher rates of mental illness, engage in more severe violence, and engage in higher rates of violence outside of the home. The pit bulls were more likely to have contempt for women but are more dependent on them and have lower rates of violence outside of the home.

Assessment Tools

There are numerous assessment tools that can be used to assess IPV and CAN. The Centers for Disease Control and Prevention *Measuring Intimate Partner Violence Victimization and Perpetration: A Compendium of Assessment Tools* (Thompson et al., 2006) is a resource that includes physical, sexual, psychological/emotional, stalking victimization, and perpetration scales.

The Revised Conflict Tactics Scales has been extensively used to assess domestic violence and measures psychological aggression, physical assault, sexual coercion, injury, and negotiation used in conflict situations (Straus, Hamby, Boney-McCoy, & Sugarman, 1996). The Parent-Child Conflict Tactics Scales provides measurements of psychological maltreatment, physical maltreatment, neglect, and sexual abuse (Straus, Hamby, Finkelhor, Moore, & Runyan, 1998).

The Personal and Relationship Profile (PRP) (Straus, Hamby, Boney-McCoy, & Sugarman, 1999) may be used to measure individual and relationship problems and risk factors for IPV. The following scales make up the PRP (Straus et al., 1999): Antisocial Personality, Borderline Personality, Criminal History, Depressive Symptoms, Gender Hostility, Neglect History, Post-Traumatic Stress, Social Desirability, Social Integration, Substance Abuse, Stressful Conditions, Sexual Abuse History, Violence Approval, Violent Socialization, Anger Management, Communication Problems, Conflict, Dominance, Jealousy, Negative Attribution, Relationship Commitment, and Relationship Distress.

In addition, Straus (2006) created the Multidimensional Neglectful Behavior Scale to measure emotional, physical, cognitive, and supervisory neglect. Multiple versions allow for administration variations with either children or adults (recalled and current neglect).

Other IPV risk assessment tools have been evaluated by Dutton and Kropp (2000) and Campbell (1999, 2005), while Hamby and Finkelhor (2001) have reviewed child victimization questionnaires.

There has been a movement toward the integration of varying types of tools for victimization studies as exemplified by the Developmental Victimization Survey program (Finkelhor, Ormrod, Turner, & Hamby, 2005). This survey includes physical assaults, bullying, teasing, sexual victimization, child maltreatment (physical, sexual, and emotional abuse, neglect, and family abduction or custodial interference), property victimization, and witnessed and indirect victimization. Using their Juvenile Victimization Questionnaire, the researchers found that 53% of their sample had been assaulted during the study year.

Paradigms and Theories

Currently, we may be in the middle of a paradigm shift in the CAN and IPV fields. A paradigm is a model used to view the world and to understand how it works. Paradigms guide our theories, research, and interventions. For example, there are medical, psychological, sociological, and legal paradigms for IPV and CAN. Supporters of different paradigms often have debates around which paradigm is the best, and this leads to competition between the supporters of the different paradigms (Kuhn, 1970; Winton, 2005). Some states have passed laws prohibiting interventions such as family therapy, anger management, or communication enhancement for IPV cases, but this is now being challenged and can be considered a paradigm conflict (see Dutton, 2008). We predict that we will see more research regarding the use of psychiatric medications in cases of IVP and CAN. For example, selective serotonin reuptake inhibitors, a class of antidepressants, may be used as part of comprehensive treatment programs (Jacobson & Gottman, 1998).

Using the case study, we will briefly describe the mental illness/psychopathology, feminist/gender-based, and intergenerational transmission of violence paradigms.

Case Summary: Part 2

Based on mental health evaluations, Mr. Jones was diagnosed with substance use disorder. He also has problems identifying and managing his emotions. Mrs. Jones was diagnosed with major depression and posttraumatic stress disorder due to her childhood sexual abuse. Ben was diagnosed with adjustment disorder. He was referred for a physical exam to rule out medical explanations for his bed-wetting. Lisa did not meet the criteria for any mental disorders but does have elevated levels of anxiety.

Mental Illness Paradigm

Mental disorders may be viewed as a cause or an effect of IPV and CAN. In the general population, men are more likely to have substance use disorders and antisocial personality disorder, while women are more likely to have depression and anxiety disorders (Kessler et al., 1994). There is a high rate of comorbidity of substance use disorders with other mental disorders (Johnson, Brems, & Burke, 2002; Kessler et al., 1994; McKeehan & Martin, 2002; Weiss, Najavits, & Mirin, 1998), and family violence has also been associated with substance abuse (Flanzer, 1993; Gelles, 1993; Jacobson & Gottman, 1998). Additionally, caregivers who abuse or neglect their children have higher rates of co-occurring mental disorders (De Bellis et al., 2001). Children who witness parental violence are at increased risk for mental health problems as well as repeating the cycle of CAN on their own children (Winton & Mara, 2001). Since co-morbidity is the norm, programs should offer a comprehensive and integrated approach addressing multiple factors (McKeehan & Martin, 2002; Wanberg & Milkman, 1998).

Kessler, Molnar, Feurer, and Appelbaum (2001) used data from the National Comorbidity Survey to assess the relationship between IPV and mental illness. They discovered intergenerational continuity of family violence for perpetrators and victims and noted that previous mental disorder among men (major depression, generalized anxiety disorder, alcohol dependence, nonaffective psychosis, dysthymia, and adult antisocial behavior) were predictors of domestic violence. Golding (1999) found that women who experienced IPV were at greater risk for posttraumatic stress disorder, depression, suicidality, and alcohol and drug abuse. Therefore, it would be important to screen for mental health disorders in all involved in IPV and CAN situations.

Some researchers use a developmental model and study research participants over long periods of time. These types of studies demonstrate that mental disorders, CAN, and IPV are related to each other in various ways over the life course. Moffitt and Caspi (1999) used their birth cohort study to assess childhood victimization, mental disorders, and adult violence. They found that male perpetrators of violence had higher rates of mental disorders than male nonperpetrators. These disorders included anxiety, depression, substance abuse (drug and alcohol dependence), antisocial personality disorder, and schizophrenia. The female victims of violence also had elevated rates of mental disorders. Additional major childhood risks for the male perpetrators of violence were poverty and low school achievement, while female perpetrators had conflicting family relationships. While both males and females engaged in violence toward each other, females were more likely to suffer physical injury.

There continues to be a lack of research on substance abuse, other mental health problems, and violence (Johnson et al., 2002). Addressing this situation, Solomon, Cavanaugh, and Gelles (2005) developed a model that focused on the interaction of types of mental disorder, support networks, history of violent behavior, and interactional and relational variables. Future research should continue to address the integration of substance abuse, other mental disorders, relationship problems, and emotions.

Studies that address the relationships between IPV and CAN and emotions are rarely presented in the professional literature. This is unfortunate, as perpetrators of IPV and CAN often have difficulties regulating and managing their emotions. Violence is one way of expressing extreme upset

(Umberson, Anderson, Williams, & Chen, 2003), and IPV offenders tend to have high levels of anger and hostility (Norlander & Eckhardt, 2005).

Focusing on emotions, Moffitt, Robins, and Caspi (2001) reported that negative emotionality (NEM) worked as a predictor of IPV. They found that "when both partners were high in NEM, the likelihood of mutual abuse increased additively" (p. 17).

A case control method with violent and nonviolent groups demonstrated that violent offenders had higher levels of global stress, hostility/anger, and alcohol problems, and were more likely to perceive threats from their partners and repress their emotions (Umberson, Williams, & Anderson, 2002).

Yelsma (1996) found that victims and perpetrators of abuse have "high levels of alexithymia, the inability to experience and express subjective emotions, lack of awareness of affective information to guide relationship talk, low levels of positive feelings about their own lives, and low levels of expression of positive emotions" (p. 157). Further studies on emotions and IPV and CAN are warranted.

Feminist Paradigms

The feminist or gender-based paradigms focus on male power, dominance, and privilege and how men have used their power to oppress women and children (Solomon, 1992; Winton & Mara, 2001). For example, according to Anderson (2002), even when there is mutual abuse, women are more likely than men to suffer negative mental health and physical health consequences.

Current feminist perspectives analyze the intersection of gender, race, and social class (Lilly, Cullen, & Ball, 2007), and many popular IPV treatment programs are based on feminist models of patriarchy or male dominance. However, this has recently been challenged, and there is a debate revolving around whether the feminist approach to IPV and CAN is based primarily on advocacy or evidence-based research, or both (Dutton, 2008; Dutton & Corvo, 2006). Focusing on IVP, Felson (2006) suggested that the gender perspective is currently being challenged by supporters of the violence perspective, and a shift from theories of sexism and patriarchy to theories of violence may be occurring.

Case Study: Part 3

Mr. Jones grew up in an alcoholic family and was often yelled at by his parents. He reports that his father "ruled the home with an iron fist." Mr. Jones left home at age 18 to attend college. He rarely talks to his parents, who currently reside in another state. Mr. Jones has an older brother who is a teacher and youth minister. His brother is always happy to lend the family some help. His brother lives in another state and visits twice a year.

Mrs. Jones grew up in a chaotic house with her mother always yelling and hitting the kids. She reports that her father was often absent from the family. She witnessed her father "beating up my mother on many occasions." When Mrs. Jones was 10 years old, her uncle sexually abused her for about 6 months. She told her mother about the abuse, but her mother told her that she was "crazy" and to "just stay away from him." Mrs. Jones has two sisters who live within an hour drive. They have similar aged children and she tries to visit them several times a month.

Intergenerational Transmission Theory

Intergenerational transmission theory is used to explain how CAN and IPV are transmitted from generation to generation. This theory is constructed from the social learning theory and is used to examine the developmental connections between CAN and IPV across the life course.

Children and adolescents who witness their parents engaging in violence may become traumatized and experience a host of negative symptoms and are at increased risk for CAN (Edleson, 1998; Ross, 1996; Smolinski, 1997; Winton & Mara, 2001). Overall, children who are physically abused, neglected, or witness parental violence are at increased risk for mental disorders, aggressive behavior, drug use, physical problems, school difficulties, teenage pregnancy, and relationship problems with their peers and adults (Barnett, Miller-Perrin, & Perrin, 2005; Wiebush, Freitag, & Baird, 2001; Winton & Mara, 2001). These children are also more likely to engage in deviant behavior and continue to engage in nonviolent and violent criminal behavior during adolescence and adulthood (Ammerman, 1990; Hotaling, Straus, & Lincoln, 1990; Kerig, 1998; McCord, 1995; Teague, Mazerolle, Legosz, & Sanderson, 2008; Widom, 1989; Winton & Mara, 2001).

In their early research, Widom and Ames (1994) reported that children who experienced sexual abuse, physical abuse, or neglect were at higher risk for juvenile or adult arrest than those in a control group. More recently, Widom and Maxfield (2001) reported that "being abused or neglected as a child increased the likelihood of arrest as a juvenile by 59 percent, as an adult by 28 percent, and for a violent crime by 30 percent" (p. 1).

Straus (2006) determined that increased levels of neglect were related to the greater likelihood of assaulting a dating partner (for both men and women). For men, the higher the level of neglect, the greater the likelihood of severely injuring a dating partner. Likewise, Heyman and Slep (2002) found that both women and men who were exposed to interparental and parent-child violence had a higher risk of abusing their children and each other.

Furthermore, mothers who experience IVP are more likely to abuse their children than those who have not experienced IPV (Coohey & Braun, 1997).

Bevan and Higgins (2002) suggested that being neglected as a child predicted IPV. Although family of origin is one of multiple risk factors, those that experienced violence in their family of origin were at greater risk for perpetration or victimization of abuse in their adult intimate relationships (Busby, Holman, & Walker, 2008). However, using meta-analysis, Stith et al. (2000) found weak to moderate relationships between family of origin violence and IPV.

While there is a clear link between being maltreated during childhood, development of mental disorders, and engaging in violent behavior as an adult, many maltreated children do not demonstrate violent or neglectful behaviors as adults. The factors that lead one to become violent or nonviolent are still being investigated. While it is important to examine the developmental links between mental disorders, CAN, and IPV (Ehrensaft, 2008), we need to avoid labeling children who were abused as potential offenders and avoid injecting biases in our research and interventions (Kaufman & Zigler, 1993; Winton & Mara, 2001).

Case Summary: Part 4

The treatment plan for the Jones family is to have Mr. and Mrs. Jones attend couples counseling, refer Mrs. Jones to a sexual abuse survivor group, and refer Mr. Jones to an outpatient substance abuse treatment program. In addition, Mrs. Jones will be referred to a health care provider to consider the use of antidepressant medication, and Ben will be referred to a health care provider to determine if there is a medical explanation for his bed-wetting. The family will be counseled about the risks of exposing their children to cigarette smoke and the risks of letting their relatively young daughter care for their son while they are away. Parenting issues will also be addressed in the couples counseling, and Mr. and Mrs. Jones will be referred to a parenting group if needed.

Conclusions

The links between IPV and CAN are complex and related to other psychological and social factors. We have shown that there are numerous risk factors across the life course that influence parenting practices and intimate relationships. Mental disorders and witnessing parental violence were two risk factors that were emphasized throughout this chapter. Other risk factors were only superficially addressed, but the complexity of these relationships has been discussed by many researchers.

Even though we have made much progress, there is still much work to be done. As Dutton (2008) states, "Our interventions for IPV are too rigid, too late, too superficial (treating symptoms), and too narrowly defined" (p. 139).

We need to look at all of the factors related to CAN and IPV. This would include biological/physical, psychological, and cultural/sociological. Linking individual, family, and community approaches will provide us with an increased understanding of violence (Sampson, 1997). Four other areas that are not covered here but certainly deserve additional attention are corporal punishment, sibling abuse, bullying by nonfamily members, and child fatalities due to abuse or neglect.

An integrated approach is needed that focuses on all types of family violence (Tolan et al., 2006). Future research might focus on both structural and agency-level variables by integrating paradigms and research findings. This may allow us to construct more effective methods of reducing the cycles of CAN and IPV.

We remain optimistically guarded that we will continue to make progress and implement evidence-based strategies. We believe that we can best accomplish this task by integrating paradigms, allowing for diversity of interventions, using evidence-based practice, and funding creative and innovative research and treatment programs.

References

Adelman, M. (2000). No way out: Divorce-related domestic violence in Israel. *Violence Against Women, 6*, 1223–1254.

Ammerman, R. T. (1990). Etiological models of child maltreatment. *Behavior Modification, 14*, 230–254.

Anderson, K. L. (2002). Perpetrator or victim? Relationships between intimate partner violence and well-being. *Journal of Marriage and Family, 64*, 851–863.

Appel, A. E., & Holden, G. W. (1998). The co-occurrence of spouse and physical child abuse: A review and appraisal. *Journal of Family Psychology, 12*, 578–599.

Barnett, O., Miller-Perrin, C. L., & Perrin, R. D. (2005). *Family violence across the lifespan: An introduction* (2nd ed.). Thousand Oaks, CA: Sage.

Bevan, E., & Higgins, D.J. (2002). Is domestic violence learned? The contribution of five forms of child maltreatment to men's violence and adjustment. *Journal of Family Violence, 17*, 223–245.

Busby, D. M., Holman, T. B., & Walker, E. (2008). Pathways to relationship aggression between adult partners. *Family Relations, 57*, 72–83.

Campbell, J. C. (1999). If I can't have you no one can: Murder linked to battery during pregnancy. *Reflections, 25*, 8–12.

Campbell, J. C. (2005). Assessing dangerousness in domestic violence cases: History, challenges, and opportunities. *Criminology & Public Policy, 4*, 653–672.

Cavanaugh, M. M., & Gelles, R. J. (2005). The utility of male domestic violence offender typologies. *Journal of Interpersonal Violence, 20*, 155–166.

Chiffriller, S. H., Hennessy, J. J., & Zappone, M. (2006). Understanding a new typology of batterers: Implications for treatment. *Victims and Offenders, 1*, 79–97.

Coohey, C., & Braun, N. (1997). Toward an integrated framework for understanding child physical abuse. *Child Abuse & Neglect, 21,* 1081–1094.

De Bellis, M. D., Broussard, E. R., Herring, D. J., Wexler, S., Moritz, G., & Benitez, J. G. (2001). Psychiatric co-morbidity in caregivers and children involved in maltreatment: A pilot research study with policy implications. *Child Abuse & Neglect, 25,* 923–944.

Dutton, D. G. (2008). My back pages: Reflections on thirty years of domestic violence research. *Trauma, Violence, & Abuse, 9,* 131–143.

Dutton, D. G., & Corvo, K. (2006). Transforming a flawed policy: A call to revive psychology and science in domestic violence research and practice. *Aggression and Violent Behavior, 11,* 457–483.

Dutton, D. G., & Kropp, P. R. (2000). A review of domestic violence risk instruments. *Trauma, Violence, & Abuse, 1,* 171–181.

Edleson, J. L. (1998). Responsible mothers and invisible men: Child protection in the case of adult domestic violence. *Journal of Interpersonal Violence, 13,* 294–298.

Ehrensaft, M. K. (2008). Intimate partner violence: Persistence of myths and implications for intervention. *Children and Youth Services Review, 30,* 276–286.

Ehrensaft, M. K., Moffitt, T. E., & Caspi, A. (2004). Clinically abusive relationships in an unselected birth cohort: Men's and women's participation and developmental antecedents. *Journal of Abnormal Psychology, 113,* 258–271.

Felson, R. B. (2006). Is violence against women about women or about violence? *Contexts, 5,* 21–25.

Finkelhor, D., Ormrod, R., Turner, H., & Hamby, S. L. (2005). The victimization of children and youth: A comprehensive, national survey. *Child Maltreatment, 10,* 5–25.

Flanzer, J. P. (1993). Alcohol and other drugs are key causal agents of violence. In R. J. Gelles & D. R. Loseke (Eds.), *Current controversies on family violence* (pp. 171–181). Newbury Park, CA: Sage.

Gelles, R. J. (1993). Alcohol and other drugs are associated with violence—They are not its cause. In R. J. Gelles & D. R. Loseke (Eds.), *Current controversies on family violence* (pp. 182–196). Newbury Park, CA: Sage.

Gewirtz, A. H., & Edleson, J. L. (2007). Young children's exposure to intimate partner violence: Towards a developmental risk and resilience framework for research and intervention. *Journal of Family Violence, 22,* 151–163.

Golding, J. M. (1999). Intimate partner violence as a risk factor for mental disorders: A meta-analysis. *Journal of Family Violence, 14,* 99–132.

Hamby, S. L., & Finkelhor, D. (2001). *Choosing and using child victimization questionnaires.* Washington, DC: U.S. Department of Justice.

Heyman, R. E., & Slep, A. M. S. (2002). Do child abuse and interparental violence lead to adult family violence? *Journal of Marriage and Family, 64,* 864–870.

Hotaling, G. T., Straus, M. A., & Lincoln, A. J. (1990). Intrafamily violence and crime and violence outside the family. In M. A. Straus & R. J. Gelles (Eds.), *Physical violence in American families: Risk factors and adaptations to violence in 8,145 families* (pp. 431–470). New Brunswick, NJ: Transaction.

Jacobson, N. S & Gottman, J. M. (1998). *When men batter women: New insights into ending abusive relationships.* New York: Simon & Schuster.

Johnson, M. E., Brems, C., & Burke, S. (2002). Recognizing comorbidity among drug users in treatment. *American Journal of Drug and Alcohol Abuse, 28,* 243–261.

Kaufman, J., & Zigler, E. (1993). The intergenerational transmission of abuse is overstated. In R. J. Gelles & D. R. Loseke (Eds.), *Current controversies on family violence* (pp. 209–221). Newbury Park, CA: Sage.

Kerig, P. K. (1998). Gender and appraisals as mediators of adjustment in children exposed to interparental violence. *Journal of Family Violence, 13*, 345–363.

Kessler, R. C., McGonagle, K. A., Zhao, S., Nelson, C. B., Hughes, M., Eshleman, S., Wittchen, H. U., & Kendler, K. S. (1994). Lifetime and 12-month prevalence of DSM-III-R psychiatric disorders in the United States: Results from the National Comorbidity Survey. *Archives of General Psychiatry, 51*, 8–19.

Kessler, R. C., Molnar, B. E., Feurer, I. D., & Appelbaum, M. (2001). Patterns and mental health predictors of domestic violence in the United States: Results from the National Comorbidity Survey. *International Journal of Law and Psychiatry, 24*, 487–508.

Kuhn, T. S. (1970). *The structure of scientific revolutions* (2nd ed.). New York: New American Library.

Kurtz, D. (1996). Separation, divorce, and woman abuse. *Violence Against Women, 2*, 63–81.

Lilly, J. R., Cullen, F. T., & Ball, B. A. (2007). *Criminological theory: Context and consequences* (4th ed.). Thousand Oaks, CA: Sage.

McCord, J. (Ed.). (1995). *Coercion and punishment in long-term perspectives.* Cambridge: Cambridge University Press.

McKeehan, M. B., & Martin, D. (2002). Assessment and treatment of anxiety disorders and co-morbid alcohol/other drug dependency. *Alcoholism Treatment Quarterly, 20*, 45–59.

Moffitt, T. E., & Caspi, A. (1999). *Findings about partner violence from the Dunedin Multidisciplinary Health and Development Study.* Washington, DC: U.S. Department of Justice.

Moffitt, T. E., Robins, R. W., & Caspi, A. (2001). A couples analysis of partner abuse with implications for abuse-prevention policy. *Criminology & Public Policy, 1*, 5–36.

Norlander, B., & Eckhardt, C. (2005). Anger, hostility, and male perpetrators of intimate partner violence: A meta-analytic review. *Clinical Psychology Review, 25*, 119–152.

Pagelow, M. D. (1993). Justice for victims of spouse abuse in divorce and child custody cases. *Violence & Victims, 8*, 69–83.

Rennison, C. M., & Welchans, S. (2000). *Intimate partner violence.* Washington, DC: U.S. Department of Justice.

Ross, S. M. (1996). Risk of physical abuse to children of spouse abusing parents. *Child Abuse and Neglect, 20*, 589–598.

Sampson, R. J. (1997). The embeddedness of child and adolescent development: A community-level perspective on urban violence. In J. McCord (Ed.), *Violence and childhood in the inner city* (pp. 31–77). Cambridge: Cambridge University Press.

Sedlak, A. J., & Broadhurst, D. D. (1996). *Third National Incidence Study of Child Abuse and Neglect.* Washington, DC: U.S. Department of Health and Human Services.

Smolinski, A. K. (1997). Emotional effects of violence in the family. In J. S. Grisolía, J. Sanmartin, J. L. Luján, & S. Grisolía (Eds.), *Violence: From biology to society* (pp. 125–129). Amsterdam: Elsevier.

Solomon, J. C. (1992). Child sexual abuse by family members: A radical feminist perspective. *Sex Roles, 27*, 473–485.

Solomon, P. L., Cavanaugh, M. M., & Gelles, R. J. (2005). Family violence among adults with severe mental illness: A neglected area of research. *Trauma, Violence, & Abuse, 6*, 40–54.

Straus, M. A. (2006). Cross-cultural reliability and validity of the Multidimensional Neglectful Behavior Scale Adult Recall Short Form. *Child Abuse & Neglect, 30*, 1257–1279.

Straus, M. A., & Gelles, R. J. (1986). Societal change and change in family violence from 1975 to 1985 as revealed by two national surveys. *Journal of Marriage and the Family, 48*, 465–479.

Straus, M. A., Hamby, S. L., Boney-McCoy, S., & Sugarman, D. B. (1996). The revised Conflict Tactics Scales (CTS2): Development and preliminary psychometric data. *Journal of Family Issues, 17*, 283–316.

Straus, M. A., Hamby, S. L., Boney-McCoy, S., & Sugarman, D. (1999). *The Personal Relationships Profile (PRP)*. Durham, NH: Family Research Laboratory, University of New Hampshire.

Straus, M. A., Hamby, S. L., Finkelhor, D., Moore, D. W., & Runyan, D. (1998). Identification of child maltreatment with the Parent-Child Conflict Tactics Scales: Development and psychometric data for a national sample of American parents. *Child Abuse and Neglect, 22*, 249–270.

Stith, S. M., Rosen, K. H., Middleton, K. A., Busch, A. L., Lundeberg, K., & Carlton, R. P. (2000). The intergenerational transmission of spouse abuse: A meta analysis. *Journal of Marriage and the Family, 62*, 640–654.

Teague, R., Mazerolle, P., Legosz, M., & Sanderson, J. (2008). Linking childhood exposure to physical abuse and adult offending: Examining mediating factors and gendered relationships. *Justice Quarterly, 25*, 313–348.

Thompson, M. P., Basile, K. C., Hertz, M. F., & Sitterle, D. (2006). *Measuring intimate partner violence victimization and perpetration: A compendium of assessment tools*. Atlanta, GA: Centers for Disease Control and Prevention, National Center for Injury Prevention and Control.

Tjaden, P., & Thoennes, N. (1998). *Prevalence, incidence, and consequences of violence against women: Findings from the National Violence Against Women Survey*. Washington, DC: U.S. Department of Justice.

Tolan, P., Gorman-Smith, D., & Henry, D. (2006). Family violence. *Annual Review of Psychology, 57*, 557–583.

Umberson, D., Anderson, K. L., Williams, K., & Chen, M. (2003). Relationship dynamics, emotion state, and domestic violence: A stress and masculinities perspective. *Journal of Marriage and Family, 65*, 233–247.

Umberson, D., Williams, K., & Anderson, K. (2002). Violent behavior: A measure of emotional upset? *Journal of Health and Social Behavior, 43*, 189–206.

U.S. Department of Health and Human Services. (2008). *Child maltreatment 2006*. Washington, DC: U.S. Government Printing Office.

Wanberg, K. W., & Milkman, H. B. (1998). *Criminal conduct and substance abuse treatment*. Thousand Oaks, CA: Sage.

Weiss, R. D., Najavits, L. M., & Mirin, S. M. (1998). Substance abuse and psychiatric disorders. In R. J. Frances & S. I. Miller (Eds.), *Clinical textbook of addictive disorders* (2nd ed., pp. 291–318). New York: Guilford Press.

Whitaker, D. J., Haileyesus, T., Swahn, M., & Saltzman, L. S. (2007). Differences in frequency of violence and reported injury between relationships with reciprocal and nonreciprocal intimate partner violence. *American Journal of Public Health, 97*, 941–947.

Widom, C. S. (1989). Child abuse, neglect, and adult behavior: Research design and findings on criminality, violence, and child abuse. *American Journal of Orthopsychiatry, 59*, 355–367.

Widom, C. S., & Ames, M. A. (1994). Criminal consequences of childhood sexual victimization. *Child Abuse & Neglect, 18*, 303–318.

Widom, C. S., & Maxfield, M. G. (2001). *An update on the "cycle of violence."* Washington, DC: U.S. Department of Justice.

Wiebush, R., Freitag, R., & Baird, C. (2001). *Preventing delinquency through improved child protection services.* Washington, DC: U.S. Department of Justice.

Winton, M. A. (2005). Treatment paradigms of sex offenders of children: An analysis of professional journals. *Aggression and Violent Behavior, 10*, 569–578.

Winton, M. A., & Mara, B. A. (2001). *Child abuse & neglect: Multidisciplinary approaches.* Boston: Allyn & Bacon.

Wolfner, G. D., & Gelles, R. J. (1993). A profile of violence toward children: A national study. *Child Abuse & Neglect, 17*, 197–212.

Yelsma, P. (1996). Affective orientations of perpetrators, victims, and functional spouses. *Journal of Interpersonal Violence, 11*, 141–161.

The Response of Child Welfare Agencies to Domestic Violence

7

MELANIE SHEPARD
GINA FARRELL

Contents

Child maltreatment and woman battering often co-occur in the same families, which can place children at risk for both physical and psychological harm. The co-occurrence of child maltreatment and domestic violence in families has been estimated to range from 30% to 60% (Office of Juvenile Justice and Delinquency Programs, 2000). In a national survey of over 6,000 families, 50% of the men who frequently abused their wives also frequently abused their children (Straus, Gelles, & Smith, 1990). More recent research suggests that when there are more severe levels of domestic violence, the child abuse is also more severe (Shepard & Raschick, 1999). Furthermore, the U.S. Advisory Board on Child Abuse and Neglect (1995) suggests that domestic violence may be the single major precursor to child abuse and neglect fatalities in the United States. Oftentimes, children may also be accidentally injured during a domestic violence incident.

The mandate of the child welfare system is to ensure that children are safe from harm. Cases in which children are exposed to domestic violence are particularly complex and challenging for child welfare professionals because the institutional practices developed within the child welfare system often do not take into account the dynamics of domestic violence. Although adult and child victims are often found in the same households, historically child protection workers and domestic violence have responded separately to them. The child welfare system has developed over the past century into a bureaucratic, largely publicly run system that is heavily governed by state and federal regulations. Domestic violence agencies are largely nonprofit and emerged from the grassroots battered women's movement of the 1970s. Differences in philosophy, mandates, training, and roles have hampered collaboration (Aron & Olson, 1997). Battered women's advocates have viewed child protection workers as unfairly penalizing woman by removing children from their care for failure to protect. On the other hand, child welfare workers sometimes view advocates for battered women as ignoring the needs of children (Shepard & Raschick, 1999). Effective intervention strategies that protect children, but do not penalize battered women, are still in developmental stages.

It should be noted that the training and education of child welfare workers, the types of services provided to families and children, and the availability of resources to address domestic violence fluctuate greatly by county and state. While there have been efforts to develop best practices (Bragg, 2003; Ganley & Schechter, 1996; National Council of Juvenile and Family Court Judges Family Violence Department, 1999), there is no uniformity in how child welfare agencies respond to domestic violence. Preliminary research findings suggest that cases in which there is domestic violence are "handled inconsistently across child welfare systems" (Kohl, Edleson, English, & Barth, 2005, p. 1169). This chapter will discuss how child welfare cases are affected by domestic violence, review practice guidelines on child welfare, and discuss an initiative to promote collaboration between the child welfare system, domestic violence agencies, and the courts.

Child Welfare Cases and Domestic Violence

Several studies in child welfare agencies have found that domestic violence has occurred in around one-third of child welfare cases (Kohl et al., 2005). In one statewide study, domestic violence was present in one in five cases referred to child protection services, and present in 47% of moderate- to high-risk cases. This study found that these cases were more likely to be open for services and to have at least one child placed out of the home (English, Edleson, & Herrick, 2005). Another study, using data from the National Survey of Child and Adolescent Well-Being, found that 14% of families investigated for child maltreatment were identified as actively experiencing domestic violence, and 19% had a history of domestic violence. Families who were actively experiencing domestic violence were more likely to have child maltreatment substantiated in child welfare investigation (Kohl et al., 2005).

Evidence suggests that child welfare professionals do not always screen for domestic violence, information is often not provided about domestic violence when cases are referred, and addressing domestic violence may not be viewed as an intervention priority (Shepard & Raschick, 1999). Child welfare professionals may be unaware of the presence of domestic violence due to a failure to disclose by family members or inadequate screening. Mothers may fear that their children will be removed from their care should they disclose the violence, or that they will face retaliation from abusers. Child welfare professionals become involved with families for a host of reasons, including child maltreatment, parental substance abuse and mental illness, truancy, and juvenile delinquency. The pressure on child welfare workers to address multiple problems in a large and demanding caseload can result in domestic violence being overlooked. Kohl et al. (2005) concluded that families with domestic violence in the child welfare system have multiple problems that contribute to the response of the child welfare system.

Many of the problems experienced by children in child welfare cases may be related to exposure to domestic violence. There is mounting evidence that exposure to domestic violence is related to emotional and behavioral problems in children (Fantuzzo & Lindquist, 1989; Jaffe, Wolfe, & Wilson, 1990). Child distress has been found to be greater where children have both witnessed domestic violence and been physically abused (Carlson, 1996). While adults may believe that they have protected their children from exposure to domestic violence, most children can give detailed descriptions of the violence experienced in their families. However, it should not be assumed that exposure to adult domestic violence in itself constitutes maltreatment, or that it will have long-term negative effects upon a child's development. Moderating variables such as age, gender, developmental stage, and the child's ability to cope can determine the extent to which exposure has been harmful, if at all (Edleson, 1999). One study found that the seriousness of child adjustment problems was related to the frequency of abuse, other negative life events, and the extent to which their mothers experienced stress and anxiety (Wolfe, Jaffe, Wilson, & Zak, 1985).

The well-being of children is closely aligned with that of their primary caregivers. In a longitudinal study of divorce, Wallerstein (1989) found that the mental health of the mother was the "most important protective factor in a child's psychological development and well-being" (p. 32). Abusers not only expose children to harm, but their abuse of primary caregivers can result in diminished parenting capacity. In a national study, Kohl et al. (2005) found that "larger proportions of primary caregivers with mental health issues, history of recent arrest, and a history of child abuse and neglect were found in families with active DV and history of DV than those families without DV" (p. 1175). Child welfare workers must find ways to both protect children and support primary caregivers who are experiencing domestic violence to address their own needs, as well as those of their children. This can be very challenging, particularly as battered women often continue to experience abuse and harassment after separation as a result of ongoing contact due to child visitation arrangements (Shepard, 1992).

Some jurisdictions use child maltreatment statutes that include the concept of "failure to protect" as the basis for removing children from homes where children are exposed to domestic violence. The challenges faced by child welfare agencies in responding to exposure to domestic violence are illustrated by the experiences of the state of Minnesota. During the 1999 legislative session the definition of *child neglect* was amended to include child exposure to domestic violence, which mandated professionals to report these cases. This resulted in many more cases being reported without new funds being allocated to investigate them. The Minnesota Social Service Association estimated that "it would cost more than $10 million to screen, assess, and provide services to these newly referred children," not to mention additional costs for community-based services and training law enforcement and county attorneys about the new law (Edleson, Gassman-Pines, & Hill, 2006, p. 170). The legislation was repealed after domestic violence advocates and child welfare agencies lobbied against it.

Federal child welfare laws place additional pressures on child welfare workers and families to act quickly to resolve issues when children are placed outside the home. Major revisions to federal child welfare law brought about by the enactment of the Adoption and Safe Families Act (AFSA) in 1997 emphasize prompt termination of parental rights in cases of abuse and neglect when children cannot safely return home. While the goals of AFSA to reduce the length of stays in foster care and improve adoption rates may benefit many children, shorter timelines can result in adult victims having between 6 and 15 months to address the damaging effects of domestic violence in their lives. According to Matthews (1999), "Adult victims of domestic violence may need considerable time to take steps necessary to ensure their own safety such as, moving, seeking a restraining order, recovering from physical and emotional trauma, finding a new job, and learning parenting skills necessary to stop the cycle of violence" (p. 56). Under AFSA, an exception to the time limits for parents who have not received the services needed for the child to return home can be granted. Because many states have major shortages of basic services needed by battered parents, often these parents may qualify for this exception. Conversely, although AFSA requires child welfare agencies to make reasonable efforts to provide services to families whose children have been removed from the home, they are not required to do so if a nonoffending parent is charged with "failing to protect" the children (Matthews, 1999). As we noted earlier, child welfare agencies may also be unaware of the extent to which problems experienced by families have been influenced by domestic violence, leading to a failure to address this issue in service plans.

Practice Guidelines for Child Welfare Professionals

A number of resource materials have been developed to provide practice guidelines for child welfare professionals when screening, assessing, and intervening in child welfare cases where there is domestic violence (Bragg, 2003; Ganley & Schechter, 1996; Minnesota Department of Human Services, 2002). Some child welfare agencies have hired domestic violence specialists and developed domestic violence teams within the child protection system (Edleson et al., 2006), although this is more often the exception than the rule.

It is recommended that routine screening for domestic violence take place for all reports of child maltreatment and on a periodic basis for all child welfare cases (Bragg, 2003). Collaboration with law enforcement is important in order to obtain information about domestic violence incidents and to consult about safety concerns. When cases are screened out for a child maltreatment assessment, it is recommended that information about domestic violence resources be provided to mandated reporters so that they may use them to refer family members to appropriate services (Minnesota Department of Human Services, 2002).

When domestic violence is identified in the screening process, it is advised that a more in-depth risk assessment for domestic violence be conducted in separate interviews with family members. When conducting a domestic violence risk assessment, Bragg (2003) recommends gathering critical information in the following areas: "the nature and extent of the domestic violence, the impact of the domestic violence on adult and child victims, the risk to and protective factors of the alleged victim and children, the help-seeking and survival strategies of the alleged victim, the alleged perpetrator's level of dangerousness, the safety and service needs of the family members, and the availability of practical community resources and services" (p. 39). Child welfare professionals should initially focus on immediate safety concerns and protective strategies, as well as provide information about domestic violence resources.

For a variety of reasons, child welfare professionals often focus their efforts on the adult victim and have less frequent contact with the alleged abuser. Interviewing alleged abusers can be challenging because they may be difficult to contact, threatening in their behavior, or generally, unresponsive. However, the failure to hold abusing partners accountable for their behavior can have the effect of blaming the victim for his or her children's exposure to domestic violence. However, care should be taken when interviewing the alleged abuser not to endanger the victim. Adult victims should be asked about any danger that such an interview might pose for them, and safety planning should take place prior to the interview. If the abuser shares information that indicates that there is imminent danger to known individuals, the child welfare professional has a "duty to warn" the victim(s) and should consult agency policies and procedures (Minnesota Department of Human Services, 2002). It is important that child welfare professionals hold abusers accountable for stopping their abusive behaviors by not allowing them to minimize their actions by justifying their violence based upon distortions of cultural practices, victim blaming, or stressful life circumstances. Bragg (2003) recommends focusing on obtaining information about alleged abusive behaviors and whether the individual accepts responsibility for this behavior. It is important to assess the abuser's willingness to seek help by attending a batterer intervention program and addressing substance abuse issues.

The information collected during the screening and assessment is used to inform decision making and to guide the intervention process. According to Bragg (2003), "CPS caseworkers should make diligent efforts to help victims protect their children before coercive measures, such as substantiation or protective custody, are considered" (p. 48). Removing children from their homes is usually unnecessary and can be traumatic for both the children and the adult victim. Consultation with supervisors and coordination of interventions with law enforcement and domestic violence service providers can help ensure that all options are pursued (Bragg, 2003). In a national study, Kohl et al. (2005) found that domestic violence by itself was not strongly associated with children being placed outside of the home. However, families actively experiencing domestic violence were among the families with the highest risk scores, which were most likely to have children placed outside the home.

Making a determination of child neglect based upon the failure to protect should be done with extreme caution because it can result in blaming the adult victim and, in some situations, strengthen the abuser's coercive control by giving credence to charges that the adult victim is an unfit parent. The result can be that the abusive partner is not held accountable for his or her actions, while the adult victim is. In addition, the adult victim is placed in an adversarial position with the child welfare system, which may prevent him or her from seeking help in the future. Before making such a determination, child welfare professionals must carefully assess whether the child is at risk because of exposure to domestic violence, the help-seeking strategies that the adult victim has used, and whether reasonable efforts have been made to protect the child. Also, it is imperative that child welfare professionals familiarize themselves with the dynamics of domestic violence so that they can appropriately assess for "reasonable" efforts. Conversely, while there has been concern that battered mothers are being faced with neglect allegations, a national study did not find that child welfare cases that included domestic violence were more likely to have neglect-related findings than other types of cases (Kohl et al., 2005).

Child welfare professionals work in tandem with other community agencies to provide services to families affected by domestic violence. Addressing factors such as the availability of safe housing, adequate income, health care services, and social support can increase the safety of families over the long term. Referrals are often made to shelter and housing services, support groups, advocacy services, child visitation centers, mental health services, financial aid, and legal resources. Attention to custody and visitation arrangements to ensure the safety of the adult victim and children is essential. Abusive partners may be court ordered or voluntarily participate in batterer intervention programs, which focus on anger management and sexist attitudes that promote the use of violence against women to maintain power and control. Child welfare professionals work with families to develop intervention plans and monitor their progress in order to safeguard the well-being of children. To effectively intervene and support families, the child welfare system must work collaboratively with other community agencies.

Promoting Collaboration: The Greenbook Project

A major federal initiative, the Greenbook Project, was undertaken to promote a collaborative community approach to families experiencing child maltreatment and domestic violence that extended beyond the child welfare system. A 1999 report (referred to as the Greenbook) by the National Council of Juvenile and Family Court Judges identifies practice and policy guidelines for child welfare systems, dependency courts, and domestic violence providers. The Greenbook provided a framework for developing interventions and measuring progress and offered communities and institutions recommendations to use as a context-setting tool to develop public policy aimed at keeping families safe and stable. The recommendations of the Greenbook focused on three primary systems: the child protection system, the network of community-based domestic violence programs, and the juvenile or other trial courts that have jurisdiction over child maltreatment cases (Schechter & Edleson, 1999).

The founding principles and recommendations of the Greenbook include collaborating for the safety, well-being, and stability of children and families; expansion and reallocation of resources to create safety, well-being, and stability; respect and dignity for all people coming before agencies and courts; commitment to building internal capacity to respond effectively to families experiencing domestic violence and child maltreatment; fact finding and confidentiality; and development of information gathering and evaluation systems to determine the intended and unintended outcomes of collaborative efforts (Schechter & Edleson, 1999). Specific Greenbook principles for guiding reforms in child welfare systems include establishing collaborative relationships with domestic violence service providers and dependency courts; taking leadership in providing services and resources to ensure family safety; developing service plans and referrals that focus on safety, stability, and well-being of all victims of family violence; and holding domestic violence perpetrators accountable (National Council of Juvenile and Family Court Judges Family Violence Department, 1999).

The U.S. Department of Justice and the U.S. Department of Health and Human Services partnered to develop a demonstration initiative to support implementation of the Greenbook recommendations and awarded grants to six sites (Schechter & Edleson, 1999). The selected sites received federal funding and technical assistance to implement the Greenbook principles and recommendations over a five-year demonstration period. In this time, sites were expected to form collaborations that would plan and implement infrastructure changes across systems to better meet the needs of victims of child maltreatment and domestic violence (Greenbook National Evaluation Team, 2008).

After the five-year demonstration initiative, a qualitative study with the framers of the Greenbook reported successes and challenges of implementing the project. One of the challenges reported in this study was the early decision regarding which systems to include in the Greenbook project and the emphasis on dependency courts, as opposed to the court system in general. According to one of the study participants, the decision to exclude the criminal court system hindered the ability of the demonstration sites to hold batterers accountable (Janczewski, Dutch, & Wang, 2008). Another challenge of the Greenbook project was the mistrust that existed between disciplines due to long-standing conflicts between the participating systems. Additionally, demonstration sites struggled with gaps in the recommendations that were not adequately addressed by the framers. For example, limited guidance for holding batterers accountable and a lack of emphasis on other important systems such as law enforcement and criminal courts created challenges for demonstration sites (Janczewski et al., 2008).

Because the federal funders of the Greenbook project required demonstration sites to spend money on system change or capacity-building activities versus direct services to families, successes in terms of broad changes that were not specific to any one system were reported. Broad improvements included increased training and skills, improved attitude and commitment of staff, improved laws and policy, and new interagency protocols (Janczewski et al., 2008). In addition, improved relationships and collaboration between systems was viewed as a success of the Greenbook project.

Conclusion

During the past decade, progress has been made in promoting greater collaboration between the child welfare system and domestic violence agencies. Child welfare agencies have received guidance in the form of training and resource materials to improve their response to cases that include domestic violence. However, much remains to be done to evaluate effective methods of intervention within the child welfare system and to develop more uniform responses across the country. Research indicates that families in the child welfare system who experience domestic violence have multiple problems and needs. Recent community-based violence prevention efforts suggest that addressing different forms of violence separately (e.g., domestic violence, child maltreatment, and youth violence) is not effective from a prevention standpoint (Bowen, Gwiasda, & Brown, 2004; Mitchell-Clark & Autry, 2004). Structural changes are needed across the broad array of human service and criminal justice systems to develop responses that can address the complex needs of families and communities who are struggling with multiple forms of violence in their lives.

References

Aron, L., & Olson, K. K. (1997). Efforts by child welfare agencies to address domestic violence. *Public Welfare, 55,* 4–13.

Bowen, L. D., Gwiasda, V., & Brown, M. M. (2004). Engaging community residents to prevent violence. *Journal of Interpersonal Violence, 19,* 356–367.

Bragg, H. L. (2003). *Child protection in families experiencing do,.nestic violence.* Child Abuse and Neglect User Manual Series. Washington, DC: National Clearinghouse on Child Abuse and Neglect Information.

Carlson, B. E. (1996). Children of battered women: Research, programs, and services. In A. R. Roberts (Ed.), *Helping battered women,* 172–187. New York: Oxford University Press.

Edleson, J. L. (1999). *Problems associated with children's witnessing of domestic violence.* Harrisburg, PA: VAWnet, a project of the National Resource Center on Domestic Violence/Pennsylvania Coalition Against Domestic Violence. Retrieved November 30, 2008, from http://www.vawnet.org

Edleson, J., Gassman-Pines, J., & Hill, M. (2006). Defining child exposure to domestic violence as neglect: Minnesota's difficult experience. *Social Work, 51,* 167–175.

English, D. J., Edleson, J. L., & Herrick, M. E. (2005). Domestic violence in one state's child protective caseload: A study of differential case dispositions and outcomes. *Children and Youth Services Review, 27,* 1183–1201.

Fantuzzo, J., & Lindquist, C. (1989). The effects of observing conjugal violence on children: A review and analysis of research methodology. *Journal of Family Violence, 4,* 77–93.

Ganley, A. L., & Schechter, S. (1996). *Domestic violence: A national curriculum for child protection services.* San Francisco: Family Violence Prevention Fund.

Greenbook National Evaluation Team. (2008). *The Greenbook initiative final evaluation report.* Fairfax, VA: ICF International.

Jaffe, P. G., Wolfe, D. A., & Wilson, S. K. (1990). *Children of battered women.* Newbury Park, CA: Sage.

Janczewski, C., Dutch, D., & Wang, K. (2008). Crafting the Greenbook: Framers reflect on the vision, process and lessons learned. *Journal of Interpersonal Violence, 23,* 981–1006.

Kohl, P. L., Edleson, J. L., English, D., & Barth, R. P. (2005). Domestic violence pathways into child welfare services: Findings from the National Survey of Child and Adolescent Well-Being. *Children and Youth Services Review, 27,* 1167–1182.

Matthews, M. A. (1999). The impact of federal and state laws on children exposed to domestic violence. *Domestic Violence and Children, 9,* 50–66.

Minnesota Department of Human Services. (2002). *Guidelines for responding to child maltreatment and domestic violence.* St. Paul: Author.

Mitchell-Clark, K. & Autry, A. (2004). Preventing family violence: Lessons from the community engagement initiative. San Francisco: Family Violence Prevention Fund.

National Council of Juvenile and Family Court Judges Family Violence Department. (1999). *Effective intervention in domestic violence and child maltreatment cases: Guidelines for policy and practice.* Reno: National Council of Juvenile and Family Court Judges.

Office of Juvenile Justice and Delinquency Programs. (2000, November). *Safe from the start—Taking action on children exposed to violence* (NCJ 182789). Washington, DC: U.S. Department of Justice.

Schechter, S., & Edleson, J. L. (1999). Executive summary. In *Effective intervention in domestic violence and child maltreatment,* 1–4. Reno, NV: National Council of Juvenile Court Judges.

Shepard, M. (1992). Child-visiting and domestic abuse. *Child Welfare, LXXI,* 357–367.

Shepard, M., & Raschick, M. (1999). How child welfare workers assess and intervene around issues of domestic violence. *Child Maltreatment, 4,* 148–156.

Straus, M., Gelles, R., & Smith, C. (1990). *Physical violence in American families: Risk factors and adaptations to violence in 8,145 families.* New Brunswick: Transaction Publishers.

U.S. Advisory Board on Child Abuse and Neglect. (1995). *A nation's shame: Fatal child abuse and neglecting the United States.* Washington, DC: Department of Health and Human Services.

Wallerstein, J. (1989). *Second chances.* New York: Ticknor and Fields.

Wolfe, D. A., Jaffe, P., Wilson, S. K., & Zak, L. (1985). Children of battered women: The relation of child behavior to family violence and maternal stress. *Journal of Consulting and Clinical Psychology, 33,* 657–665.

The Connection Between Domestic Violence and Homelessness

8

CHARLENE K. BAKER

Contents

Introduction

Within the United States, approximately one in five women reports being physically assaulted by an intimate partner at some point in her lifetime (Tjaden & Thoennes, 1998). In particular, domestic violence made up 20% of violent crime against women in 2001 (Rennison & Welchans, 2000). Each year, domestic violence results in an estimated 1,200 deaths and 2 million injuries among women (National Center for Injury Prevention and Control, 2003). Domestic violence has been linked with adverse physical health outcomes in abused women, such as gynecological problems, headaches, back pain, gastrointestinal distress, and sexually transmitted diseases (Campbell et al., 2002; Centers for Disease Control and Prevention 2008; Coker, Smith, Bethea, King, & McKeown, 2000; Sutherland, Bybee, & Sullivan, 1998). In addition to the physical consequences of domestic violence, there are also psychological and social consequences, such as depression, posttraumatic stress disorder, and social isolation (Dutton et al., 2006; Golding, 1999; Jones,

Hughes, & Unterstaller, 2001; Raj & Silverman, 2002; Rose & Campbell, 2000).

Another set of consequences relate to the survivors' economic well-being. In particular, economic consequences include lost work productivity, inability to pay bills, credit problems, and homelessness (Baker, Cook, & Norris, 2003; Browne & Bassuk, 1997; Browne, Salomon, & Bassuk, 1999; Byrne, Resnick, Kilpatrick, Best, & Saunders, 1999; Lloyd & Taluc, 1999; Swanberg, Logan, & Macke, 2005; Tolman & Rosen, 2001). For example, research shows that one in six women who report domestic violence report time lost from paid work (National Center for Injury Prevention and Control, 2003). Furthermore, another study shows that female victims of domestic violence were only one-third as likely to work at least 30 hours per week for 6 months or more the following year than women who did not experience such abuse (Browne et al., 1999). Past exposure to domestic violence has also been shown to predispose women to unemployment and poverty (Byrne et al., 1999). In fact, rates of domestic violence among welfare recipients are quite high (Brandwein, 1999; Tolman & Rosen, 2001), and in one study almost half of women who received welfare benefits cited domestic violence as a factor in their need for assistance (Raphael, 1996).

This chapter focuses on women who have experienced domestic violence, and the connection with one economic consequence: homelessness.[1] Specifically, this chapter explores: (1) evidence related to the intersection between domestic violence and homelessness, (2) factors that give rise to this intersection (individual level, social level, organizational/systems level, and national level), and (3) recommendations and strategies to reduce homelessness among women who have experienced domestic violence.

Domestic Violence and Homelessness: Establishing the Connection

Many research studies have described the relationship between domestic violence and homelessness (Browne & Bassuk, 1997; Bufkin & Bray, 1998; Goodman, 1991; Metreaux & Culhane, 1999; Shinn et al., 1998; Toro et al., 1995; Zorza, 1991). According to one study conducted in 10 locations around the United States, 25 out of 100 homeless mothers had been physically abused within the year leading up to the study (National Center of Family Homelessness & Health Care for the Homeless Clinician's Network, 2003). Domestic violence was also associated with a failure to receive subsidized housing among women who were homeless (Shinn et al., 1998). But, not only is there a correlation between domestic violence and homelessness—there is also evidence to suggest that domestic violence is among the leading causes of homelessness nationally for women (U.S. Conference of Mayors–Sedexho, 2005). Moreover, some studies have suggested that one in four homeless women are homeless because of violence committed against them (Jasinski, Wesely, Mustaine, & Wright, 2002; Levin, McKean, & Raphael, 2004; Wilder Research Center, 2007; Institute for Children and Poverty, 2002).

Fewer studies have examined how domestic violence is related to other forms of housing problems that fall just short of homelessness, such as housing instability, which can include sacrificing bills to pay rent, eating less or skipping meals to pay rent, doubling up with family or friends, being threatened with eviction, or experiencing credit problems (Baker et al., 2003; Tolman & Rosen, 2001). One study showed that up to 50% of women seeking services from domestic violence shelters, welfare offices, and the criminal justice system reported at least one housing problem, such as difficulty paying rent, being denied housing or threatened with eviction, or having to move because of partner harassment (Baker et al., 2003). In another study, after adjusting for age, race/ethnicity, marital status, and poverty, women who experienced domestic violence in the last year had almost four times the odds of reporting housing instability than women who had not experienced domestic violence (Pavao, Alvarez, Baumrind, Induni, & Kimerling, 2007).

Connections Between Domestic Violence and Homelessness

There is no question that domestic violence and homelessness are prominent social problems facing our society today. The question lies in the intersection of these two social problems and the reasons behind this intersection. To answer this question it is necessary to think broadly. Each social problem has many hypothesized causes, as explanations range from those at the individual level to the societal level. In addition to a causal relationship, there are many factors associated with each social problem that are simply intertwined or correlated. The complexity is thus increased 10-fold when considering all of these relationships.

To illustrate this complexity, it is helpful to consider the many issues that domestic violence survivors face in their attempts to gain safety and obtain stable housing. These can include mental health issues such as depression, posttraumatic stress disorder, or substance abuse resulting from repeated victimizations over months/years; the continued stalking women face by their abusers after separating from them; women's need to focus energy on their children's recovery, especially if the children witnessed the violence or were abused themselves; their attempts to find a job that pays a livable wage (which is especially difficult if they lack previous job experience); their need to reach out to formal systems for help and the difficulties in obtaining tangible assistance from these systems; and ultimately their inability to find affordable housing because of the issues just described, not to mention the limited number of units available (Choi & Snyder, 1999).

Given the space constraints of this chapter, it is not possible to go into depth on each of these topics. Rather, the discussion is framed in terms of an ecological model while highlighting a few select factors at each level of the model (see Figure 8.1). The ecological model suggests that an individual is surrounded by increasingly broader contexts that shape his or her behavior (Bronfenbrenner, 1979). In this example, the individual is surrounded by her social systems, including friends and family. Moving outward, the social system is bound by a set of organizational/system policies and procedures. Finally, at the outermost level are national influences that affect the behavior of all other levels. In sociological terms, these can be referred to as micro, meso, and macro levels of explanation. To help anchor the discussion, the different factors will be discussed from the standpoint of how they are related to homelessness among women who have experienced domestic violence. Therefore, the chapter examines factors that may relate to whether domestic violence survivors become homeless in the course of gaining safety from their abusers.

Individual-Level Factors

Within the research on individual-level factors, some have suggested that it is important to consider previous experiences of victimization, as it has been shown to be a risk factor for current victimization (Basile, 2008; Kimerling,

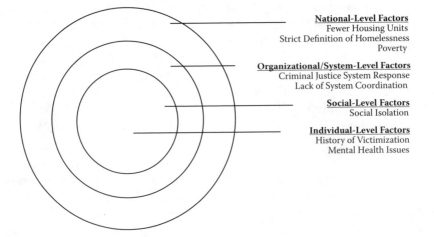

National-Level Factors
Fewer Housing Units
Strict Definition of Homelessness
Poverty

Organizational/System-Level Factors
Criminal Justice System Response
Lack of System Coordination

Social-Level Factors
Social Isolation

Individual-Level Factors
History of Victimization
Mental Health Issues

*This figure does not include an exhaustive list of factors

Figure 8.1 Suggested ecological model of factors associated with the connection of domestic violence and homelessness.

Alvarez, Pavao, Kaminski, & Baumrind, 2007). The question then posed is: How is victimization, and especially repeated victimization, associated with homelessness? Evidence suggests that women who have been repeatedly victimized are also at risk for a range of mental health problems, including PTSD, depression, and substance abuse (Green et al., 2000; Kimerling et al., 2007). Such problems may make it more difficult for women to maintain stable employment (Moe & Bell, 2004; Swanberg et al., 2005). They also make it more difficult for women, especially low-income women, to find and maintain stable housing (Phinney, Danziger, Pollack, & Seefeldt, 2007). Therefore, it appears that some of the consequences associated with domestic violence may also be related to women's difficulties in securing and maintaining housing after separating from their abusive partners. That is not to say that all survivors have mental health problems. Nor is it accurate to point to these issues as the sole reason for homelessness among survivors. Moving outward from the center of the ecological model in Figure 8.1, it is also important to consider social factors.

Social-Level Factors

For women who are trying to separate from an abusive partner, it is difficult for them to do so without help. Women in abusive relationships often report that during the relationship their partners would deny them access to money or other resources. Rather, women were given only a small allowance as a way to control their activities. Therefore, women who leave their abusive partners often need a variety of resources, ranging from emotional support to more tangible support, such as money for rent and utilities, and help finding employment, child care, and transportation (Adams, Sullivan, Bybee, & Greeson, 2008; Tan, Basta, Sullivan, & Davidson, 1995).

One option to obtain these resources is to seek support from family or friends. In fact, among low-income women in Baltimore who experienced physical or sexual violence in adulthood, family and friends were identified as typical sources of help when attempting to leave a violent relationship (O'Campo, McDonnell, Gielen, Burke, & Chen, 2002). In particular, tangible support has been shown to moderate the relationship between lifetime trauma and PTSD (Glass, Perrin, Campbell, & Soeken, 2007). This is an important finding, given the relationship between mental health issues and homelessness cited above. However, often abusers isolate women from family and friends. In some cases, after the separation women isolate themselves out of fear that their abusive partner will threaten or physically hurt their family and friends (Riger, Raja, & Camacho, 2002). Therefore, women may lack the informal support needed to escape the abuse. Without access to support from family and friends, women may be forced to turn to formal systems for help.

Organizational/System-Level Factors

Within formal systems there are often policies and procedures that must be followed. Accordingly, the organizational/system-level factors that put domestic violence survivors at risk for homelessness may stem from the policies and procedures within a particular system. Depending on what formal system they seek help from, women may or may not receive the services they need to secure stable housing away from the abuser. One formal system that women access for help is the criminal justice system. Although this system does not provide housing to women, their response has been linked with homelessness among women (Baker et al., 2003; Bufkin & Bray, 1998). Battered women seek help from the criminal and civil justice systems for protection against abuse and to hold their partners accountable for the abuse. However, these systems have been widely criticized for poor treatment of women and an inability to protect women, both of which could be key intervening variables in women's homelessness (Bufkin & Bray, 1998). For example, in a study of 50 battered women, 50% reported that police officers minimized their injuries, 33% encountered objectionable questions and comments by judges, and 51% reported that prosecutors asked whether they provoked their abuse (Erez & Belknap, 1998). Given these experiences, women may seek help initially, but if treated poorly, they may be less likely to contact the police again (Fleury, Sullivan, Bybee, & Davidson, 1998). Consequently, women may need to relocate to gain safety; however, relocation may lead to homelessness if women are unable to find affordable housing.

Furthermore, in the civil justice system, women's petitions for protection orders do not necessarily guarantee protection from their partners. In some cases, police officers do not arrest men for violating protection orders (Finn & Colson, 1998; Harrell & Smith, 1996; Kane, 2000). Without an arrest, it may be more difficult to hold men accountable for the violence perpetrated against their partners, which may force the woman to leave her home, again putting her at risk for becoming homeless (Mullins, 1994; Zorza, 1991).

Another organizational/system-level factor that may exacerbate women's housing instability stems from a lack of coordination between the domestic violence service system and the housing/homelessness service system. Despite evidence on the link between domestic violence and homelessness, there is limited collaboration between the two systems, which is likely a result of their different goals. Furthermore, there are also issues within each system that are important to consider.

On one hand, domestic violence shelters are focused on safety planning and a wide array of advocacy services that victims need and want, including housing. However, the presence of a history of homelessness combined with mental illness or chemical dependency may eliminate women in current abusive relationships from domestic violence services. Some domestic violence emergency shelters and transitional housing programs run by domestic violence shelters specifically exclude women with mental health or substance abuse issues (Baker, Holditch Niolon, & Oliphant, 2009; Melbin, Sullivan, & Cain, 2003). Other programs have specific eligibility criteria that women must meet before being admitted (e.g., having children, over the age of 18, legal immigrant). Even if women are admitted to these programs, they may face other challenges. Transitional housing programs often impose rules that women must follow, such as attending weekly support groups, submitting to staff inspections of their apartments, and having no overnight visitors—even family members. These rules are sometimes viewed as excessive and may lead to women's dissatisfaction and exit from the programs (Melbin et al., 2003).

By contrast, housing service providers are focused on a move to stable housing and improved financial stability. The presence of current physical danger may eliminate domestic violence survivors from admission into homeless shelters or housing programs. In addition, housing providers may not be aware of the continuing effect of past abuse on women's present psychological and physical health, which can affect women's ability to remain stably housed.

Also, the presence of a criminal record may limit women's ability to access permanent housing (public or private). However, having a criminal record is not uncommon among battered women because of arrests that are related to the abuse (e.g., women may be forced to participate in illegal activities by their partners) or surviving the abuse (Richie, 1996). Often a criminal history prohibits women from being eligible for public housing.

Even for women who have secured housing, there are still risks. Women may face eviction because landlords hold them accountable for any criminal act committed by a family member, which includes abusive partners and ex-partners (Renzetti, 2001). Although the Violence Against Women Act (VAWA) in its 2005 reauthorization[2] prohibits such practices, there are still reports of public housing administrators (and private housing landlords who are not required to adhere to VAWA mandates) evicting women who call the police when their abuser comes to their home and threatens or physically assaults them.

Therefore, we see two separate systems, with different perceptions about the clients they serve. Within these systems there is a tendency to compartmentalize women as experiencing either domestic violence or homelessness. Women who have been victimized *and* who are homeless fall through the cracks of both systems, and are less likely to receive the services they need to gain safety and economic stability.

National-Level Factors

As discussed throughout this chapter, women who want to separate from their abusers face a dilemma. In attempts to prevent revictimization, women may be forced to separate from their abusive partners, an act that is usually linked to leaving their homes. Thus, to increase their safety, women also increase their risk of becoming homeless because housing options away from their abusers are limited. This risk is even more pronounced for low-income women (Menard, 2001). Therefore, one national-level factor to consider is the number of low-income housing units available, with evidence suggesting that there are fewer available each year (Choi & Snyder, 1999). In addition, federal housing programs (e.g., Section 8), developed to assist families by paying a portion of their rent, have waiting lists of more than two years (Choi & Snyder, 1999), while other housing lists have simply been closed to new applicants (Hammeal-Urban & Davies, 1999). Survivors of domestic violence may be given preference for housing; however, only about 35% of public housing authorities maintain this preference (Martin & Stern, 2005).

Another national-level factor relates to how homelessness is defined. Women who are doubling up with family or friends after fleeing their abusers have not been considered homeless. Without this designation, women are not eligible for many types of housing-related services. Recent legislation has sought to change the definition of homelessness. On May 20, 2009, President Obama signed into law a bill to reauthorize the McKinney-Vento Homeless Assistance Programs, which included the expansion of the definition of homeless to include people precariously housed, such as those doubled up with friends or relatives or living day-to-day in motels, with money and options running out. The effect of this legislation on precariously housed survivors of domestic violence remains to be seen.

The final national-level factor is the most difficult to address. At its core, homelessness is driven by poverty. Certainly there are other circumstances, only a fraction of which have been described above, but poverty is an overwhelming contributor to homelessness. While this chapter has focused on the intersection between domestic violence and homelessness, the contextual backdrop of poverty cannot be dismissed. In fact, poverty is a risk factor for both homelessness and domestic violence. Research suggests that poverty increases the risk of domestic violence, especially severe violence (Browne, 1995; Browne & Bassuk, 1997). In trying to escape the violence, poor women are disproportionately at risk for homelessness compared to women with more resources. The positive relationship between gaining safety and living in poverty is compounded for minority and immigrant women, who are at an even higher risk for homelessness because they are already more likely to be living below the poverty level than white women (Caiazza, Shaw, & Werschkul, 2004; Smith Nightingale & Fix, 2004). Therefore, some researchers have suggested that the connection between domestic violence and homelessness may be a result of the failed communication between the domestic violence movement and the antipoverty movement (Margulies, 1995; Meier, 1997).

Recommendations for Reducing Homelessness Among Domestic Violence Survivors

This section makes recommendations for how service providers, researchers, and advocates might move forward to reduce homelessness among survivors who seek safety from their abusive partners. The proposed recommendations do not necessarily correspond with each level of the ecological model. Rather, the recommendations are focused at the organizational/systems level and national level because ultimately it requires a contextual shift by our systems and society rather than individual-level changes to achieve this goal.

Not surprisingly, the first recommendation is that domestic violence and homelessness should be addressed simultaneously. Some might say that this is intuitive; however, much of what we do is to compartmentalize services instead of taking a more holistic approach. Without a holistic approach, women and children who are the most vulnerable may not receive the services they need because they do not fit neatly within either system paradigm. This will require a paradigm shift, not only for service providers but also for those who fund social programs. Eligibility criteria that programs use are often a direct result of funding requirements. For example, housing programs receiving Temporary Aid for Needy Families (TANF)[3] money may not be allowed to admit women without children. Other funders may require that funds not be used to provide housing assistance to undocumented immigrants. Thus, the current paradigm of system and service compartmentalization will need to be replaced with a new paradigm that examines and embraces the intersections of domestic violence and other social problems, while also considering how these intersections are affected by issues such as racism, sexism, and classism (Sokoloff & Dupont, 2005).

Following from the first recommendation is the need for a coordination of services and protocols between domestic violence and homeless/housing service systems. One possibility for building these efforts is for both coalitions to develop a set of guidelines for services that could be made available to survivors of domestic violence who are tenants in permanent housing operated by mainstream housing providers. Cross-trainings between these different systems could then be offered to help implement these service guidelines. The hope is that this collaboration might lead to other landlord/ service provider partnerships that may foster a continuing relationship and understanding between domestic violence providers and apartment owners and housing management organizations.

A third recommendation emphasizes the importance of educating our criminal justice system about the role they play, not only in preventing domestic violence but also homelessness. Research has shown that positive police intervention reduced women's odds of homelessness after separating from their partners (Baker et al., 2003). This is an important message to disseminate to both new and experienced police officers. Also, while I have focused in this chapter on the criminal justice system and its treatment of survivors, other systems, like the medical system or welfare system, have a role to play as well. In this way, it is not the specific system that matters but rather the response from the system to women's help seeking.

As an example, in 1996 the Personal Responsibility and Work Opportunity Reconciliation Act (P.L. 104-193) passed. Under this new law, work requirements and time limits for the receipt of welfare benefits were implemented (Josephson, 2007). With limitations placed on their ability to secure benefits, domestic violence survivors now have fewer options by which to escape the abuse. The law did include a family violence option whereby women who are victims of domestic violence can be temporarily exempted from the work requirements and time limits. The majority of states have adopted this option; however, case workers are often responsible for screening women. The issue is that many caseworkers have not been trained on how to screen women, and even if trained, screening would be difficult because caseworkers are overworked and have too little time to manage their caseloads as it is. Some caseworkers also believe that women claim to be victims of domestic violence simply to get out of work requirements, and they therefore do not screen women consistently.

In both of these systems (i.e., criminal justice system and welfare system), help-seeking women receive the message that they are on their own, due to either the lack of services available from formal systems or mistreatment by these systems. Without help from formal systems women may be forced to stay in abusive relationships or risk a plethora of negative outcomes, including homelessness (Cooley, Jones, Onge, & Wilcox, 1997). Therefore, raising awareness among system personnel and holding systems accountable for their protocols and actions (or inaction as the case may be), as well as advocating policies that support, not hinder, women's abilities to escape abuse and secure economic stability, are critical to reducing homelessness among domestic violence survivors.

A final recommendation relates to the structure and availability of housing options for women fleeing domestic violence. For the most part there are three options: emergency shelter, transitional housing, and permanent housing. Traditionally, in an emergency shelter women are allowed to stay only

30 to 60 days. This short amount of time may not be enough for women to recover emotionally and economically after experiencing abuse for months and often years. As a result, many women return to their abusers (Davies, Lyon, & Monti-Catania, 1998) because they have nowhere else to go after their shelter stay. Transitional housing programs offer women a place to stay for 1 to 2 years; however, there are fewer programs, and often women are expected to meet rigid eligibility criteria before being granted admission. Finally, there is permanent housing, from either public housing authorities or private landlords.

In recent years the focus seems to be shifting from emergency shelter to longer-term housing with the understanding that stability as well as safety is critical to recovery. This is not to say that emergency shelters and transitional housing programs are not needed; however, there is an increasing need for permanent solutions. Therefore, to meet the long-term needs of survivors it will be necessary to secure more permanent housing options. This becomes even more important for low-income women, who have even fewer affordable housing options available to them. In response to this need, some domestic violence providers, in both rural and urban areas, are beginvning to create their own housing options for women. Service providers are now expanding their roles to include managing apartment buildings so that units are available to survivors at a subsidized rate. Others are writing for grant funding to build their own apartment buildings, realizing that existing units are insufficient to meet the need. This is only the beginning; service providers, policy makers, and funding agencies will need to continue to think outside the box to increase the availability of permanent housing options for survivors.

Conclusion

The intersection between domestic violence and homelessness has been discussed a great deal in the literature. Explanations for this relationship range from the individual level to the societal level. However, solutions to these two intransigent social problems will require creativity and broad-level thinking. They will also require a paradigm shift away from the current practice of compartmentalizing survivors into women who are either victims of domestic violence or homeless. Rather, it is critical that we create a holistic approach that considers women's simultaneous experiences in order to create a response that supports women as they seek both safety and economic stability.

Endnotes

1. Although research shows that men are also victims of domestic violence, the focus of this chapter is on the economic consequences experienced by female survivors of male violence against women.

2. The 2005 Reauthorization of the Violence Against Women Act (VAWA) includes several housing provisions that protect domestic violence survivors. One provision prohibits evictions based on real or perceived domestic violence, dating violence, or stalking (sexual assault is specifically not included in these provisions). Another is that a family with a Section 8 voucher may move to another jurisdiction if the family has complied with all other obligations of the program and is moving to protect the health or safety of an individual who is or has been the victim of domestic violence, dating violence, or stalking—even if moving otherwise would be a lease violation. VAWA also provides other potential relief, as it gives public housing authorities (PHAs) flexibility that can help domestic violence survivors. For example, PHAs may bifurcate leases, turn the voucher/apartment over to the survivor if she was a household member but not on the lease, and grant emergency transfers.

3. Previously known as Aid to Families With Dependent Children (AFDC), Title I of the Personal Responsibility and Work Opportunity Reconciliation Act (P.L. 104-193) gave fixed block grants to states to provide temporary assistance for needy families. In an effort to end welfare dependency, under TANF, those receiving benefits are required to work. In addition, the law instituted time limits within which individuals are eligible for benefits.

References

Adams, A. E., Sullivan, C. M., Bybee, D., & Greeson, M. R. (2008). Development of the scale of economic abuse. *Violence Against Women, 14*, 563–588.

Baker, C. K., Cook, S. L., & Norris, F. H. (2003). Domestic violence and housing problems: A contextual analysis of women's help-seeking, received informal support, and formal system response. *Violence Against Women, 9*, 754–783.

Baker, C. K., Holditch Niolon, P., & Oliphant, H. (2009). A descriptive analysis of transitional housing programs for survivors of intimate partner violence in the U.S. *Violence Against Women, 15*, 460–481.

Basile, K. C. (2008). Histories of violent victimization among women who reported unwanted sex in marriages and intimate relationships. *Violence Against Women, 14*, 29–52.

Brandwein, R. A. (1999). *Battered women, children, and welfare reform: The ties that bind*. Thousand Oaks, CA: Sage.

Bronfenbrenner, U. (1979). *The ecology of human development: Experiments by nature and design*. Cambridge, MA: Harvard University Press.

Browne, A. (1995). Reshaping the rhetoric: The nexus of violence, poverty, and minority status in the lives of women and children in the United States. *Georgetown Journal on Fighting Poverty, 3*, 17–23.

Browne, A., & Bassuk, S.S. (1997). Intimate violence in the lives of homeless and poor housed women: Prevalence and patterns in an ethnically diverse sample. *American Journal of Orthopsychiatry, 67*, 261–278.

Browne, A., Salomon, A., & Bassuk, S. S. (1999). Impact of recent partner violence on poor women's capacity to maintain work. *Violence Against Women, 5*, 393–426.

Bufkin, J. L., & Bray, J. (1998). Domestic violence, criminal justice responses and homelessness: Finding the connection and addressing problem. *Journal of Social Distress and the Homeless, 7*, 227–240.

Byrne, C. A., Resnick, H. S., Kilpatrick, D. G., Best, C. L., & Saunders, B. E. (1999). The socioeconomic impact of interpersonal violence on women. *Journal of Consulting and Clinical Psychology, 67*, 362–366.

Caiazza, A., Shaw, A., & Werschkul, M. (2004). *Women's economic status in the states: Wide disparities by race, ethnicity, and region.* Washington, DC: Institute for Women's Policy Research.

Campbell, J., Snow Jones, A., Dienemann, J., Kub, J., Schollenberge, J., O'Campo, P., et al. (2002). Intimate partner violence and physical health consequences. *Archives of Internal Medicine, 162*, 1157–1163.

Centers for Disease Control and Prevention. (2008). Adverse health conditions and health risk behaviors associated with intimate partner violence—United States, 2005. *Morbidity and Mortality Weekly Report, 57*, 113–117.

Choi, N. G., & Snyder, L. (1999). Voices of homeless parents: The pain of homelessness and shelter life. *Journal of Human Behavior in the Social Environment, 2*, 55–77.

Coker, A. L., Smith, P. H., Bethea, L., King, M. R., & McKeown, R. E. (2000). Physical health consequences of physical and psychological intimate partner violence. *Archives of Family Medicine, 9*, 451–457.

Cooley, T., Jones, E., Onge, A. S., & Wilcox, L. (1997). *Safety and self-support: The challenges of welfare reform for victims of domestic abuse.* Bangor: Maine Coalition for Family Crisis Services.

Davies, J. M., Lyon, E., & Monti-Catania, D. (1998). *Safety planning with battered women: Complex lives, difficult choices.* Thousand Oaks, CA: Sage Publications.

Dutton, M. A., Green, B. L., Kaltman, S. I., Roesch, D. M., Zeffiro, T. A., & Krause, E. D. (2006). Intimate partner violence, PTSD, and adverse health outcomes. *Journal of Interpersonal Violence, 21*, 955–968.

Erez, E., & Belknap, J. (1998). In their own words: Battered women's assessment of the criminal processing systems' responses. *Violence and Victims, 13*, 251–268.

Finn, P., & Colson, S. (1998). Civil protection orders. In *Legal interventions in family violence: Research findings and policy implications* (NCJ 171666, pp. 43–47). Washington, DC: National Institute of Justice.

Fleury, R. E., Sullivan, C. M., Bybee, D. I., & Davidson, W. S. (1998). "Why don't they just call the cops?": Reasons for differential police contact among women with abusive partners. *Violence and Victims, 13*, 333–346.

Glass, N., Perrin, N., Campbell, J. C., & Soeken, K. (2007). The protective role of tangible support on post-traumatic stress disorder symptoms in urban women survivors of violence. *Research in Nursing & Health, 30*, 558–568.

Golding, J. M. (1999). Intimate partner violence as a risk factor for mental disorders: A meta analysis. *Journal of Family Violence, 14*, 99–132.

Goodman, L. A. (1991). The prevalence of abuse among homeless and housed poor mothers: A comparison study. *American Journal of Orthopsychiatry, 61,* 489–500.

Green, B. L., Goodman, L. A., Krupnick, J. L., Corcoran, C. B., Petty, R. M., Stockton, P., et al. (2000). Outcomes of single versus multiple trauma exposure in a screening sample. *Journal of Traumatic Stress, 13,* 271–286.

Hammeal-Urban, R., & Davies, J. (1999). *Federal housing and domestic violence: Introduction to programs, policy, and advocacy opportunities* (Report 8). National Resource Center on Domestic Violence. Harrisburg, PA.

Harrell, A., & Smith, B. (1996). Effects of restraining orders on domestic violence victims. In E. S. Buzawa & C. G. Buzawa (Eds.), *Do arrests and restraining orders work?* (pp. 214–242). Thousand Oaks, CA: Sage.

Institute for Children and Poverty. (2002). *The hidden migration: Why New York City shelters are overflowing with families.* New York: Institute for Children and Poverty.

Jasinski, J. L., Wesely, J. K., Mustaine, E., & Wright, J. D. (2002). *The experience of violence in the lives of homeless women: A research project* (NCJRS 211976). Washington, DC: U.S. Department of Justice.

Jones, L., Hughes, M., & Unterstaller, U. (2001). Post-traumatic stress disorder (PTSD) in victims of domestic violence. *Trauma, Violence, & Abuse, 2,* 99–119.

Josephson, J. (2007). The intersectionality of domestic violence and welfare in the lives of poor women (pp. 83–101). In N. J. Sokoloff (Ed.), *Domestic violence at the margins: Readings on race, class, gender, and culture.* Piscataway, NJ; Rutgers University Press.

Kane, R. J. (2000). Police responses to restraining orders in domestic violence incidents: Identifying the custody-threshold thesis. *Criminal Justice & Behavior, 27,* 561–580.

Kimerling, R., Alvarez, J., Pavao, J., Kaminski, A., & Baumrind, N. (2007). Epidemiology and consequences of women's revictimization. *Women's Health Issues, 17,* 101–106.

Levin, R., McKean, L., & Raphael, J. (2004). *Pathways to and from homelessness: Women and children in Chicago shelters.* Chicago: Center for Impact Research.

Lloyd, S., & Taluc, N. (1999). The effects of violence on women's employment. *Violence Against Women, 5,* 370–392.

Margulies, P. (1995). Representation of domestic violence survivors as a new paradigm of poverty law: In search of access, connection, and voice. *George Washington Law Review, 63,* 1071–1104.

Martin, E. J., & Stern, N. S. (2005). Domestic violence and public and subsidized housing: Addressing the needs of battered tenants through local housing policy. *Clearinghouse Review: Journal of Poverty Law and Policy, 38,* 551–560.

Meier, J. (1997). Domestic violence, character, and social change in the welfare reform debate. *Law & Policy, 19,* 205–263.

Melbin, A., Sullivan, C. M., & Cain, D. (2003). Transitional supportive housing programs: Battered women's perspectives and recommendations. *Affilia, 18,* 1–16.

Menard, A. (2001). Domestic violence and housing: Key policy and program challenges. *Violence Against Women, 7,* 707–720.

Metreaux, S., & Culhane, D. P. (1999). Family dynamics, housing, and recurring homelessness among women in New York City homeless shelters. *Journal of Family Issues, 20,* 371–396.

Moe, A. M., & Bell, M. P. (2004). The effects of battering and violence on women's work and employability. *Violence Against Women, 10*, 29–55.

Mullins, G. P. (1994). The battered woman and homelessness. *Journal of Law and Policy, 3*, 237–255.

National Center for Injury Prevention and Control. (2003). *Costs of intimate partner violence against women in the United States*. Atlanta, GA: Centers for Disease Control and Prevention.

National Center of Family Homelessness & Health Care for the Homeless Clinician's Network. (2003). *Social supports for homeless mothers*. New Centre, MA: National Center on Family Homelessness.

O'Campo, P., McDonnell, K., Gielen, A., Burke, J., & Chen, Y.H. (2002). Surviving physical and sexual abuse: What helps low-income women? *Patient Education and Counseling, 46*, 205–212.

Pavao, J., Alvarez, J., Baumrind, N., Induni, M., & Kimerling, R. (2007). Intimate partner violence and housing instability. *American Journal of Preventive Medicine, 32*, 143–146.

Phinney, R., Danziger, S., Pollack, H. A., & Seefeldt, K. (2007). Housing instability among current and former welfare recipients. *American Journal of Public Health, 97*, 832–837.

Raj, A., & Silverman, J. (2002). Violence against immigrant women: The roles of culture, context, and legal immigrant status on intimate partner violence. *Violence Against Women, 8*, 367–398.

Raphael, J. (1996). *Prisoners of abuse: Domestic violence and welfare receipt*. Boston: Northeastern University Press.

Rennison, C. M., & Welchans, S. (2000). *Intimate partner violence* (NCJ 178247). Washington, DC: Bureau of Justice Statistics, U.S. Department of Justice.

Renzetti, C. M. (2001). "One strike and you're out": Implications of a federal crime control policy for battered women. *Violence Against Women, 7*, 685–698.

Riger, S., Raja, S., & Camacho, J. (2002). The radiating impact of intimate partner violence. *Journal of Interpersonal Violence, 17*, 184–205.

Richie, B. E. (1996). *Compelled to crime: The gender entrapment of battered black women*. New York: Routledge.

Rose, L. E., & Campbell, J. (2000). The role of social support and family relationships in women's responses to battering. *Health Care for Women International, 21*, 27–39.

Shinn, M., Weitzman, B., Stojanovic, D., Knickman, J. R., Jimenez, L., Duchon, L., et al. (1998). Predictors of homelessness among families in New York City: From shelter request to housing stability. *American Journal of Public Health, 88*, 1651–1657.

Smith Nightingale, D., & Fix, M. (2004). Economic and labor market trends. *The Future of Children, 14*, 49–59.

Sokoloff, N. J., & Dupont, I. (2005). Domestic violence at the intersections of race, class, and gender. Challenges and contributions to understanding violence against marginalized women in diverse communities. *Violence Against Women, 11*, 38–64.

Sutherland, C., Bybee, D., & Sullivan, C. (1998). The long-term effects of battering on women's health. *Women's Health: Research on Gender, Behavior, and Policy, 4*, 41–70.

Swanberg, J. E., Logan, T. K., & Macke, C. (2005). Intimate partner violence, employment, and the workplace: Consequences and future directions. *Trauma, Violence, & Abuse, 6*, 286–312.

Tan, C., Basta, J., Sullivan, C. M., & Davidson, W. S. (1995). The role of social support in the lives of women exiting domestic violence shelters. *Journal of Interpersonal Violence, 10*, 437–451.

Tjaden, P., & Thoennes, N. (1998). *Prevalence, incidence, and consequences of violence against women: Findings from the National Violence Against Women Survey.* Washington, DC: U.S. Department of Justice, Office of Justice Programs.

Tolman, R. M., & Rosen, D. (2001). Domestic violence in the lives of women receiving welfare: Mental health, substance dependence, and economic well-being. *Violence Against Women, 7*, 141–158.

Toro, P. A., Owens, B. J., Bellavia, C. W., Daeschler, C. V., Wall, D. D., Passero, J. M., et al. (1995). Distinguishing homelessness from poverty: A comparative study. *Journal of Consulting and Clinical Psychology, 63*, 280–289.

U.S. Conference of Mayors–Sedexho. (2005). *Hunger and homelessness survey: A status report on hunger and homelessness in America's cities, a 24-city survey.* Washington, DC: Author.

Violence Against Women and Department of Justice Reauthorization Act of 2005. (2006). Public Law 109-162.

Wilder Research Center. (2007). *Overview of homelessness in Minnesota 2006: Key facts from the statewide survey.* Saint Paul, MN: Wilder Research.

Zorza, J. (1991). Woman battering: A major cause of homelessness. *Clearinghouse Review, 25*, 420–429.

The Relationship Between Substance Abuse and Domestic Violence

9

JOSEPHINE KAHLER
SHIRLEY GARICK
GODPOWER O. OKEREKE

Contents

Overview

There is a strong correlation between domestic violence and substance abuse. Many studies have shown that substance abuse of any type may lead to domestic violence since it lowers the inhibitions of the user. Fals-Stewart, Golden, and Schumacher (2003) found that alcohol and cocaine use were associated with a constant increase in the daily likelihood of male-to-female physical aggression; however, cannabis and opiates were not significantly associated with this type of violence. Most domestic violence—as distinguished from other forms of family violence—takes place within an intimate partner relationship. Easton, Weinberger, and George (2007) point out that substance abuse and domestic violence most commonly occur among men seeking substance abuse treatment. They further allude to the fact that alcohol dependence and intimate partner violence (IPV) are a major public health threat, which is being encountered in the criminal justice system and substance abuse treatment facilities.

Domestic Violence

An epidemic of domestic, spousal, and intimate partner abuse is occurring in the United States due to the frequency of battering among spouses or significant others. According to Campbell et al. (2003), a woman is battered every 15 seconds, and battering in the United States is the leading cause of injury to women between the ages of 15 and 44. Multiple terms are used interchangeably within the realm of IPV. Martin (1998) defines battering, which is part of spousal abuse, as the affliction of injury or physical pain intended to cause harm from punching, slapping, biting, and hair pulling. Many of the battering incidents involve more serious assaults, which include choking, kicking, breaking bones, stabbing, shooting, or forcible restraints. Campbell and Humphreys (1993) also define battering as repeated physical or sexual assault of an intimate partner within the context of coercive control. Gelles and Straus (1998) point out that most women hit men in self-defense, and most men initiate the physical abuse. Women, due to their smaller size and relatively lesser strength, are more prone to serious injury and death as a result of male-initiated violence (Browne & Herbert, 1997; Sadock, 1989). Many of these result from conflict tactics, which range from shoving to pushing and from choking to severe battering. These victims may suffer from broken limbs, fractured ribs, internal bleeding, and brain damage. Injuries may also be inflicted on the face and breast, and if the woman is pregnant, her abdomen is battered.

National statistics show there is truly cause for alarm within the substance abuse arena. Most of the substance abuse starts in the teenage years and continues on into adulthood. According to the National Institute on Drug Abuse (NIDA), since 1992, most children between the ages of 12 and 17 have doubled their use of marijuana. Conceivably, any type of drug abuse is potentially implicated in other social problems, such as violent crime and domestic violence.

Victim Profiles of Domestic Violence

Dickstein and Nadelson (1989) described battered women as representing all ages, racial, educational, religious, and social/economic groups. They may be married or single, business executives, or housewives. Walker (1979) pointed out that battered women had lower self-esteem, commonly adhered to feminine sex role stereotypes, and frequently accepted blame for their batterers' actions. They commonly exhibit feelings of fear, anger, shame, guilt, and may be isolated from family and support systems. Many of these victims grew up in abusive homes and may have left those homes, even married, at a very young age in order to escape the abuse. Other symptoms may include withdrawal from socializing, self-blame, denial of abuse, and making excuses for the abuser. These abused individuals may also say, "What did I do to make him react so violently?" and families may also reinforce this self-questioning.

According to Campbell et al. (2003), most women will stay with their male partners because of children, financial problems, fear of living alone, emotional dependence on the abuser, a belief that divorce is shameful, or fear of reprisal from the abuser. Most battered victims view their relationship as male dominated. As the battering continues, their ability to recognize available options and to make decisions for themselves and their children could develop into a phenomenon of learned helplessness (Walker, 1979). This phenomenon occurs when an individual fails to understand that regardless of his or her behavior, there is usually an undesirable or unpredictable outcome. According to Barnett (2001), women will mainly stay with the abuser out of fear for their lives or their children's lives, as the batterer gains more power and control with the use of intimidation, saying, for instance, "I'll kill you and the kids if you don't do as I say." As these threats continue, this compounds the victim's low self-esteem and she sees no way out. She may try to leave only to return and be confronted by her abuser and the psychological power he holds over her. In extreme cases, she may be murdered when attempting to leave or after having left. Other authors, such as Moss (1991), cite three more reasons for a woman staying in the marriage: a lack of a support network for leaving, religious beliefs, and a lack of financial independence to support herself and her children. The victims of domestic violence may include men, live-in same-sex partners, children within a family, or anyone close to the domestic situation.

Some researchers have examined how alcohol, cocaine opiates, and cannabis related to domestic violence (Fals-Stewart et al., 2003). Interestingly, alcohol had the strongest correlation, with cocaine being second, with likelihood of severe violence. The study looked at day-to-day use, and on days when both alcohol and cocaine were used, the drug used close to the violent event was considered related to the event. The use of opiates and cannabis was not associated with any IPV. Although this study was lengthy, the authors suggested it is not conclusive, as they could not rule out other noncausal events. This might include all types of mental illness, including sociopathic behaviors.

Clinical Findings in Domestic Violence

Police officers, social workers, and health care providers see a panoply of behaviors from abused women. The clinical picture of these victims will include physical, emotional, and psychological injuries. Most victims are treated in the emergency room for physical injuries. Assessment for intimate partner abuse should be mandatory and take place in whatever setting the victim chooses to seek for help. When injuries are not obvious, risk assessment instruments are used to gauge the history of abuse and the potential for violence within the victim's intimate partner relationship.

Several themes expressed by victims who have been in spousal abusive relationships have been identified by Hall (2003) and Smith (2003). These include lack of relational authenticity, immobility, emptiness, and disconnection. Answers to questions about these types of relationships should be assessed for feelings of being controlled, or needing to control. A relationship is more likely to be violent when it is characterized by a partner's excessive jealousy, emotional immaturity, neediness, strong feelings of inadequacy, low self-esteem, and poor problem-solving and social skills (Hattendorf & Tollerud, 1997). The victim may be asked about how the couple solves their problems, and if one partner needs to have the final say or uses forceful verbal aggression, he or she can also be considered abusive and possibly dangerous.

Another approach would be to ask the individual whether the arguments involve "pushing or shoving." As the interview continues, questions about violence within the relationship help to normalize the patient's experience and lessen the stigma of disclosure. If the patient hesitates, looks away, or displays other nonverbal behavior, or reveals risk factors for abuse, he or she may be asked again later in the interview about physical violence (Poirier, 2000). A number of clinics, hospitals, and doctors' offices ask women about safety issues as part of the overall health history or intake interview. Due to the delicate and sensitive nature of the topic, with many abused women being embarrassed about admitting to a problem, health care workers must be careful with their questioning approach. One technique used is the acronym SAFE, which stands for stress/safety, afraid/abused, friends/family, and emergency plan. The first two categories are designed to detect abuse, and if abuse is present, questions in the other two categories are asked of the patient. Ashur (1993) denotes that the usefulness of these questions allows the health care provider to paraphrase or edit them as needed for any given situation. If abuse is revealed from questioning, the health care provider's first response is critical. An abused woman should realize she is not alone and should not be afraid to reveal the frequency of the abuse. Careful recording is essential to identify the extent and type of abuse along with documentation using a body map to identify the location of contusions, bruises, or cuts for potential legal actions related to the violence. Other recordings of old and new injuries must be documented, and obtaining the patient's permission to take x-rays as well as photographs is essential. The health care provider must also obtain the abuser's name and how he injured her, with the use of direct quotes from the patient. Inclusive with this is patient teaching and giving her referrals to social services, plus reassurance that her confidentiality is ensured, according to Berlinger (2004). Janssen, Holt, and Sugg (2002) indicate the health care provider has an ethical duty to diagnose and treat domestic violence victims, pointing out that some have been held liable in the past for failure to ask about abuse. Introducing the concept of domestic violence is an overlooked health issue and has been compared to "opening Pandora's box."

Unlike other health risks for which providers order routine screening, exposure to spousal abuse is known to be often avoided due to exposure to embarrassing situations. The excuse often given is that the health care provider does not feel competent in dealing with abuse once it is identified (Janssen et al., 2002). For example, battering during pregnancy often leads to miscarriage and still birth, as well as future psychological and physical problems for the woman (Mattson & Rodriguez, 1999; Scobie & McGuire, 1999). Given this likelihood, assessment forms for abuse screening are often included in patient charts and initiated on the arrival of the patient to the postpartum unit from the delivery suite.

When to Suspect Domestic Abuse

The police officer, social worker, or health care provider should suspect spousal abuse in any individual who has the following characteristics: unexplained bruises, lacerations, burns, fractures, or multiple injuries in various stages of healing (particularly in areas normally covered by clothing); delays seeking treatment for an injury; appears embarrassed, evasive, anxious, or depressed; has a partner who is reluctant to leave the victim alone and is domineering, uncooperative, or insists on answering all of the questions for the individual. One should also remember that some abusers are excessively solicitous of the victim by stating their partner has a psychiatric history or problems with alcohol or drugs.

Health providers in this situation should trust their instincts in cases of suspected abuse even when these symptoms may not be present. It is important for the safety and care of the abused to be given assurances of confidentiality that her abuser will not be made aware of any information shared with the provider. Providers must also bear in mind that nonverbal behavior, including facial expressions, are a reflection of one's sincerity. Any questions should be posed in an open-ended fashion and in an empathetic and non-judgmental manner to place the abused person at ease (Jansser et al., 2002).

One of the key attributes of the provider should be that of good listener. The provider should offer written materials on the phases and progression of abuse and characteristics of victims and abusers and the reasons victims stay. It is important for the victim to devise a safety, so the provider can and discuss with her the effects of abuse on the children in the home (Berlinger, 2004). Stalans and Richie (2007) explain that the linkage between substance use/abuse and intimate partner violence does vary within groups. Individuals who live in poverty may face various forms of discrimination, and who are low-wage earners, may be vulnerable to IPV victimization. Cunradi, Caetano, and Schafer (2002) points out that women living in poverty are very vulnerable to and have a far higher rate of IPV. Other indicators include high school dropouts who live in a stressful environment where the daily struggle to earn a living wage may take its toll, with IPV being a part of the situation.

Cycles of Violence

This battery may include violent sexual assault as well as physical violence, and it may go on for days, after which the abuser may be extremely apologetic, promising to never do this again. According to Walker (1979), the cycle of violence has three phases. The first is the tension-building phase, in which the woman senses an increase in the man's frustration. He becomes angry with little provocation, but after lashing out at her he may be quick to apologize. At this point the victim may become very compliant and nurturing, trying to anticipate his every whim in order to prevent his anger from escalating. Minor battering incidents may occur during this phase, and in a desperate attempt to avoid more serious confrontations, the woman accepts the abuse as legitimately directed toward her. Her ability to reason is impaired when she assumes the guilt for the abuse. The battering incidents continue to escalate as the tension mounts and the woman anticipates an explosion. The tension building phase might last from a few weeks to even years. As this phase intensifies, the woman becomes greatly impaired by not recognizing that the abuser's jealousy and possessiveness has increased along with threats of abuse and brutality to maintain control and captivity of the victim.

During the second phase, the battering phase, the most violent behavior occurs, lasting for the shortest duration. The triggering event occurs and violence most often begins with the batterer justifying his behavior to himself, where in reality, he has lost control. It might begin with the batterer wanting to teach her a lesson or the woman intentionally provoking the behavior of the abuser. The woman will often initiate phase 2 when the situation has become unbearable, knowing once it is over, things will be better. During this phase the beatings are severe and physical damage will occur as drugs and alcohol may be involved. The victim survives by dissociating from her body despite the severity of abuse. Victims usually seek help when the injury is severe or they fear for their lives and their children. In the apologetic phase (commonly regarded as the honeymoon phase), battererers become extremely loving and contrite. Promises of forgiveness and change in behavior are made by the abuser, along with every bit of charm he can muster. The batterer believes he can now control his behavior, and since he has taught his victim a "lesson," he believes she will not act up again. The victims' feelings are played on by the abuser, and she desperately wants to believe she can change his behavior. Magical thinking is used by the victim, who focuses on the loving phase of the relationship and hopes against hope that the previous phase will not be repeated. This phase may last briefly and be almost undetectable, but in most incidences the cycle all too soon begins again.

Women and men need to understand this cycle of violence and be willing to leave or have the spouse seek help. Lore and Schultz (1993) conclude there is evidence to suggest that social pressure may be used on abusers to help them control their behavior.

Overall, health care professionals must be aware of the signs of abuse through careful observation of the individual and his or her spouse, since many of the victims overuse the health care system with multiple prehypocondrical complaints. Many of the symptoms of emotional and physical abuse are atypical chest pain, asthma, recurrent headaches, somatic complaints with no identifiable cause, eating disorders and other gastrointestinal complaints, anxiety/panic attacks, depression, drug overdose, forgetfulness, hopelessness/suicide attempts, guilt, low self-esteem, sleep disturbances, and an inability to make decisions.

Although domestic and intimate partner violence is considered a crime in the United States, there may be need for the victim to obtain a restraining order from the county of residence to legally prohibit the abuser from contacting or approaching the victim. However, a temporary restraining order provides only limited protection. Holt, Kernie, Lamley, Wolf, and Rivara (2002) found permanent protection orders were less likely to be violated, while the likelihood of abuse increased with temporary restraining orders, even when relationships had ended. Mullen, Pathe, Purcell, and Stuart (1999) report that stalking or other communication attempts may be attempted following the issuance of a restraining order. Many times victims may move into a shelter; however, most shelters have a waiting list and this provides only a temporary respite. Thus, for the overall safety of the abused victim, the importance of recognition, assessment, and implementation of action by health care providers cannot be overemphasized. Asking the correct questions, careful observation, and following the right reporting and recording procedures may mean the difference between life and death for these victims.

The Linkage of Substance Abuse and Domestic Violence

Boles and Miotto (2003) conclude that "given the different degrees and nature of stress, substance abuse or use may or may not have the same relationship with intimate partner violence (IPV), across all social classes, races, and environments" (p. 11). They further point out that the relationship within a domestic situation may be so stressful that alcohol and other substances may be abused to cope with the situation, and thus act as a partial impetus for IPV. Many researchers have found that during partner conflict there is generally a great deal of talk regarding money and how it is spent in relationship to alcohol and illicit substance abuse. In two separate reports Caetano and colleagues (Caetano, Cunradi, Clark, & Schafer, 2000; Caetano, Schafer, & Cunradi, 2001) investigated the role of race/ethnicity in IPV. Their findings suggested that heavy alcohol use among Hispanics played a strong role in IPV but not with Caucasian men. After controlling multiple indicators such as employment, impulsivity, presence of children, and approval of wife beating, alcohol abuse was a significant predictor of IPV for African American men and women. Responses to stress may vary among ethnic groups and are not conclusive (Cao, Adams, & Jensen, 1997). These ethnic studies have not examined whether drug abuse in subcultures explains the relationship between illicit drug abuse and domestic violence, and if these subcultures vary across race.

Distinguishing Addictions From Occasional and Recreational Use

According to Stalans and Ritchie (2007), there are many variables that affect drug use and abuse and IPV. Some of these variables are socioeconomic status, racial status, and environmental indictors of a drug-supportive culture. These items coupled with other mediating factors, such as depression, psychopathology (like bipolar personality), violence in the family of origin, social norms approving of violence, high level of marital and relationship conflict, plus a low income, may determine whether the drug abuse becomes a way of life, or is placed into a recreational environment. However, the outcome of violence is persistent whether it is occasional or recreational use, which is the order of the day. As pointed out by Bennett (1995) and Daly and Pelowski (2000), substance abuse may not cause violence, but if the drug is used persistently and left untreated, the batterer's judgment becomes impaired and his or her ability and willingness to participate in treatment programs is lacking. Stalans and Ritchie (2007) point out that any type of illicit drug use is a stronger predictor of IVP than alcohol alone. Roberts (1988) and Wilson et al. (2000) suggest that once the batterer has experienced the euphoria of illicit drug use, the IVP becomes more pronounced. Apparently occasional drug usage assuages the neurological symptoms that are prominent in the user. This, however, generally progresses into dependency and abuse if not terminated by treatment or mediated by some form of social intervention (i.e., family, intimate partners/significant others, or friends). The Stalans and Richie study (2007) explains that occasional use of marijuana (one a month) does not lead to as much violence as regular/abusive use of marijuana. Even with recreational use of this particular drug, inhibitions become lowered and IPV could still occur. Many studies point to the violence and the severity of the violence being related to drug abuse, which in many cases the batterers are abusing multiple substances.

Mental Health and Treatment Issues

A number of large-scale epidemiologic studies have promoted the significance of cumulative adversity of batterers being at risk for mental health problems (Lloyd & Turner, 2003). These findings are also consistent with studies on the neurobiology of depression and anxiety disorders with adverse life experiences in childhood, which are associated with lasting changes in the hypothalamic-pituitary-adrenal axis neural circuitry. They may in turn heighten the vulnerability for depression, posttraumatic stress disorder, bipolar disorder, and other mental health problems (Heim & Nemeroff, 2001). This sensitization hypothesis has produced research showing that individuals with a history of child abuse exhibit heightened physiological and behavioral reactivity to psychosocial stressors (Heim et al., 2000; Koopman, Gore-Felton, Classen, Kim, and Spiefel, 2001). Evidence from these studies suggests that cumulative exposure to multiple life stresses may indeed be predictive for attempts at self-medication through alcohol and drug activity, which further complicates the possible adherence to treatment. Arata, Langhinrichsen-Rohling, Bowers, and O'Farrill-Swails (2005) did a retrospective study of college students and found that students with multiple types of abuse in childhood (i.e., sexual abuse, neglect, emotional and physical abuse) had greater symptoms of depression and other mental health issues, including substance abuse. Easton et al. (2007) found there was little difference between alcohol/drug IPV and treatment issues. The study pointed to very little compliance, and that many of the participants often missed their sessions. Treatment outcomes addressing anger management were more impaired in pre- and posttreatments with the alcohol plus drug groups, which pointed to the need for additional intervention for alcohol plus drug group individuals. Interestingly, most of the individuals were referred by the criminal justice system for substance abuse, after being arrested for domestic violence. The Easton study findings suggest concurrent use of alcohol and drugs leads to and is associated with violent behavior. Pennings, Leccese, and de-Wolff's (2002) study also found that concurrent alcohol and drug use led to violent thoughts and threats, which in turn led to violent behaviors. Parrott and Giancola (2004) suggested that an individual's "anger proneness" might be involved when trying to assess substance-induced aggression. Easton found that over time, treatment for alcohol and alcohol plus cocaine/cannabis use improved over time, but that 12-week evidence-based treatments generally mediated overt physical and verbal aggression as well.

Case Study

T.S., a 57-year-old Caucasian male, suffers from bipolar disorder. He was diagnosed while in his early 20s and has taken his medication off and on over the course of 30 years. He is known for his erratic behavior at times, which is accentuated when consuming large quantities of alcohol. When the drinking binges occur, he will become loud, verbally abusive, and obnoxious, making insulting remarks and trying to be the "life of the party." His early childhood was one of parental alcohol abuse and neglect starting in infancy, followed by a series of foster homes and finally adoption by a caring family at the age of 14. After high school, a stint in the military helped pay his college tuition, where he attained a degree in accounting. He has held several comptroller positions, worked long hours, and always strived to do the best job he could to please his superiors. Two years ago he suffered a head injury that proved to be detrimental. He had married and was a new father of a beautiful but colicky baby, which resulted in his loss of sleep. He was also treated for back strain caused by his accident and became addicted to painkillers. When he felt he was losing control of his environment he supplemented with alcohol and found himself "spinning out of control." He lost his job and sunk into a state of severe depression. T.S. checked himself into a drug and alcohol rehab program and made efforts to regulate his medication for high blood pressure and diabetes—but to no avail. The depression continued as he was hired and fired from a series of jobs due to the inability to concentrate and deal with pressure. His marriage failed and he contemplated suicide.

References

Arata, C., Langhinrichsen-Rohling, J., Bowers, D., & O'Farrill-Swails, L. (2005). Single versus multitype maltreatment: An examination of the long-term effects of child abuse. *Journal of Aggression, Maltreatment and Trauma, 11*, 29–52.

Ashur, M. L. C. (1993). Asking questions about domestic violence: SAFE questions. *Journal of the American Medical Association, 269*, 2367.

Barnett, O. W. (2001). Why battered women do not leave, part 2. *Trauma, Violence, and Abuse, 2*, 3–35.

Bennett, L. W. (1995). Substance abuse and the domestic assault of women. *Social Work, 40*, 760–772.

Berlinger, J. (2004). Taking an intimate look at domestic violence. *Nursing, 34,* 42–55.

Boles, S., & Miotto, K. (2003). Substance of violence: A review of the literature. *Aggression and Violent Behavior, 8,* 155–174.

Browne, K., & Herbert, M. (1997). *Preventing family violence.* New York: John Wiley & sons.

Caetano, R., Cunradi, C. B., Clark, C. L., & Schafer, J. (2000). Intimate partner violence and drinking patterns among white, black, and Hispanic couples in the United States. *Journal of Substance Abuse, 11,* 123–138.

Caetano, R., Schafer, J., & Cunradi, C. B. (2001). Alcohol-related intimate partner violence among white, black, and Hispanic couples in the United States. *Alcohol Research and Health, 25,* 58–65.

Campbell, J. C., et al. (2003). Risk factors for femicide in abusive relationship: Results from a multisite case control study. *American Journal of Public Health, 93,* 1089–1097.

Campbell, J. C. & Humphreys, J. (1993). *Nursing care of survivors of family violence.* St. Louis: Mosby.

Cao, L., Adams, A., & Jensen, V. J. (1997). A test of the subculture of violence thesis: A research note, *Criminology, 35,* 367–379.

Commission on Domestic Violence. (1999). *Statistics on domestic violence.* Retrieved from http://www.abanet.org.domviol/stats/html

Cunradi, C. B., Caetano, R., & Schafer, J. (2002). Socioeconomic predictors of intimate partner violence among white, black, and Hispanic couples in the United States. *Journal of Family Violence, 17,* 553–559.

Daly, J. E., & Pelowski, S. (2000). Predictors of dropout among men who batter: A review of studies with implications for research and practice. *Violence and Victims, 15,* 137–160.

Dickstein, L. J., & Nadelson, C. C. (Eds). 1989. *Family violence: Emerging issues of a national crisis.* Washington, DC: American Psychiatric Press.

Easton, C. J., Weinberger, A. H., & George, T. P. (2007). Age of onset of smoking among alcohol-dependent men attending substance abuse treatment after a domestic violence arrest. *Addictive Behaviors, 32,* 2020–2031.

Fals-Stewart, W., Golden, J., & Schumacher, J. A. (2003). Intimate partner violence and substance use: A longitudinal day to day examination. *Addictive Behaviors, 28,* 1555–1574.

Gelles, R. J., & Straus, M. A. (1998). *The definitive study of the causes and consequences of abuse in the American family.* New York: Simon & Schuster.

Hall, J. M. (2003). Positive self-transitions in women child abuse survivors. *Issues of Mental Health Nursing, 24,* 647.

Hattendorf, J., & Tollerud, T. R. (1997). Domestic violences: Counseling strategies that minimize the impact of secondary victimization. *Perspectives in Psychiatric Care, 33,* 14–23.

Heim, C., & Nemeroff, C. B. (2001). The role of childhood trauma in the neurobiology of mood and anxiety disorders: Preclinical and clinical studies. *Biological Psychiatry, 49,* 1023–1039.

Heim, C., Newport, D. F., Heit, S., Graham, Y. P., Wilcox, M., Bonsall, R., et al. (2000). Pituitary-adrenal and autonomic responses to stress in women after sexual and physical abuse in childhood. *Journal of the American Medical Association, 284,* 592–597.

Holt, U. L., Kernie, M. A., Lamley, T., Wolf, M. E., & Rivara, F. P. (2002). Civil protection orders and risk of subsequent police-reported violence. *Journal of the American Medical Association, 288,* 589–594.

Janssen, P. A., Holt, V. L., & Sugg, N. K. (2002). Introducing domestic violence assessment in a postpartum clinical setting. *Maternal and Child Health Journal, 6,* 195–201.

Koopman, C., Gore-Felton, C., Classen, C., Kim, P., & Spiefel, D. (2001). Acute stress reactions to everyday stressful life events among sexual abuse survivors with PTSD. *Journal of Child Sexual Abuse, 10,* 83–99.

Lloyd, D. A., & Turner, R. J. (2003). Cumulative adversity and posttraumatic stress disorder: Evidence from a diverse community sample of young adults. *American Journal of Orthopsychiatry, 73,* 381–391.

Lore, R. K., & Schultz, L. A. (1993). Control of human aggression: A comparative perspective. *American Psychologist, 48,* 16–25.

Martin, M. (1998). Battered women. In N. Hutchings (Ed.), *The violent family: Victimization of women, children and elders.* New York: Human Sciences Press.

Mattson, S., & Rodriguez, E. (1999). Battering in pregnant Latinos. *Issues in Mental Health Nursing, 20,* 405–422.

Moss, V. A. (1991). Battered women and the myth of masochism. *Journal of Psychosocial Nursing, 29,* 18–23.

Mullen, P. E., Pathe, M., Purcell, R., & Stuart, G. W. (1999). Study of Stalkers. *American Journal of Psychiatry, 156,* 1244–1249.

Parrott, D. J., & Giancola, P. R. (2004). A further examination of the relationship between trait anger and alcohol related aggression: The role of anger control. *Alcoholism, Clinical and Experimental Research, 28,* 855–864.

Pennings, E. J. M., Leccese, A. P., & de-Wolff, F. A. (2002). Effects of concurrent use of alcohol and cocaine. *Addiction, 97,* 773–783.

Poirier, N. (2000). Psychosocial characteristics discriminating between battered women and other women psychiatric inpatients. *Journal of the American Psychiatric Nurses Association, 6,* 144.

Roberts, A. (1988). Substance abuse among men who batter their mates: The dangerous mix. *Substance Abuse Treatment, 5,* 83–87.

Sadlock, V. A. (1989). Rape, spouse abuse and incest. In H. J. Kaplan & B. J. Saddlock (Eds.), *Comprehensive textbook of psychiatry* (Vol. 1, 5th ed.). Baltimore: Williams & Wilkins.

Scobie, J., & McGuire, M. (1999). Professional issues: The silent enemy: Domestic violence during pregnancy. *British Journal of Midwifery, 7,* 259–262.

Smith, M. E. (2003). Recovering from intimate partner violence: A difficult journey. *Issues in Mental Health Nursing, 24,* 543.

Stalans, L. J., & Richie, J. (2007). Relationship of substance use/abuse with psychological and physical intimate partner violence: Variations across living situations. *Journal of Family Violence, 23,* 9–24.

Walker, L. E. (1979). *The battered woman.* New York: Harper & Row.

Wilson, P., McFarlane, J., Malecha, A., Watson, K., Lemmey, D., Schultz, P., et al. (2000). Severity of violence against women by intimate partners and associated use of alcohol and/or illicit drugs by the perpetrator. *Journal of Interpersonal Violence, 15,* 996–1008.

Domestic Violence in Gay, Lesbian, Bisexual, and Transgender Persons

10

Populations at Risk

CHRISTOPHER W. BLACKWELL

Contents

Introduction

Domestic violence (DV) presents a unique problem in gay, lesbian, bisexual, and transgender (GLBT) communities across the United States. While GLBT survivors and perpetrators of DV share characteristics similar to those of heterosexuals, there are also significant differences, which emphasize the need to address DV within this population from a unique approach. This chapter will discuss the topic of DV in GLBT populations and explore disparities within the social service and criminal/justice systems, which weaken law enforcement and social service professionals' abilities to respond effectively to DV.

Defining DV in GLBT Persons

Perhaps the most commonly applied definition and measures of DV within gay populations is that provided by Burke (1998), who asserted:

Gay domestic violence [is] defined as a means to control others through power, including physical and psychological threats (verbal and non-verbal) or injury (to the victim or to others), isolation, economic deprivation, heterosexist control, sexual assault, vandalism (destruction of property) or any combinations of methods. (p. 164)

Prevalence of DV Within GLBT Persons

It is important to recognize that within the general population, up to 10% of individuals identify their sexual orientation as one other than heterosexual (Duthu, 2001; Seidel, Ball, Dains, & Benedict, 2006). While there are existing data that indicate DV is an issue among GLBT persons, there is a relative lack of scholarly research to assess DV within these populations (Kulkin, Williams, Borne, Bretonne, & Laurendine, 2007; West, 2002; Burke, Jordan, & Owen, 2000). However, research does suggest the occurrence of DV within GLBT persons is at least equal to that of heterosexuals (Merrill & Wolfe, 2000). For instance, Barnes (1998) estimated that 25% of GLBT people are battered by their partners. Breaking this prevalence down further, West's (2002) meta-analysis of research assessing lesbian DV suggested 30% to 40% of lesbians had experienced physical abuse, including pushing, shoving, and slapping. This same study revealed a wide range of sexual violence experienced by lesbians, including forced kissing, breast and genital fondling, and oral, anal, or vaginal penetration. When West (2002) included psychological dimensions of abuse (i.e., threats and verbal abuse, name calling, yelling, and insults), prevalence rose to 80%. Merrill and Wolfe (2000) reported that approximately 26% of gay men had used violence in their current or most recent male-male relationship, while roughly 25% of their partners had as well. Scrutinizing this data further, 87% of gay male survivors reported recurrent physical abuse, 85% reported recurrent emotional abuse, 90% identified financial abuse, and 73% reported one or more types of sexual abuse.

Transgender is a term used to describe an individual who, although biologically is one sex, identifies psychologically as the opposite sex. These persons may choose to express characteristics of that opposite but self-identified sex, including dressing in the clothing of the identified sex, wearing makeup or other physically enhancing accessories, altering name to a more gender-appropriate one, or living out every aspect of his or her life as that identified sex. There has been very little inquiry into the prevalence of DV among transgendered populations. The only study found in the comprehensive literature review of Bornstein, Fawcett, Sullivan, Senturia, and Shiu-Thornton (2006) was that of Courvant and Cook-Daniels (1998), which estimated that 50% of transgender persons reported being raped or assaulted by an intimate partner. Thirty-one percent of these study participants also identified themselves as survivors of DV. Aside from relationship issues, transgender persons have higher rates of discrimination in employment, and consequently may be at a significant socioeconomic disadvantage (National Center for Transgender Equality, 2008). Transgender persons, especially youth, may be rejected by their friends and families and find themselves homeless. This often forces them into sex work, which may dramatically increase their susceptibility to violent crimes (Gay and Lesbian Medical Association, 2008).

The Role of Culture and Ethnicity in GLBT DV

It is imperative to indicate that GLBT persons often have social and cultural memberships that transcend the identity of their sexuality or sexual orientation (Erbaugh, 2007). As there are multiple subcommunities within the GLBT community itself, DV among these groups might pose unique considerations that have yet to be widely studied empirically. For example, bisexual and transgender individuals often report a feeling of marginalization within the greater GLBT community and in a broader social context (Bornstein et al., 2006). Bisexual and transgender survivors of DV have reported increased coercion from their perpetrators for not meeting role expectations as being either transgender or bisexual. Even more, bisexuals are often framed as being more promiscuous with both men and women and, perhaps consequently, more deserving of the DV inflicted upon them (Bornstein et al., 2006). Of equal significance are the cultural and ethnic groups to which GLBT persons also identify. Because some cultures place even more stigma on a GLBT identity, it is essential to consider the impact this might have on reporting incidences of victimization and the likelihood that a survivor will utilize criminal justice and social service systems.

In terms of group differences in relating to and acceptance of GLBT lifestyles, research has consistently indicated higher levels of homophobia among African Americans and heterosexuals who identify with a conservative Christian ideology (Finlay & Walther, 2003; Lewis, 2003). Therefore, it could be reasonably postulated that GLBT DV survivors—who are also members of these communities—may be less likely to seek assistance from law enforcement and other social service providers out of fear their GLBT identity could be revealed to family members and friends who may react negatively. Cross-culturally, samples of Asian individuals in China indicate levels of homophobia that are statistically similar to those of American and Western heterosexuals (Lim, 2002).

Understanding DV in Gay and Lesbian Persons From a Theoretical Perspective

A theoretical model is often useful when attempting to describe and explain a certain phenomenon. Theories help to derive hypotheses that can then be tested through applied research. One particular theoretical framework employed to explain DV in gay and lesbian persons is the disempowerment theory. A basic premise of disempowerment theory is that those who feel inadequate, or feel they lack self-efficiency, are at risk of using unconventional power assertion, including violence (Archer, 1994). These same individuals oftentimes overcompensate by exerting control over the persons who they perceive as threatening or who might expose their insecurities (Gondolf, Fisher, Fisher, & McPherson, 1988). Physical and emotional abuse in gay and lesbian relationships has been effectively conceptualized in a power/control paradigm. Additional support and validation for this notion is provided by McKenry, Serovich, Mason, and Mosack (2006), who found it highly applicable to this field of study.

Disempowerment theory explains gay and lesbian domestic violence in terms of one of three classifications or clusters: (1) individual, (2) family of origin, and (3) intimate relationship characteristics (McKenry et al., 2006). Individual characteristics increase a person's risk for domestic violence based on personality-oriented factors such as self-concept or degree of attachment. Family of origin factors occur during childhood, in which individuals learn conflict resolution and coping mechanisms through the modeling of the adults around them. Many persons transfer these methods into adulthood and employ them in their own relationships. Perhaps this provides some explanation as to why DV is perpetuated in certain families (i.e., an intergenerational transmission of violence). Finally, intimate relationship characteristics refer to qualities of romantic relationships that increase the likelihood an individual will use violence against an intimate partner. Examples found in the literature include status inconsistency—such as differences in physical size—attractiveness, job status, relationship stress or dissatisfaction, and imbalances in dependency between the members of the relationship (McKenry et al., 2006; Gelles, 1999; Rutter & Schwartz, 1995; Lockhart, White, Causby, & Isaac, 1994; Meyers, 1989; Renzetti, 1989).

Other theories generally used to explain DV among heterosexuals have also been applied to explain DV among homosexual populations (Jackson, 2007). For instance, deterrence theory suggests that individuals are less likely to commit criminal acts, including DV, due to fear of sanctions (Jackson, 2007). When swift and strong penalties for criminal behavior do not exist, or the individual is impervious to its consequences, some individuals might resort to violence. This theory implies that because the criminal justice system is largely designed on a heterosexist model, with most jurisdictions inadequately capable of responding to same-sex DV, perpetrators are more likely to commit it because police are often reluctant to get involved and policy makers are yet to draft GLBT-specific legislation to punish such acts (Jackson, 2007).

Finally, researchers have suggested substance abuse plays a possible role in GLBT DV. Specifically, the data appear to indicate that gay men and lesbians have higher rates of substance abuse and alcoholism than heterosexuals (Jackson, 2007). While certainly not all perpetrators of DV are under the influence of substances at the time of the incident, substances like alcohol and other illicit drugs can decrease inhibitions and may increase the probability for a violent outburst (Jackson, 2007). However, it must be emphasized that substance use and abuse doesn't serve as a precise etiology for DV among GLBT persons; it is more likely to be an exacerbating factor (Jackson, 2007). Moreover, correlation does not prove causation.

The Social Service and Criminal/Justice Response to GLBT DV: Perpetuating the Problem

While addressing domestic violence in the general heterosexual population provides a big challenge, meeting the social service and criminal/justice needs of gay, lesbian, bisexual, and transgender survivors of DV presents an even greater challenge to social service and criminal/justice systems based on a heterosexual model of care (Simpson & Helfrich, 2005). Cultural mythological beliefs and stereotypes of GLBT individuals not only perpetuate misunderstanding of DV among social service and criminal/justice professionals, but also may add to the pathology of GLBT DV. West (1998) hypothesized that aggressors might actually use society's heterosexist myths and beliefs about DV in GLBT persons to suppress their victims from coming forward to legal authorities or seeking help from social service providers. For example, a popular myth in American society is that DV in heterosexual couples results from the construction of a patriarchal view of opposite-sex relationships, in which traditional male-dominant and female-submissive roles yield an explanation for why male aggressors inflict physical, emotional, or sexual harm on their female partners (Simpson & Helfrich, 2005).

When this myth is then applied to same-sex partners, however, DV becomes an almost impossible phenomenon to explain as the traditional male-female gender roles of a heterosexual relationship do not exist. Thus, social service providers and criminal/justice practitioners often underestimate or completely dismiss DV among same-sex partners. The perspective of

DV as an issue reserved for heterosexual couples has resulted in significant disparities between services provided to heterosexual survivors and homosexual or transgender survivors.

Attitudes and perceptions among the general population could also lead to perpetuation of myths regarding same-sex DV and a weakened societal response. Some individuals believe gay male relationships are less permanent and should therefore be of less concern than heterosexual relationships (Seelau, Seelau, & Poorman, 2003). This translates into a significantly lower level of empathy toward men in abusive relationships from the general population, which is especially problematic in gay male relationships, where both batterer and survivor are men (Seelau et al., 2003).

There is little concentration in the research literature regarding referral services and social services provided to GLBT survivors of DV. Although few researchers have focused on lesbian DV, Rose (2003) found some community-oriented police interventions were effective in dealing with GLBT DV on a broader scale. First, having a specifically designated liaison who responds to GLBT-related issues of DV within police departments was found to be effective. Survivors could call a hotline set up to respond to GLBT DV cases. Callers to such a hotline don't have to fear possible homophobic and unfair treatment by the police since the liaison answering the call is sensitive to GLBT issues (Rose, 2003). Another effective approach is to ensure Domestic Violence Assault Team (DART) personnel are specifically trained on GLBT DV incidents. Oftentimes, the police department's GLBT liaison is responsible for instituting such training (Rose, 2003). Responders to incidences of GLBT DV should be educated to look for signs of a same-sex relationship within the setting (for example, looking at photographs within the residence and assessing the number of bedrooms) to correctly identify cases of GLBT DV and not just violence among "roommates." While these strategies are effective once GLBT DV has been discovered, reporting of such incidences still poses a significant dilemma in and of itself.

The National Coalition of Anti-Violence Programs (2002) reported that the range of DV incidences among gays and lesbians that are reported to the criminal/justice system lies somewhere between 20% and 50%. In addition, poorly worded and ill-defined statutes often enable members of the judicial system to make decisions open to subjective interpretation and bias. Furthermore, several states specifically exclude GLBT persons in their DV regulations, and law enforcement personnel often lack training and education in culturally sensitive issues related to the GLBT community (Burke, Jordan, & Owen, 2002; National Coalition of Anti-Violence Programs, 2001; Hodges, 2000). Constitutional amendments outlawing the recognition of same-sex relationships in certain states also have the potential to weaken the ability of criminal/justice professionals to respond effectively to DV within same-sex couples and transgender persons (Fairchild, 2005). For example, such amendments could make laws that enhance the penalties for assault in situations of DV nonapplicable to same-sex partners (Fairchild, 2005).

The work of Simpson and Helfrich (2005) highlights some of the major problems of the American social service system in responding to DV in GLBT persons. Their work identified three major barriers to social service access: (1) systemic barriers, (2) institutional barriers, and (3) individual barriers. Systemic barriers were those obstacles created from a heterosexually dominated American culture and included social and cultural attitudes toward same-sex relationships. Use of heterosexually focused theoretical models to explain DV in GLBT persons and assumptions of the dynamics of violence in these persons were also identified as systemic barriers to service access. While reformation of these was largely seen as requiring significant societal change, they are often cited as the source of a large amount of frustration among providers attempting to care for GLBT survivors of DV, especially in terms of interorganizational and departmental collaboration.

Institutional barriers are those that happen specifically within agencies as a result of inadequate policies and procedures. Examples include ambiguous and inconsistent policies that might allow discrimination of a GLBT DV survivor. In these instances, screening tools that are used to help justify service inclusion are often worded using opposite-sex terminology and can be used to exclude a GLBT survivor from services. This can be corrected by ensuring agencies use gender-neutral terminology in their screening methods or use tools that allow for inclusion of GLBT survivors. The National Coalition of Anti-Violence Programs (2008) has a tool that incorporates not only assessment of DV incidences, but also violence and harassment against GLBT individuals altogether. Another institutional barrier is an almost automatic referral to agencies that exclusively provide services to GLBT persons (Simpson & Helfrich, 2005). Because such few agencies exist across the United States for lesbians, and even fewer for gay men or transgender persons, they can be easily overwhelmed and are often operating with fewer resources than other agencies. Therefore, it is essential to have staff with the knowledge and expertise to appropriately handle situations of GLBT DV.

Finally, individual barriers must be addressed to optimize care for GLBT survivors of DV. Internalized homophobia (i.e., self-hatred of a homosexual's own sexual orientation), anticipation of discrimination, and concerns about the revelation of a survivor's sexual orientation have all been identified as individual barriers to service access. For instance, lesbians will often identify their perpetrators as male to avoid issues of discrimination and avoid being "outed" as a homosexual (Simpson & Helfrich, 2005). Lesbians often fear they will not be accepted by heterosexual survivors. Likewise, they are frequently concerned other females might misperceive them as making sexual propositions, which could result in difficulties in placing them in rooming quarters with other females. In addition, GLBT survivors of DV are often subjected to the religious and personal biases of staff personnel. Therefore, it is essential that social service providers establish a trusting relationship with clients and remove any religious or personal biases they may have. Clients should be welcomed into a service agency and should be able to openly discuss their situation free of the fear of discrimination or suboptimal care. If a provider is unable to provide care to a GLBT client, then he or she needs to discuss this with a supervisor to ensure the client is referred to an appropriate provider who can best provide care to the client.

Conclusion

This chapter has provided an overview of the issue of DV among GLBT populations. Data related to the prevalence of DV in GLBT relationships have been discussed. Multiple theoretical frameworks, including the disempowerment theory, deterrence theory, and role of substance abuse, have been provided as models to help explain why DV among GLBT persons exists. Finally, the social service and criminal/justice response to DV and problems within these systems have been outlined. In closing, it is essential that policy makers, medical, law enforcement, and social service professionals comprehend and address DV in GLBT persons. As emphasized in this work, a one-size-fits-all mentality to addressing DV is not working and only perpetuates the disparities (in treatment and services) experienced by GLBT survivors.

Setting aside personal biases and ensuring all clients are treated equally and equitably is just the beginning of ending the cycle of DV in GLBT persons. Professionals must work to eliminate institutional biases and clients' individual biases, which also inhibit the optimal delivery of service to GLBT survivors. Finally, this is an area of much needed research. Future scholars should continue to assess the causes of DV among GLBT persons and assess the best ways to prevent it. Evidence-based data are badly needed to define which methods are best to screen and treat those who are survivors of DV. Only careful and culturally sensitive approaches to addressing this issue will ultimately be deemed most efficacious.

References

Archer, J. (1994). Power and male violence. In J. Archer (Ed.), *Male violence* (pp. 310–332). New York: Routledge.

Barnes, P. (1998). It's just a quarrel. *American Bar Association Journal, 84*, 24–25.

Bornstein, D. R., Fawcett, J., Senturia, K. D., Sullivan, M., & Shiu-Thornton, S. (2006). Understanding the experience of lesbian, bisexual, and trans survivors of domestic violence: A qualitative study. *Journal of Homosexuality, 51*, 159–181.

Burke, T. W. (1998). Male to male gay domestic violence: The dark closet. In N. Jackson & G. Oates (Eds.), *Violence in intimate relationships: Examining psychological and sociological issues* (pp. 161–179). Boston: Butterworth-Heinemann.

Burke, T. W., Jordan, M. L., & Owen, S. S. (2000). A cross-national comparison of gay and lesbian domestic violence. *Journal of Contemporary Criminal Justice, 18*, 231–257.

Courvant, D., & Cook-Daniels, L. (1998). Trans and intersex survivors of domestic violence: Defining terms, barriers, and responsibilities. In *National Coalition Against Domestic Violence 1998 conference handbook*. Denver, CO: NCADV.

Duthu, K. F. 2001. Why doesn't anyone talk about gay and lesbian domestic violence? In N. Lerman (Ed.), *Domestic violence law* (pp. 191–203). St. Paul, MN: West Group.

Erbaugh, E. B. (2007). Queering approaches to intimate partner violence. In L. O'Toole (Ed.), *Gender violence: Interdisciplinary perspectives* (pp. 451–459). New York: University Press.

Fairchild, D. (2005). Gay-marriage bans—The boomerang effect. *Time, 165*, 17.

Finlay, B., & Walther, C. (2003). The relation of religious affiliation, service attendance, and other factors to homophobic attitudes among university students. *Review of Religious Research, 44*, 370–393.

Gay and Lesbian Medical Association. (2008). Ten things transgender persons should discuss with their health care providers. Retrieved September 8, 2008, from http://glma.org/index.cfm?fuseaction=Page.viewPage&pageID=692

Gelles, R. J. (1999). Male offenders: Our understanding from the data In M. Harway & J. M. O'Neil (Eds.), *What causes men's violence against women?* (pp. 36–48). Thousand Oaks, CA: Sage.

Gondolf, E. W., Fisher, W. W., Fisher, E., & McPherson, J. R. (1988). Radical differences among shelter residents: A comparison of Anglo, Black, and Hispanic battered. *Journal of Family Violence, 3*, 39–51.

Hodges, K. M. (2000). Trouble in paradise: Barriers to addressing domestic violence in lesbian relationships. *Law & Sexuality, 9*, 311–331.

Jackson, N. A. (2007). Same-sex domestic violence: Myths, facts, correlates, treatment, and prevention strategies. In A. Roberts (Ed.), *Battered women and their families* (pp. 451–470). New York: Springer Publishing.

Kulkin, H. S., Williams, J., Borne, H. F., Bretonne, D., & Laurendine, J. (2007). A review of research on violence in same-gender couples: A resource for clinicians. *Journal of Homosexuality, 53*, 71–87.

Lewis, G. B. (2003). Black-white differences in attitudes toward homosexuality and gay rights. *Public Opinion Quarterly, 67*, 78–89.

Lim, V. (2002). Gender differences and attitudes towards homosexuality. *Journal of Homosexuality, 43*, 85–89.

Lockhart, L. L., White, B. W., Causby, V., & Isaac, A. (1994). Letting out the secret: Violence in lesbian relationships. *Journal of Interpersonal Violence, 9*, 948–963.

McKenry, P. C., Serovich, J. M., Mason, T. L., & Mosack, K. (2006). Perpetration of gay and lesbian partner violence: A disempowerment perspective. *Journal of Family Violence, 21*, 233–243.

Merrill, G. S., & Wolfe, V. A. (2000). Battered gay men: An exploration of abuse, help seeking, and why they stay. *Journal of Homosexuality, 39,* 1–30.

Meyers, B. (1989). *Lesbian battering: An analysis of power.* Unpublished doctoral dissertation, Indiana University of Pennsylvania.

National Center for Transgender Equality. (2008). *Issues: Discrimination.* Retrieved September 8, 2008, from http://nctequality.org/Issues/Discrimination.html

National Coalition of Anti-Violence Programs. (2001). *Lesbian, gay, bisexual, and transgender domestic violence in 2001.* New York: Author.

National Coalition of Anti-Violence Programs. (2002). *Lesbian, gay, bisexual, and transgender domestic violence in 2002.* New York: Author.

National Coalition of Anti-Violence Programs. (2008). *Lesbian, gay, bisexual, and transgender domestic violence in 2007.* Retrieved September 8, 2008, from http://www.ncavp.org/common/document_files/Reports/2007HVReportFINAL.pdf

Renzetti, C. M. (1989). Building its second closet: Third party responses to victims of lesbian partner abuse. *Family Relations, 38,* 157–163.

Rose, S. M. (2003). Community interventions concerning homophobic violence and partner violence against lesbians. *Journal of Lesbian Studies, 7,* 125–139.

Rutter, V., & Schwartz, P. (1995). Same-sex couples: Courtship, commitment, and context. In A. E. Auhagen & M. von Salisch (Eds.), *The diversity of human relationships.* Cambridge: Cambridge University Press.

Seelau, E. P., Seelau, S. M., & Poorman, P. B. (2003). Gender and role-based perceptions of domestic abuse: Does sexual orientation matter? *Behavioral Sciences and the Law, 21,* 199–214.

Seidel, H. M., Ball, J. W., Dains, J. E., & Benedict, G. W. (2006). *Mosby's guide to physical examination.* St. Louis: Mosby.

Simpson, E. K., & Helfrich, C. A. (2005). Lesbian survivors of intimate partner violence: Provider perspectives on barriers to accessing services. *Journal of Gay & Lesbian Social Services, 18,* 39–59.

West, C. (1998). Leaving a second closet: Outing partner violence in same-sex couples. In Jana L. Jasinski and Linda M. Williams (Eds.), *Partner violence: A comprehensive review of 20 years of research* (pp. 184–209). Thousand Oaks, CA: Sage.

West, C. M. (2002). Lesbian intimate partner violence: Prevalence and dynamics. *Journal of Lesbian Studies, 6,* 121–127.

Spouse Violence Among Police Officers
Work-Family Linkages

11

LEANOR BOULIN JOHNSON

Contents

Historical Context

Prior to the 1970s most studies on U.S. workers took a segmentation approach—ignoring as sources of stress the family and often even the work environment. The family unit was assumed to be isolated from work by virtue of its specialization, particularly family division of labor based on gender. The labor force, dominated by men, meant that working men could compartmentalize their lives focusing on work while at work and then leaving work to relax in a home, made comfortable by a full- or part-time housewife or stay-at-home mother. This was considered comfortable by a full- or part-time housewife or stay-at-home mother. When workers' stress emerged, individual characteristics such as personality and coping skills were assumed to be at the root. Thus, stress prevention strategies focused on helping workers cope with job demands. Without question, the importance of individual differences cannot be ignored. However, scientific evidence suggests that certain working conditions are stressful to most people (Strong & DeVault, 1992, p. 380). Such evidence argues for primary prevention strategies that emphasize redesigning working conditions (e.g., level of job autonomy, safety, task meaning, deadlines, and production expectations). Whether the primary cause of job stress lies in worker characteristics or working conditions, the impact of work stress on nonwork domains received little attention (Strong & DeVault, 1992).

By the following decade, the segmentation model began to lose credence against the tide of the women's movement, upsurge in dual-worker families, and rising divorce rates among families with children. The work-family linkage now took on an "in your face" tension, forcing employers to acknowledge this linkage for both males and females. Several studies supported a spillover effect that assumes that experiences at work carry over into family life (e.g., Crosby, 1984; Karney & Bradbury, 1995; Maslach, 1982; Neff & Karney, 2007; Rook, Dooley, & Catalano, 1991). Because of the heightened potential for stress to negatively affect family dynamics, high-stress occupations caught the attention of many social scientists, especially family researchers.

Despite the recognition of work-family linkages and focus on high-stress occupations, family violence remained relatively obscure. In fact, prior to the *Journal of Marriage and the Family* 1971 special issue on family violence, not one article in this leading family publication contained the word *violence* in its title. Since then, the number of texts and journals giving attention to domestic violence markedly increased. In 1974 Sociological Abstracts citations showed only nine domestic violence articles. By 1998, the number of citations had increased by 228. However, partly because the police profession represents "law and order," it appeared oxymoronic to speak of "police spouse abuser"; thus, none of these articles dealt with police families (Johnson, Todd, & Subramanian, 2005). Even as we crafted our study of work-family stress among police officers and their spouses, no thought was given to the possibility that any of our 735 police officers perpetrated violence against their family members. Yet, through interviews, several police spouses in the early stages of our study spontaneously told their stories of abuse. Thus began our inquiry as to how those sworn and empowered to enforce law, prevent crime, and preserve peace could themselves be perpetrators of the most intimate of crimes—domestic violence.[1]

We began with an examination of organizational culture, cost and rewards structure, and occupational gendering. Among the theories used to explain intimate partner violence, those that have special relevance to the culture of policing include mechanical solidarity, exchange theory, and feminist theory. Each is examined in the following section.

Police Culture

Mechanical Solidarity

According to Emile Durkheim (1933) mechanical solidarity exists when a society (typically small in size) exhibits cohesion and integration as a result of its members' homogeneity. In defending the group's common consciousness and collective practices, rules develop that stunt individuality, insulate the group, and block outside intrusion. These rules become the group's distinguishing cultural characteristics. Similarly, every organization can be seen as a society with a common consciousness evident by a subculture of values, rules, and norms that shape the appropriate behavior, attitude, and emotions for its members. The highly organized and traditional structure of police departments is no exception. While the more than 17,000 U.S. police agencies vary in size, culture, and philosophy, a common normative thread permeates the lives of their 732,000 sworn employees[2]—isolation and solidarity. It is within this insulated circle that recruited civilians train to perfect core elements of masculinity: authority, power, control, dominance, aggression, and dispassionate behavior. When mastered, these essential traits make a competent street cop. Yet, at the same time, they are diametrically opposed to the traits needed to be effective in the home. Unfortunately, the police community, characterized by isolation and secrecy, provides a perfect incubator for protecting officers who choose to misplace aggression and misuse authority within their homes.

The injection of hypermasculinity begins in the academy, followed by booster shots throughout the officer's career. An old police recruiting poster that reads "For Men Only: A Job For Men If You Can Qualify" drives home the message that although masculine traits characterize law enforcement, maleness does not automatically ensure admittance to the "blue brotherhood" (Tapper & Culhane, 2007). In the academy each civilian must prove to peers and the upper brass his or her hypermasculinity, a task more challenging for females. In our survey, the majority of the female (54%) and a large minority of the male (39%) officers stated that they acted tougher than they felt. Regardless of their comfort level, acting tough, suppressing emotions, being aggressive, and internalizing their entitlement to authority ultimately becomes part of their identity.

After the completion of their tenure as a rookie and a few years of street patrol, officers encounter a sufficient number of crisis situations to know which skills to hone. Without question they place highest priority on skillfully maintaining control of all situations and obtaining conformity from others through command presence, aggressive body language, verbal aggression, assaultive behavior, or deadly force. Officers who lose control not only endanger themselves, but also send signals to fellow officers that he or she cannot be trusted.

The premium placed on control partially explains the resistance departments had to researchers who studied police work-family linkages. Making this point, one sergeant emphatically stated,

> Link? There is no link. Any officer who can't control his domestic affairs by keeping his family in line can't possibly be fit for duty and needs to get out! (Source anonymous)

Most police families clearly understand the expectation for segmenting work and home as well as the secrecy expected when family problems arise. In our survey, 51% (with an additional 15% unsure) of our 479 police spouses believed that their mate's police career would be hurt if family concerns of a negative nature reached the department. Thus, denying work-family linkages becomes a matter of occupational survival. In this reality it is understandable that a solid majority of male (55%) and a large minority of women (37%) officers state that their family has to be held at a high standard because of their police profession.

Life on the streets further builds on this general attitude of family-work segmentation. On a regular basis, cops encounter a wide variety of unsavory individuals behaving at their worst. They must be on constant guard against unpredictable and potentially dangerous persons. This alertness creates a type of "street high" while on the job and an off-duty depression as the body attempts to homeostatically revitalize. Hypervigilance leads officers to not only find their home life less interesting, but conditions them to become overly suspicious of civilians, including family members (Gilmartin, 1986). Slowly, the emotional loyalty to work begins to trump that of home. A feeling of "us versus them" is compounded by the irregular working hours (particularly shift work), extended periods of overtime, and holiday duties, which diminish opportunities to develop off-duty friendships with nonpolice (Russel & Beigel, 1990; Violanti, 2000). Not surprising, prior to age 40 most police officers center their social life exclusively within the police subculture (Shernock, 1995).

With weak ties to nonpolice groups, officers become trapped by the reverberation of their common consciousness and collective practices, and thereby blinded to alternative ways of handling conflict. For example, our study found that those officers who interact with civilians showed lower stress and strain symptoms. Yet, when confronted with the advantages of diversifying their social life, most officers resisted. They argued that civilian friends always try to get something from them (e.g., fix a ticket) or offend their ego by sharing their anti-law enforcement experiences, or they attempt to probe into the "confidential" world of policing. They emphatically stated that fellow officers have their back in life-and-death situations; thus, their fellowship takes priority. After all, few occupations can claim that their employees would lay down their life for a co-worker. In essence, policing becomes the officer's demanding "mistress" that is protected from all external intrusion.

In exchange for their fellow officers' protection, officers tacitly agree to never "blow the whistle," or testify against a fellow officer. Secrecy and loyalty bind their brotherhood. Families also become part of this secrecy. In exchange for the spouse's loyalty, the department pledges to never forsake the officer or his or her family; even after death, the loyalty continues. But in return, what happens in the police family must stay there. Unfortunately, this also means that any transference of unwanted job behavior into the home too often goes undetected (Johnson et al., 2005).

Spouses frequently complain of their mate's inability to turn off the job. In fact, a significant number of officers in our sample report feeling that they can never shake off the feeling of being a police officer. At least a third of our 735 officers stated that at home their job conditions them to want to do things by the book, to treat the family the way civilians are treated, to be overcritical, and to expect the last word on how things are done. Nearly 50% of officers reported the latter two work spillover effects. For far too many officers the specific "take charge" behavior effective on the street continues at home, that is, the in-your-face loud commanding voice, dominating posture, cross-examinations, expectations for immediate compliance, threats of physical violence—"I don't care what you think, do it or else" (Bradstreet, 1994). Sixty percent of our female spouses complained of this type of verbal violence that for some rivals physical abuse.

> Sometimes I wish he would just hit me and get it over with. I can't take the verbal insults. He knows just how to threaten, belittle, and mess with my mind.[4]

Granting this "wish" to even one spouse would be unthinkable. Yet, our data revealed that at least 10% (45 or more) of the spouses experienced physical violence and more than 40% (294 or more) of our officers reported that they had gotten out of control and behaved violently toward their mate.[5] Given the premium placed on control, losing or the potential threat of losing control kicks in a knee-jerk response of regaining it by any means. In most cases the tactic does not include physical violence, since job-related psychological manipulation generally works (Wetendorf & Davis, 2006). The fact that officers receive a significant number of domestic violence calls that result in arrest, raises the expectation that few would cross the line from law enforcer to perpetrator. While the majority do not cross over, a significant minority do. Exchange theory is another framework for understanding why some officers cross that line, thereby risking their jobs and reputation.

Exchange Theory

Maximizing rewards and minimizing cost undergirds the basic assumption of exchange theory. Based on past experiences, individuals make choices that they believe to be physically and psychologically rewarding. They will provide reciprocity to those who have helped them in anticipation that the reciprocity will continue in an equitable manner. In contrast, cost may be anything that the individual deems repugnant, such as some onerous duty or demeaning status. It may also consist of rewarding feelings or positions that must be given up when selecting some competing alternative (Ingoldsby, Smith, & Miller, 2004).

Police officers violate their partner's psychological and physical well-being because of the low cost incurred—the "code of silence" and "camaraderie" work to protect them from being arrested, and if arrested, they believe that prosecution will be unlikely, particularly prior to the year 2000.[6]

One woman formerly married to a cop tells her story of abuse:

The first time I attributed his violent behavior to job stress. The next time I called for help and the entire squad turned up. The house was in disarray— phone pulled out of the wall, glass broken, and more. His squad helped clean up and there was no arrest.

This same spouse describes her cost in calling for help:

At 3:00 a.m. my husband's sergeant calls me and says that I need to be a better wife and that I am no longer part of the police family if I'm reporting.... When I went to internal affairs I found that of the 22 domestic violence incidents I reported, only 5 had case numbers.... The captain described me as a lunatic and not to be taken seriously.... Even after I moved into my own apartment, the police did nothing as he continued with phone threats and harassment.

Civilian victims often mention that prior to them making a 911 call for help, their abusing spouse prepares for that moment by conditioning his squad to the "fact" that his wife is unpredictable and crazy.[7] Sometimes the officer will make a preemptive strike by calling 911 and requesting a restraining order against her, even though it is she who needs the protection. The following testimony demonstrates how perpetrating officers further weaken their spouse's resolve to report by threats:

The police are my buddies, they won't believe you. You can't hide. I know all the battered women's shelter locations. I have access to information to track you down wherever you run. If I lose my job I will kill the children, you, and myself. I know how to injure you and get away with it. Your case will never hold up in court, I know the judicial system. (National Center for Women and Policing, 2008; Wetendorf, 2000)

With a significant portion of an officer's training devoted to lethal and nonlethal use of force, evidence collecting, and judicial law procedures, such threats must be taken seriously. For example, those resorting to physical coercion may inflict nonobservable injuries (e.g., including pressure point maneuvers to the armpit or nose), thereby weakening the case for any criminal charges brought against them. The more offending officers believe the facts support their threats, the lower their perceived cost of committing domestic violence.

According to Wetendorf (2006, p. 79), the challenge becomes even greater for women officers.

When a civilian woman married to a cop needs help, she thinks, "but he is the police." When a female officer needs help, she thinks, "… but I am the police."

Feminist Theory

The last theoretical perspective used to amplify the context of intimate partner violence among police officers is feminist theory, which best explains the dilemma female officers encounter when seeking help. Three major assumptions undergird this theory: (1) power issues characterize male-female relationships, (2) society constructs gender so that males dominate females, and (3) gender inequality results from the belief that men and women contrast each other in personalities, abilities, skills, and traits. Furthermore, society places higher value on the traits of reason, objectivity, independence, and aggression (male traits) than on the submissive, supportive, nurturing, emotional, and subjectivity traits socially expected of females (Strong & DeVault, 1992 pp. 78–79).

In applying gender theory to work and family, feminists perceive that both at work and at home, there is a division of labor that distinguishes men's work from women's work, with the latter devalued. Since both males and females learn to relate as male and female first, and second as co-worker, traditional sex-role expectations spill over into the work environment. When women enter traditionally male occupations, such as law enforcement, messages and expectations for behavior become particularly confusing, as evidenced by the following remarks of a female officer.

I was just about to enter a dark alley to investigate a robbery in progress, when my male backup motioned for me to fall back. He said I might get hurt. I did not know whether to be flattered at his chivalry or angry at his lack of confidence in me! (Johnson, 1995, p. 594)

Unfortunately, reactions to role ambiguity too often go beyond chivalry. Among males in our sample, nearly 50% believed that their work became more dangerous as a result of women entering the force (less than 5% of females agreed). As a result, some males express their resistance by excluding women from the protection of camaraderie (e.g., blocking calls for help by jamming their radio), verbal abuse, and unwanted sexual attention (including assault).

Those women officers who endure sexual harassment at work aren't assured that home will be a safe, supportive haven. As a group, women officers, compared to male officers, receive less emotional and instrumental support in the home. In our interviews women officers told us that their husbands/mates, even those who seem to be proud of their profession, did not want to hear about their work. Further, these women live in a conflicting and singular duality—wielding the authority of the badge at work, while trying to meet the expectation of submission and supportive nurturing behavior at home. The following assertion sheds light on this duality:

My husband is a construction worker. Realizing that our income would double if I trained to become a police officer he agreed that I should enter the academy. Everything was fine, until I came home wearing the uniform … he got in a physical fight with me to show me that I wasn't as tough as he and the academy wasn't preparing me for the streets.

While both male and female officers possess the potential of bringing the job home, females do not share males' sense of entitlement to authority that society legitimizes. In various ways female officers get the message that their opinion, dominance, and authority may carry weight on the street, but not in the home. Three women officers married to officers shared these incidents:

Officer 1:

We can work the same beat, experience similar traffic violations, and the same number of irate citizens, but when we get home he expects me to listen to him. He says my day could never be as unpleasant as his; and even if it was, it is my job to listen. (Johnson, 1995, p. 594)

Officer 2:

One evening we got into a dispute about how he should have handled a stop. The next thing I knew I was waking up from being knocked out cold.

Officer 3:

My former husband was on the force for nine years. When I went to work he wasn't happy … tension escalated. He followed me at my parents' home and at the academy … in the parking lot he began yelling at me, calling me foul names ... at home he took my 9-millimeter gun and grabbed me trying to make me shoot him. The gun discharged and the bullet went through the wall and just missed my two-year-old daughter's bed. I got suspended for not reporting the discharge.... No one would look at the injuries on my back.

My sergeant tells me to keep it quiet; just call his supervisor. Both the supervisor and my husband tried to dissuade me. They said I had a hidden agenda ... that I was 29 having a mid-life crisis. I wrote out my own police report, because no one would do it.

When family dynamics move from disagreements over who should be supportive to physical violence, female officers find their recourse restrained by gender role spillover. The police culture attaches a strong stigma to the label of "victim." Being a victim is the antithesis of being an officer. In the larger society, victimization largely describes females and not males. Female officers work hard to inculcate masculine traits, so that they can prove their ability to survive and thrive in the male world of policing. Whether they suppress femininity completely or covertly retain it by wearing fancy feminine underwear beneath their masculine uniform, their outward appearance in posture and language projects a stern toughness. Reporting their victimization thwarts all their efforts to be accepted and taken seriously as a cop.

Wentendorf (2006, pp. 81–82) cites examples illustrating the cost abused police women incur when reporting:

If women in policing admit to or acknowledge the victimization piece, they are pushed out of the pack—shunned. You want to be able to continue to excel and advance. If you are now a victim, they won't touch you with a ten-foot pole.

My personal hell was out on the table for all to speculate about. I knew my peers would label me "A Victim." These words just made me want to scream as loud as I could, "It's okay that this could happen to your sister, your daughter, your friend or anyone else that means something to you? But it's not okay because I am a cop?" ... I knew there would be speculation, "How could she let this happen? She should know better, she's a cop.... She must have done something to make him do it. How could she do this to another cop."

Female officers believe that the brotherhood protects them if an unrelated civilian attacks, but they do not expect the same reaction when it's a fellow officer. They have first-hand knowledge about how both males and females feel about intimate partner violence. Officers frequently sympathize with the abuser: "He's an asshole, but she's a lunatic too." "What a bitch! If she were my wife, I'd have hit her, too." Reporting abuse means being labeled not only a victim, but a vindictive witch for setting up her husband, and even worst yet, a traitor for setting up a cop. Even female officers may see her as a liability, by reporting she makes all female officers look weak (Wetendorf, 2006).

Those courageous officers who report may be told the department does not concern itself with off-duty behavior—another tactic for denying the link between work and family. In 1989 the Chicago Police Department took this position and learned a painful lesson. The case involved domestic violence between two police officers. The department ignored the reporting female officer, who subsequently turned up murdered (Kremer, 2008).

In terms of prevention and intervention measures, off-duty behavior should not be any less valued than on-duty behavior. Violence flows interactively across both domains. Officers violent in one domain have a high probability of being violent in the other domain. Among the 40% of intimate partner abusers who self-identified in our sample, the overwhelming number violated citizens and vice versa. Media attention to police street brutality would lead one to believe that violence against citizens has the highest association with domestic violence. While a high degree of correlation exists between officer street violence and spouse abuse, the few officers (particularly females) who act violently toward a fellow officer represent the greatest danger to their mates. Of this group, 81% of the males and 91% of the females also behaved violently toward their spouse/mate. Considering the premium placed on camaraderie, one can expect that any officer who turns on their life-and-death support system will demonstrate an extreme lack of control in all other interactions. This holds especially true for women who must work hard for group approval. Officers fighting other officers represent a warning sign to family life interventionists that family abuse may be present.[8]

Our study did not test whether an officer lashing out against a fellow officer becomes more vulnerable to having his or her violence against an intimate partner reported. If such officers tend to be reported, most likely their behavior would be handled internally. In doing so, discipline based on job misbehavior rather than that within the home often takes priority. Unfortunately, both nonabusive and abusive officers find the rewards of protecting the "blue wall of secrecy" far more compelling than the reward of controlling their behavior or that of their fellow officers. Overall, prior to the year 2000, the rules that insulated the police community and blocked outside intrusion continue to provide the optimal opportunity for officers to abuse in silence.

Academic and Legislative Response

Breaking the Silence

Beginning in the early 1990s the cost-reward balance began to shift. A few researchers began documenting the frequency and unique aspect of intimate partner violence within police families. Johnson's (1991) testimony before Congress caught the attention of federal lawmakers as she documented the work-family linkage and the hidden crime of police domestic violence abuse. Neidig, Russell, and Seng's (1992) study showing more than 40% of 425 officers surveyed reporting violent intimate partner violence (ranging from pushing to using a gun) revealed statistics similar to Johnson's. The National Institute of Justice funded Robyn Gershon's study, "Project Shields" (2000), that replicated some of the seminal research on the police stress-domestic violence nexus revealed by Johnson's (1991) National Institute of Mental Health study. Gershon focused not only on sources of stress, but also on innovative intervention strategies (Gershon, 2000). In addition, several national conferences increased public and organizational awareness (e.g., 1999 National Institute of Justice Conference, 1998/1997 National Center for Women and Policing Conferences, FBI 1998 National Conference on Domestic Violence in Law Enforcement, 1997 International Association of Chiefs of Police Summits, 1991 National Fraternal Order of Police Annual Convention).

At the macro level, federal and state legislators began formulating more stringent laws. In 1996, the Lautenberg Amendment to the 1968 Gun Control Act increased the cost of perpetrating domestic violence. The 1968 Gun Control Act made it a felony for anyone—except military and police personnel—convicted of a "misdemeanor crime of domestic violence" to ship, receive, or possess firearms or ammunition. The 1996 amendment expanded the group of firearm-prohibited persons to include military and police. Anyone who knowingly supplies guns or ammunition to prohibited persons also commits a felony. Further, the amendment prohibited guns/ammunition to those under a domestic restraining order as well as those who have ever been convicted of a "misdemeanor crime of domestic violence," regardless of whether it occurred prior to or after the 1996 legislation (Halstead, September 1, 2001; Lautenberg Amendment 1996; 18 USC §925). With this amendment law enforcement agencies became responsible for reviewing the domestic violence criminal records of all their employees. Ultimately, some departments dismissed convicted officers, if they could not find duties for them that did not require a firearm. Domestic violence could no longer be considered a private matter with no occupational repercussion. Within the world of law enforcement, work linkage to intimate family violence received federal legislative recognition.

Since its inception the Lautenberg Amendment has drawn its fair share of critics.[9] Challengers believe the law runs contrary to the Second Amendment (right to bear arms) and unduly interferes with the ability of law enforcement to execute their job. Despite challenges, the Lautenberg Amendment remains law. Symbolically, 1996 represents a paradigmatic shift—where carrying arms for public interest no longer trumped family safety. However, proponents of the law lament over its poor enforcement. Drawing examples from numerous high-profile cases, they believe that offenders circumvent the lifetime ban intention of the law by having their criminal records expunged. Scientific studies and inspector general investigations also give support to their concerns.

Kappeler (1999) empirically investigated the impact of the Lautenberg Act on policing in Kentucky. The results showed Kentucky police agencies to be largely unaffected by the Act. Of the small percentage of police departments uncovering domestic violence convictions, the majority had their convictions expunged from their records. Kentucky handling of convicted officers patterned that of police agencies nationwide. Of the 23 domestic violence complaints filed against Boston police employees during the 1998–1999 period, none resulted in criminal prosecution. Similarly, in 2007, the Los Angeles Police Department (LAPD) sustained 12 of 27 allegations (representing 11 employees). If history repeats itself, discipline will be light. For example, during the 1990–1999 period, of 91 sustained cases 75% had no mention of the allegation in their performance evaluation, and 29% received promotions, including 6 who were promoted within two years of the incident (National Center for Women and Policing, 2008).

In 1999–2000, the television show *60 Minutes* aired the story of Bob Mullally, a legal consultant who leaked to the press the LAPD personnel files for the years 1990 to 1993. These files showed the mishandling of LAPD cases involving more than 70 LAPD officers investigated for rape and battery of their wives and girlfriends. In 2006, Mullally served 45 days in federal prison for violating a civil protective order when he exposed the confidential files. However, despite the Lautenberg Amendment, all of the exposed police officers escaped prosecution and many continued to carry firearms (Ortega, 2001).

Based on these cases, federal law appears necessary, but insufficient for protecting law enforcement families. In order to curb the criminal elements within the ranks, the blue wall of silence needs to crack and the police departments need to raise the cost of police-perpetrated violence.

Model Departmental Policies and Programs

The International Association of Chiefs of Police (IACP) recognized the need for departmental-level action. Consequently, it created a model policy on how to handle cases of domestic violence within police agencies. The policy, effective July 2003, addresses prevention through hiring and training practices, provides instruction for supervisors on how to intervene when warning signs emerge, institutionalizes a structured response to reported officer-perpetrated domestic violence incidents, and offers guidelines for conducting administrative and criminal investigation.

The IACP comprehensive policy specifically aims at cracking the blue wall of police culture, which encourages police to protect one another, even when they break the law. Explicitly attacking loyalty over integrity, Section IV-B6 of the policy states that all officers will be subject to severe discipline or dismissal if they (1) fail to report knowledge of abuse or violence involving a fellow officer, (2) fail to cooperate with an investigation of a fellow police officer, (3) interfere with cases involving themselves or a fellow officer, or (4) intimidate/coerce witnesses or victims (i.e., surveillance, harassment, stalking, threatening, or falsely reporting).

In sum, the IACP reinforced the need for every U.S. police department to take a zero-tolerance approach (Frazier, 1999). According to the U.S. Department of Justice Bureau of Statistics, within the United States nearly 13,000 general purpose local police departments with 100 or more officers serve populations in diverse communities. Crafted as a model, the IACP policy can be adapted to these agencies' unique environment. Importantly, the mere existence of a model protocol promoted by a professional law enforcement leader such as the IACP makes those departments without a policy or an insufficient one more vulnerable to liability (International Association of Chiefs of Police, 2003). The IACP emphasizes that reasons for adopting a policy should not be limited to liability risk—the issues of community trust and leadership must be maintained and in some cases restored.

Chicago Police Department

In one year, the Chicago Police Department (CPD) lost three officers who killed their spouses and then themselves. These Brame-like tragedies[10] pressured the department to take a zero-tolerance policy, with firing as the consequence. However, when they fired the next offending officer, he retaliated by abducting and murdering his spouse. In 1993 the CPD learned from its failed attempts and developed an innovative program that now serves as a national model. Kremer (2008) reports several distinguishing features of the Chicago program—discretionary arrest, expeditious reporting, independent investigators, and public/employee awareness.

No Mandatory Arrest

After the 1981–1982 Minneapolis Domestic Violence Experiment (Minneapolis Experiment) found arrest to be the most effective police response to domestic violence calls, 23 states and the District of Columbia proscribed mandatory (presumptive) arrest policies. Unlike these states, Illinois' state law does not stipulate that offenders must be arrested. An officer first determines whether arresting will compromise the victim's safety and then makes a decision whether to arrest. While not mandatory, the state encourages arrest after securing the victim's safety. Chicago's domestic advocates prefer this approach because, for a variety of reasons, victims appear more willing to call 911 for help. They argue that victims feel that calling the police and placing their partner in jail for a few hours may only increase their partner's anger, putting them in greater danger. The CPD received some empirical support from a National Institute of Justice-sponsored research that replicated the Minneapolis Experiment in six cities (Atlanta, Charlotte, Colorado Springs, Omaha, Milwaukee, and Miami) during the 1985–1990 period. At least two of these studies showed mandatory arrest effective for only those who remained employed. These data suggest that, although arrest alone may deter some men, an unemployed suspect tends to become even more violent after an arrest (Sherman et al., 1992; Pate & Hamilton, 1992; Kremer, 2008).

Fedders (1997) also questions the universal effectiveness of mandatory arrest. She argues that abused women engage in a cost-benefit analysis to determine whether police presence or an arrest benefits their situation. Thus, if dependent on his income, an abused woman may merely want to diffuse an explosive situation or frighten her batterer into ceasing his abuse rather than have him arrested. Or she may not want her children to witness their father's arrest, a compounded concern for police spouses. Women in relationships with Black or Mexican American men may not welcome help from a system that they deem disproportionately procures harsh prosecutorial treatment on abusive men of color, regardless of whether the badgerer carries a badge.[11]

In the case of women married to police officers of color, they may experience a triple guilt trip from turning on both an officer and intimate partner as well as exposing yet one more person of color to an unjust prosecuting system. Women living in poverty and high-crime areas may not call 911 because they assume that the responding officers believe they can tolerate a higher degree of violence and thus will not appreciate their desperation. In sum, because police must determine probable cause, regardless of the state's mandatory arrest policy, the intersection of racism and classism may operate to make officers discount the testimonies of lower-class women and women of color. While the help-seeking concerns vary, similar to other women, safety reigns as the consistent concern for battered women of color (Weisz, 2005).

This cost-benefit analysis from a woman's perspective does not necessarily reflect the fact that mandatory arrest may be for many offenders the best antidote for recidivism, or that it may make no difference to the majority (Maxwell, Garner, & Fagan, 2001). However, from CPD's perspective the question of whether arrest prevents future aggression misses the antecedent issue—if abused women do not feel safe reporting because they know a mandatory arrest policy exists, then this obviates any discussion of arrest effectiveness. In essence, women needing help will not come to the attention of those who can provide assistance.

One-Hour Rule

In line with the IACP model, if the perpetrator also carries a badge, then a supervisor must be involved in assisting in the write-up. The Chicago policy stipulates that the write-up must be done within one hour in order to deflect the alleged abuser's efforts to call in favors. If the reporting officer waits too long, he or she could be given as much as a month's suspension without pay.

Independent Investigators

Within the Office of Professional Responsibility, the CPD established an independent unit staffed by six civilians who exclusively investigate allegations for disciplinary action, as opposed to criminal charges. Though the police department pays their salary, they do not share information with the department. The unsworn staff jurisdiction includes gathering facts as well as calling the supervisor to request that the suspect relinquish weapons and refrain from contacting the victim. Since victim safety receives priority, as soon as knowledge of an alleged abuse reaches the staff, they dispatch investigators to interview witnesses to see whether the officer should face department discipline (albeit, the staff can neither subpoena nor prepare court cases). With the standard for discipline lower than that for criminal convictions, an officer may be disciplined or dismissed even after the dismissal of criminal charges. While the officer can appeal, ultimately the decision of the Office of Professional Standards (OPS) domestic violent unit goes to the civilian police board, which makes final discipline decisions. Concurrent with the independent investigators' work, other police units determine whether to order the suspect to undergo psychiatric and physical exams or enter treatment. So that victims feel safe, a victim advocate with a law degree provides free counseling in a secret location. The annual abuse reports average about 1 in every 54 officers (about 250 cases) on the 13,500-person force. The Chicago program appears to be the only one in the nation whose structure convinces victims to come forward (Kremer, 2008).

Posting Policies

The CPD widely disseminates the IACP model policy as well as its own policies and procedures to the public, its officers, and all CPD employees. These policies, the 24-hour complaint line, as well as the procedures relevant to a victim's case serve to reassure the victim that his or her case will be taken through a due process with his or her safety as the paramount concern.

Conclusion

These model policies and programs complement the Lautenberg Act, providing a more comprehensive approach to officer-perpetrated domestic violence. They provide details on firm, written, and publicized department policies and protocols for dealing with abuse after the fact. However, prevention programs hold the greatest promise for developing and maintaining healthy police families. Prevention must begin in the academy and continue throughout the officer's career. The academy curriculum ranges from hundreds to more than 1,000 hours, depending on the municipality. Relatively few of these hours focus on work-family issues. Most involve families only on graduation day (Kirschman, 1997). A sergeant in charge of a two-hour family seminar this author attended spent the entire time providing details on the rigorous training the graduating recruits endured. When a wife interrupted to comment that her husband had changed, becoming more dispassionate, moody, and quick tempered, the sergeant immediately replied, "Don't worry, this will pass in a few weeks."

Seven years later a significant number of these same officers, blindsided by the job's insidious invasion into the core of their being, will most likely seek refugee in counterproductive behavior and activities or begin looking for jobs outside of law enforcement. This can be avoided or minimized if recruits receive awareness of how the job may change them or feed their desire for control in intimate relationships. If the academy fails to provide an adequate foundation for emotional family survival, many concerned departments encourage attendance at one-day in-service continuing education classes, designed for both officers and families.

In giving focus to the troubled side of police family interactions, it is easy to forget that domestic violence constitutes less than half of police families. Thus, while professional training and credibility uniquely posture officers who batter to misuse cultural norms and institutional support, clearly the police culture does not necessarily transform nonbatterers into batterers. Hundreds of families in our sample struggle and thrive in their intimate relations. In seminars, interviews, and survey reports they shared their anxiety, fears, communication issues, and frustration with the police administration. Less than 30% of spouses in our sample believe that the police department really cares about the welfare of its officers, and more than 80% believe that the department makes policies and demands inconsiderate of family well-being. Concurrently, the spouses expressed their survival techniques, love and support for their spouse and his or her work, as well as their hope for the department's greater sensitivity to their needs.

Developing a healthy law enforcement family begins by first recognizing and valuing the work-family linkage. The input of families should be sought by departments when seeking guidance in designing interventions for troubled families, as well as healthy families in need of enrichment. Departments would do well to institutionalize an advisory board with official representation from both male and female civilian spouses (similar to the military ombudsman model). Such a board could provide the necessary forum for a proactive approach with regard to departmental policies that affect police families as well as provide ongoing assessment of issues affecting the psychological health of their officers and significant others, reduce the negative view spouses hold of the department, provide spouses with a broader appreciation of policing, expand the spouses' support system, and overall create positive work-family linkages. With the collaborative efforts of legislators, police organizations, police agencies, family practitioners, educators, officers, and their families, strategies can be created for maintaining strong noncombative relationships.

Endnotes

1. Note that our study, funded by the National Institute of Mental Health (NIMH), consisted of 735 police officers and 479 spouses. Unless otherwise cited, all statistical data referencing our study are derived from this National Institute of Mental Health (NIMH) data set. For a detailed description of our sample and couple data, see Beehr, Johnson, & Nieva (1995) and Johnson et al. (2005).
2. See Reaves (2007) for more statistical profile detail.
3. Gershon's (2000)[3] study found officers with high stress to be three times more likely to abuse their spouse/partner.
4. Jacobson and Gottman's (1998) decade study found emotional abuse harder to endure than being beaten, despite the pain and bruises inflicted by punching, kicking, and chocking. Given the officer's training in use of force and control, what officers may consider nonviolent, the average citizen may consider violent. Kirschman (1997) cites two prominent Los Angeles County Sheriff psychologists who note that for cops, restraining someone probably rates a 2 on a 10-point use-of-force scale; grabbing, pushing, and shoving also rank similarly low; punching, grappling, or using a restraint hold might equal a 5 or 6; and drawing and shooting a weapon a 10. However, raising their voices and using intimidating nonverbal tactics would not even rate a 1.
5. While the spouse's questionnaire specifically asked about the type of violence, the officers responded to a more general question as to whether in the last six months prior to the survey they got out of control and behaved violently toward their spouse/mate.
6. The 1996 Lautenburg Amendment to the Gun Control Act of 1968 establishes a comprehensive regulatory scheme designed to prevent the use of firearms by anyone convicted of a domestic violence misdemeanor or who has a protective order issued against them. Greater detail of this amendment can be found later in this chapter.

7. Unless otherwise stated, this article focuses on male perpetrators and female victims; this does not deny the research supporting unidimensional violence by females.

8. Radical feminist paradigms focus exclusively on male intimate violence, thus ignoring empirical studies showing domestic violence among women, especially with lesbian relationships. For a critique of the feminist worldview, see Dutton and Nicholls (2005).

9. See Edwards' (1997) congressional testimony for further details on the Lautenberg controversy.

10. On April 26, 2003, Chief David Brame of the Tacoma, Washington, police department fatally shot his wife (Crystal Judson) and then himself with his children nearby. Not acting on warning signs, the department agreed to settle a multi-million-dollar suit and promised changes in policies and procedures. In December 2005, Congress passed the Crystal Judson bill to fund domestic violence programs nationwide (Sand, 2005).

11. For stressors unique to Black police officers see Johnson (1989) and Dulaney (1996).

References

Beehr, T. A., Johnson, L. B., & Nieva, V. F. (1995). Occupational stress: Coping of police and their spouses. *Journal of Organizational Behavior, 16*, 1–25.

Bradstreet, R. (1994). Cultural hurdles to healthy police families. In J. T. Reese & E. Scrivner (Eds.), *Law enforcement families: Issues and answers* (pp. 19–25). Washington, DC: U.S. Government Printing Office.

Crosby, F. (1984). Job satisfaction and domestic life. In M. D. Lee & R. N. Kanango (Eds.), *Management of work and personal life* (pp. 41–60). New York: Prager.

Dulaney, W. M. (1996). *Black police in America*. Indianapolis: Indiana University Press.

Durkheim, E. (1933). *The division of labor in society* (George Simpson, Trans.). New York: Macmillan.

Dutton, D. G. & Nicholls, T.L. (2005). The gender paradigm in domestic violence research and theory. Part 1. The conflict of theory and data. *Aggression and Violent Behavior, 10*, 680–714.

Edwards, D. (1997, March 5). *National network to end domestic violence*. Testimony before the Subcommittee on Crime Judiciary Committee, U.S. House of Representatives. Retrieved December 27, 2007, from http://judiciary.house.gov/legacy/319.htm

Fedders, B. (1997). Lobbying for mandatory-arrest policies: Race, class, and the politics of the battered women's movement. New York University *Review of Law and Social Change, 281*, 291–296.

Frazier, T. C. (1999, May 6). *Baltimore Police Department—General order G-11: Domestic incidents—Reporting/arrest criteria*. Retrieved December 27, 2008, from http://www.mcdaa.org/defenseatty/general%20orders%20baltimore%20city%20police/g-11.pdf

Gershon, G. (2000). *Law enforcement and family support: Project Shields*. Washington, DC: National Institute of Justice, U.S. Department of Justice.

Gilmartin, K. (1986). Hypervigilance: A learned perceptual set and its consequences on police stress. In J. Reese & H. Goldstein (Eds.), *Psychological services for law enforcement* (pp. 443–448). Washington, DC: U.S. Government Printing Office.

Halstead, T. J. (2001, September 1). *Firearms prohibitions and domestic violence convictions: The Lautenberg Amendment.* CRS Report to Congress. Retrieved December 19, 2008, from http://www.peaceathomeshelter.org/DV/readings/federal/lautenberg.pdf

Ingoldsby, B., Smith, S., & Miller, J. (2004). *Exploring family theories.* Los Angeles: Roxbury.

International Association of Chiefs of Police. (2003). *Domestic violence by police officers: A policy of the IACP response to Violence Against Women Project.* Alexandria, VA: Author.

Jacobson, N., & Gottman, J. (1998). *When men batter women: New insights into ending abusive relationships.* New York: Simon & Schuster.

Johnson, L. B. (1989). The employed black: The dynamics of work-family tension. *Review of Black Political Economy, 17,* 69–85.

Johnson, L. B. (1991). On the front lines: Police stress and family well-being. Hearing before the Select Committee on Children, Youth, and Families. House of Representatives, One Hundred and Second Congress, First Session. (May 20), 36–48. Wshington, DC.: U.S. Government Printing Office.

Johnson, L. B. (1995). Police officers: Gender comparisons. In W. G. Bailey (Ed.), *The encyclopedia of police science* (pp. 591–598). New York: Garland.

Johnson, L. B. (2000). Burnout and work and family violence among police: Gender comparisons. In D. C. Sheehan (Ed.), *Domestic violence by police officers* (pp. 108–114). Washington D.C.: U.S. Government Printing Office.

Johnson, L. B., Todd, M., & Subramanian, G. (2005). Violence in police families: Work-family spillover. *Journal of Family Violence, 20,* 3–12.

Kappeler, V. E. (1999). Kentucky's response to the Lautenberg Act: Curbing domestic violence. *Kentucky Justice & Safety Research Bulletin, 1,* 1–12.

Karney, B. R., & Bradbury, T. N. (1995). The longitudinal course of marital quality & stability: A review of theory, method, and research. *Psychological Bulletin, 118,* 3–34.

Kirschman, E. (1997). *I love a cop: What police families need to know.* New York: Guilford.

Klein, E., Campbell, J., Soler, E., & Ghez, M (Eds.). (1997). *Ending domestic violence: Changing public perceptions/halting the epidemic.* Thousand Oaks, CA: Sage.

Kremer, L. (2008). *Victims come first.* The News Tribune. Retrieved December 27, 2008, from http://www.thenewstribune.com/news/projects/david_brameldomestic _violence/story/366513.html

Maslach, C. (1982). After-effects of job-related stress: Families as victims. *Journal of Occupational Behavior, 3,* 63–77.

Maxwell, D. C., Garner, J. H., & Fagan, J.A. (2001). *The effects of arrest on intimate partner violence: New evidence from the Spouse Assault Replication Program.* Washington, DC: National Institute of Justice.

National Center for Women and Policing. (2008). *Police family violence fact sheet.* Retrieved December 27, 2008.

Neff, L., & Karney, B. R. (2007). Stress crossover in newlywed marriage: A longitudinal and dyadic perspective. *Journal of Marriage and the Family, 69,* 594–607.

Neidig, P. H., Russell, H. E., & Seng, A. F. (1992, Fall/Winter). Interspousal aggression in law enforcement personnel attending the Fraternal Order of Police Biennial Conference. *National Fraternal Order of Police Journal,* pp. 25–28.

Ortega, T. (2001, January 11). *Blind justice*. NewTimesLA.com. Retrieved December 27, 2008, from NewTimesLA.com.

Pate, A. M., & Hamilton, E. E. (1992). Formal and informal deterrents to domestic violence: The Dade County spouse assault experiment. *American Sociological Review, 57*, 591–697.

Reaves, B. (2007). *Census of state and local law enforcement agencies, 2004* (Bureau of Justice Statistics Bulletin NCJ212749). Washington, DC: U.S. Department of Justice.

Rook, K., Dooley, D., & Catalano, R. (1991). Stress transmission: The effects of husbands' job stressors on the emotional health of their wives. *Journal of Marriage and the Family, 53*, 165–177.

Russel, H. E., & Beigel, A. (1990). *Understanding human behavior for effective police work* (3rd ed.). New York: Basic Books.

Sand, P. (2005, December 19). *Congress passes Crystal Judson bill to help stop abuse*. The News Tribune. Retrieved December 27, from http://www.thenewstribune.com/news/projects/david_bramel/story/367687.html

Sherman, L. W., Schmidt, J. D., Rogan, D. P., Smith, D. A., Gartin, P. R., Cohn, E. G., et al. (1992). The variable effects of arrest on criminal careers: The Milwaukee domestic violence experiment. *Journal of Criminal Law & Criminology, 83*, 137–169.

Shernock, S. (1995). Police solidarity. In W. G. Bailey (Ed.), *The encyclopedia of police science* (2nd ed., pp. 610–623). New York: Garland.

Strong, B., & DeVault, C. (1992). *The marriage and family experience*, 5th ed. New York: West Publishing.

Tapper, J. & Culhane, M. (2007, January 29). *She's the chief: From high school dropout to the capital's first female police chief*. Retrieved December 27, 2008, from http://abcnews.go.com/Nightline/Story?id=2821100&page=1

Violanti, J. M. (2000). A partnership against police domestic violence: The police and health care systems. In D. C. Sheehan (Ed.), *Domestic violence by police officers* (pp. 353–365). Washington, DC: U.S. Government Printing Office.

Weisz, A. (2005). Reaching African American battered women: Increasing the effectiveness of advocacy. *Journal of Family Violence, 20*, 91–99.

Wetendorf, D. (2006). *Crossing the threshold: Female officers and police-perpetrated domestic violence*. Arlington Heights, IL: Diane Wetendorf.

Wetendorf, D., & Davis, D. L. (2006). *Advocate and officer dialogues: Police-police perpetrated domestic violence*. Arlington Heights, IL: Diane Wetendorf.

Domestic Violence[1] Policy

Navigating a Path of Obstacles

12

CYNTHIA BROWN

Contents

Introduction

Historically, reproof has not been our legal system's response to domestic abuse (Lemon, 1996). For centuries authorities and the law tolerated, if not lauded, a husband's violence against his wife, as long as the husband's beating was a form of chastisement addressing an alleged offense by his spouse. Only when anger served as the motivation for the beating did a husband's violence toward his spouse garner criticism. Authorities disapproved of beatings out of anger because they viewed the husband's conduct as an abuse of his status, not because of concerns for the well-being of the wife (Amussen, 1994). It was not until the 1960s and the birth of a women's rights movement that the issue of domestic violence received national attention in the United States. It was only 40 years ago that our legal system acknowledged domestic violence as a serious harm and proscribed domestic violence as conduct in conflict with the law. Since that time the U.S. Supreme Court, the Congress, our state courts and legislatures have all promulgated a body of criminal, tort, and family laws that almost universally condemn domestic violence (Schneider, 2002). The path to condemnation, however, has been far from what could be considered a well-worn route (Lemon, 1996). While the last four decades have resulted in incredible social change in domestic violence law, the path of our nation's domestic violence policy more closely resembles one akin to an obstacle course.

History Repeats Itself

Over 2,700 years ago during the reign of Romulus in 753 b.c., the Romans adopted the *laws of chastisement*, accepting and condoning wife abuse. Roman society regarded the husband as the sole head of his household, and the marital power of the husband was absolute (Stedman, 1917). A Roman wife was her husband's inseparable possession, and as such, the husband could be held responsible for any crimes his wife might commit. The laws of chastisement arose as a means of protecting a man from the harm caused by his wife's misdeeds. This legal mechanism conferred authority to husbands, permitting wife beating with a rod or stick so long as the circumference was no greater than the girth of the base of the man's right thumb. "The rule of thumb," as the law became known, established a tradition that can be traced throughout most of Europe and into English common law (Straus and Gelles, 1986). Some maintain, however, that the rule of thumb was used more so in an allegorical sense rather than actual practice. Nonetheless, scholars still tend to disagree on how far authorities allowed a husband to go with his acceptable beatings. Some insist that the laws of chastisement possessed the husband with the right to beat, divorce, or murder his spouse for offenses that negatively impacted his honor or jeopardized his property rights (Okun, 1986). Others challenge the existence under Roman law of a husband's legal right to cause permanent injury or death (Hunter, 1980).

Notwithstanding the disagreement concerning the early limits on a husband's beating of his spouse, the later period of Roman law curtailed much of the previous authority a husband possessed over his wife. During the 600 years that followed the adoption of the laws of chastisement, Rome experienced significant changes in the family structure. Women gained more freedom and became entitled property owners in their own right. While husbands' chastisements were not prohibited, with these changes women received the right to sue their husbands if the beatings were unjustified (Tierney, 1982).

The wife's divestiture from her husband's authority was short-lived, however. As Christianity grew, church fathers took advantage of their popularity and reestablished the husband's patriarchal authority. The early Roman and Jewish law found favor with early Christian leaders who revived the principles, but over the course of time, the Christian church reacted with more ambivalence toward husband-initiated abuse. There have been times when the church encouraged husbands to demonstrate compassion for and moderation in punishment of their wives. There have also been times when the church supported the husbands' corporal punishment of their wives (Smith, 1988).

In the early 15th century, Bernard of Siena, a reformist friar later sainted, promoted compassion, urging his male parishioners to treat their wives with as much mercy as they would provide their hens and pigs. Reversing his predecessor's advice, Friar Cherubino of Siena published the *Rules of Marriage* later in the 15th century, vesting men with the authority to serve as the judges of their wives and to deliver beatings with a stick if a wife behaved offensively. Cherubino's rules included the following instructions:

> When you see your wife commit an offense, don't rush at her with insults and violent blows.... Scold her sharply, bully and terrify her. And if this doesn't work ... take up a stick and beat her soundly, for it is better to punish the body and correct the soul.... Readily beat her, not in rage but out of charity ... for her soul, so that the beating will rebound to your merit and her good. (England, 2009:2)

English law also tolerated and approved men's violence toward women, repeating the early Roman tradition throughout the 17th, 18th, and 19th centuries. The early common law of England mirrored the early Roman perspective of women and considered the wife as a property interest belonging to the husband. Perpetuating the rule of thumb, the law of England gave a husband the legal right to chastise his wife with a switch no larger than his thumb as necessary to maintain family discipline (Schneider, 2000). This authority was part of the "law of moderate correction" and allowed men to beat and abuse their wives in public without fear of interference from others (Stedman, 1917). In fact, old English common law tolerated a husband's murder of his wife without requiring any punishment for the act (Buzawa, 2003).

An acknowledged Anglo-American legal scholar, Sir William Blackstone wrote that a husband and wife were one, and that one was the husband. He acknowledged that a husband had a right to chastise his wife (Siegel, 1996). However, he also described the practice as antiquated and asserted that the practice persisted primarily among the British lower classes:

> But, with us, in the politer reign of Charles the Second, this power of correction began to be doubted; and a wife may now have security of the peace against her husband; or, in return, a husband against his wife. Yet the lower rank of people, who were always fond of the old common law, still claim and exert their ancient privilege: and the courts of law will still permit a husband to restrain a wife of her liberty, in case of any gross misbehavior. (Blackstone, 1979)

By the late 19th century women began to see reform in their treatment. With Queen Victoria's ascension to the throne, English lawmakers began enacting reforms relative to women. Women in England could no longer be kept under lock and key, and life-threatening beatings became recognized as justifiable grounds for divorce (England 2007; Buzawa and Buzawa, 2003).

Not unlike its English heritage, throughout a large part of legal history in the United States, a husband's right to chastise his wife was an acknowledged and approved practice. Anglo-American common law provided the husband with superiority over his wife in almost all aspects of the relationship. He acquired rights to her person, to the value of her labor—whether paid or unpaid—and the property she brought with her into the marriage. The husband also became legally responsible for his wife's conduct. The wife, on the other hand, was required to obey and serve her husband (Kent, 1827).

Instructed by the common law, the Supreme Court of Mississippi delivered this country's first court decision recognizing the husband's right to chastise his wife (*Bradley v. State*, 1824). The court held that a husband should still be permitted to exert the right to moderately chastise his wife in cases of great emergency, without subjecting himself to vexatious prosecution for assault and battery, resulting in the discredit and shame to all parties concerned. However, there is evidence within the opinion that the continued status of chastisement in the state was in doubt. The trial court in *Bradley* refused to instruct the jury that the defendant husband could not be found guilty of assault and battery if the jury found that the victim was, indeed, his wife. The state's supreme court upheld the trial court's ruling.

The temperance and abolitionist protests of the antebellum era provided the first organized protest against wife beating. The protesters did not question the husband's proclaimed authority over his wife, but challenged the violence that drunken husbands often inflicted on their families. Through these discussions of the social evils of alcohol printed in newspapers, poems, songs, and novels, protesters initiated public conversation about wife beating in a movement that was simultaneously radical and conservative. The denunciation of alcohol served as a vehicle for publicly discussing the unattractive social conditions of family life in an effort to protect the sanctity of the family life (Siegel, 1996).

The 19th century, an era of feminist agitation for reforms of the marriage laws, resulted in further progress. Though authorities in England and in the United States declared that husbands' chastisements of their wives would no longer be allowed, nearly a century passed with little or no intervention in cases involving marital violence. The privacy of the family and the importance of domestic harmony presented continuing obstacles guiding authorities to grant perpetrators formal and informal immunities from prosecution. Little impinged the continuing household violence (Siegel, 1996).

In addition to the temperance and abolitionist movements of the 19th century, women's rights advocates began speaking out at first throughout the Northeast and Midwest.

During the mid-1800s advocates espoused a Declaration of Sentiments and began identifying chastisement as part of a political system of male dominance, challenging the marital status rules of the common law and seeking the right to vote for women. In response, state legislatures and courts began to recognize a wife's right to hold property in marriage, the right to their earnings, and the right to file suit in their own names (Siegel, 1994).

These movements certainly influenced the Mississippi high court, which 70 years following *Bradley* repudiated its earlier "revolting precedent" writing that "this brutality found in the ancient common law, though strangely recognized ... has never since received countenance; and it is superfluous to now say that the blind adherence shown in that case to revolting precedent has long been utterly repudiated, in the administration of criminal law in our courts" (*Harris v. State*, 1894).

In 1864, 30 years prior to *Harris v. State*, the North Carolina Supreme Court issued the following decision:

> A husband is responsible for the acts of his wife, and he is required to govern his household, and for that purpose the law permits him to use towards his wife such a degree of force as is necessary to control an unruly temper and make her behave herself; and unless some permanent injury be inflicted, or there be excess of violence, or such a degree of cruelty as shows that it is inflicted to gratify his own bad passions, the law will not invade the domestic forum or go behind the curtain. It prefers to leave the parties to themselves, as the best mode of inducing them to make the matter up and live together as man and wife should. (*State v. Black*, 1864)

The North Carolina court refused, however, to sanction battery that "was so great and excessive as to put life and limb in peril, or where permanent injury to the person was inflicted, or where it was prompted by a malicious and wrongful spirit, and not within reasonable bounds" (*State v. Edens*, 1886, 696). Years later, the North Carolina court went even further, wholly renouncing the rule of thumb, holding that "the old doctrine that a husband has a right to whip his wife provided he used a switch no larger than his thumb, is not law in North Carolina. Indeed, the courts have advanced from that barbarism until they have reached the position that the husband has no right to chastise his wife under any circumstances" (*State v. Oliver*, 1874, 62). At that time the court regarded the *Oliver* decision "as the latest and best judicial expression of the law conforming to the sentiment of the most enlightened statesmen and jurists of the age" (*Powell v. Benthall*, 19, 154).

By the late 19th century, the American legal system had repudiated the doctrine of marital chastisement. This repudiation is, however, misleading as an indicator of how America's legal system responded to marital violence. Though legislators and jurists fervently condemned the chastisement doctrine, they habitually condoned the husband's chastising conduct, an impediment that perpetuates itself throughout most of the 20th century (Siegel, 1996).

In the 20th century, progress for women continued in educational, financial, and social equality with men, but unfortunately the obstacles continued as well. Cultural biases deeply ingrained in the legal tradition persisted and burdened women who were victims of domestic violence, sexual assault, and stalking (Valente, Hart, Zeya, & Melafyt, 2001). In California, for example, as recently as 1951, state law continued to give men complete legal control over all of their wives' earnings. Another example is provided by laws in most states in this country. Until 1988, most states' laws presumed that married women were the legal dependents of their husbands. This presumption took precedent unless evidence to the contrary was presented in court (Kay, 1988).

States' Response

The social activism of the 1960s highlighted oppressed groups, including children and women. This, and the added disenchantment with the traditional family, which also began in the 1960s, facilitated the acknowledgment of negative features of family life, including violence. As a result, the late 1960s saw a dramatic increase of pleas from battered women requesting safe shelter and protection from their partners. With no place to refer battered women, volunteers at women's centers across the country began opening their own homes to these victims of violence. Very quickly the demand became greater than available homes. Efforts to organize community assistance led to wide recognition that the legal and social service systems offered little assistance to abused women. More than homes serving as a refuge were needed. Legal services attorneys and practitioners met continuing challenges of inadequate remedies for women whose husbands employed violence as a means of coercion and control (Hart, 1992).

As a result, the 1970s brought the first significant challenges to the legal system's limited concept of women's rights. Lawyers and battered women advocates insisted that the law no longer could condone husbands' chastisements and coercive controls exercised against their wives. Further, these individuals worked to refocus the legal system's emphasis from one on the victim's behavior to one on the perpetrator's misconduct. By pushing for new state legislation, they began the journey to change the legal culture that blamed women for the violence inflicted upon them (Valente et al., 2001).

The first important change in state law was the promulgation of statutes that permitted victims of domestic violence to obtain civil protection orders (sometimes referred to as injunctions, restraining orders, protection from abuse orders, harassment orders, stalking orders, stay-away orders, no-contact orders, protection orders incorporated into divorce decrees, conditions of release orders, and probation orders) issued by a judge usually in family court. Prior to the creation of the civil protective or restraining order system, battered women had to initiate divorce proceedings before requesting protection from our legal system (Valente et al., 2001). Thus, civil protection orders were the first step toward advancing the autonomy and independence of the battered woman from her abuser (Hart, 1992).

The new remedy was designed to constrain an abusing husband from interfering with or disrupting the lives of his wife and children. It provided mothers with the authority to act as the primary caretaker of her children, further constraining or limiting the father from taking the children in an effort to force reconciliation or penalize his wife. Consequently, this remedy that did not displace an abused wife from her home but could compel the abusing spouse to relocate. It also aided in providing stability and predictability for an abused woman and her children (Dalton & Schneider, 2001).

To garner the protection provided by the order, a victim files a petition requesting the court to protect her from acts, such as physical abuse, threats of harm, or harassing actions, committed by her spouse, ex-spouse, or intimate partner, subject to state law provisions. The court usually schedules a hearing, notifies the alleged abuser, receives testimony and evidence, and issues findings on whether domestic violence occurred. If the evidence supports a finding of domestic abuse, the judge then issues a protective order that outlines what an abuser can and cannot do. The orders may provide any number of allowable remedies necessary to protect the victim. A state's protective remedies may include ordering the abuser to refrain further violent or threatening behavior, ordering the abuser to refrain from all contact with the victim, ordering the abuser to relocate from the home with the victim, and providing custody of any children to the nonabusive parent (Valente et al., 2001).

The application of protective orders to domestic violence was a progressive step and provided victims the ability to control the initiation of the court processes. There was no longer the need to wait on a prosecutor to proceed with a criminal action. The abused had immediate entry into a legal forum and the possibility of its protections. Further, the amount of proof necessary to avail oneself of the law's protections was significantly reduced in civil court, compared to that required in criminal court. Also important is the social change brought by the acknowledgment by our legal system's guardians that certain patterns of actions engaged in by a spouse or other intimate partner constituted a prohibited activity known as domestic abuse (Valente et al., 2001). By 1994, every state and the District of Columbia had enacted a domestic violence statute providing protection from abusive acts perpetrated or threatened by a member of the family or household.

Federal Response

Eventually, states' legislative changes to family and criminal laws concerning domestic violence proved inadequate to wholly resolve the problems that arose in these and sexual assault cases. Protection order statutes evolved separately across the states, and a protection order statute was specific to the state in which it originated, and though perhaps similar to another jurisdiction's statutes, rarely contained identical laws. Likewise, the statutory sanctions differed across jurisdictions. Often victims from differing states did not have access to the same levels of protection, and consequently, heightened protections were not available to all victims. Some jurisdictions allowed protective orders only for victims of heterosexual relationships; others included only victims in relationships where the partners cohabitated. Some states offered protections for victims of same-sex relationships or dating relationships. Another consequence of these differences is most jurisdictions did not recognize the protective orders issued by other states. The result was that authorities refused to enforce those protections issued by sister jurisdictions (Valente et al., 2001). Additionally, state legislatures lacked the authority to require other states to enforce their laws. Enforcement was uneven and little could be accomplished by the states (Renzetti, Edelson, & Bergen, 2001).

Another issue arose in jurisdictions where judges continued to make judgments based on the historical gender-dominant view that subordinated women to men. In these jurisdictions, judges declined to invoke or enforce their state's protective laws, leaving battered women with little recourse for assistance (Renzetti et al., 2001). Consequently, even where protections were established, those entrusted with delivering protection did not always act to do so.

At a minimum, all victims did not receive consistent degrees of protection. Uneven state laws and immovable judges contributed to the inequities but presented only two examples of the continuing barriers advocates battled in their efforts to ensure uniform protections for victims of domestic violence. The state law inequities presented a particularly troublesome obstacle. The decentralization efforts of our country's original legal architects worked to ensure that the individual states maintained the necessary powers to determine the laws specific to them. The creation and implementation of family law had historically been the province of the states (*In re Burrus*, 1890).

The state law inequities presented a particularly troublesome obstacle. The decentralization efforts of our country's original legal architects worked to ensure that the individual states maintained the necessary powers to determine the laws specific to them. The creation and implementation of family law had historically been the province of the states (*In re Burrus*, 1890). Domestic violence falls within the parameters of family law, and therefore is left exclusively to the state legislatures to address. Typically, domestic violence would not have been a matter even considered approachable by Congress. Unfortunately, the continuing inequities among the states and the rising challenges presented by domestic violence and sexual assault cases demonstrated that the individual states were ill-equipped to entirely resolve the issues solely through changes to the states' family and criminal laws (Renzetti et al., 2001).

The states' legal interventions marked progress but demonstrated the limits of the states' abilities to combat domestic violence (Kelly, 2003). Broader help was needed, and victim advocates targeted Congress for assistance. A series of U.S. Supreme Court decisions helped to make a congressional approach feasible. First, the court judicially recognized that situations existed in which federal law rather than state law might better address some family law concerns (*Hisquierdo v. Hisquierdo*, 1978).

Second, a line of Supreme Court cases resulted from the civil rights movement, which began in the 1950s. These established that the Constitution empowered Congress with the legislative authority to address unequal or discriminatory treatment as violations of an individual's civil rights. The uneven protections afforded domestic violence victims resulting from the various state protective remedies provided advocates with evidence of discriminatory impact. This provided the requisite threshold to argue the necessity of invoking Congress's authority to enact legislation to protect individuals from state action that would "deny any person within its jurisdiction the equal protection of the laws" (U.S. Constitution, 14th Amendment, Section 5; Renzetti et al., 2001).

Most notably, decades of cases stemming from the Depression era had determined that the Constitution established congressional authority to address legislation on issues that affected interstate commerce (U.S. Constitution, Article I, Section 8, Clause 3; *Heart of Atlanta Motel, Inc. v. U.S.*, 1964) A possible solution arose if domestic violence, sexual assault, and stalking presented issues that also affected interstate commerce. If so, then these issues appropriately fell within the discretion of Congress (Valente et al., 2001).

Relying on these and other interpretations by the U.S. Supreme Court, victim advocates approached Congress, calling attention to the prevalence of violence being perpetrated against women and requesting it address the inconsistencies and gaps in state laws addressing violence against women. Advocates also sought funding to train law enforcement, prosecutors, and court personnel about domestic violence, sexual assault, and stalking in hopes that better understanding of these issues would improve responses to these acts (Valente et al., 2001).

From 1990 to 1994, Congress convened hearings to determine whether domestic violence, sexual assault, and stalking affected interstate commerce sufficiently to trigger its authority to enact legislation concerning these issues. The hearings generated great debate and controversy, but they also resulted in significant research about the victims of domestic violence. The research revealed that millions of women each year in the United States were victims of domestic violence, that domestic violence was the leading cause of injury to American women, and that the annual cost of domestic violence in health care, investigative and protective services, lost worker productivity, and to the criminal justice system (including law enforcement and the courts) exceeded $5 billion (Valente et al., 2001).

The Conference of Chief Judges and the Judicial Conference of the United States entered the debates in opposition to the proposed civil rights legislation, asserting that it could "cause major state-federal jurisdictional problems and disruptions in the processing of domestic relations cases in state courts" (Crimes of Violence Motivated by Gender, 1993, p. 80). The state court judges were concerned that federal domestic violence legislation "would impair the ability of state courts to manage criminal and family matters traditionally entrusted to the states" (Crimes of Violence Motivated by Gender, 1993, pp. 83–84). No one criticized the proposed legislation's intent of protecting women. The argument centered on the creation of a federal cause of action to address domestic violence, sexual assault, and stalking that usurped the interest of the states and threatened to create a deluge of new cases for the federal judiciary who were not well equipped to handle them (Siegel, 1996).

Former Senate Judiciary Committee chairman Senator Joseph Biden, the bill's original sponsor, joined with Senator Orrin Hatch (then ranking minority member of the committee) to draft a version of the proposed legislation that would defer to the states their traditional role in regulating matters of marriage and divorce, and also that would offer some protection to the federal dockets from overcrowding with cases that the new legislation might create.

In 1994, Congress passed the Violence Against Women Act (VAWA) as Title IV of the Omnibus Crime Control and Law Enforcement Act of 1994, and with its enactment the first federal legislation to specifically target the problem of violence against women came into existence (Violence Against Women Act, 1994). The resulting statute provided that "all persons within the United States shall have the right to be free from crimes of violence motivated by gender" (Violence Against Women Act, 1994; Siegel, 1996). It is the embodiment of a group of individually conceived, debated, and negotiated legislative pieces that addressed domestic violence[2] and sexual assault.

VAWA is the most publicized portion of the Violent Crime Control and Law Enforcement Act, which is a comprehensive piece of federal legislation intended to "allow grants to increase police presence, to expand and improve cooperative efforts between law enforcement agencies and members of the community to address crime and disorder problems, and otherwise to enhance public safety" (Stevenson, 1997, pp. 855–856). The primary purpose of VAWA is to provide local authorities with the resources to protect women from assaults and acts of rape by spouses or intimate partners (Siegel, 1996). The provisions introduced in VAWA include funding for women's shelters, establishing the National Domestic Violence Hotline, providing rape education and prevention programs, and training for federal and state judges (Schneider, 2000).

VAWA also includes multiple provisions aimed at raising awareness of the existence of violence against women (Feeney, 2007), and further provides female domestic violence victims a level of protection never before afforded to them (Siegel, 1996). Five predominant sections of the legislation, however, have perhaps had the greatest impact on improving the handling of crimes of violence against women in the United States. The first of these is the "full faith and credit provision," requiring states, territories, and tribes to enforce protection orders originating in other jurisdictions as vigorously and as completely as they would their own (18 USC §§2265, 2266). The second is the creation by Congress of a crime to commit domestic violence across state lines. Prior to this piece of federal legislation, states and territories possessed the authority to address only those crimes committed wholly within their borders (18 USC §§2261, 2262). Relatedly, VAWA also makes it a crime to violate the terms of a protection order in the course of crossing state, territorial, or tribal lines (18 USC §2262).

VAWA's third influential provision addresses battered immigrant women (18 USC §1154(a)(1)(A)(i)–(iii)). Before this legislation, a spouse seeking permanent legal residence in the United States had to rely on a spouse who was already an American citizen or legal permanent resident to file *and* follow through on the immigration petition. VAWA's provision permits a battered immigrant who satisfies the threshold requirements to apply for legal permanent residency without the spouse's assistance through self-petitioning. Similarly, there is also a VAWA provision enabling battered immigrant women who are subject to deportation to petition the Immigration and Naturalization Service for a cancellation of removal, eliminating the threat of deportation.

A fourth significant provision of VAWA is a 1994 amendment to the Gun Control Act (18 USC §921, *et seq.*). The amendment includes four firearm prohibitions related to domestic violence, making it a federal crime to possess a firearm or ammunition if one is subject to certain types of protective orders or has been convicted of certain types of misdemeanor domestic violence crimes (18 USC §922(g)(1)–(9)) It is also unlawful to transfer a firearm or ammunition to another who is known to be subject to certain types of protective orders.

A fifth provision of great import was the creation of three new federal grant programs administered by the U.S. Department of Justice's Violence Against Women Office. These include the Grants to Encourage Arrest (42 USC §3796hh), the Law Enforcement and Prosecution Grants to Reduce Violent Crimes Against Women (popularly known as the STOP Violence Against Women Formula Grant Program and the STOP Violence Against Indian Women Grant Program, 42 USC §3796gg), and the Rural Domestic Violence and Child Abuse Enforcement Assistance Grants (42 USC §13971).

These programs have generated hundreds of millions of dollars to local programs to provide direct services to victims of domestic abuse.

Arguably the most innovative and controversial aspect of VAWA was its development of a civil rights remedy for gender violence that allowed victims of domestic abuse to sue for damages in civil court (Violence Against Women Act, 1994). The U.S. Supreme Court overturned this provision of the act, holding that Congress lacked the authority to implement such a law. The Supreme Court invalidated VAWA's civil rights provision on the ground that gender-motivated domestic violence crimes are not considered economic activity. Consequently, Congress did not have the authority under the Commerce Clause to enact a civil rights provision such as provided for in VAWA. Further, the court found that the provision exceeded Congress's power under Section 5 of the 14th Amendment (*United States v. Morrison*, 2000). All other provisions of the act remained effective.

Congress reauthorized the VAWA in 2000 and included crimes of dating violence[3] and stalking.[4] It reauthorized VAWA again in 2005, expanding on the progress achieved over the last decade since the original enactment. In 2005, Congress included important new housing provisions, which mark the first federal housing protections for victims of domestic violence, dating violence, and stalking. VAWA became effective on January 5, 2006, with the new housing programs, which began on October 1, 2006. These provisions included funding for housing services, including grant programs for public and assisted housing agencies to address domestic violence through agency policy changes, training, and best practices; amendments to the McKinney-Vento Homeless Assistance Act to ensure safety and confidentiality for victims in the Homeless Management Information System; amendments to ensure that the needs of domestic violence victims are considered in the local planning processes; requirements for VAWA implementation for public housing authorities; new grant program to ensure local community collaboration in developing long-term affordable housing for domestic violence victims; and protections against discriminatory denials and evictions in public and Section 8 housing for victims of domestic violence, dating violence, and stalking (Violence Against Women Act, 2006).

VAWA's passage and the lengthy road to its enactment provided monumental strides in raising awareness of issues regarding domestic violence, dating violence, sexual assault, and stalking. Advocates worked for change and achieved substantiation for the harmful conduct suffered by victims at the hands of their abusers. Statistical and empirical data were gathered, presented, and preserved to demonstrate the crimes of violence against women and successfully assisted in raising concerns to a new national interest. Further, the creation of new federal crimes shifted how violative conduct was addressed at the state level. Further still, VAWA has spawned a climate of victim safety and offender accountability (Valente et al., 2001).

Endnotes

1. The American Bar Association (ABA) Commission on Domestic Violence has defined domestic violence as follows:

   A pattern of behavior that one intimate partner or spouse exerts over another as a means of control. Domestic violence may include physical violence, coercion, threats, intimidation, isolation, and emotional, sexual or economic abuse. Frequently perpetrators use the children to manipulate victims: by harming or abducting the children; by threatening to harm or abduct the children; by forcing the children to participate in abuse of the victim; by using visitation as an occasion to harass or monitor victims; or by fighting protracted custody battles to punish victims. Perpetrators often invent complex rules about what victims or the children can or cannot do, and force victims to abide by these frequently changing roles.

   The ABA cautions readers to consider this broader definition in conjunction with state and federal law definitions (American Bar Association, 2003).

2. *Domestic violence*, as defined in VAWA,

   includes felony or misdemeanor crimes of violence committed by a current or former spouse of the victim, by a person with whom the victim shares a child in common, by a person who is cohabitating with or has cohabitated with the victim as a spouse, by a person similarly situated to a spouse of the victim under the domestic or family violence laws of the jurisdiction receiving grant monies, or by any other adult person against a victim who is protected from that person's acts under the domestic or family violence laws of the jurisdiction receiving grant monies. (Violence Against Women Act, 1994)

3. The VAWA defines *dating violence* as

   violence committed by a person who is or has been in a social relationship of a romantic or intimate nature with the victim, and where the existence of such a relationship shall be determined based on a consideration of the following factors: the length of the relationship, the type of relationship and the frequency of interaction between the persons involved in the relationship. (Violence Against Women Act, 2000)

4. The VAWA defines *stalking* as follows:

   To follow, pursue or repeatedly commit acts with the intent to kill, injure, harass, or intimidate; or to place under surveillance with the intent to kill, injure, harass, or intimidate another person; and in the course of, or as a result of, such following, pursuit, surveillance, or repeatedly committed acts, to place a person in reasonable fear of the death of, or serious bodily injury to, or to cause substantial emotional harm to: that person; a member of the immediate family of that person; or the spouse or intimate partner of that person. (Violence Against Women Act, 2000)

References

American Bar Association. (2003). *Teach your students well: Incorporating domestic violence into law school curricula* (DOJ Grant 98-WL-VX-0032). Chicago: ABA Printing Department.

Amussen, S. D. (1994). Being stirred to much unquietness: Violence anddomestic violence in early modern England. *Journal of Women's History 6*, 70–89.

Blackstone, W. (1979). *Commentaries on the laws of England* (Book I). Chicago: University of Chicago Press. (Original work published 1765).

Bradley v. State. (1824). 2 Miss. (Walker) 156.

Buzawa, E. S. & Buzawa, C. G. (2003). *Domestic violence: The criminal justice response.* Thousand Oaks, CA: Sage.

Crimes of violence motivated by gender. Hearing before the Subcommittee on Civil and Constitutional Rights of the House Committee on the Judiciary, 103rd Congress, 1st Session 80. (1993). Statement by Conference of Chief Justices on S. 15, Violence Against Women Act of 1991, adopted by the State-Federal Relations Committee of the Conference of Chief Justices at meeting in Scottsdale, AZ, on January 31, 1991.

Dalton, C., & Schneider, E. (2001). *Battered women and the law.* New York: Foundation Press.

Dugan, L. (2002). *Domestic violence legislation: Exploring its impact on domestic violence and the likelihood that police are informed and arrest* (DOJ 196853). College Park, MD: Department of Criminology and Criminal Justice.

Feeney, D., Jr. (2007). Ensuring the domestic violence victim a means of communication: Why passing legislation that criminalizes impairing another's communication is the next logical step in combating domestic violence. *Seton Hall Legislative Journal, 32,* 167.

Harris v. State. 71 Miss. 462, 14 So. 266 (1894).

Hart, B. (1992). State codes on domestic violence: Analysis, commentary and recommendations. *Juvenile and Family Court Journal, 3,* 23–24.

Heart of Atlanta Motel, Inc. v. United States. 379 U.S. 241 (1964).

Hisquierdo v. Hisquierdo. 439 U.S. 572 (1978).

Hunter, W. A. (Ed.), The Edinburgh University Calendar 1882–1883. (1882). *Introduction to Roman Law,* p. 70.

In re Burrus. 136 U.S. 586 (1890).

Kelly, K. (2003). *Domestic violence and the politics of privacy.* Ithaca, NY: Cornell University Press.

Kent, J. (1827). *Commentaries on American law.* New York: O. Halstead.

Lemon, N. K. D. (1996). *Domestic violence law reader.* Bethesda, MD: Austin & Winfield Publishers.

Lemon, N. K. D. (2001). Statutes creating rebuttable presumptions against custody to batterers: How effective are they? *William Mitchell Law Review 28,* 601–676.

Miller, N. (2002). *Review of state laws relevant to violence against women (domestic violence, sexual assault, stalking, and related laws).* Alexandria, VA: Institute for Law and Justice.

Okun, L. (1986). *Woman abuse: Facts replacing myths.* Albany: SUNY Press.

Powell v. Benthall. 136 N. C. 145, 48 S. E. 598 (1924).

Renzetti, C. M., Edelson, J. L., & Bergen, R. K. (Eds.) 2001. *Sourcebook on violence against women.* Thousand Oaks, CA: Sage.

Schneider, E. M. (2000). *Battered women and feminist lawmaking.*

Schneider, E. M. (2002). Battered women and feminist lawmaking. *Women's Rights Law Reporter, 23,* 243.

Siegel, R. B. (1994). The modernization of marital status law: Adjudicating wives' rights to earnings, 1860–1930. *Georgetown Law Journal, 82,* 2127.

Siegel, R. B. (1996). "The rule of love": Wife beating as prerogative and privacy. *Yale Law Journal, 105,* 2117.

State v. Black. 60 N.C. 262, 86 Am. Dec. 436 (1864).

State v. Edens. 95 N. C. 696, 59 Am. Rep. 294 (1886).

State v. Oliver. 70 N. C. 60 (1874).

Stevenson, G. B. (1997). Federal antiviolence and abuse legislation: Toward elimination of disparate justice for women and children. *Willamette Law Review, 33,* 847.

Straus, M. A., & Gelles, R. J. (1986). Societal chagne in family from 1985 as revealed in two national surveys. *Journal of Marriage and Family, 48,* 3:207–220.

Tierney, K. T. (1982). The battered woman movement and the creation of the wife beating problem. *Social Problems, 29,* 3:207–220.

U.S. Constitution, 14th Amendment, Section 5.

U.S. Constitution, Article I, Section 8, Clause 3.

United States v. Morrison. 529 U.S. 598 (2000).

Valente, R. L., Hart, B. J., Zeya, S., & Melafyt, M. (2001). *The Violence Against Women Act of 1994: The federal commitment to ending domestic violence, sexual assault, stalking, and gender-based crimes of violence.*

Violence Against Women Act of 1994. 42 USCA §13981 (West 1995).

Civil Protection Orders Against Domestic Violence

13

The Fight Against Domestic Violence by Orange County, Florida

ROBERT T. MAGILL
WALTER KOMANSKI

Contents

Introduction

"… and they lived happily ever after."

This is perhaps the most famous, and most cliché, ending of numerous fairy tales, and is usually the goal of every marital relationship. Unfortunately, for far too many partners, there is to be an ending far from happy. Disagreements dissolve into bitter arguments. Tempers flare out of control. One or both turn to alcohol or other drugs for relief, only to discover such distractions exacerbate the situation. The long exposure to domestic violence comes full circle, and the son abuses his wife just as his father did to his mother. In the case of others, the relationship dissolves into abuse quickly, long before the opportunity to "live happily ever after" even arises, while other personal interactions, wholly unromantic in nature, can also collapse into violence, leaving a victim fearful that harm may soon return again.

To seek solace, a victim of violence, either domestic in nature or just simply interpersonal, is able to seek not only the assistance of law enforcement, but also the protection of the courts in the form of a protection order. Such protection orders prevent, by threat of imprisonment, any further physical contact or even communication by the abuser toward a victim. These protection orders are a civil remedy, obtained not in a criminal court, but instead from a domestic relations judge, who can enter a temporary protection order within hours. Such emergency orders are available in all 50 states, and recent studies reveal that many times a civil protection order is sought in lieu of reporting the violence to law enforcement (Keilitz, Hannaford, & Efkeman, 1997, p. 12).

Once a civil petition for protection is filed, a court official will typically review the petition and either dismiss it or grant a temporary order preventing the abuser from having any further contact with the victim. As soon as practicable, the court will next hold a hearing, offering both the victim and the accused an opportunity to be heard. After each party has presented its case, the court will then either deny the petition and dismiss the action, or enter a permanent injunction for a period of time, which may be custom tailored to address any issues between the parties, such as property distribution or visitation for children. In order to provide examples of the mechanics of this legal procedure, this chapter will not only address nationwide issues in obtaining a civil protection order, but also focus on the court system in Florida, with a specific spotlight on the domestic violence courts in Orange County, Florida.

Statistical Examination

Unhappily, far too many victims do not avail themselves of the remedy of a civil protection order. The National Violence Against Women Survey of 2000 found that only 16.4% of rape victims, 17.1% of assault victims, and 36.6% of stalking victims sought such protection. Different studies show that somewhere between 12% and 22% of women who suffer domestic violence abuse seek the assistance of protection orders (Klein, 2008, p. 58). Once a victim chooses to seek the assistance of the courts, however, help is usually provided. In 2007, for example, a total of 6,281 petitions for protection were filed in Orange County, Florida, 5,434 (or 86.5%) of which were either denied (but scheduled for a hearing) or granted on a temporary basis. (More on how a petition can by denied but scheduled for a hearing can be found later in this chapter.) In either case, a hearing before the court was scheduled within 15 days of the petition being reviewed, and after being heard, 1,480 permanent injunction orders were issued.

It is incumbent upon the victim to appear before the court or the temporary protective order will automatically expire. In 2007, of the 5,434 cases scheduled to be heard by the Orange County court, only 2,508 (or 46%) were actually heard. After being heard by the court, a permanent injunction was granted 58% of the time, for a total of 1,480 permanent injunctions ordered. The remaining petitions were dismissed, either because the petitioner requested the dismissal or because the petitioner failed to appear at the hearing to determine whether a permanent injunction was appropriate.

Types of Injunctions

A victim of violence is afforded four avenues of protection under Florida law. What is commonly referred to as a restraining order is, in Florida, legally referred to as an injunction, and can be obtained to protect a victim from domestic, repeat, dating, or sexual violence. The circumstances experienced by the victim will determine the form of injunction to be pursued, and it is important that a victim petition for the correct type of injunction, as each has differing requirements of proof.

Possibly the most well-known type of injunction is that which is designed to prevent domestic violence. Under §741.28, Florida Statutes, Florida law specifically defines domestic violence as any assault, battery, stalking, kidnapping, false imprisonment, or other criminal offense that causes an injury or death of one family household member by another. A family member is specifically defined as "spouses, former spouses, persons related by blood or marriage, any person who is or was residing within a single dwelling with petitioner as if a family, or a person with whom the petitioner has a child in common." If the perpetrator of the violent act falls within this definition of family member, it is sufficient for the petitioner to allege that threats of violence were made that caused the petitioner to be reasonably fearful that an actual act of violence was imminent. In other words, the petitioner can allege assault and need not allege a physical attack or multiple acts of violence.

Multiple acts of violence or stalking are, however, required in order to file for protection against repeat violence, which is addressed under a completely different statute, §784.046, Florida Statutes. Simply alleging threats of violence or a fear of impending violence is not sufficient for this type of injunction; two or more actual incidents of violence must have occurred. Additionally, one of those acts must have occurred within six months of the filing of the petition, and the act must have been directed toward the petitioner or an immediate family member of the petitioner. This form of injunction was created to protect against violence committed by individuals who do not fall under the definition of family members. In the words of Florida Administrative Judge Amy Karan, "Repeat violence cases have become mostly love triangle cases (new girlfriend v. old girlfriend, former husband v. new husband, etc.), employer-employee and co-worker relationships, schoolmates, neighborhood disputes, and roommates who do not have a dating or intimate relationship" (Karan & Lazarus, 2008, p. 191).

If the petitioner is currently in an intimate relationship with the alleged attacker, or has just ended the relationship, it would be appropriate to seek an injunction for protection against dating violence. Defined in §784.046(d) of the Florida Statutes, dating violence means "violence between individuals who have or have had a continuing and significant relationship of a romantic or intimate nature." To determine whether the relationship of the parties rises to that level, several factors are enumerated for the court to consider, which include whether there was any mutual expectation "of affection or sexual involvement between the parties" and whether the "frequency and type of interaction between the persons involved" indicated a continuous relationship, which must have existed within the six months preceding the filing of the petition. Dating violence does not include violence occurring in a casual acquaintanceship or "between individuals who have only engaged in ordinary fraternization in a business or social context." In other words, dating violence is between people who consider themselves "boyfriend" and "girlfriend" and not just "friends." Also, as with petitions for protection against domestic violence, dating violence petitions need only petition a reasonable belief of imminent violence and need only allege one act of such violence in order to meet the statutory threshold. It is also permitted, under the statute, for a parent of a minor involved in a dating relationship to bring such a petition to the court on that child's behalf.

The last form of injunction that may be heard by a Florida court is one for protection against sexual violence. Referring to definitions provided in other sections of Florida law, §784.046(1)(c), Florida Statutes, defines sexual violence as any one incident of sexual battery, lewd or lascivious conduct committed upon or in the presence of a person younger than 16 years of age, luring or enticing a child, sexual performance by a child, or any other felony wherein a sexual act is committed or attempted. A unique element of this type of injunction is the requirement, under §784.046(2)(c), that the petitioner must have reported the act to law enforcement or the respondent in the petition has been previously sentenced and is serving a jail sentence that will expire within 90 days of the filing of the petition. As many of the acts detailed under the statute are committed against minors, it is, of course, acceptable for a parent or legal guardian to bring the petition to the court on behalf of a child victim.

Seeking Assistance and Filing the Petition

In Orange County, victims of domestic violence can seek the assistance of counselors at Harbor House, a shelter located within the courthouse itself. At Harbor House, victims can find the support needed to overcome the trauma they have experienced. Counselors at Harbor House are able to help victims obtain professional care and satisfy any special needs they may have, including alternative housing, create and implement a safety plan geared toward the prevention of further violence, and provide aid in obtaining all legal protections available to them. Counselors can also collect any evidence of the violence, most often in the form of photographs of the victim, which will be used later by the court. But, perhaps the best intangible item Harbor House, and the similar offices throughout the state of Florida, can offer is the safety and comfort so desperately needed by victims of domestic violence—someone at Harbor House will listen, will comfort, will counsel, and will help to make life safe again. To secure that safe future, one of the first steps a counselor at Harbor House does is to encourage and even take the victim to the third floor of the Orange County courthouse and through the door of the clerk's injunctions office. (It is appropriate to note that, while we use the word *she* here, not all victims of domestic violence are women. Many men, in fact, seek the assistance of Harbor House and there is, of course, absolutely no shame in doing so.) (Oksnar, personal communication, October 27, 2008).

It is, of course, not necessary, or even appropriate, for every victim of a violent act to first seek the assistance of Harbor House prior to walking through the clerk's door. Some individuals have resources that others lack. Also, there are, as discussed above, other forms of violence against which someone would seek protection other than domestic in nature. But, though not all forms of violence are domestic in nature, the procedure to obtain whichever type of injunction is roughly the same for everyone in this office. And, for each type of injunction, there are no filing fees charged or any court costs assessed (§741.30(2)(a) and §784.046(3)(b), Florida Statutes).

A friendly deputy clerk is the first person who greets any entrant to this office and who will offer clerical assistance to anyone who wishes to file a petition for an injunction. A few questions from the clerk will determine which of the types of injunctions should be pursued, and the clerk will continue to ask questions in order to complete the information necessary to prepare the statutorily mandated form of the petition. These questions are very basic in nature, such as name, address, workplace, and description of the respondent, as well as similar basic information of the petitioner. At no time does a clerk offer any advice as to how to answer the questions, nor, of course, is any advice of a legal nature given. The assistance provided is merely clerical and meant only to elicit responses to properly complete the form of the petition on the clerk's computer system. It is the responsibility of the petitioner to properly answer the questions and to handwrite an affidavit that details the reasons for the filing of the injunction. This part of the petition is most important, as it is to these allegations a judge will later look to determine whether the granting of a temporary injunction is appropriate. A Harbor House counselor is likely to assist in the completion of the petition, and if photographs were taken of any injuries, those will be included with the petition. Also, if law enforcement was called to the scene of the incident and a report or arrest record is in the possession of a petitioner, copies of those reports or records are also included with the petition (Oksnar, personal communication, October 27, 2008).

Once all the questions have been completed, and the affidavit has been finalized, the clerk will print out the form for the petitioner to review. Any changes necessary will then be made, and a final form will be executed by the petitioner before the clerk, who acts as the notary for the petitioner's signature. At this point, the case now leaves the hands of the petitioner and takes a "behind the scenes" path for the next hour or two.

Ex Parte Review

A petition for injunction will now become a formal court file and, along with any other cases that may have previously or contemporaneously been filed between these parties or by this petitioner, will be forwarded to court administration for formal processing. At this stage, each case is tentatively scheduled for a hearing date, which must, by statute, occur within 15 days, as no temporary injunction, if granted, can last for more than those 15 days (§741.30(5)(b) and §784.046(6)(c), Florida Statutes). Three forms are then prepared, each reflecting the possible dispositions of the petition: a temporary injunction order; a denial of the petition, with the legal grounds for the denial; or a notice of hearing, providing not a temporary injunction, but an opportunity for the parties to appear before a judge and explain the case in more detail. These files and possible orders are then taken to a judge on a roughly hourly basis during normal working hours and, in the case of injunctions being sought outside of business hours, upon their completion to a judge who remains available to review them 24 hours a day (Oksnar, personal communication, October 27, 2008).

In Orange County, each petition is then reviewed by a judge from the domestic violence division. Though the petitions are not all for injunctions against domestic violence, these judges are assigned all injunction petitions for review for the sake of expediency. Under §741.30(5)(a), Florida Statutes, a court may grant at an *ex parte* proceeding a temporary injunction for protection against domestic violence when "it appears to the court that an immediate and present danger of domestic violence exists." There are enumerated in §741.30(6)(b), Florida Statutes, 10 factors the court *must* consider in determining whether a petitioner has a reasonable fear or cause to fear an immediate and present danger of domestic violence. Some of the factors include the relationship status of the parties; whether the respondent has committed other acts of violence, such as threatening to harm or actually harming any other family member or any children, as well as killing or injuring a family pet; whether any prior injunctions have been filed or granted; and any criminal history of the respondent. Of course, the court may also consider any other relevant matters that may demonstrate a petitioner's reasonable fear. Although not specifically required to, these factors will also be considered when deciding whether to grant a temporary injunction for protection against repeat, dating, or sexual violence. (§784.046(6)(a), Florida Statutes, only holds that such an injunction may be granted when "it appears to the court that an immediate and present danger of violence exists.").

Before a judge reviews whether any "immediate and present danger of violence exists," the first step is, of course, to ascertain that standing is appropriate for the type of injunction being sought. As discussed above, each type of injunction has specific requirements. For example, it would be inappropriate to file for protection against domestic violence for a violent act by a former boyfriend who is no longer living with the petitioner and with whom there are no children. The statutory definition of "family member" does not include such a person. Repeat violence, however, would be the appropriate injunction in such a situation. Additionally, a petitioner seeking an injunction to protect his or her minor child must properly note that the petition is being brought on behalf of that child; many times a parent will inadvertently misfile the petition and seek an injunction between the parent and respondent and not between the child and respondent. Such a lack of standing, obviously, will lead to the dismissal of the petition on legal grounds.

If standing is properly plead, the judge will then review the affidavit for the existence of immediate and present danger of violence, taking into consideration each of the relevant elements of §741.30(6)(b), if appropriate, and any other important issues. Perhaps the best method of demonstrating this process is through examples.

CASE A

Sally, the petitioner, alleges that she is a victim of domestic violence. Her former boyfriend, Jim, is the father of their one-year-old son, Freddie, and they all lived together until two weeks ago, when Sally and Freddie moved out of the apartment and moved in with her parents. She left, she says, because Jim recently became addicted to prescription pain medication, which he takes while excessively drinking beer. In this state he becomes belligerent and, on two occasions, has hit her. The last straw was when she found out he used rent money to illegally buy more pain medication. On the morning of the filing of her petition, she states that she had to go to their apartment to get some of Freddie's clothes. Jim, thankfully, was not there, so she was able to get the clothes and leave. At a stop sign down the street, however, Jim was riding in a car with his new girlfriend and saw Sally. He jumped out of the car, approached the front of Sally's van, preventing her from moving forward. It was obvious to Sally that Jim was under the influence of either alcohol or drugs. He screamed obscenities and for her to get out of the van. When she refused, he pulled a gun out of his pocket and began screaming more obscenities at her, threatening to shoot her and Freddie. In order to try and get away, Sally began backing the van up, hoping to turn around in a driveway. Jim jumped on the hood of the van and, with the gun and his boots, shattered and kicked in the windshield, sending shattered glass all over Sally and their son. Jim at this point lost his balance and fell off the van. Sally, now in tears, grabbed her phone and called 911. Seeing this, Jim ran away, toward his apartment, while the new girlfriend drove off in a different direction. Though she wanted to drive as far away as possible, the 911 dispatcher told Sally to remain at the scene and a police officer quickly arrived. After seeing the van and hearing Sally's description of the events, the police officer and Sally drove to the apartment together, where they found Jim feigning sleep. After questioning Jim, the police officer found probable cause and arrested Jim, giving to Sally a copy of the arrest report. At the officer's suggestion, Sally went to the courthouse and filed a petition for injunction against domestic violence.

This case is relatively straightforward. The first step, of course, is to analyze whether the proper petition has been filed. In this case, the parties used to live together as a family and have a child in common, so the standing requirements are in two respects satisfied. The next step is to examine whether an act of violence or threat of domestic violence has occurred, or whether the petitioner has a reasonable fear that an act of domestic violence will occur. During this examination, the judge should keep in mind the many factors that must be considered under the statute. Some of the factors relevant here are whether the respondent has used or threatened to use any weapons, such as guns or knives; whether the respondent has destroyed any personal property; and whether the respondent has engaged in any behavior or conduct that leads the petitioner to have reasonable cause to believe that she is in imminent danger of becoming a victim of domestic violence. Obviously, the facts of this case easily satisfy each of these considerations. A key additional element to Sally's case is the fact that law enforcement was contacted and took action. If the actions of a respondent rise to the level of providing law enforcement with probable cause that a crime was committed, it is likely that a judge will find a reasonable fear of further domestic violence and grant a temporary injunction.

CASE B

Thad and Lois had been dating for over two years. Though each maintained their own residences throughout their intimate relationship, it was common practice for each of them to stay at the other's residence overnight. Thad would often stay at Lois's house, and she would occasionally stay with him at his condominium. But, never did either party consider themselves to be living together at any point in the relationship. After Thad and Lois broke up, Lois began a new relationship with Morris. Unfortunately, Thad did not like this new boyfriend or the fact that he had lost Lois, and began acting in a manner that forced both Lois and Morris to seek protection orders. Lois, owing to her prior intimate relationship with Thad, filed a petition for injunction against domestic violence (*Slovenski v. Wright*, 849 So.2d 349 (Fla. 2nd DCA 2003)).

It should be obvious in this scenario that Lois lacked proper standing to file a petition for injunction against domestic violence. Although she and Thad had an intimate relationship that involved each staying overnight at the other's residence, Lois' petition is improper because they were not living together as if a family and were not "currently residing or have in the past resided together in the same single dwelling unit" (§741.28(3), Florida Statutes). As the Second District Court of Appeals points out, the appropriate petition would have been for protection against repeat violence.

Lack of standing, like in Lois's case, is one of the many legal reasons a court could cite as the reason for denying a petition. Other reasons could include a failure to allege two separate incidents of violence when petitioning for an injunction against repeat violence, a failure for a parent to have called law enforcement when petitioning on behalf of a child believed to have been a victim of sexual violence, and a failure to establish a dating relationship. But, whatever the legal reasons for denying the petition, the order of denial must specifically state, in writing, the reason(s) for the denial. If the only reason given is lack of appearance of an immediate and present danger of domestic violence, the petition may be denied, but the court must set a full hearing on the matter with notice to the respondent for the earliest possible time (§741.30(5)(b), Florida Statutes; see also *Cuiska v. Cuiska*, 777 So.2d 419 (Fla. 1st DCA 2000).) A full hearing is also scheduled, within 15 days, in the event the judge finds a reasonable appearance of immediate and present danger of continuing violence and enters the temporary injunction. This is because, pursuant to §740.30(5)(c), Florida Statutes, no temporary injunction may be in force and effect for longer than 15 days, unless extended by court order based on a showing of "good cause," including failure to obtain service of process.

Whatever the decision of the judge, the signed order, along with the court file, is returned to court administration for disposition. If the petition was denied, the order of denial is copied and forwarded to the clerk's office or to Harbor House (if appropriate) to give to the petitioner and the case will be closed. If the petition is denied, but scheduled for a hearing, the order is likewise forwarded to the petitioner, and the court file remains open until disposed of by the judge at the hearing. If a temporary injunction is granted, the petitioner will be given a certified copy and instructed to carry the injunction with him or her. This is in the event the respondent violates the terms of the injunction and the petitioner is forced to seek the assistance of law enforcement. A certified copy of a temporary injunction will assist any law enforcement officer in finding probable cause to arrest the respondent for contempt of court, should the respondent violate the terms of the injunction. Both the temporary injunction and a notice of hearing will be forwarded to the Orange County sheriff's office, or other appropriate law enforcement agency, for personal service on the respondent (Oksnar, personal communication, October 27, 2008).

Formal Hearing

As mentioned before, most of the temporary injunctions granted in Orange County during 2007 were dismissed for failure of the petitioner to appear at the scheduled hearing time. In fact, 54% of the temporary injunctions granted expired or were dismissed because the petitioner failed to appear at the hearing to seek a permanent injunction. A survey headed by Susan Keilitz et al. (1997) on behalf of the National Center for State Courts in 1997, which was conducted in Denver and Washington, D.C., indicates a number of factors that are likely to explain the reasons victims choose not to pursue a permanent protective order. These reasons are likely similar to the experiences of individuals in Orange County (Oksnar, personal communication, October 27, 2008). While a centralized process for obtaining orders, such as the system employed in Orange County, provide, in the words of Ms. Keilitz and her team, a "salutary effect on women's decisions to return for a permanent protection order," other factors, such as relief from the abuse, reconciliation, or persuasion, provided a greater influence upon a woman's decision to not appear before the court (Keilitz et al., 1997, pp. 46–47). Specifically, the survey revealed that 36% of women who failed to appear before the court did so as a result of the abuser abandoning his actions against the victim. Put simply, he stopped bothering her. In 17% of the cases the petitioner and respondent reconciled, although, given that a small percentage (2 to 4%) of women reported being either threatened or coerced into dropping the matter, it is likely that many of those reporting reconciliation were equally threatened or coerced into doing so. The balance were dropped either because service could not be made on the respondent (17% of the time), or the respondent had left the area (10%), the process was too much work or trouble (11%), the respondent agreed to seek counseling (4%), or for various other reasons (1%) (Keilitz et al., 1997, p. 47).

When a petitioner and respondent do appear for a hearing, they will encounter in Orange County a system vastly different from most other jurisdictions in the state. While Orange County does share the scheduling practice of setting multiple hearings for two time slots, one beginning at 8:30 a.m.

and the other at 1:30 a.m., the similarities to the actual procedure followed end there. Most other jurisdictions hold all injunction hearings in the same large courtroom, and require all petitioners to sit on one side of the courtroom's gallery and respondents to sit across from them on the other side. This situation invites many respondents to "stare down" their victims and creates a very uncomfortable situation for petitioners, not to mention added burdens on law enforcement officers and the court itself to maintain order and decorum. Additionally, the cases are called one at a time and heard in front of other individuals. As Orange County court administrator Mollie Oksnar put it, "Everyone gets to hear everyone's business." Until recently, this was the method employed by the domestic court in Orange County as well (Oksnar, personal communication, October 27, 2008).

But, approximately two years ago, the system changed in the Orange County courthouse. There now exists two separate offices on the 16th floor, one for each party, ensuring that petitioners and respondents will await their cases in separate rooms. Once their case is called, the respondent is usually sent in the courtroom first and seated before the petitioner is permitted entry. This ensures the civility of the hearing, as no respondent is afforded an opportunity to stare down or otherwise attempt to intimidate a petitioner without attracting the attention of the court or court deputies. Obviously, such tactics are not accepted and are quickly rectified. At the conclusion of the hearing, the petitioner is asked to wait outside the courtroom for a copy of the court's order, and the respondent is directed to the back gallery of the courtroom to also await a copy of the order. Additionally, the respondent must wait at least 20 minutes after receiving the court order, to allow ample time for the petitioner to leave the courthouse property. These logistical changes have improved the safety and comfort levels for petitioners and all involved in these proceedings (Oksnar, personal communication, October 27, 2008).

The actual procedure of the formal hearing is not unlike that of any other court hearing. It is much more common for parties to appear without attorneys at these hearings, though attorneys are sometimes present. A petitioner who has sought the assistance of a shelter (such as Harbor House) can elect to have a counselor sit at the table next to him or her during the hearing. Though the counselor cannot in any way offer any assistance during the hearing itself, he or she can be there to offer moral support and, after the hearing, may answer any questions the petitioner has concerning the process. These counselors, of course, are not lawyers, and do not offer legal advice. They will, if requested, put a petitioner in contact with an attorney (Oksnar, personal communication, October 27, 2008).

After a brief introduction by the judge of the process, the petitioner will be asked if he or she would like the injunction to be extended for a period of time or to be dismissed. Sometimes, for various reasons, many of which are addressed above, the petitioner will ask that the petition be dismissed. More often than not, however, an extension of the injunction will be requested. If the respondent is at the hearing, he or she will be asked if there are any objections to the continuation of the injunction. If the respondent accepts the entry of an injunction and offers no contest to its entry, a final injunction will be granted. If, however, the respondent contests the matter, testimony will be taken from both sides and the judge will determine the merits of the petitioner's claims. If there are no attorneys involved, the judge will ask questions of both parties and any witnesses, in order to determine what happened. If attorneys are involved, questions will come from them in order to establish the position of their respective clients.

It is, just as with any court proceeding, incumbent for the petitioner to meet the burden of proving that the injunction should be granted on a permanent basis. The burden to be met is very low, as a petitioner need only show by greater weight of the evidence that he or she has been or has reasonable cause to believe that he or she will become a victim of domestic violence, further incidents of repeat violence, dating violence, or that the petitioner was a victim of at least one incident of sexual violence. A simple, but very effective way to explain this to nonlawyers, such as unrepresented parties, is to say that the arguments of each party are like two perfectly balanced weights placed on a scale. The burden is met if a piece of evidence in any way tilts the scale in one party's favor, just as a weight would be tipped if a feather were added.

Evidence addressing any of the enumerated factors listed in §741.30(6)(a), discussed above, is appropriate to accept, as is any form of evidence that supports the claims of the petitioner or the respondent. Also, in cases involving allegations of domestic violence, the court is required to consider any custody issues for any children the parties may have, child support and visitation rights, property distribution, and right of entry into any marital home. Again, examples may offer the best method of understanding the process.

CASE C

Giselle and Patrick's marriage collapsed into divorce. The divorce was not exactly amicable, but neither was it particularly nasty. It is, however, complicated by the fact that they both attend the same college and occasionally bump into each other. Giselle claims that, on four occasions, Patrick's conduct amounted to either stalking or physical violence. On the first occasion, she discovered Patrick's car parked right next to hers in the school parking lot, something not likely to occur randomly, as the parking lot was quite large and Patrick could have availed himself of other lots nearby. The second occasion actually included three times when she saw Patrick looking at her in the same building where they were both attending separate classes. On the last of these moments, he greeted her in passing. The third incident involved Patrick offering Giselle a birthday card as they crossed in a hallway. Not taking the card, Giselle continued walking away. The last confrontation occurred at the conclusion of a lecture each attended. While Giselle tried to get out of the room, Patrick did not move out of her way, forcing Giselle to physically shove him aside so she could leave. After this last incident, Giselle went to the courthouse and filed a petition for injunction against domestic violence (*Farrell v. Marquez*, 747 So.2d 413 (Fla., 5th DCA 1999)).

The standing issue in this case is easily satisfied, as the parties are former spouses, a relationship specifically referred to in the statute. The trickier issue is whether Patrick's actions rose to the level of domestic violence. Based upon the allegations made by Giselle alone, it would appear reasonable to find that Patrick was indeed stalking her and had even possibly restrained her from leaving the lecture hall. As a result, a temporary order was issued, but at the hearing two weeks later, Giselle's allegations failed to meet the statutory standard. This is a perfect example of why injunctions are granted initially on a temporary basis, and why parties are required to appear before the court to explain the situation prior to the entry of a final injunction. At the hearing, Giselle admitted that Patrick was not in his car when she returned to hers and that Patrick's car was in no way impeding or blocking her car. Also, at the conclusion of the lecture, Giselle admitted on cross-examination that there were people surrounding Patrick, all trying to get handouts near the exit. Patrick was not impeding her exit, but was himself unable to move, owing to the large crowd. It was, in fact, Giselle who physically shoved her way past Patrick, and not Patrick acting in any manner to forcefully impede Giselle's exit. Although the lower court did grant the petition and entered an injunction against Patrick, the appeals court overturned the decision and dismissed the injunction, finding that Giselle was not a victim of domestic violence and did not have reasonable cause to believe she was in imminent danger of becoming a victim of any act of domestic violence.

Final Injunctions

If the petitioner has satisfied the burden of proof and the court has found after the hearing that the petitioner was, or has reasonable fear that she or he will become, a victim of domestic violence, a final injunction for protection against domestic violence (or other appropriate injunction) will be entered. The Supreme Court of Florida has provided a standardized form and requires that all jurisdictions use those forms when issuing injunctions (Fla. Fam. Law R. of P. 12.610(c)(2)(A)). These forms address all matters that the court was required to consider during the hearing, including child custody, visitation, child support, property distribution, exclusive or joint use of the marital home, alimony, and the rights and responsibilities of each party concerning the matters contained in the injunction. In fact, under §741.2902(2)(b), Florida Statutes, the court is required to "ensure that the parties understand the terms of the injunction, the penalties for failure to comply, and that the parties cannot amend the injunction verbally, in writing, or by invitation to the residence." The injunction's period of effectiveness is not limited by any statute, and may, according to the terms of the form itself, "be effective indefinitely, until modified or dissolved by the judge at either party's request, upon notice and hearing, or expire on a date certain at the judge's discretion" (Florida Supreme Court Approved Family Law Form 12.980(e)). Typically, injunctions are granted for a set period of time, such as six months, one or two years, or until further order of the court. They are, of course, able to be modified, after appropriate hearing and notice to each party.

When explaining the terms of the injunction, it is usually helpful to explain to the parties, through the use of another analogy, that this is only a temporary solution to a more complicated problem. Often, parties appearing at an injunction hearing are couples who are married, were married, or have children or even paternity issues. In other words, they have issues that are more properly heard by a domestic court, who is better equipped to deal with those types of problems. For example, it is not the purview of a domestic violence court to resolve a paternity issue. The domestic violence injunction hearing is much like a visit to an emergency room. The violent incident between the parties is like an automobile accident, and there are certain injuries that must be immediately addressed. But, just like an emergency room cannot deal with long-term care and refers patients to other medical care, a domestic violence hearing can do only so much. For many parties, it is advisable that they seek a more long-term solution, such as divorce, paternity, or other domestic relations, that can more effectively address matters, such as long-term child support, visitation schedules, alimony, and other related matters.

Enforcement

Without some form of enforcement provision, the entire process of obtaining an injunction for protection against violence would be moot. After all, how is a simple piece of paper going to protect anyone? What protects victims is the fact that the injunction ensures, in writing, that should any further acts of violence or any provision of the injunction be violated, punishment of the respondent will be swift. Florida Statute §741.31 holds that a violation of any provision of an injunction for protection against domestic violence can be prosecuted as a civil contempt of court proceeding, or prosecuted as a misdemeanor crime through the state attorney's office. A violating respondent may be forced to pay a monetary fine of up to $1,000 or even serve up to one year in jail (§741.283, Florida Statutes). Though a civil court is not precluded from simply levying a monetary fine for a willful violation of an injunction, the legislature of Florida has made its intention clear by stating in §741.2901(2), Florida Statutes, that "criminal prosecution shall be the favored method of enforcing compliance with injunctions for protection against domestic violence." This is important, as national research indicates that civil protection orders are violated within 6 months 35% of the time and within 12 months 60% of the time (Klein, 2008, p. 58).

Unique "Challenges"

Owing to the nature of the injunction proceeding, it has become far too frequent for some individuals to seek their long-term relief from the short-term process of an injunction. For example, an injunction petition is free, whereas filing fees for a formal divorce action in Florida can cost over $400. It is possible for a petitioner to quickly resolve all divorce issues through the injunction process. A temporary injunction can be granted in a very short period of time (about 2 hours), and within 15 days, a hearing before the judge is required to be scheduled. It is possible for an ambitious petitioner to get all the relevant matters of a divorce resolved within 15 days and free of charge. The only missing element, of course, is the burden of proving the petitioner was or has reasonable fear of becoming a victim of domestic violence.

As an illustration, consider the completely fictional marriage between Bob and Wendy. Their relationship had obviously fallen apart. They constantly verbally argued with each other, even in front of the children, but never had one physically threatened or actually harmed the other. During one nasty fight, however, Bob, in complete exasperation, threw up his hands, exclaiming, "Well, what do you want me to do?" When he did this, he inadvertently hit Wendy on the side of her arm. This was too much for Wendy, and she left the house, immediately going to the courthouse to file an injunction petition. Based on the apparently credible allegations of Wendy, who claimed that Bob had intentionally struck her arm and had repeatedly threatened her, the court granted a temporary injunction, requiring Bob to leave the house immediately. Instantly, Wendy has what she really most wants—Bob out of the house and the children under her exclusive care and custody.

After two weeks, Wendy and Bob appear before the court at a formal hearing to determine whether a permanent injunction should be entered. Again, at this point, Wendy has expended no money and is on the verge of obtaining a court order addressing all issues: custody, visitation, distribution of personal property, exclusive use of the marital home, even alimony. But, there exists the stumbling block of no actual violence from which she needs protection.

It is, therefore, incumbent upon the domestic violence judge to ensure, through evidence and testimony, that actual incidents of violence occurred and that the petitioner has reasonable cause to fear that she will again be the victim of domestic violence. When Wendy is asked about the incident, she will, of course, likely paint a verbal picture that best supports her allegations. Bob will refute the allegations, and it is the judge's responsibility to "read between the lines" and discover the true intent of parties. Sometimes, the intent of the parties becomes quickly obvious. For example, if Wendy was represented by counsel and the first issue the attorney addressed during direct examination of Bob was the amount of his employment compensation, rather than addressing the alleged incidents of violence, it is fairly obvious what is happening.

This is, as one can imagine, a delicate balance. After all, should the allegations of the petitioner in this scenario be true, denying an injunction could well place the petitioner in a very bad situation: the victim of domestic violence who has no protection from a now very upset respondent. Happily, these situations do not often occur, and more often than not, careful questioning of the parties and any witnesses, along with a judge's experience and observations, usually reveals the deficiency of any actual violence. This is yet another reason why the injunction hearing process is so critical.

Conclusion

There are, unfortunately, real situations that call for the assistance of civil protection orders. Some people find themselves caught in a cycle of violence from which there appears no escape. Others, such as young children, are exposed to things they should never see or experience. For each of these people, however, there are two courses of action, one through the criminal justice system and the other through the civil courts. A civil protection order, unlike criminal proceedings, can address each case individually, and tailor an injunction for protection against violence to the needs of the petitioner. They also provide peace of mind, for they are proof that someone listened to them, heard their cry for help, and offered a helping, protective hand.

References

Karan, A., and Lazarus, L. (2008). Florida's four orders of protection against violence: Distinguishing the difference. In *Florida's domestic violence benchbook: September 2008* (pp. 187–195). Office of the State Courts Administrator, State of Florida.

Keilitz, S., Hannaford, P. L., & Efkeman, K. S. (1997). *Civil protection orders: The benefits and limitations for victims of domestic violence* (NCJ 172223). Williamsburg, VA: National Center for State Courts, Retrieved from http://www.ncjrs.gov/pdffiles1/pr/172223.pdf

Klein, A. R. (2008, April). *Practical implications of current domestic violence research. Part III: Judges* (NCJ 222321). Washington, DC: National Institute of Justice. Retrieved from http://www.ncjrs.gov/pdffiles1/nij/grants/222321.pdf

Cases Cited

Cuiska v. Cuiska. 777 So.2d 419 (Fla. 1st DCA 2000).
Farrell v. Marquez. 747 So.2d 413 (Fla. 5th DCA 1999).
Slovenski v. Wright. 849 So.2d 349 (Fla. 2nd DCA 2003).

Statutes and Other Authorities

Section 741.28, Florida Statutes, 2008.
Section 741.283, Florida Statutes, 2008.
Section 741.2901, Florida Statutes, 2008.
Section 741.31, Florida Statutes, 2008.
Section 784.046, Florida Statutes, 2008.
Fla. Fam. Law R. of P. 12.610(c)(2)(A), 2008.
Florida Supreme Court Approved Family Law Form 12.980(e), 2004.

Prosecuting Domestic Violence Cases
Issues and Concerns

14

WALTER KOMANSKI
ROBERT T. MAGILL

Contents

Introduction

A natural response for any victim of a violent act is to immediately seek the assistance of law enforcement. In the context of domestic violence, however, some victims hesitate. After all, who really wants to call the police on their spouse? And, many believe that this was just an isolated incident and will never happen again. But, all too frequently, the violence returns and, eventually, law enforcement must be contacted to end the abuse. Unlike any other crime, there are two avenues available to protect a victim of domestic abuse from further violence. Protection in the form of a civil injunction order may be sought, as can punishment of the perpetrator through the criminal justice system. Once involved, many issues and concerns arise regarding the appropriateness of prosecuting an act of domestic violence. The most important aspect a prosecuting attorney will look for when prosecuting a domestic violence case through the criminal court is something called convictability, a combination of evidence, witness and victim credibility, and the culpability of the perpetrator. This chapter will focus on this idea of convictability, and address the many issues and concerns raised during the criminal prosecution of a domestic violence crime.

Statistical Discussion

In 2005, the National Crime Victimization Survey (NCVS) released a report of domestic violence rates for the years 1993 to 2005. Basing the analysis on a population segment of 1,000 persons of age 12 or older, the survey revealed violence rates for intimate partners or relatives stood at 5.9 out of 1,000 for female victims and 2.1 for males. Approximately one-third of domestic violence victims reported actual physical violence, with the balance reporting only threats of violence or death (Klein, 2008b, p. 7). It should be noted, however, that a different survey, the National Violence Against Women Survey (NVAWS), revealed that only 27% of women and 13.5% of men who were assaulted actually reported the incident(s) to law enforcement. This apparently indicates that the crime of domestic violence is underreported. Equally troublesome is the finding that initial attacks are not commonly reported. Victims typically suffer multiple assaults before the authorities are contacted (Klein, 2008b, p. 10).

The NVAWS also reveals that less than 20% of women reported intimate partner rapes to police. Different state-based studies, on the other hand, appear to point toward more prevalence of such attacks. A Texas study, for example, found that almost 70% of women seeking a protective order had been raped. Studies conducted in Massachusetts and Colorado, while indicating sexual assault rates lower than Texas, uncovered the disturbing fact that such attacks are not often reported, which probably explains the lower national findings. For example, interviews with women conducted at the conclusion of their case seeking protective orders in Massachusetts revealed an unwillingness to report any sexual assault in their initial petitions, while similar interviews with women in Colorado discovered a reporting rate of only 4% (Klein, 2008b, p. 8).

If the matter is reported to the proper authorities, it is comforting to know that prosecution rates for the crime of domestic violence have steadily increased over the years. In the past it was common practice for state prosecutors to either automatically dismiss or *nolle prose* almost all domestic violence cases. But such inaction is now increasingly rare and exceptional. It is more common today for state and local authorities to routinely prosecute such cases. An analysis of over 100 studies conducted in over 170 urban jurisdictions throughout the United States reveals a national average rate of 63.8% of all arrests for domestic violence being prosecuted (Klein, 2008a, p. 41).

The disparity of prosecution rates stems not only from each jurisdiction's variation of defining domestic violence, but also upon whether a jurisdiction employs a specialized domestic violence prosecution program. One of the first jurisdictions to create such a specialized program, often referred to as a "no drop" policy (which will be discussed in more detail below), was San Diego's City Attorney's Office. That office recently boasted a prosecution rate of 70% of those arrested for domestic violence. Following San Diego's example, specialized prosecutors in Omaha, Nebraska, prosecuted 88% of all police domestic violence arrests, while Everett, Washington, has seen its rate of dismissals fall from a high of 79% to a low of 29%. Such specialized programs also benefit the prosecution of civil protection order violations. Between 1992 and 1995, 60% of the approximately 15,000 violations of civil protection orders issued in Massachusetts were prosecuted criminally (Klein, 2008a, p. 41).

As noted earlier, the prosecution against domestic violence has the uncommon feature of prosecution through both the criminal and civil court systems. Research indicates that many of the perpetrators of domestic violent acts quickly become aware of this fact first hand. For example, 65% of respondents to civil injunction proceedings in Wilmington, Delaware, Denver, and Washington, D.C., also had an equivalent criminal proceeding pending against them stemming from the same incident. In Texas, slightly over 70% of civil respondents also faced criminal charges, while a Massachusetts study revealed an even greater percentage of 80%. This high level of overlap is likely the result of victims receiving encouragement from arresting officers to pursue a civil remedy in addition to the state pursuit of the criminal penalty (Klein, 2008b, p. 57).

However, much like the failure of victims to report initial incidents of violence to the police, civil protection orders are typically not immediately pursued. National surveys report only approximately 17% of assault victims and 36% of stalking victims seek protection orders after the original incident, and only 40% of women entering a battered woman's shelter obtained a civil protection order prior to entering the facility (Klein, 2008b, p. 58). These low reporting rates are likely the result of victims seeking self-assistance, such as leaving the home or getting the abuser to leave. A Boston study indicated that 68% of women had left their abuser at least once prior to the filing of a petition for a civil protection order. Other courses of action indicate that approximately 30% sought independent professional counseling and 25% contacted a victim hotline or sought shelter (Klein, 2008b, p. 58).

Once a civil petition for protection is filed, a court official will typically review the petition and either dismiss it or grant a temporary order preventing the abuser from having any further contact with the victim. As an example of this process, the circuit court in Orange County, Florida, which has created a specialized domestic violence court, requires one judge to review petitions on a roughly hourly basis, ensuring that petitions for protection against domestic violence are reviewed quickly. If the petitioner alleges sufficient facts to warrant court action, a temporary injunction order is issued and a formal hearing before the court is set to determine whether a permanent injunction is necessary to protect a victim from further harm. In 2007, a total of 6,281 petitions for protection were filed, 5,434 (or 86.5%) of which were either granted or scheduled for a follow-up hearing before the court to determine the appropriateness of issuing a permanent injunction. Such a hearing before the court usually occurs within two to three weeks. It is incumbent upon the victim to appear before the court at that time or the temporary protective order will automatically expire. In 2007, of the 5,434 cases scheduled to be heard by the court, only 2,508 (or 46%) were heard by the court. The balance were dismissed, typically for failure of the petitioner to appear at the hearing.

A survey headed by Susan Keilitz, Hannaford, and Efkeman (1997) on behalf of the National Center for State Courts in 1997, which was conducted in Denver and Washington, D.C., indicates a number of factors that are likely to explain the reasons victims fail to pursue a permanent protective order. While a centralized process for obtaining orders, such as that employed in Orange County, Florida, and Denver, provide, in the words of Ms. Keilitz and her team, a "salutary effect on women's decisions to return for a permanent protection order," other factors, such as relief from the abuse, reconciliation, or persuasion, provided a greater influence upon a woman's decision to not appear before the court (Keilitz et al., 1997, pp. 46–47). For example, 35.5% of women who failed to appear before the court did so as a result of the abuser abandoning his actions against the victim. Put simply, he stopped bothering her. In 17% of the cases the petitioner and respondent reconciled, although given that a small percentage (2 to 4%) of women reported being either threatened or coerced into dropping the matter, it is likely that many of those reporting reconciliation were equally threatened or coerced into doing so (Keilitz et al., 1997, p. 47).

If the petitioner does appear before the court seeking a permanent protection order, it is the burden of that individual to demonstrate to the court, through the greater weight of the evidence, that a permanent order is in the best interests of preventing further violence. This is accomplished through presentation of testimony and evidence, with an opportunity for the respondent to persuade the court that the order is not required. If the court finds in favor of the petitioner and a permanent order is granted for a specified period of time, it will, in contrast to the general provisions of the temporary order, typically offer specific provisions tailored to the needs of the participants, such as permitting the respondent to reenter any joint residence to retrieve personal belongings and establishing visitation and child support, if required, and any form of nonhostile contact, if appropriate (Keilitz et al., 1997, p. 48). Once granted, however, civil protection orders are far from offering complete protection for the victims of domestic violence. National research indicates that civil protection orders are violated within 6 months 35% of the time and 12 months 60% of the time (Klein, 2008a, p. 58). Violations of a civil protection order are considered a criminal matter and are therefore pursued through the criminal justice system.

Criminal Prosecution

Intake and Review

In addition to receiving protective order violations from the civil court, state prosecutors, such as the state attorney's office in Orange County, Florida, receive criminal domestic violation cases directly from the arresting law enforcement agency (Orange County State Attorney's Office, personal communication, September 17, 2008). The prosecutor's role in criminal domestic violence cases is one of great importance and great deference, especially in the initial stages of the case. In the words of Professor Cassia Spohn (2004, p. 3), a prosecutor "decides who will be charged, what charge will be filed, who will be offered a plea bargain, and the type of bargain that will be offered." In the process of making those decisions, a prosecutor usually receives broad discretion. There are typically no legislative guidelines imposed on how those decisions are to be made, as prosecutors are essentially immune from judicial review. As the U.S. Supreme Court held in *Bordenkircher v. Hayes* (434 U.S. 357, 364), "So long as the prosecutor has probable cause to believe that the accused committed an offense defined by statute, the decision whether or not to prosecute, and what charge to file or bring before a grand jury generally rests entirely in his discretion."

Given such broad authority, it is only natural to wonder what elements a prosecutor considers when deciding whether or not to prosecute. Citing various studies in this area, Professor Spohn concludes that prosecutors are most concerned with avoiding uncertainty "by filing charges in cases in which the odds of conviction are good and by rejecting charges in cases for which conviction is unlikely" (Spohn & Holleran, 2004, p. 3). Factors used to avoid such uncertainty include an evaluation of the culpability of the defendant and the character and credibility of the victim. State Attorney Jason Fiesta, working in Orange County, Florida, adds one additional piece to consider: victim cooperation. "In my experience that is the biggest hurdle" to successful prosecution, he admits. Yet he is careful to point out that victim cooperation, while an important hurdle to jump, is not an absolute determinative factor, noting, "If they're cooperative that's not a 'golden key' to prosecution either." Other factors, like evidentiary support, are also considered (Fiesta, personal communication, September 17, 2008). Attorney Barbara Smith of the American Bar Association agrees. After analyzing surveys of other jurisdictions, she concluded that prosecutors "were rational decision-makers who were most likely to proceed without the victim's cooperation if they had a strong case based on other evidence" (Smith, 2001, p. 78). An analogy provided by State Attorney Michelle Latham, who also works in Orange County, Florida, is quite helpful in understanding the importance, but not necessarily critical, make-or-break nature, of victim cooperation. Without a cooperative victim, "You're basically prosecuting almost like you would a homicide, because you have to factor the victim out and you have to see if there's enough evidence of a crime without her there" (Latham, personal communication, September 17, 2008).

This, of course, reveals what may be a stronger factor, to which Fiesta, Latham, and other Orange County state attorneys all agree: strength of evidence. If there is enough evidence, even with an uncooperative or resistant victim, "we're going to prosecute" (Fiesta, personal communication, September 17, 2008). Studies of other jurisdictions also appear to agree that strength of evidence is a very strong factor, but do not place a greater emphasis on one element. Instead, it is the combination of elements that is determinative. Charges are more likely to be filed with strong physical evidence connecting the perpetrator to the victim and the crime, but other elements, such as a defendant's prior record and the victim's credibility or possible contribution to the incident, are equally important. The formula is best stated in Professor Spohn's conclusion "that prosecutors' concerns about convictability lead them to file charges when they believe the evidence is strong, the suspect is culpable, and the victim is blameless" (Spohn, 2004, p. 5).

A policy of strongly pursuing a case based upon convictability elements rather than victim cooperation is sometimes referred to as a no-drop policy. As discussed previously, one of the first jurisdictions to employ such a policy was the San Diego City Attorney's Office in the 1980s. The successful increase in conviction rates experienced by that office resulted in two-thirds of 142 major prosecutor's offices throughout the United States following suit and adopting a similar policy in the years since (Smith, 2001, p. 1). San Diego's City Attorney's Office enjoyed high success rates on cases taken to trial, even without victim statements or victim testimony. In contradiction to the experiences expressed by some of Florida's state attorneys, this high success rate in San Diego's no-drop policy seems to support a conclusion offered by Professor Klein that "either lack of victim cooperation is exaggerated or that victims are not the key variable in successful prosecution programs" (Klein, 2008a, p. 52).

It should be pointed out, though, that the term *no drop* is a bit misleading, as not every single case is fully prosecuted and some are, in fact, dropped. After conducting a review of various no-drop jurisdictions on behalf of the American Bar Association, attorney Smith's team concluded that "the first lesson we learned is that no-drop is more a philosophy than a strict policy of prosecuting domestic violence cases. None of the prosecutors pursued every case they filed" (Smith, 2001, p. 78). Ms. Smith's team appears to agree with the conclusions of Professor Spohn that the analysis is one that includes many factors, noting that prosecutors tend to look into the prior record of the defendant, other forms of evidence like photographs or eyewitness testimony, and the relationship between the defendant and the victim. "In other words," Ms. Smith concludes, "the term, 'evidence-based' prosecution, probably fits practices at our sites better than the phrase, 'no-drop'" (Smith, 2001, p. 78).

While the San Diego experiences have provided an increase in prosecutions against domestic violence for most of the various jurisdictions that followed suit, a small minority have met with unsatisfactory results. Prosecutors in Milwaukee, for example, originally employed a threshold of requiring victim cooperation before pursuing a domestic violence case. However, owing to low prosecution rates, the policy changed and cases were pursued without victim cooperation as long as sufficient evidence was collected to ensure higher conviction rates. Interestingly, these changes did not result in higher prosecution rates, nor did the rate of victim cooperation increase. In fact, victims reported dissatisfaction with prosecutors and believed that these actions did not make them safer from further abuse. Without cooperative victims Milwaukee prosecutors were forced to rely upon other evidence, such as photographs, 911 recordings or transcripts, or police officer testimony. At times, they found themselves facing defense attorneys more willing to take cases to trial rather than agree to plea bargains. As a result, the prosecutor's office was faced with needing to expend more resources than available, leading to no increase in trials or prosecutions against domestic violence defendants, as demonstrated by the drop in overall convictions from 69% to 52% after implementation of the policy. In addition, the time from filing to disposition doubled (Smith, 2001, p. 2).

Happily, this experience appears to be an aberration. The analysis conducted by Ms. Smith's team concluded that adopting such an evidence-based prosecution policy dramatically boosted convictions in most of the other study sites. Extraordinarily large increases in conviction rates, declines in processing time, and large increases in trials were experienced by two sites analyzed by Ms. Smith's team. This enthusiasm is tempered, however, as the increases in domestic violence criminal trials may only be "a temporary phenomenon that will decline as defense attorneys come to accept the fact that the rules of the game have changed and come to realize that, even when victims are uncooperative, prosecutors can still win trials" (Smith, 2001, p. 78). This appears to already be occurring in San Diego, where trial rates have dropped to a mere 2% of all cases over the past 10 years (Klein, 2008a, p. 45).

Another tool prosecutors can use to determine the convictability of a case comes from the civil protection petitions and orders. When a violation of such an order is referred to the prosecutor's office, each element of that civil case is reviewable and can assist a prosecutor in pursuing the criminal domestic violence charges. For example, the civil protection case can assist prosecutors in assessing the risks posed by a particular defendant against a victim, as well as fleshing out the details of the incident(s). Additionally, there is the unintended benefit of providing prosecutors with a means to pursue a defendant for other criminal actions, such as probation violation. In Massachusetts, for instance, the affidavit filed in support of a civil protection petition can be used as evidence against someone for violating probation (Klein, 2008a, p. 12).

Evidence Collection

If a no-drop policy is more appropriately referred to as evidence-based prosecution, it is obvious that the collection of evidence plays a critical role in pursuing domestic violence cases. On this subject, the element of victim cooperation again comes into play, justifying the emphasis placed on cooperation by the Orange County state attorneys, and offering a factor not considered by Professor Klein. As a prime example, when prosecuting stalking cases, a lack of victim cooperation will essentially prevent any prosecution, as the evidence in the case is usually only provided by the victim. In such cases, State Attorney Fiesta reports that victim cooperation is typically present, and the victim is usually able to provide the needed information, such as the "names of their friends, their coworkers, who witnessed the calls, or the harassing, or the following." Indeed, he notes that the victims "become our helpers in prosecuting their case," collecting such other evidence as phone message recordings or actual calls made by the defendant" (Fiesta, personal communication, September 17, 2008).

When pursuing assault and battery cases, however, cooperation is usually not forthcoming, leaving prosecutors to rely on other means to obtain evidence. When describing the task of prosecuting a battery case without victim cooperation, Florida state attorney Lindsey Gergley notes no case is ever simple. "It's not cut and dry ever," she says, forcing prosecutors "to be creative in your ways of getting evidence into the case through different channels" (Gergley, personal communication, September 17, 2008). Evidence is usually collected by the arresting agency and most commonly consists only of a tape of the emergency call made to 911, some physical injury, and occasionally, an admissible excited utterance. Other times, in the words of attorney Latham, "We'd be lucky to have photographs," taken either at the scene by law enforcement or of the victim by a shelter agency such as Harbor House of Central Florida (Latham, personal communication, September 17, 2008).

But, of all the usually available evidence, in Latham's opinion, the 911 call is the key piece of evidence when the victim of domestic violence is unwilling to cooperate (Latham, personal communication, September 17, 2008). To highlight the importance of the 911 call, Professor Klein agrees, advising prosecutors to specifically ask "law enforcement to catalogue and maintain 911 tapes of domestic violence calls as they may contain possible excited utterance evidence because a majority of reported incidents is made by victims" (Klein, 2008a, p. 12). Those emergency calls can also, if conducted properly, provide prosecutors with the names and contact information of third-party witnesses who may be making the call. These individuals can serve as another useful piece of evidence (Klein, 2008a, p. 12). Third-party witnesses, such as neighbors, friends, or relatives, can assist the prosecution of a case by proving the relationship between the defendant and an uncooperative victim. Additionally, if these witnesses saw the actual incident(s) of abuse, they can also testify to the actual domestic violence. It is not unheard of for a witness completely unrelated to any of the parties to the case to come forward to testify. "You'd be surprised," Latham exclaimed when asked. "We have a lot of—it seems a lot more often now—we have a lot of independent witnesses that are willing to come in and testify; just civilian people that happened to see the incident happen." Such witnesses are, obviously, invaluable, as they present an uninterested and uninfluenced witness to the crime (Latham, personal communication, September 17, 2008).

Sadly, though, many cases involving uncooperative or unavailable victims simply fail to offer enough independent evidence for a prosecutor. In 2002, a study of over 6,000 domestic violence police reports revealed the following woeful evidentiary elements: "victim photos (17%), crime scene photos (16%), suspect photos (3%), physical evidence collected (8%) and weapons (11%), medical reports in (9.4%), witness reported (37%), suspect statements (18%), and signed victim statements (53%)." Professor Klein, who reported on these statistics, laments that the "Rhode Island data are not unique" (Klein, 2008a, p. 50). But, for cases with sufficient evidence, with or without a cooperative victim, State Attorney Fiesta speaks for most state prosecutors: "We're going to prosecute."

Plea Bargaining

Inevitably, a defendant facing a strong case or a state prosecutor willing to take the case before a jury will attempt to avoid the risks of jail through plea bargaining. Florida law provides an example of how plea offers can differ, depending upon the charges made against a defendant and the circumstances of each case. Defendants in Florida facing any charge for domestic violence and who have caused bodily injury are required, by §741.283, Florida Statutes, to attend a batterer's intervention program for 26 weeks. For misdemeanor charges such as battery or stalking, according to State Attorney Donna Hung, first offenders are usually offered 12 months probation on top of the intervention program. In addition, court costs and any costs incurred during the prosecution of the case will also have to be reimbursed, and depending on the circumstances of the case, the defendant may also have to agree to attend Alcoholics Anonymous, undergo drug treatment and evaluations, and attend parenting classes. The goal, according to State Attorney Hung, is "to do the right thing for everybody involved with our plea offers" (Hung, personal communication, September 17, 2008). As for defendants facing felony charges, like abuse on children or sexual abuse, the plea offers from state attorneys like Linda Drane Burdick will depend upon whether any permanent physical injuries were sustained by the victim. If there are no permanent injuries on the victim, a first-time offender will likely only face substantial probation time, in addition to the same programs discussed above, if applicable. Of course, the batterer's intervention program is required. If, on the other hand, the victim sustains permanent injury, jail time will be imposed, pursuant to the statutory guidelines (Drane Burdick, personal communication, September 25, 2008). As some domestic violence crimes carry sentences of up to 15 years, any offered jail time will likely be substantial.

Trial Preparation for the Victim

If no plea bargain can be reached, or the state or a defendant prefers to take the matter before a jury, it is imperative for the state prosecutor to prepare a cooperative victim or any witnesses for their testimony. In order to assist in this matter, a specialized advocacy program has been developed in Orange County, Florida. Victim advocates, like Cindy Dubrouillet, work directly alongside (and even in the same offices) as the prosecutors, acting as a sort of liaison between victims and state attorneys. They also assist victims who qualify in obtaining compensation from the Federal Victim Compensation Fund for any counseling or other professional assistance needed while recovering from the domestic violence they have experienced (Dubrouillet, personal communication, September 25, 2008).

Of special concern for the advocates as well as the state attorneys are the victims of child abuse. The role of an advocate is especially acute in this regard, as the first contact a child abuse victim typically has with the state attorney's office will be with an advocate (Dubrouillet, personal communication, September 25, 2008). The state attorney's office in Orange County includes a play area for very young children, in an effort to make a child as comfortable as possible prior to any questioning about his or her experiences. Typically, attorneys and advocates will join the child in the play area and attempt to build rapport with him or her. Once a friendly and trusting relationship is created, the attorneys will appropriately introduce what attorney Drane Burdick refers to as "warm-up questions," such as determining that the child can differentiate between right and wrong. Once that barrier has been crossed, more detailed questions relating to the events giving rise to the charges will be introduced. The goal of the state attorneys at this point is to ensure that the child can relate the events in adequate detail and confirm the facts of any police report or other evidence to be used at trial. But the overriding goal of any child interview is to build rapport with the child, so that he or she is as comfortable as possible during testimony (Drane Burdick, personal communication, September 25, 2008). To bolster a child's comfort, Ms. Dubrouillet will often take him or her into the courtroom prior to the trial and point out the many features of a courtroom, including where everyone will sit and what is expected to occur (Dubrouillet, personal communication, September 25, 2008).

While pretrial interviews with adult victims of domestic violence are not normally that detailed (and usually don't involve the use of a play area), it is most helpful for state attorneys to have some form of personal interaction with them prior to trial as well. State Attorney Fiesta reports that he will typically go over what questions he plans on asking the victim while on the stand, such as the basic information of what happened and where. After that has been established, attorneys will then attempt to "color it in" by asking, "Did you attack the defendant before he attacked you? Did you have a weapon in your hand? How far apart were you? Were you talking or arguing at the time?" The purpose of these questions is to make certain that the jury understands the situation was not created by the victim and that the victim is blameless for the defendant's crimes, as well as deflecting any attempts by defense counsel to raise a "self-defense" argument (Fiesta, personal communication, September 17, 2008).

Equally important to preparing the victim for what will be asked and what can be said is educating the victim on what *can't* be said. State Attorney Gergley says she makes certain that the victim understands any prior incidents can't be referred to or discussed. Additionally, the challenge of getting a nonattorney to understand the basics of hearsay must be addressed— things said by others cannot be a part of the victim's testimony. The most difficult aspect for a victim to understand, though, is that he or she should only answer the questions being asked and not to "go into anything else," like prior batteries or something someone else said. The incident being prosecuted has to be discussed "in a vacuum," and that is a hard concept for some victims to understand (Gergley, personal communication, September 17, 2008).

If the crime being prosecuted is the violation of a civil protection order, a victim's testimony can be used to educate a jury on the process of obtaining an injunction and why the defendant's violation is criminal. Preparing a victim in this regard, obviously, becomes important as well. Setting the scene of the crime through questioning is relatively simple, as all that needs to be asked are questions to show that the injunction was in place, the defendant and victim were at the location, and the defendant acted in a manner that violated the terms of the injunction. The difficulty comes in trying to get a jury to believe that the defendant's actions rise to the level of criminal activity. "It's extremely difficult to get a jury to buy into this idea that this paper says he can't do this and when he does it he should be punished," explains Fiesta. To educate a jury in this regard, questions are generally geared toward getting the victim to describe how the injunction was imposed, while avoiding the inadmissible reasons why the injunction was imposed. The questions elicit responses that inform the jury that each party had to appear in court, were afforded an opportunity to explain their case to the court, and once the order was entered, each side was informed of the terms of the order and told what they could or could not do and that there would be consequences for any violation (Fiesta, personal communication, September 17, 2008).

Jury Selection

As with any trial, the selection of the jury can be the most important part of any domestic violence case. There are, however, certain unique aspects of a jury that domestic violence attorneys will look to address. For example, when prosecuting a misdemeanor battery case, Florida state attorney Crystal Segui looks to make sure, as much as possible, that a potential juror understands that something as innocuous as a little push can actually become criminal battery. It is also important to try to gauge whether or not the juror is going to trust this particular victim or the witnesses to be presented (Segui, personal communication, September 17, 2008).

Child abuse cases also look for these elements as well, but state attorneys prosecuting a child abuse case will also hope to include jurors who have some experience with children, regardless of gender. Interestingly, State Attorney Drane Burdick reports that many defense attorneys will attempt to exclude women as much as possible, a technique that, in her experience, yields no added benefit for the defense (Drane Burdick, personal communication, September 25, 2008).

Successful Prosecution Rates

Just as with most criminal prosecutions, the majority of domestic violence cases are resolved through the plea bargaining process. Contributing to this fact is, no doubt, the statistical reality that most domestic violence cases that are taken before a jury overwhelmingly result in convictions. Professor Klein's studies reveal that jury acquittals "are rare," documenting rates as low as 1.6% in North Carolina to a scant high of 5% in Ohio. "A study of felony domestic violence prosecutions in Brooklyn, New York found a similarly low 'not guilty' rate of only 2%" (Klein, 2008a, p. 42). If a defendant is being prosecuted in a jurisdiction that features a specialized domestic violence program, such as that found in San Diego or Omaha, Nebraska, a conviction is even more likely and, owing to the expedited trial dockets, will come at a relatively quick time. For example, in San Diego the average processing time for a domestic violence case is an almost unheard of 32 days. In Omaha, only 43 days are needed to prosecute such a case. "These specialized programs," conclude Professor Klein, "apparently create their own momentum," which provides benefits, as such short times "both reduce victim vulnerability to threats and chances of reconciling with the abuser pending trial" (Klein, 2008a, p. 53). State Attorney Segui reports equal success with the prosecution of civil injunction violations, noting that juries, once they understand the nature of the crime, are usually sympathetic and willing to prosecute acts as simple as getting too close or a defendant making a telephone call (Segui, personal communication, September 17, 2008).

Punishment

Sentencing for domestic violence crimes varies not only according to the severity of the crime, but, of course, from jurisdiction to jurisdiction. As mentioned before, Florida, for example, has a mandatory statutory jail term of five days for crimes involving injuries and attendance in a batterer's intervention program irrespective of injury to the victim, under §741.283, Florida Statutes. This punishment is in addition to the sentencing guidelines provided by other statutes, which vary according to the severity of the crime. For a battery misdemeanor, which is the most common form of domestic violence prosecuted, a defendant could be found guilty of a first-degree misdemeanor and face up to one year incarceration and a $1,000 fine. The same punishment is awaiting a civil injunction violator under §741.31, Florida Statutes. For felony domestic violence, such as child abuse, which is addressed in §827.03, Florida Statutes, a defendant could be found guilty of a third-degree felony, and face up to five years in prison and a fine not to exceed $5,000. For felonies involving sexual assault, guilty parties have committed a second-degree felony and face up to 15 years incarceration and a $10,000 fine. Any domestic violent act that results in the death of the victim is prosecuted as a homicide and the defendant faces the possibility of a capital punishment. Actual sentences, reports State Attorney Hung, will depend upon the discretion of the trial judge, who will base the decision upon the facts of each case and, sometimes, upon testimony received from the victim.

California Penal Code Section 1203.097 requires a substantial mandatory sentence, which includes three years probation, the issuance of a criminal protective order preventing further contact with the victim, the completion of a batterer program of "no less than a year," community service, restitution, and in lieu of a fine, payment of up to $5,000 to a battered women's shelter. While quite severe, it should be noted that most defendants avoid this punishment by pleading guilty to non-domestic violence crimes (Klein, 2008b, p. 43).

Just as the sentencing guidelines for each crime vary, so do the actual sentences imposed. For example, a 2002 study of the Brooklyn Misdemeanor Domestic Violence Court revealed "of those pleading or found guilty, 51% received a conditional discharge, 35% received jail, 7% received probation, 5% were ordered to complete community service, and 1% were fined." A similar study in Chicago found about one-third of defendants receiving a conditional discharge, and about 23% receiving jail time, including time served pending trial (Klein, 2008b, p. 42). Like the requirement in Florida that a defendant attend a batterer's intervention program, most other specialized prosecution courts require batterer treatment programs or other programs when appropriate, such as alcohol treatment, parenting classes, or mental health evaluation (Klein, 2008b, p. 43).

Unique Issues in Domestic Violence Prosecutions

Crawford v. Washington and the Right to Confrontation

In 2004, the U.S. Supreme Court altered the prosecution procedures of many criminal cases, including domestic violence, when it issued the landmark case of *Crawford v. Washington* (541 U.S. 36 (2004)). Under the court's ruling, any out-of-court testimonial statement of a witness who is absent from trial is to be admitted only where the declarant is unavailable and only when the defendant has had a prior opportunity to cross-examine the declarant. The impact of this ruling on domestic violence cases is most acutely felt in cases where a victim is unwilling to testify against his or her abuser, as any statement made by that victim, especially to police officers and even to medical experts, could be deemed "testimonial" and therefore inadmissible.

While State Attorney Latham reports that the restrictions of requiring cross-examination aren't really a problem, the difficulty arises out of the Supreme Court's unwillingness to concretely define what constitutes a "testimonial statement." Specifically, the question of whether statements made to police officers at the scene are testimonial, and therefore only admissible if the victim is going to be available for confrontation through cross-examination, remains unclear. Prior to *Crawford*, in the event a victim was unwilling to testify against his or her abuser, arresting officers could testify in greater detail concerning the events they witnessed under the excited utterances exception to hearsay exclusions. State attorneys could ask questions like: "What was her demeanor? Was she crying? What did she tell you? So the jury got to hear the whole story from the police officer. You can't do that anymore" (Latham, personal communication, September 17, 2008).

State Attorney Fiesta also points out that *Crawford* has impacted the use of the key piece of evidence: 911 calls. While court rulings have held 911 calls made by the victim to not be testimonial, "if somebody else called 911 other than the victim, or somebody who didn't see [the incident], that call is no good to us for evidence and all we have is the statement of the officer [of the victim's comments made] in an excited state. But right now, under the current rulings from the [district courts], we can't use that." Such rulings currently hold that statements made to arresting officers are testimonial in nature and therefore inadmissible even under the excited utterance exception. This "has been very limiting" to the prosecution of cases without victim cooperation (Fiesta, personal communication, September 17, 2008).

Professor Klein agrees that the *Crawford* ruling has imposed new obstacles that must be overcome by prosecutors, and advises that now "prosecutors must work with law enforcement to gather as much evidence as possible and accurately identify all potential witnesses and ways to contact them or third parties that will remain in touch with them." Important witnesses would include any individual who spoke with the victim at the time of the incident, as statements made to such individuals at the time of the incident are nontestimonial and probably admissible (Klein, 2008a, p. 51).

Interestingly, when asked if *Crawford* has had any negative effect on the prosecution of child abuse cases, State Attorney Drane Burdick replied with an emphatic "absolutely not." As she explained, this is because her office almost always makes a child victim available for cross-examination during the discovery process, most commonly through deposition. Also, it is normal procedure to put any child victim on the witness stand for live testimony during the trial, when appropriate, giving the defendant yet another opportunity to confront his accuser (Drane Burdick, personal communication, September 25, 2008).

Medical Experts

Perpetrators of domestic violence, as the name of the crime implies, often inflict bodily harm on their victims. As a result, one of the first places a victim of domestic violence will seek assistance is from a medical care provider, who can, along with treating injuries, provide invaluable legal evidence. It is important, therefore, for physicians and other health care providers to understand that they must carefully document a victim's injuries, so that such evidence can be used later to prosecute the person responsible. This is the conclusion stated by senior Harvard research scientist Nancy E. Isaac and law professor V. Pualani Enos of Northwestern University (2001). They note that many medical records contain various flaws that prevent their proper use in subsequent criminal proceedings, including incomplete or inaccurate records and, most often, illegible notes from the treating medical professional (Isaac & Pualani Enos, 2001). In fact, one study examined by Professor Klein discovered nearly one-third of medical notes made as a result of domestic violence-related treatments were deemed illegible and useless (Klein, 2008a, p. 51). Properly prepared and legibly written medical records "can corroborate police data. It constitutes unbiased, factual information recorded shortly after the abuse occurs, when recall [by the victim] is easier" (Isaac & Pualani Enos, 2001, p. 2). Additionally, many medical records also include photographs of the victim's injuries, which "capture the moment in a way that no verbal description can convey" (Isaac & Pualani Enos, 2001, p. 2).

While some medical professionals may be reluctant to appear in court for a variety of reasons (Isaac & Pualani Enos, 2001, p. 2), they are frequently used with success by many prosecuting offices. Florida state attorney Drane Burdick has often used the expert testimony of medical doctors as well as nurse practitioners in cases involving child abuse and sexual assault cases. While records are also used, it is more often the practice of prosecutors pursuing felony domestic violence cases to use the live testimony of these medical professionals during the trial (Drane Burdick, personal communication, September 25, 2008).

Victim Requests to Abandon Prosecution

For a variety of reasons, it is not uncommon for a victim of domestic violence to request, or even demand, that the prosecution be abandoned. Many victims cite fear of falling victim to further violence, as well as retaliation should the defendant be found not guilty. These fears are not unfounded, as multiple studies "broadly concur that abusers who come to the attention of the criminal justice system who reabuse are likely to do so sooner rather than later" (Klein, 2008b, p. 41).

State Attorney Gergley has also experienced other, more practical, reasons motivating a victim to request the case be dropped. Many calls have been received begging that the defendant be released, because the house bills aren't getting paid. In one instance, a victim claimed she was forced to spend all night fanning cockroaches off her children because the electric bill had been shut off. But, in this instance, "we know the defendant has repeatedly beaten her." Such moments cause a prosecutor to question which is worse: protecting the victim from further abuse or causing financial or even residential harm to the victim (Gergley, personal communication, September 17, 2008). While the moral dilemma may cause some anxiety among many prosecutors, State Attorney Latham is quick to point out that no case has been dropped in favor of allowing the crime to continue, and the other prosecutors in this division readily agreed. These issues of hardship are not ignored, as they are presented to the court to consider during the sentencing process and may result in the defendant receiving probation in favor of jail time. But they do not prevent the prosecution of the crime (Latham, personal communication, September 17, 2008).

Prosecution Perspectives

Public Role of Prosecutor

When asked what role she plays with the state attorney's office, Victim Advocate Cindy Dubrouillet provided an answer that went well beyond the normal logistical answer. While it is true that she serves as an advocate for the victims of domestic violence, assisting them with monetary and legal needs, she also attempts to stop the cycle of violence in the lives of those she assists. This, she hopes, is accomplished when a child sees that the violent behavior of a father or mother is *not* the "right" way to act; in fact, it is "wrong." Doing so, she believes, ensures that at least this child will not become a future abuser and saves them from a dismal future (Dubrouillet, personal communication, September 25, 2008).

She also assists other adult victims and even perpetrators of domestic violence through the teaching parenting classes, which offer to many parents invaluable lessons on how to raise a family and be a good parent. These are lessons not typically taught to these parents by their own parents when they were children. Instead, they fell victim to the cycle of violence, which, hopefully, these classes stop (Dubrouillet, personal communication, September 25, 2008).

Underlying Causes of Domestic Violence

In addition to this cycle of violence inadvertently taught through many generations of family members, there is one other major factor prevalent through many domestic violence cases. "As with criminality in general, there is a high correlation (but not necessarily causation) between substance/alcohol abuse and domestic violence for both abusers and, to a lesser extent, victims," concludes Professor Klein. This conclusion stems from many national studies, one of which found up to 92% of assailants admitted to using drugs or abusing alcohol within 24 hours of committing the assault (Klein, 2008b, p. 18). In California, approximately 38% of domestic violence arrests involved drugs and alcohol, while almost 66% of calls in North Carolina for domestic assaults involved alcohol at the scene (Klein, 2008b, pp. 18–19).

When asked if alcohol played a role in their cases, just about all of the Florida state attorneys prosecuting misdemeanor domestic violence cases in Orange County replied with an emphatic affirmative. It was more common than not that the defendant and victim were consuming alcohol or other substances during the incident, and most defendants have a prior criminal history of possession charges or violent crimes related to substance abuse. Other substances commonly abused and frequently involved in domestic violence cases include prescription drugs, as well as illegal street drugs (Latham et al., personal communication, September 17, 2008).

Public Perceptions

The use of specialized domestic violence prosecution teams has resulted not only in an increase in the successful prosecution of domestic violence cases, but also by improving the public's general perception of state prosecutors. Professor Klein has found that "victims generally report satisfaction with domestic violence prosecutions conducted by specialized prosecution teams." Such satisfaction, he believes, may result in future cooperation with other victims, thus increasing the probability of greater success in prosecution (Klein, 2008a, p. 58). As an example, a study conducted in Alexandria, Virginia, showed about 9 out of 10 victims found prosecutors either very or somewhat helpful. That number was higher than that given to police or even victim advocates, and was much higher than the 67% rating given to prosecutors in Virginia Beach, who do not employ a specialized team of domestic violence prosecutors or advocates (Klein, 2008a, p. 58).

State attorneys in Orange County state they have experienced calls of both overzealousness and leniency. Most accusations of being overzealous, at least in State Attorney Latham's experience, come from victims who wish the case to be dismissed and will ask loaded questions like, "Why are you out to get us?" Additionally, some jurors express during *voir dire* a frustration that their time is being wasted on a simple push or telephone call (Latham, personal communication, September 17, 2008). On the other hand, State Attorney Segui notes that a cooperative victim will likely want his or her abuser to receive the absolute maximum punishment allowable and become frustrated when a plea bargain is made for less (Segui, personal communication, September 17, 2008).

Summary

As demonstrated here, there are many issues that must be addressed when prosecuting the crime of domestic violence. Prosecutors must sometimes face the reality that putting a perpetrator of domestic violence behind bars may cause severe hardship for the victim and her family. Legal hurdles, such as the requirements of confrontation, must be overcome. Evidence of the crime must be strong, and believable witnesses are always helpful. Each of these elements can be summed up under the term *convictability*. Simply defined, this is the idea that each of the individual parts of the case—evidence, witness believability, blamelessness of victim, and culpability of the defendant—is strong enough to ensure that a defendant accused of committing the crime of domestic violence will receive appropriate justice. It is the responsibility, and great challenge, of a prosecuting attorney to fully explore each of these issues and increase the level of convictability to its highest degree.

References

Isaac, N. E., & Pualani Enos, V. (2001, September). *Documenting domestic violence: How health care providers can help victims* (NCJ 188564). Washington, DC: U.S. Department of Justice, Office of Justice Programs. Retrieved from http://www.ncjrs.gov/pdffiles1/nij/188564.pdf

Keilitz, S., Hannaford, P. L., & Efkeman, K. S. (1997). *Civil protection orders: The benefits and limitations for victims of domestic violence* (NCJ 172223). Williamsburg, VA: National Center for State Courts, Retrieved from http://www.ncjrs.gov/pdffiles1/pr/172223.pdf

Klein, A. R. (2008a, April). *Practical implications of current domestic violence research. Part II: Prosecution* (NCJ 222320). Washington, DC: National Institute of Justice. Retrieved from http://www.ncjrs.gov/pdffiles1/nij/grants/222320.pdf

Klein, A. R. (2008b, April). *Practical implications of current domestic violence research. Part III: Judges* (NCJ 222321). Washington, DC: National Institute of Justice. Retrieved from http://www.ncjrs.gov/pdffiles1/nij/grants/222321.pdf

Smith, B. E., et al. (2001). *An evaluation of efforts to implement no-drop policies: Two central values in conflict* (NCJ 187772). American Bar Association. Retrieved from http://www.ncjrs.gov/pdffiles1/nij/grants/187772.pdf

Spohn, C., & Holleran, D. (2004). *Prosecuting sexual assault: A comparison of charging decisions in sexual assault cases involving strangers, acquaintances, and intimate partners* (NCJ 199720). Retrieved from http://www.ncjrs.gov/pdffiles1/nij/199720.pdf

Cases Cited

Bordenkircher v. Hayes. (1978). 434 U.S. 357.
Crawford v. Washington. (2004). 541 U.S. 36.

Statutes

Section 741.283, Florida Statutes, 2008.
Section 741.31, Florida Statutes, 2008.
Section 827.03, Florida Statutes, 2008.

Defending Individuals Charged With Domestic Violence

15

JOHN V. ELMORE

Contents

Introduction

Defending individuals charged with domestic violence presents unique challenges for the defense attorney. The defendant, who is, in most cases, a male accused of committing an act of violence against a girlfriend or spouse, is emotionally charged and irrational. Domestic violence cases are often assigned to judges in specialized courts who place a higher priority on solving problems of domestic violence than affording the accused the presumption of innocence. Prosecutors' offices often have specialized units as well that are assigned to prosecute allegations of domestic violence. Armed with a multidisciplinary team of investigators and social workers, prosecutors often have a "no drop" policy in domestic violence cases, with additional resources to prosecute domestic violence cases (Feige, 2004, p. 1).

For the purpose of this chapter, the federal definition of *domestic violence* is used as defined in Section 6 of Title 18, United States Code, which provides in pertinent part,

> For the purpose of this clause, the term "crime of domestic violence" means any crime of violence against a person or former spouse of the person by an individual with whom the person shares a child in common, by an individual who is cohabitating with or has cohabitated with the person as a spouse, by an individual similarly situated to the spouse of the person under the domestic violence or family violence laws of the jurisdiction.

Role of the Defense Attorney

The role of the defense attorney in a domestic violence case is to represent the best interests of a client. The defense attorney's duties in a domestic violence case include securing the client's release on bail, conducting a complete investigation of the case, advising the client to seek appropriate counseling, if necessary, filing discovery and pretrial motions, negotiating pleas, and conducting a trial if the matter is not dismissed or resolved at earlier stages of the proceedings. "The basic duty of defense counsel owes to the Administration of Justice and as an officer of the court is to serve as the accused counselor and advocate with courage and devotion and to render effective representation" (ABA Criminal Justice Standard 4-1.2(b)).

Attorneys should carefully screen domestic violence cases before accepting them. Moreover, they should exercise caution about representing defendants that have unreasonable expectations concerning the outcome of their case. Anecdotally, attorneys should not accept cases when they are convinced that the client will not follow their advice and seek to resolve the case in a logical and reasonable manner. For example, I recall one such instance where I refused to represent a potential client (who appeared to be a fireman) who had unreasonable expectations about his case. The fireman was arrested for hitting his girlfriend in the head with a lead pipe. In my opinion, his judgment was clouded due to his anger at his accuser. The fireman explained to me that his new girlfriend and his ex-girlfriend were roommates. He escorted his new girlfriend to the apartment that she shared with his ex-girlfriend in order to retrieve her belongings. The two women got into a fistfight. The fireman hit his ex-girlfriend in the head with a lead pipe in an attempt to break up the fight. The ex-girlfriend required medical attention, which included staples to close the wound on her head. The fireman was convinced that he had a solid self-defense claim and wanted complete exoneration of the charges, even if it meant going to a jury trial. He refused to accept my instructions that he had the right to use physical force to break up the fight—but not with a lead pipe, which, under the law, is deadly physical force. The use of deadly physical force to break up a fight between the two women was excessive and therefore unlawful. I felt that it was better for him to hire another lawyer who would take his money and be the attorney of record when the fireman went to jail and lost his job.

Establishing the Trust of the Accused

"Defense counsel should seek to establish a relationship of trust and confidence with the accused and should discuss the objectives of the representation" (ABA Criminal Justice Standard 4-3.1(a)). The successful defense of an individual accused of domestic violence begins with establishing the trust of the accused. In my experience, the typical defendant in a domestic violence case is involved in a toxic relationship where there are emotional issues that could not be resolved in an amicable manner, which may have triggered an incident and resulted in an arrest.

A domestic violence defendant is generally not familiar with the criminal justice system—unless he is the proverbial "frequent flier." The experience of being arrested, fingerprinted, held overnight in a holding cell with career criminals, deprived of a meal, a shower, and sanitary toilet conditions is not pleasant. When combined with the potential end of a romantic relationship, the separation from home and children, and financial issues that naturally flow from the breakup of a relationship, the accused may become an emotional time bomb. The defense attorney must recognize that the accused is experiencing myriad combinations of factors, including bouts of depression, fear, anxiety, anger, guilt, and shame. Oftentimes, the incident that led to the accused arrest was caused in part by the accused irrational and emotional response to a problem. The attorney must convince the client that it is in the client's best interest to exercise sound judgment and logic in all aspects of the case as well as in future dealings with the accuser. Failure of the accused to base decisions on logic rather than emotion could have a detrimental impact on the outcome of the case.

As a defense attorney, one of the best tactics used to gain a client's trust and confidence is to be a good listener. It is far more important to let the client know how much you care than it is to let him know how much you know. Good listening skills create confidence and trust with the client, which is necessary to reach a successful resolution of the case. For example, during the initial client interview, let the client vent and get all of his problems off his chest. At this stage, attorneys should attempt to find out who the client is and what is troubling him. Domestic violence incidents are often the symptoms of other problems. Possible root causes of the incident that led to the arrest of the accused may include alcohol or drug abuse, depression, jealousy, finances, job insecurity, difficulties with children or in-laws, sexual dysfunction, infidelity, or unresolved anger. Having the ability to identify the root causes of the problem will aid in developing a defense strategy and, more importantly, improve the quality of the client's life.

After allowing the client to vent his frustration and showing the client that the attorney has legitimate concern for the accused as a person, the next step for the practitioner is to explain the legal system. The mini-lecture on the criminal justice system should include the roles of the defense attorney, prosecutor, and judge; plea bargaining; bail; the elements of each crime the defendant is accused of and possible defenses; the importance of abiding by restraining orders; the penalties the accused is facing if convicted: the court-sanctioned batterer intervention program; and counseling.

The accused, who generally enjoys good standing in the community, has much to lose if convicted of a domestic violence crime. The accused faces the loss of his home—should the court issue a permanent order of protection—which bars him or her from the residence of the accuser. Separation from children and other family members is a major problem facing the defendant, as a criminal conviction can have an adverse effect on child custody and visitation in the event that there is a separation or divorce. Generally, family court judges determine child custody issues on what is in the best interest of the child. Judges often consider a parent convicted of domestic abuse as being unfit to be a custodial parent or unfit to have unsupervised visitation of children. The accused also risk the possibilities of termination from employment. Frequent court appearances, court-mandated counseling, and negative publicity associated with an arrest have often led to loss of employment of persons accused of domestic violence, many of whom were falsely accused. Counsel must advise his client that he or she is aware of all the above concerns.

After the practitioner has allowed his client to vent and thoroughly explained the criminal process to the accused, the next step is to learn the details about the incident that led to the arrest. Here, particular attention should be exercised in determining whether the accused's version of the event constitutes a legal defense or a mitigating factor that can be used in negotiating a favorable plea bargain or sentence. For instance, I once represented a man accused of assaulting his wife who was addicted to cocaine. I learned that the wife squandered the couple's life savings to support her drug habit and he injured her when trying to prevent her from leaving the house to purchase more cocaine. I used the mitigating information that I learned from my client to convince prosecutors to resolve the case in a manner that did not result in my client receiving incarceration or a criminal conviction.

Legal defenses such as self-defense, necessity, defense of third persons, diminished capacity, and property should also be explored. In many instances, false allegations of domestic violence are motivated by a spouse seeking to obtain an advantage in a matrimonial or custodial proceeding. Counsel should make arrangements to obtain copies of family court and matrimonial court documents at the initial client interview. In my career, I have observed an extreme case where a jilted lover had self-inflicted wounds and falsely reported abuse. In these jilted lover cases, emails, text messages, twittering, and telephone recordings often contain evidence to support a defense that the claims of abuse are false.

The client should be given instructions on how to conduct himself during the duration of the pending criminal charges. The most important instruction a client can receive is to obey all court orders and to not engage in any conduct that will result in the client's rearrest. Courts often issue orders of protection (or restraining orders) against defendants accused of domestic violence. The restraining orders bar the accused from having any contact with the complainant and bar the defendant from the complainant's house and place of business. Violations of the court's order can lead to additional charges and incarceration, including felony contempt of court. Judges do not take kindly to defendants who violate restraining orders and often revoke bail. Bail revocation and incarceration often result in termination of employment of offenders because they cannot show up for work while they are in jail. Defendants who lose their job often lose their ability to afford private counsel.

The most detrimental impact that a violation of a restraining order has on the defense is that the prosecution, in many instances, no longer needs the cooperation of the victim to prove that the defendant committed a crime. For instance, if a police officer testified to say that he saw the accused leaving the victim's home or place of business in violation of the restraining order, the prosecutor would only need the testimony of the police officer and proof that the defendant was served with the restraining order in order to get a conviction.

The accused should also receive some general instructions when charged in *any* criminal case:

1. Make all court appearances on time.
2. Dress and act professionally while in court.
3. Act nice to everyone in the courtroom, including the prosecutor, court personnel, and the judge, even if you feel they treat you nasty.
4. If applicable, make all court-ordered child support payments, as courts will view the accused in a negative light if he has not followed orders issued by other courts.
5. If applicable, enroll in anger management counseling, alcohol or drug counseling, or other appropriate counseling.
6. If unemployed, get a job even if it is for minimum wage.
7. Do not discuss your case with anyone other than your attorney unless your attorney directs you otherwise.
8. Follow all court orders.

9. Do not use alcohol or drugs while the case is pending.
10. Always tell the truth when discussing the case with your attorney.

Bail

Securing bail is essential in domestic violence cases for many reasons. A defendant released on bail has easy access to his attorney and can assist in the preparation of his defense. While out on bail, the accused can take steps toward rehabilitation, including counseling, which will aid in securing a favorable plea bargain. It is more difficult for a judge to sentence a defendant to incarceration who has been free on bail than one who appears in court in a prison jumpsuit and shackles. The likelihood of a defense attorney's success in defending a domestic violence case is increased when the client's release on bail is secured.

A prosecutor's and a judge's greatest fear in a domestic violence case is to have the accused released on bail go out and kill or injure his or her significant other. In 2001, 1,247 women and 440 men were killed by an intimate partner (Rennison & Welchans, 2000). In such instances, the media, the public, and most importantly, the victim's family demand to know why the system released a person accused of domestic violence while doing nothing to protect the victim. For the defense attorney, the fear that prosecutors and judges have about the potential of violence must be reduced (or alleviated) in order to have the accused released on bail.

Controlling the demeanor of the defendant appearing before the judge is the most important tool the defense attorney has to convince the court to release the defendant. My experiences have taught me that at the time of the arrest, people accused of domestic violence are in an emotional state somewhat analogous to a can of gasoline near an open flame ready to explode. It is important to spend time with clients before arraignment and stress how important it is for them to appear relaxed and calm with the court. Defendants accused of domestic violence often are angry and direct their anger toward the court. If a defendant acts angry toward a judge, the judge will set a high bail that will prevent the defendant's release. Therefore, clients are instructed to appear calm at arraignment and not say anything that is not responsive to questions addressed to them by the court. Defendants should look the court in the eye and speak in a clear, relaxed voice. Generally, the court will ask the accused if he or she understands the nature of the charges against him or her and his or her rights. Defendants should be counseled about their rights before arraignment so that the process will run smoothly.

During bail argument, defense attorneys make all of the usual arguments that are made in any criminal case by stressing the client's strong community ties, reputation, character, employment, length of residency, and the likelihood of his appearance in future court appearances (NYS Criminal Procedure Law §510.30.2(a)). In domestic violence cases, if the defendant has firearms, it is wise to volunteer the information to the court and make suggestions for the surrender and safekeeping of firearms while the charges are pending. Of equal importance, attorneys should stress to the court that they have counseled their client about the consequences of having offensive contact with the complainant and that they are confident that there will be no offensive contact.

The importance of having family members present—to support the accused—in the court at arraignment and bail hearings cannot be overstated. Family members should be prepared to address and assure the court that they are willing to provide a temporary residence for the accused if the court deems it necessary. In many cases, it would be unwise for a judge to allow a defendant to return home when he is faced with allegations of domestic violence because of the likelihood that it will happen again. The judge's goal of giving domestic violence defendants a cooling off period can be realized by directing the accused to stay with relatives while the case is pending.

The prosecutor's most potent weapon in convincing the court to remand the defendant without bail is pleas from the alleged victim to keep the defendant incarcerated. If there are no visible signs of injury, defense counsel can argue that the complainant's claims are exaggerated or false. In some instances, it may be appropriate to have a family member or mutual friend intervene and persuade the complainant to not advocate against the release of the accused. There are circumstances where, despite defense counsel's best efforts, the court will set a high bail that the accused cannot make.

Investigating the Case

> Defense counsel should conduct a prompt investigation of the circumstances of the case and explore all avenues leading to the facts relevant to the merits of the case and the penalty in the event of conviction. The investigation should include efforts to secure information in the possession of the prosecution and law enforcement authorities. (ABA Criminal Justice Standards 4-4.1(9))

After arraignment, a thorough investigation must be conducted. If the defendant has been injured, it is important to get photographs as well as medical documentation of the injuries. If there were witnesses to the incident, they should be interviewed by counsel in the presence of a third party, preferably a private investigator. It is also essential to get medical records and photographs of injuries of the accuser.

The background of the complainant and prosecution witnesses and defense witnesses should be thoroughly investigated. If the complainant or other prosecution witnesses have been arrested in the past, defense counsel should obtain more than a rap sheet. It is essential to obtain arrest reports, accusatory instruments, allocutions, and transcripts of the plea, when applicable. Many times, witnesses have memory lapses when asked about criminal convictions. An extremely effective cross-examination technique of witnesses who have forgotten about previous convictions is to recite the entire plea allocation of the witness that was given under oath to a judge. Later, counsel can point out to the jury how conveniently the witness forgot about the criminal conduct that was admitted to under oath in a court. How reliable can such a witness be who has forgotten the underlying conduct of a criminal conviction?

Defense counsel should determine whether the accuser has reported incidents of abuse in the past. If prior allegations of abuse were false or withdrawn, such information is very useful on cross-examination. The best source to find out about false reports of abuse is from the client. Discovery demands can be made of the prosecution, and subpoenas of the local police department can also uncover such information.

The Internet is a valuable investigative tool. News articles, MySpace and Facebook sites, and dating sites contain a wealth of information about a witness that, if accessed and utilized, can undermine his or her credibility. Many seasoned defense attorneys are not as computer-savvy as younger people. Senior attorneys are advised to utilize the services of a young attorney or paralegal to conduct Internet research of witnesses.

I recall conducting a background check on a prosecution witness on whom the assistant district attorney had given me a rap sheet that listed a couple of petit larceny convictions and a burglary conviction. I was able to obtain all of the court records of the individual as well as arrest reports and news articles. From the information gathered, I was able to learn that during the Christmas season, the witness committed a series of burglaries and stole Christmas presents. Several house burglaries were dismissed and covered by the plea of guilty to one burglary. Many of the victims were relatives of the witness. Had I not done a diligent background of the witness and relied solely on the rap sheet that the prosecution had supplied, the jury would have simply known that the witness was convicted of stealing and burglary. On a more humorous note, during cross-examination, in addition to obtaining a complete understanding of the witness misconduct, the jury was able to learn that the newspapers dubbed the witness as the "Grinch Who Stole Christmas."

Meeting With the Accuser

Defense attorneys are advised, if possible, to meet with an alleged domestic violence victim. Extreme caution must be exercised when having discussions so they are not violations of any ethical rules governing attorney conduct. An attorney must never advise the witness to not cooperate with the prosecution and never advise the witness to lie or commit perjury. Such conduct can result in disbarment (ABA Criminal Justice Standard 4-4.4(d)).

Victims of domestic violence are often ambivalent about prosecuting cases in court and often seek to drop the charges. Several factors can lead the victim to lack confidence in the criminal justice system. These include procedural delays, complex court proceedings, discourteous court employees, and misinformation about the court system given by the abuser or uninformed service provider (*Domestic Violence Benchbook* 1.7.2).

According to the National District Attorneys Association's Policy on Domestic Violence (2004, p. 4), "a victim of domestic violence may often express hostility towards the police and the prosecutor over the arrest and prosecution of the offender. In the end a victim of domestic violence may refuse to cooperate; recant his/her initial version of the abuse; or in the end display reluctance to participate in the criminal justice system." To alleviate these concerns, and if given the opportunity, I generally explain to the alleged domestic violence witness (who does not want to cooperate with the prosecution) that I represent the defendant and not the accuser. I instruct the witness that anything I say to him or her should be interpreted to be what is in the best interest of my client only and not the witness's best interest. I do not discourage the witness from cooperating with the police or prosecution. Rather, witnesses are told they also have the right to fully cooperate with the prosecution or the defense. Generally, a witness has a right to not talk to the police, prosecutors, defense attorneys, or defense investigators if they choose not to. The prosecution and defense both have the authority to subpoena a witness to the stand in court under oath before a judge or jury. Neither the prosecution nor the defense can force a witness to discuss a case in their office, and the police do not have the right to enter the witness's home to talk. Witnesses have the right to speak to or refuse to speak to either side if they wish.

In the event that the witness wishes to recant his or her testimony, the defense attorney can make arrangements for a private investigator to take the witness's statement outside of my presence. If the witness needs the assistance of an attorney, I will refer the witness to an attorney that will aggressively protect the interests of the witness. I do not want to be placed in a position where the prosecution could call me as a witness surrounding the circumstances of the taking of the statement. I advise the investigator to caution the witness against committing perjury. I also instruct my investigator to not take a statement if something happens during the course of the interview that leads the investigator to conclude that the witness is committing perjury in the statement that recants the earlier statement.

I recall representing a police officer accused of assaulting his wife. The officer was arrested, fingerprinted, and released on bail with the condition that he surrender all of his weapons and refrain from contact with his wife. The officer was suspended from his job and separated from his wife and children. The prosecution made a plea offer that was not acceptable to my client or his wife. The prosecution pursued the matter in an aggressive manner that displeased the victim. The victim felt that the prosecution did not represent her best interests. During a visit to my office, she told me that she wanted to switch sides and defend her husband. The woman claimed that the police pressured her to make a false statement. I believed her. Despite the no contact order, the couple had secretly reconciled their differences. The police officer's wife did not want him fired from his job and certainly did not want him to go to jail. She felt that court-mandated counseling was unnecessary because a couple of prayer sessions with their pastor seemed to work.

I referred the woman to a very good lawyer who did a wonderful job in representing her. The attorney sent a letter to the prosecutor noting his representation and directed the prosecution to have no contact with the witness without his consent. Through the attorney, the witness was noncooperative with the prosecution. The lawyer for the police officer advocated to the court and the prosecution his client's desire to drop the charges. Eventually the charges were dismissed.

Pretrial Motions

In a domestic violence case, counsel should make all pretrial motions that would be made in any criminal case, for example, a motion for discovery, to suppress statements, to suppress physical evidence, and in some instances, to dismiss on speedy trial grounds. It is very important to demand all police reports, photographs, witness statements, 911 recordings, tapes of police radio transmissions, medical records, and their list of expert witnesses. All of these items received from the prosecution should be examined closely. Counsel should pay particular attention for inconsistent statements made by the accuser and police. Often the accuser's statements to medical personnel will vary significantly from what he or she told the police. Any inconsistent statements should be used on cross-examination of the accuser if the case proceeds to trial.

Plea Bargaining

Plea bargaining in domestic violence cases requires a special sensitivity because the outcome of the case can have a long-lasting impact on the family unit. Children's relationships with both parents are affected by the outcome of the case as well as the financial stability of the family unit.

Defense counsel should enlighten the prosecution of the irrevocable effects that a trial will have on the family. Counsel should portray the incident as an isolated outburst and not a pattern of destructive behavior. Most people have lost their tempers at some time in the heat of the moment and have done things they have come to later regret. If counsel can convince the prosecution that the incident will not be repeated, negotiations for a pretrial settlement may be feasible.

Many inexperienced attorneys engage in plea discussions with the prosecution at the bench in the courtroom. Well-seasoned attorneys will schedule an office visit with the prosecution attorney to discuss resolving the case. Defense attorneys who take the initiative to meet privately with prosecutors will often obtain a better result for their client than they would if they tried to negotiate the case at a court proceeding.

Plea bargaining in the courtroom at a calendar call presents problems. The prosecutor generally has a heavy calendar. Police officers, defense attorneys, witnesses, and crime victims are all competing for the prosecutor's time. Defense counsel arguments for a better plea offer are not always heard or understood by prosecutors at calendar call because there is too much going on at one time. An attorney who takes the time to schedule a private meeting with the prosecutor can be assured that the prosecutor has the time to consider another point of view. Furthermore, even if negotiations in a private setting are unsuccessful, defense counsel can seize the opportunity to probe the prosecutor for evidence and strategy the prosecutor will use if the matter goes to trial.

Sometimes plea bargain discussions occur in the judge's chambers. There are instances when it is clear that the judge considers the prosecutor's view to be unreasonable. The judge's belief of a just resolution of the case may be consistent with defense counsel's view. Defense counsel should consider waiving a jury trial in this instance because of the strong likelihood that the outcome of the trial will be consistent with the judge's sense of fairness. A jury may find the defendant guilty of a more serious crime than what the judge believes is fair.

Successful plea bargaining of a domestic violence case may require enrolling the client in counseling to deal with anger management and dispute resolution issues. I stress the importance of the successful completion of these programs to clients. If they are *not* enthusiastic about attending the programs, a good defense attorney should instruct them that they must act enthusiastic and pretend to be interested in the program. If they find themselves with a counselor that they do not like, they should not display animosity toward the counselor. Successful completion of the program will require complete cooperation. The better the client's attitude and cooperation, the shorter the program will be. Unbeknownst to many, clients that fail to coop-erate often have the time extended or start the process over again when they are referred to other programs.

In plea negotiations, it may be appropriate to question the character of the accuser. Inconsistent statements are relevant concerning the character of the accuser. Minimize the suffering if it is supported by medical records or pho-tographs. If counsel is aware of drug abuse, alcohol abuse, or psychological issues involving the accuser, defense counsel should be prepared to discuss a plan to address counseling for those problems. It is appropriate for counsel to argue that the trauma of trial may victimize the accuser again. Often pros-ecutors and judges can be swayed to become more lenient when they believe a trial will be harmful to the accuser whose credibility is at issue.

The Jury Trial

Jury Selection

An overwhelming majority of domestic violence cases are dismissed or result in plea bargains. In the rare instance a domestic violence case goes to trial, it is probably one where either the defendant or the accuser is noncooperative or the defendant is truly innocent and prepared to take the stand to proclaim innocence. Otherwise, the jury will be left with some evidence of physical abuse, such as photographs or medical records and the accuser's testimony that the defendant caused the injury.

During jury selection, counsel must be keenly aware that people are pre-disposed to believe the word of the weaker sex who is alleged to have been abused by a member of the stronger sex. During the *voir dire* process, defense counsel should fashion questions to draw out the biases that most people have in domestic violence cases and have those individuals excused from the jury trial for cause. For example, a potential juror that would not consider a claim of self-defense in a case where a man is accused of assaulting a woman should be excused for cause. A tactic to lure prosecution-prone witnesses to be challenged for cause is to get them to admit that they understand what self-defense is. Then ask them if there are circumstances when a man has the right to hit a woman. If the witness responds no, then the witness has made it clear that he or she will not objectively consider self-defense. This witness should be excused for cause. The side that receives the most challenges for cause has an obvious advantage.

Counsel should begin planting the seeds of the defense theory during jury selection. For instance, if there is a claim of self-defense or a claim of false accusation to obtain an advantage in matrimonial or family court, the jury panel should be introduced to the defense during the *voir dire* process.

The panel should be asked if they have ever said or done things to family members that they have later regretted.

The defense theory should be integrated into all phases of the trial, including opening and closing statements and direct and cross-examination of all witnesses. When jurors are exposed to the theory of defense at jury selection and defense counsel consistently integrates the defense at all phases of the trial, the theory becomes reality in the minds of the jurors.

Finally, the instructions that the judge gives the jury should verify that there is a legal basis for the defense theory of the defense. In closing argument, defense counsel should reference the legal instructions that the judge will give them that are consistent with the theory of defense. "Whether the instruction is on the credibility of the witnesses, preponderance of the evidence/elements of neglect, a special instruction on the right to defend oneself based upon apparent necessity, 'duress' or 'choice of evils,' there is some instruction that contains within it a reference to the concepts embraced by the chosen theme line and the theory" (Pozner & Dodd, 1993, p. 66).

Cross-Examination of the Alleged Victim

The alleged victim in a domestic violence case is the prosecution's star witness and, in many instances, the only eye witness to the event that led up to the defendant's arrest. The successful cross-examination of the accuser can likely be a fatal blow to the prosecution's case.

Cross-examination of the accused in a domestic violence case is difficult. The examination must be consistent with the theory of defense. Defense counsel must not be overly aggressive during cross-examination in the manner one would examine a police informant or a veteran detective because of the risk that the fact finder will be overly sympathetic to the accuser. Defense counsel should treat the accuser with respect. Questions should be delivered in a deliberate fashion for the purpose of getting the witness to admit to facts that are favorable to the defense theory of the case. Questions should be leading and framed for the witness to respond with either a yes or no.

Sometimes, inexperienced defense attorneys allow the witness on cross-examination to testify about everything that he or she testified to on direct examination. A properly conducted cross-examination will limit the witness testimony to repeating areas covered by direct examination that are favorable to the defense. The examiner will utilize inconsistent statements to impeach the witness in areas that are harmful to the defense. All written statements should be scrutinized for inconsistencies. Emphasis on inconsistent statements during cross-examination is essential. Motivations to fabricate to gain an advantage in matrimonial or family court are common themes to explore. Proof that the defendant was injured creates an inference that the accuser was the aggressor. Explore the character of the accused when appropriate. The cross-examination should conclude with areas such as bias, motivation to lie, and issues of credibility.

The Defendant Takes the Stand

Unless the testimony of the accuser is so bad for the prosecution that it is considered a "slam dunk" for the defense, I believe that in most cases the defendant should take the stand. I believe that there are two sides to every allegation of domestic violence, and when juries hear both sides, they are more likely to acquit.

Any client who takes the stand in a criminal case should be extremely well prepared to testify. Preparation includes numerous dry runs of both direct and cross-examination. During preparation, the witness should become familiar with all previous statements that he has given in the past. In domestic violence cases, defense counsel should familiarize the witness with all of the documents signed in matrimonial or family court. Many of the documents the client previously signed may not have been read thoroughly or completely understood when executed. Counsel should also familiarize the defendant with all of the reports and paperwork that he filed in the criminal case that is on trial.

The client should be instructed to be relaxed and calm through the testimony. The witness should look the jury in the eye when answering questions. He or she should be trained to listen to the questions and think before giving answers. The answers should be responsive to the question. The answers must be truthful. If the witness is caught telling a small lie, there is a danger the jury will disbelieve his entire testimony and convict. In most instances, the direct examination should conclude with the defendant expressing his love for the accuser.

It is important that the defendant not lose his or her temper or display hostility at any time during the trial, including cross-examination. The prosecutor will cross-examine the defendant with questions designed to provoke an angry response. If the defendant acts angry, the jury will conclude from the behavior that the defendant is predisposed to violence and will likely convict.

Evidentiary Issues at Trial

Prosecutors often try to bring in hearsay evidence when there is a reluctant complaining witness in domestic violence cases. For 25 years, prosecutors used the authority of *Ohio v. Roberts* (448 U.S. 56 (1980)) to introduce hearsay evidence such as 911 calls or excited utterances to police officers in domestic violence cases when the victim refused to testify (Raeder, 2005). Prosecutors have utilized experts on battered women's syndrome to explain why the victim recanted his or her testimony or is uncooperative.

Crawford v. Washington (541 U.S. 36 (2004)) has limited the prosecutor's ability to use out-of-court statements against the accused. In *Crawford*, the wife refused to testify about the cause of her injuries, citing marital privilege. The prosecution submitted the wife's statement to the jury. The U.S. Supreme Court held that the admission of the wife's out-of-court statement violated the defendant's Sixth Amendment right of confrontation because there was no opportunity for the defense to cross-examine the wife. Therefore, defense attorneys citing *Crawford* should vigorously oppose the admission of all out-of-court statements of the accused. This should include the admission of 911 tapes and statements to police officers. Defense counsel should argue that the admission of out-of-court statements of the accuser violates their client's Sixth Amendment constitutional right to confront the accuser. A judicial order precluding the admission of hearsay statements from the complainant will disarm the prosecution of a potentially lethal weapon.

Conclusion

One of the best pieces of advice for defense attorneys representing defendants accused of domestic violence is to not get emotionally involved with the client or the case. Defense lawyers should exercise sound judgment, intellect, diligence, and logical reasoning when defending allegations of domestic violence. Obtaining the trust and confidence of the accused is extremely important, as is a thorough investigation and preparation of the case. It will take time and patience to establish the trust of the accused, particularly those who are accused of domestic violence and have never before been exposed to the criminal justice system.

Negotiate with the prosecutor in private at the prosecutor's office. At a private meeting with the prosecutor, attempt to portray the client as a human being and the incident that resulted in arrest as an isolated one. Demonstrate that prosecution of the matter will be harmful to the family unit and that alternative means such as family counseling are more appropriate. If the matter proceeds to trial, integrate the theory of defense into all phases of the trial. When appropriate, have the defendant prepared to take the stand. In many cases, the best defense weapon that a defense attorney has is the accuser who no longer trusts the criminal justice system and refuses to cooperate with the prosecution. In domestic violence cases, it is not unusual for the accuser to become a part of the defense team.

References

ABA criminal justice standards: Defense function approved. (1991, February). Standard 4-1.2(b).

ABA criminal justice standards: Defense function approved. (1991, February). Standard 4-3.1(a).

ABA criminal justice standards: Defense function approved. (1991, February). Standard 4-4.1(9).

ABA criminal justice standards: Defense function approved. (1991, February). Standard 4-4.3(d).

ABA criminal justice standards: Defense function approved. (1991, February). Standard 4-4.4(d).

Crawford v. Washington. (2004). 541 U.S. 36.

Feige, D. (2004). Domestic silence: The Supreme Court kills evidence-based prosecution. *Jurisprudence: The Law, Lawyers, and the Court.* Retrieved January 25, from http://www.slate/id/209704

National District Attorneys Association's policy on domestic violence. Adopted October 23, 2004, by the Board of Directors in Monterey, CA. Retrieved January 25, 2009, from http://www.ndaa.org/pdf/domestic_violence_policy_oct_23_2004.pdf [p. 4].

New Mexico domestic violence benchbook: Overview of domestic violence. Section 1.7.2. Retrieved January 25, 2009, from http://jec.unm.edu/resources/benchbooks/dv/ch_1.htm

NYS criminal procedure law §510.30.2(a).

Ohio v. Roberts. (1980). 448 U.S. 56.

Pozner, L., & Dodd, R. (1993). *Cross-examination: Science and techniques* (p. 66). Michie Company Law Publishers.

Raeder, S. (2005). Domestic violence, child abuse, and trustworthy exceptions after *Crawford. American Bar Association of Criminal Justice Magazine, 20,* 1.

Rennison, C. M., & Welchans, S. (2000). *Intimate partner violence, 1993–2001* (NCJ 197838, Statistics Crime Data Brief 920031). U.S. Department of Criminal Justice, Bureau of Justice. Retrieved January 15, 2009, from http://www.ojp.usdoj.gov/bjs/abstract/ipv01.htm

U.S. Code, Title 18, Section 6.

Court-Ordered Treatment Programs
An Evaluation of Batterers Anonymous

16

REBECCA BONANNO

Contents

Introduction

Programs designed to change the attitudes and behaviors of abusive men have existed in the United States for more than three decades. In the early to mid-1990s, spurred by shifts in societal attitudes about and legal responses to domestic violence, local jurisdictions saw a dramatic increase in the number of these programs. Primarily delivered in group settings to men mandated to attend, batterer intervention programs (BIPs) now serve thousands, if not hundreds of thousands, of offenders each year whose abusive acts toward their partners have landed them in the criminal justice system. Judges have come to rely on such programs, often delivered by community agencies and paid for by participant fees, as alternatives to incarceration, punishment, means of holding offenders accountable for their actions, and treatment. The extent to which BIPs are used for each of these purposes varies with the particular philosophical stances and political interests of each jurisdiction's stakeholders. Because so many communities have made BIPs an integral part of their response to domestic violence, and because the safety of families is a primary goal of the intervention, the stakes are high for these services. As such, BIPs have been studied extensively in the last 15 years. Without question, services have expanded nationwide. Yet, in spite of the numerous examinations of BIPs, there remains little in the way of strong empirical evidence of what strategies are effective in changing attitudes and behaviors, reducing recidivism, and increasing victim and family safety. This paper will provide a brief history of the BIP; an overview of the current state of the field; current controversies among service providers, researchers, and criminal justice professionals; and a review of what renowned researchers and practitioners in the field foresee as the future of the BIP.

BIPs in Historical Context

To understand the history of the BIP, we look to the women's liberation movement in the United States and the battered women's movement it spawned. Prior to the 1970s, the abuse of a woman by a male partner was mostly thought to be a private family matter. When police were called to homes because of domestic disputes, men were routinely encouraged (though not forced) to briefly leave the home to "cool off" and take the proverbial "walk around the block." The women's movement of the 1970s is credited with removing the cloak of domestic privacy and the shame that often accompanied it and bringing male violence and control of women into the light of public view. Feminist activists began to argue that problems like wife abuse and sexual assault were not simply "family problems" but symptoms of a society in which male dominance was achieved and enacted on the bodies of women without protection or recourse. They brought these issues out of the hidden domestic sphere and into public discourse, at first in consciousness-raising groups and self-published writings and eventually in rallies and marches on the street and government hearings.

Increased public awareness about violence against women enabled battered women and their supporters to form their own social movement through which they called for changes in legal protections, police responses, and judicial action. Grassroots action also sought to confront societally sanctioned abuse of women by addressing abusive men themselves. In the mid- and late 1970s, programs like EMERGE in Boston, AMEND in Denver, and RAVEN in St. Louis were developed to "resocialize" men to think about how they used abusive behavior to dominate and control women (Gondolf, 2002). These groups viewed wife battering as an expression and an extension of men's power over women in society. By the mid- to late 1980s, there was an estimated 200 to 300 batterer treatment programs in the United States (Hamberger, 2005). Despite the role of feminist activists in the development of the early BIPs, such programs were not universally accepted within the battered women's movement. Some advocates for victims' rights and protections worried that the paltry available resources would be diverted away from victims' services like shelters and legal assistance to support services for abusive men. Some also were concerned that treating individual men failed to address the larger societal attitudes that they believed encouraged violence against women, and that BIPs offered little more than false hope to women who believed their partners were "cured" of violence after receiving batterers' services.

As the battered women's movement continued to press for greater institutional responses to domestic violence, BIPs claimed a higher place in the criminal justice system and in communities at large. Perhaps the most significant reform in domestic violence policy has been the widespread implementation of mandatory arrest policies in the late 1980s to mid-1990s. Under these policies, police are required to arrest individuals when they believe there is probable cause that a crime has occurred and that the defendant has perpetrated it (Buzawa & Buzawa, 2003). The theoretical bases for mandatory arrest are twofold: (1) This policy limits the discretion of police officers to make arrests based on their own personal attitudes and beliefs about domestic violence, which may be biased toward the perpetrator, and (2) it relieves victims of the burden of pressing charges against their abusers on their own when they may not feel safe enough to do so. Like so many domestic violence policies, mandatory arrest is not without controversy. Some argue that unintended consequences of mandatory arrest policies negatively affect women and communities of color (Bourg & Stock, 1994; Hanna, 1996; Chesney-Lind, 2002; Ross, 2007), while others say that mandatory arrest has little effect in improving safety or deterring abuse (Buzawa & Buzawa, in Gelles & Loseke, 1993). Regardless of their merits or detractions, these policies have had a major impact on BIPs. One study examined the effects of mandatory arrest on BIP referrals and found that referral rates doubled within one year of the implementation of mandatory arrest policies and remained at that rate for two subsequent years (Hamberger & Arnold, 1990). This trend brought unprecedented numbers of domestic violence offenders into the criminal justice system—a system already made crowded by new laws mandating harsh sentences for drug offenders—and forced judges to figure out what to do with them. Particularly in cases in which incarceration was determined to be unwarranted, BIPs became the first choice for the judicial system.

Models of Intervention

In the 1980s, as the battered women's movement began receiving government funding and gained in institutional legitimacy, interventions with both victims and batterers increasingly came to be delivered by mental health and social service professionals, rather than by victims and advocates. In some communities, with this new professional influence came a shift away from consciousness raising and mutual support toward psychologically oriented services (Schecter, 1982). In batterers groups this often meant the introduction of cognitive-behavioral techniques that attempt to identify and interrupt the thinking that underlies undesirable behavior and replace the undesired behaviors with more adaptive ones (Healy, Smith, & O'Sullivan, 1998). Cognitive-behavioral anger management programs have caused particular controversy among feminist victims' advocates because the approach assumes that anger, rather than a sexist desire to exert power and control of female partners, is the cause of abusive behavior. What is typically referred to as the psychodynamic or insight-based approach to batterer intervention is even more controversial in the field. Like psychotherapeutic treatments for other behavioral or emotional difficulties, these "talk" therapies assist individuals in working through internal conflicts, past traumatic experiences, and stressful life events. Some in the field have argued that when abusive behavior is framed as a psychological problem, batterers are provided with excuses for their behavior and may fail to take responsibility for their harmful and intentionally abusive actions (Adams, in Yllo & Bograd, 1988). Further, it is suggested that focusing on psychological etiologies of abuse undermines the progress feminist activists have made in calling attention to the sexist ideologies that create and support violence against women (VCS, 2005).

The most well-known type of intervention with batterers is typically referred to as the Duluth model. Developed by a group of domestic violence advocates in Duluth, Minnesota, this model includes a psychoeducational curriculum that involves confronting abusive men about their violent behavior and its consequences, teaching them that their behavior stems from a desire to control their female partners, and encouraging them to take responsibility for controlling their behavior. The Domestic Abuse Intervention Project describes the curriculum as follows:

> A central assumption is that nature and culture are separate. Men are cultural beings who can change because abusive behavior is cultural, not innate. Facilitators engage men in dialogue about what they believe about men, women, marriage and children. Curriculum exercises engage men in critical thinking, and self-reflection; identify the contradictions; and explore alternatives to abuse. (Domestic Abuse Intervention Program, n.d.)

Delivered in groups, usually in 1- to 1½-hour weekly sessions over a period of about 6 months (Gondolf, 2002), these programs are typically administered by community domestic violence agencies. Cognitive-behavioral techniques to interrupt faulty thinking and stop abusive behavior are a part of Duluth model intervention.

Duluth-type programs are the most widely recognized approach to batterer intervention. But many local jurisdictions throughout the country implement Duluth-like services—that is, programs that incorporate the model's fundamental gender-based ideology and cognitive-behavioral strategies—without following the model explicitly or precisely. In states that set standards and guidelines for BIPs, Duluth model principles are often found (Gondolf, 2002). Most programs tend to focus on helping batterers to take responsibility for their abusive behavior, expand their understanding of what constitutes abuse, and learn new skills to replace aggressive and controlling behaviors (Gondolf, 1997). What differs across programs is the emphasis placed on skills training, cognitive strategies, gender-role restructuring, power and control motives for abuse, patterns for family interaction, or the role of past person trauma (Saunders, 2001).

The term *Duluth model* has come to be synonymous with confrontational, group intervention focusing on the power and control motive for domestic violence. However, Duluth program developers have always maintained that such an intervention cannot stand alone; batterer interventions are most appropriate and effective when integrated into wider institutional responses from law enforcement, the judicial system, and community services, what has come to be known as the *coordinated community response* to domestic violence (Pence & McMahon, 1997). This approach is based on the idea that institutional practices and systems (pro-arrest policies, prompt referral to programs, swift prosecution, sentencing recommendations, coordination among criminal justice agencies, etc.) are crucial in keeping victims safe (Pence & McMahon, 1997; Gondolf, 2002; Shepard, Falk, & Elliott, 2002). Without coordinated and responsive systems in place to send the message that domestic violence is a serious crime and to provide appropriate monitoring and sanctions, batterer treatment can be only so effective in reducing recidivism and increasing safety.

One recent development in batterer intervention is the New York model, a set of principles that are rooted in Duluth's feminist ideology, but make no claims of actually changing the attitudes of abusive men. This model emphasizes batterer accountability in the context of the criminal justice system and de-emphasizes batterer services as treatment for individual pathologies. One of the primary goals of the New York model is to create and promote a batterer program that supports the social change efforts of the battered women's movement (VCS, 2005). The model's guiding principles include:

- Domestic violence is rooted in the historical precedent that accepted men controlling their female partners.
- Only court-mandated participants are enrolled.
- Batterers programs exist as part of a coordinated community response to domestic violence.
- Batterers programs are educational classes, not treatment.

- To view batterers programs as treatment or rehabilitation is to suggest that battering is the result of pathology.
- While the New York model asserts that individual men can change their behavior, there is no reliable evidence to suggest that a class is an effective mechanism for change.

This approach focuses not on attitude and behavior change, but serves "to extend judicial monitoring ... and as a mechanism for offender accountability" (VCS, n.d.). Despite the promotion of this approach through training and outreach offered by the model's developers, the New York model has yet to receive much attention in the research literature on BIPs. However, in the current environment of doubt about the effectiveness of BIPs, programs that make no claims of "changing" batterers are likely to appeal to judges looking for programs to assist in monitoring offenders, yet are wary of relying on interventions that lack empirical support. As such, the field may see more New York model programs emerge in the coming years.

BIP Evaluations

Considering the primary role mandated BIPs have come to occupy in the criminal justice system's response to domestic violence, it is reasonable to expect that victims and their advocates, judges, community leaders, researchers, and policy makers all want to know if these programs are actually effective in reducing abusive behavior and increasing victim and community safety. Unfortunately, results of BIP evaluations do not provide a clear answer about their effectiveness. While some evaluations have found small positive effects (Palmer, Brown, & Barrera, 1992; Tutty, Bidgood, Rothery, & Bidgood, 2001), others, like the experimental studies of programs in Broward County, Florida, and Brooklyn, New York, carried out by the National Institute of Justice, concluded that batterers who completed the programs showed no differences in attitudes, beliefs, or behaviors (Jackson, Feder, Davis, Maxwell, & Taylor, 2003).

A recent meta-analysis by Babcock, Green, and Robie (2004) examined data from 22 studies evaluating domestic violence treatment efficacy. The studies included in the analyses were either experimental or quasi-experimental designs and evaluated Duluth/feminist-based psychoeducational programs, cognitive-behavioral programs, and other approaches, including couples therapy, supportive therapy, relationship enhancement, and programs that combined different types of services. Not all of the programs evaluated were mandatory for participants. Overall, the authors found that "the effects due to treatment were in the small range, meaning that the current interventions have a minimal impact on reducing recidivism beyond the effect of being arrested" (p. 1024). The quasi-experimental studies examined (those that compared either treatment completers with noncompleters or treated offenders to a matched group of nontreated offenders) showed slightly higher effect sizes than those of the experimental studies; the differences in effect sizes were not significant. No significant differences were found in effects sizes when Duluth-type programs were compared with cognitive-behavioral treatments, the two most common intervention types, which represented 30 of the 37 programs included in analysis.

Babcock et al. (2004) caution readers not to accept the null hypothesis—that BIPs are ineffective in reducing recidivism—too quickly. First, they point out that even a small effect size, such as the 5% decrease in the likelihood that a woman will be reassaulted by a partner who went to treatment, may still equate to an increase in safety for some victims (in this case, an estimated 42,000 women per year based on all reported cases of domestic violence in the United States). Second, the authors warn that any meta-analysis is only as good as the individual studies it examines. Methodological issues present in the 22 studies, such as variability in what constituted treatment completion and the absence of controls for the number of sessions completed by participants (the so-called dose effect), may contribute to the smaller effect sizes. Further, they remind the reader that, in these studies, as in any other real-world evaluation of BIPs, "effect size due to treatment from court mandated batterers is confounded with the strength of the coordinated efforts of the police, probation, and legal system" (p. 1048). Isolating the treatment effect of the intervention is almost impossible in the context of the coordinated community response to domestic violence, which has become the norm, thanks to local, state, and federal policies, in communities throughout the country.

In another meta-analytic review of 10 quasi-experimental and experimental evaluations of BIPs, Feder and Wilson (2005) found that official reports (arrests or official complaints made to police) suggested a slight decrease in reoffending after program participation. However, when victims' reports of offender violence were taken into account, these modest effect sizes disappeared. Like Babcock et al. (2004), Feder and Wilson were quick to point out their concerns about the studies that comprised the meta-analysis, including the use of highly restrictive inclusion criteria that may have biased the sample and reduced the generalizability of the results; reliance on official reports of domestic violence, which may not capture the true amount or severity of ongoing violence among the samples; the low response rates of victims in follow-up data collection; and the use of program dropouts as control groups. In the end, Feder and Wilson conclude that their meta-analysis "does not offer strong support that court-mandated treatment to misdemeanor domestic violence offenders reduces the likelihood of further reassault" (p. 257).

Studies such as these have been the targets of criticism from both advocates of the Duluth model and programs like it (Minnesota Program Development, n.d.) and researchers who have pointed out the methodological problems that are difficult to avoid in program evaluation of this kind. Gondolf (2004) has argued that most evaluations have not addressed the problems of differences in implementation across sites, the impact of concurrent criminal justice interventions such as probation supervision and court action, the absence of pure control groups, and the range of participant outcomes that could be viewed as constituting success. In response to these methodological issues, Gondolf (2004) worked with the Centers for Disease Control to design a multisite evaluation to address these methodological issues; from that study it was concluded that "at least some programs are effective in stopping assault and abuse and that batterer intervention programs in general show some promise" (p. 616). Among the study's noteworthy findings are (1) that reassault and other forms of abuse during the first year after program intake de-escalated and remained at lower levels over the three years that followed, and (2) that the overwhelming majority of men in the sample (80% to 90% in 30- and 48-month follow-ups) were not violent for a sustained period. On the other hand, during the first 15 months after program intake, over one-third of the men reassaulted a partner and nearly half reassaulted during the full four-year follow-up of the study.

Predictors of Program Success and Failure

Researchers interested in finding out what characteristics increase the likelihood that an abuser will complete and have success in a batterers program have looked at a variety of variables. Most quantitative researchers have defined success in terms of recidivism rates, that is, rates of reassault, as reported by batterers or victims, or official reports of rearrest or violations of probation. Risk factors for program dropout or recidivism include unemployment and unstable employment history, being unmarried, young age, criminal history, and substance abuse problems (Hanson & Wallace-Cappretta, 2004; Cissner & Puffett, 2006). Results from Gondolf's multisite evaluation discussed above found that drunkenness during the follow-up period and the women's perceptions of their own safety were the most substantial predictors of reassault (2004). Heckert and Goldolf (2004) have attempted to develop a robust model that would help those in the field predict risk of reassault among batterers based on individual characteristics. However, they warn that high-risk batterers are not easy to identify and that risk assessment instruments should be used with caution.

Current State of the Field

There is no national organization or association of BIP service providers, nor is there a federal government agency that tracks BIPs around the country. In the absence of any unifying body, BIPs tend to operate independently and are accountable only to their local, or sometimes, state agencies, making it difficult for researchers and policy makers to examine national trends in service delivery. In the first study of its kind of since the 1980s, a recent national survey (Dalton, 2007) has begun to fill in the details about what is happening in BIPs nationwide. Dalton drew his sample from lists of BIPs provided by state organizations, coalitions, and networks and from state governments. From questionnaires mailed to 312 programs in 2002, the final sample consisted of 150 programs from 36 states.

Results reveal a fairly diverse and expansive national landscape of BIP providers. A large majority (87%) of the programs surveyed had been operating for three years or more. About a third provided services under the auspices of another organization (some of which were battered women's shelters), and the remaining programs were free-standing organizations. The programs were provided by an almost even mix of for-profit and nonprofit agencies. Whereas some programs received local, state, or federal government funding, private donations, or assistance from the United Way, the operating budgets of most providers depended on client fees.

The average number of referrals reported by the surveyed agencies for the year prior to the study was 262.7, with the judicial system (courts, probation, parole, etc.) providing the largest proportion of referrals. Program length averaged 31.5 weeks, with a standard deviation of 12.2 weeks, and the majority lasted 24 weeks or more. Thirty-nine programs described different "tracks" of services based on various client criteria, such as substance abuse problems and seriousness of offenses. Agencies reported an impressively high completion rate with a mean of 62% and a surprising (and perhaps overly optimistic) recidivism rate of 16% for male clients. Dalton states that, when asked, most BIP directors surveyed did not report that they collected recidivism data, yet most had an opinion about clients' recidivism. He notes that these opinions are considerably more hopeful than the literature on BIPs suggests they should be.

Unfortunately absent from Dalton's study are data on the types of intervention models used by the programs surveyed, and questions remain about the prevalence and quality of specific types of programs throughout the country. For example, how many of the BIPs surveyed describe themselves as Duluth model programs? How closely do they follow the model, and do they incorporate other strategies? Readers of the BIP literature would also be interested to know about the type and extent of training BIP providers receive. These issues are ripe for further research and would help to expand our understanding of what is actually happening in field.

For those in the field who believe that batterers can and sometimes do change as a result of intervention, one salient question is: How does this change occur? The process through which change takes place among batterers in BIPs has been the focus of several qualitative studies (Pandya & Gingerich, 2002; Scott & Wolfe, 2000; Silvergleid & Mankowsi, 2006, MacPhee-Sigurdson, 2004). These authors try to pull apart the processes taking place in the batterers group to bring about the hoped for psychological, social, and behavioral changes in its members. Pandya and Gingerich (2002) conducted a microethnography of a group of six BIP participants and found that the men attributed changes in themselves to gaining greater self-knowledge, acknowledging that they have a problem, identifying what specifically that problem is (substance abuse, anger, poor communication skills, etc.), and learning new adaptive interpersonal skills. Scott and Wolfe (2000) conducted semistructured interviews with nine men who had changed their abusive behavior according to their own reports and those of their counselors and partners. The researchers identified 21 distinct variables related to change, the most significant of which were (1) taking responsibility for past behavior; (2) empathy for their victims; (3) reduced dependency, which the authors described as the men's realization that they were self-sufficient and responsible for their own behavior, and that their partners were also autonomous individuals with the right to make their own decisions; and (4) communication, in particular learning conflict management and resolution skills and developing better listening abilities.

Silvergleid and Mankowsi (2006) interviewed 9 batterers group participants and 10 facilitators to identify and describe key change processes. They broke their findings down into four categories:

1. Community-level and extratherapeutic influences, including the criminal justice system, child protective services, and fear of the loss of their partners
2. Organizational-level influences, specifically the influence of the individual facilitators and their ability to balance support and confrontation
3. Group-level processes, which include the participants' provision (like the facilitators) of support and confrontation, sharing and hearing the stories of others, and modeling nonabusive behaviors and attitudes
4. Individual psychological development, such as learning new interpersonal and emotion management skills, gaining self-awareness, and deciding to change

Schrock and Padavic (2007) used extensive nonparticipant observation to explore how masculinity is constructed and negotiated in a Duluth-based batterer intervention program. They found that the (all-male) group participants only rhetorically and superficially took responsibility for their behavior while showing no indication that their attitudes or beliefs about women and relationships had changed as intended by the program. Group facilitators challenged the participants on their use of sexist language, such as referring to their partners using possessives (i.e., "my lady"), but in many other ways they simply reinforced the participants' traditional ideas about gender roles. Facilitators used tactics such as shaming or cajoling to get their points across, while the participants resisted through disengagement or diversion. Schrock and Padavic conclude that the implementation of Duluth model interventions, and not the curriculum itself, is problematic.

Standards

Despite the absence of clear empirical evidence of whether and what types of BIPs are most effective, many states—30, at last count—have developed standards by which those BIPs receiving referrals from government agencies will operate. Content analyses of these state standards (Austin & Dankwort, 1998; Maiuro, Hagar, Lin, & Olson, 2001) have revealed the varying degrees to which states seek to control the content, format, and delivery of services to batterers. Standards in some states are voluntary, but in others are mandated through oversight or specific legislation (Maiuro et al., 2001). The most consistent elements of the state standards for BIPs pertained to the modality in which services are to be provided, specifically in groups (90% of states emphasized or required the group modality and 43% specifically preclude couples treatment) (Maiuro et al., 2001). Other domains of batterer's treatment specified in state standards include program length, education and training of facilitators, philosophy, intake procedures, and completion criteria (Austin & Dankwort, 1999).

There is considerable controversy about the wisdom of implementing standards for BIPs. Though it seems that common sense would advise policy makers to take measures to ensure program accountability, provide guidance to practitioners, and limit questionable interventions, some in the field believe that too little is known about the effectiveness of the most commonly implemented interventions to make a case for standardizing them. Gelles (2001) argues that even the most rigorous evaluations of BIPs provide too little consistency as to the effectiveness of these programs to warrant researchers and policy makers giving a "seal of approval" to any particular types of interventions. In creating standards for BIPs, models of interventions are provided with undeserved legitimacy, which may prove to be harmful to victims of abuse, Gelles suggests. Geffner and Rosenbaum (2001) wonder if the implementation of standards has the impact on improving services that many assume it to have, a question they say requires further study.

As a compromise between those who decry the absence of any standards for BIPs as dangerous and others who claim that the implementation of standards may be equally or perhaps more dangerous, the Maryland Attorney General's and Lt. Governor's Family Violence Task Force developed standards that intentionally do not include "rigidly prescribed program models or practices" (Murphy, 2001, p. 251). Instead, this group chose to implement operating guidelines that specify only that those programs eligible for court referral maintain a focus on ending abuse and on preventing abusers from evading or minimizing their responsibility for aggressive behavior. This middle ground seems to encapsulate what little consensus exists in the field of batterer intervention and may be the best way forward in the standards debate.

The Future of BIPs: Recommendations From the Literature

One of the primary (and often critiqued) assumptions of the common approaches to batterer intervention is that abusive men are similar enough to one another in behavior and motivation that one approach to correcting abuse would work for the majority of abusers. Both the Duluth and New York models, for example, presume that domestic violence is a social problem, rather than a psychological one, and that abusive men come to be so through social learning. By extension then, it is assumed that ending abuse requires a social intervention—hence the gender-based psychoeducational interventions. Many researchers and theorists have argued, however, that the concept of *the batterer* as a man who uses abusive behavior as a means of exerting power and control over his female partner is overly simplistic and fails to adequately describe the range of etiologies and expressions of abuse found among this population of men (Dutton & Nicholls, 2005; Gelles & Cavanaugh, 2005). Several typologies of batterers have been developed based on personality and psychopathological characteristics and severity, frequency, and generality of abuse (Holtzworth-Munroe & Stuart, 1994; Johnson, 1995; see Capaldi & Kim, 2007, for review). Other researchers suggest the need for interventions that address the substance abuse problems of abusive men as well as their violent behavior (Moore & Stuart, 2004). Interventions tailored to address the various problems, needs, and cultural backgrounds of abusive men have been recommended by many in the field and may prove to be a major focus of research and program development in the next several years (Healy, Smith, & O'Sullivan, 1998; Stuart, Temple, & Moore, 2007).

Motivational counseling techniques have also been suggested for use in BIPs to increase the batterer's internal desire for change (Murphy & Baxter, 1997; Stuart et al., 2007). The literature on batterers documents their use of minimization and denial when asked about their abusive behavior (Henning, Jones, & Holdford, 2005; Smith, 2007); the confrontational strategies employed by facilitators of some feminist-based interventions may only serve to increase resistance to treatment among men who do not believe themselves to have a problem with violence. Examples of motivational strategies include creating a supportive and cooperative environment in treatment groups and using nonconfrontational approaches to help the participants identify their own reasons to change harmful behaviors. The transtheoretical model of change, also known as the stages of change model (Prochaska & DiClemente, 1982), has been utilized and studied extensively with substance abusing and other populations and offers a framework for helping individuals who are resistant to treatment to move toward internal motivation for change. Some believe that this model may improve the effectiveness of treatment of court-ordered batterers (Daniels & Murphy, 1997; Begun, Shelley, Strodthoff, & Scott, 2001; Eckhardt, Babcock, & Homack, 2004).

Couples (also called conjoint) treatment for domestic violence is about as controversial a topic as exists in the domestic violence field, but one which some say warrants further consideration. Among victims' advocates, many practitioners, and some researchers, couples therapy has been considered politically incompatible with the goals of the battered women's movement in that it assumes that both batterer and victim require treatment to correct a relationship problem rather than focusing on holding abusers accountable for their behavior. Some believe that couples treatment places female victims at increased risk for further abuse should an abuser retaliate for something said or done during therapy, and it is reasonable to assume that such risk exists for some couples with high levels of violence. Research has shown, however, that conjoint treatment—implemented with caution—can be effective in reducing relationship violence (Brannen & Rubin, 1996; O'Leary, 2001). O'Leary and others (Stuart et al., 2007) point out that since much of the violence seen in relationships is mutual, couples without histories of serious violence are likely to benefit from making a joint decision to eliminate aggression and improve relationship skills. O'Leary calls for caution in implementing treatment with couples, including making every effort to ensure that the female partner feels in no way coerced into or threatened by treatment, and asks that practitioners and advocates in the field remain open to the possibilities of conjoint therapy.

Conclusion

Batterer intervention, which began with small community groups in the 1970s, has expanded to become one of society's first-line weapons in the war against domestic violence. From program models and philosophies to standards and evaluation, BIPs spark seemingly endless controversy among researchers, practitioners, activists, and policy makers. To the frustration of many in the field, after three decades since their inception, there are more questions about BIPs and their effectiveness than there are answers. The controversy surrounding batterer interventions has, however, maintained a high level of interest and motivation for ongoing research and innovation in the field. Further study and development of BIPs will remain necessary as long as the criminal justice system continues to rely on these interventions as a means of increasing family and community safety.

References

Adams, D. (1988). Treatment models for men who batter: A profeminist analysis. In *Feminist perspectives on wife abuse,* Ed. K. Yllo & M. Bograd (176–199). Newbury Park, CA: Sage Publications.

Austin, J. B., & Dankwort, J. (1999). Standards for batterer programs: A review and analysis. *Journal of Interpersonal Violence, 14,* 152–168.

Babcock, J. C., Green, C. E., & Robie, C. (2004). Does batterers' treatment work? A meta-analytic review of domestic violence treatment. *Clinical Psychology Review, 23,* 1023–1053.

Bourg, S., & Stock, H. V. (1994) A review of domestic violence arrest statistics in a police department using a pro-arrest policy: Are pro-arrest policies enough? *Journal of Family Violence, 9,* 177–189.

Brannen, S. J., & Rubin, A. (1996). Comparing the effectiveness of gender specific and couples groups in a court mandated spouse abuse treatment program. *Research on Social Work Practice, 6,* 405–424.

Buzawa, E. S., & Buzawa, C. G. (1993). The scientific evidence is not conclusive: Mandatory arrest is no panacea. *Current controversies on family violence.* In R. J. Gelles & D. R. Loseke (Eds.), (337–356). Newbury Park, CA: Sage Publications, Inc.,

Buzawa, E. S., & Buzawa, C. G. (2003). *Domestic violence: The criminal justice response* (3rd ed). Thousand Oaks, CA: Sage.

Capaldi, D. M., & Kim, H. K. (2007). Typological approaches to violence in couples: A critique and alternative conceptual approach. *Clinical Psychology Review, 27,* 253–265.

Chesney-Lind, M. (2002). Criminalizing victimizations: The unintended consequences of pro-arrest policies for girls and women. *Criminology & Public Policy, 2,* 81–91.

Cissner, A. B., & Puffett, N. K. (2006). *Do batterer program length or approach affect completion or re-arrest rates? A comparison of outcomes between defendants sentenced to two batterer programs in Brooklyn.* Center for Court Innovation. Retrieved December 1, 2008 from www.courtinnovation.org

Dalton, B. (2007). What's going on out there? A survey of batterer intervention programs. *Journal of Aggression, Maltreatment & Trauma, 15*, 59–74.

Domestic Abuse Intervention Program. (n.d.). *Countering confusion about the Duluth model.* Retrieved December 1, 2008, from www.theduluthmodel.org

Dutton, D. G., & Nicholls, T. L. (2005). The gender paradigm in domestic violence research and theory: Part 1. The conflict of theory and data. *Aggression and Violent Behavior, 10*, 680–714.

Eckhardt, C. I., Babcock, J. K., & Homack, S. (2004). Partner assaultive men and the stages and processes of change. *Journal of Family Violence, 19*(2), 81–93.

Feder, L., & Wilson, D. B. (2005). A meta-analytic court-mandated review of batterer intervention programs: Can courts affect abusers' behavior? *Journal of Experimental Criminology, 1*, 239–262.

Geffner, R. A., & Rosenbaum, A. (2001). Domestic violence offenders: Treatment and intervention standards. *Journal of Aggression, Maltreatment & Trauma, 5*, 1–9.

Gelles, R. J. (2001). Standards for programs for men who batter? Not yet. *Journal of Aggression, Maltreatment & Trauma, 5*, 11–20.

Gelles, R. J., & Cavanaugh, M. M. (2005). The utility of male domestic violence offender typologies: New directions for research, policy, and practice. *Journal of Interpersonal Violence, 20*, 155–166.

Gondolf, E. W. (1997). Batterer programs: What we know and need to know. *Journal of Interpersonal Violence, 12*, 83–98.

Gondolf, E. W. (2002). *Batterer intervention systems: Issues, outcomes and recommendations.* Thousand Oaks, CA: Sage.

Gondolf, E. W. (2004). Evaluating batterer counseling programs: A difficult task showing some effects and implications. *Aggression and Violent Behavior, 9*, 605–631.

Hamberger, L. K. (2005). Men's and women's use of intimate partner violence in clinical samples: Toward a gender sensitive analysis. *Violence and Victims, 20*, 131–151.

Hamberger, L. K., & Arnold, J. (1990). The impact of mandatory arrest on domestic violence perpetrator counseling services. *Family Violence Bulletin, 6*, 10–12.

Hanna, C. (1996, June). No right to choose: Mandated victim participation in domestic violence prosecutions. *Harvard Law Review, 109*, 1849–1910.

Hanson, R. K., & Wallace-Cappretta, S. (2004). Predictors of criminal recidivism among male batterers. *Psychology, Crime & Law, 10*, 413–427.

Healy, K., Smith, C., & O'Sullivan, C. (1998). *Batterer intervention: Program approaches and criminal justice strategies.* National Institute of Justice, U.S. Department of Justice. Retrieved November 24, 2005, from www.ncjrs.gov/txtfiles/168638.txt

Heckert, D. A., & Gondolf, E. W. (2004). Battered women's perception of risk versus risk factors and instruments in predicting repeat reassault. *Journal of Interpersonal Violence, 19*, 778–800.

Henning, K., Jones, A. R., & Holford, R. (2005). "I didn't do it, but if I did I had a good reason": Minimization, denial, and attributions of blame among male and female domestic violence offenders. *Journal of Family Violence, 20*, 131–139.

Holtzworth-Munroe, A., & Stuart, G. L. (1994). Typologies of male batterers: Three subtypes and the differences among them. *Psychological Bulletin, 116*, 476–497.

Jackson, S., Feder, L., Davis, R., Maxwell, C., & Taylor B. (2003). *Batterer intervention programs: Where do we go from here?* Washington, DC: National Institute of Justice.

Johnson, M. P. (1995). Patriarchal terrorism and common couple violence: Two forms of violence against women. *Journal of Marriage and the Family, 57,* 283–294.

MacPhee-Sigurdson, M. (2004). Exploring perceptions of men who completed a group program for partner abuse. *Envision: The Manitoba Journal of Child Welfare, 3*(2). Retrieved December 1, 2008, from http://www.envisionjournal.com/application/Articles/65.pdf

Maiuro, R. D., Hagar, T. S., Lin, H.-H., & Olson, N. (2001). Are current state standards for domestic violence perpetrator treatment adequately informed by research? A question of questions. *Journal of Aggression, Maltreatment & Trauma, 5,* 21–44.

Minnesota Program Development, Inc. (n.d.). Recent research: Countering confusion about the Duluth model. Retrieved Feb. 12, 2006 from www.duluth-model.org

Moore, T. M., & Stuart, G. S. (2004). Illicit substance use and intimate partner violence among men in batterers' intervention. *Psychology of Addictive Behaviors, 18,* 385–389.

Murphy, C. M., & Baxter, V. A. (1997). Motivating batterers to change in the treatment context. *Journal of Interpersonal Violence, 12,* 607–619.

Murphy, C. M. (2001). Toward empirically based standards for abuser intervention: The Maryland model. *Journal of Aggression, Maltreatment & Trauma, 5,* 249–264.

O'Leary, K. D. (2001). Conjoint therapy for partners who engage in physically aggressive behavior: Rationale and research. *Journal of Aggression, Maltreatment & Trauma, 5,* 145–164.

Palmer, S. E., Brown, R. A., & Barrera, M. E. (1992). Group treatment program for abusive husbands: Long-term evaluation. *American Journal of Orthopsychiatry, 62,* 276–283.

Pandya, V., & Gingerich, W. J. (2002). Group therapy intervention for male batterers: A microethnographic study. *Health & Social Work, 27,* 47–55.

Pence, E., & McMahon, M. (1997). *A coordinated community response to domestic violence.* Duluth, MN: National Training Project.

Prochaska, J. O., & DiClemente, C. C. (1982). Transtheoretical therapy: Toward a more integrative model of change. *Psychotherapy: Theory, Research, and Practice, 20,* 161–173.

Ross, L. E. (2007). Consequences of mandatory arrest policies: Comments, questions, and concerns. *Law Enforcement Executive Forum, 7,* 73–85.

Saunders, D. G. (2001). Developing guidelines for domestic violence offender programs: What can we learn from related fields and current research? *Journal of Aggression, Maltreatment & Trauma, 5,* 235–248.

Schecter, S. (1982). *Women and male violence: The visions and struggles of the battered women's movement.* Boston: South End Press.

Schrock, D. P., & Padavic, I. (2007). Negotiating hegemonic masculinity in a batterer intervention program. *Gender & Society, 21,* 625–649.

Scott, K. L., & Wolfe, D. L. (2000). Change among batterers: Examining men's success stories. *Journal of Interpersonal Violence, 15,* 827–842.

Shepard, M. F., Falk, D. R., & Elliott, B. A. (2002). Enhancing coordinated community responses to reduce recidivism in cases of domestic violence. *Journal of Interpersonal Violence, 17,* 551–569.

Silvergleid, C. S., & Mankowski, E. S. (2006). How batterer intervention programs work: Participant and facilitator accounts of processes of change. *Journal of Interpersonal Violence, 21,* 139–159.

Smith, M. E. (2007). Self-deception among men who are mandated to attend a batterer intervention program. *Perspectives in Psychiatric Care, 43,* 193–203.

Stuart, G. S., Temple, J. R., & Moore, T. M. (2007). Improving batterer intervention programs through theory-based research. *Journal of the American Medical Association, 298,* 560–562.

Tutty, L. M., Bidgood, B. A., Rothery, M. A., & Bidgood, P. (2001). An evaluation of men's batterer treatment groups. *Research on Social Work Practice, 11,* 645–670.

VCS, Inc. (2005). *VCS Community Change Project Domestic Violence Program for Men: Accountability to the battered women's movement.* Retrieved December 1, 2008, from http://www.nymbp.org/reference/AcctBWMovement.pdf

VCS, Inc. (n.d.). Retrieved December 1, 2008, from http://www.nymbp.org/principles.htm

Community Supervision of Domestic Violence Offenders

Where We Are and Where We Need to Go

17

LYNETTE FEDER

Contents

Introduction

Research indicates that intimate partner violence (IPV) affects an estimated 3 to 4 million women yearly (Tjaden & Thoennes, 2000; Plichta & Falik, 2001). Additionally, studies demonstrate that individuals who have been victims of domestic violence are at greater risk of future violence (Langan & Innes, 1986), especially among those experiencing the most severe instances. In 2004, there were 1,544 deaths due to domestic violence (Centers for Disease Control and Prevention [CDC], 2006). And an 11-city study of intimate partner femicide found that the majority (67% to 80%) involved physical abuse prior to the murder (Campbell et al., 2003; Glass et al., 2003). The societal and individual costs of this violence are enormous, reaching an estimated $67 billion per year (Miller, Cohen, & Wiersema, 1996), with mental health care costs being the largest proportion of the increased health care expenditures associated with intimate partner violence (Wisner, Gilmer, Saltzman, & Zink, 1999). Adding to the costs of intimate partner violence, research has found that approximately 3 to 10 million children live in domestically

247

violent households (Socolar, 2000). Shockingly, approximately 10% of teenagers nationwide report being physically hurt by their boyfriend or girlfriend in the last 12 months (CDC, 2008).

Despite these numbers, violence committed against intimate partners was largely ignored until recently. Over the last 30 years, however, this topic has begun to receive increased attention from practitioners, researchers, and policy makers, all attempting to lessen its frequency, severity, and/or consequence. When the problem of domestic violence first emerged from behind closed doors, there was little in the way of research to structure policies and programs. Practitioners and policy makers had to act quickly given both the seriousness and urgency of this problem. However, in the intervening years, research has become available. Sadly, though, when research findings run contrary to institutionalized beliefs, they are often dismissed, leaving established practices in place. This is especially true as researchers call into question the effectiveness of these policies and programs. Instead of being openly curious about what will work, many in the domestic violence field hold on to beliefs about what they think should work. It is within this context that this chapter will discuss the probationary programs presently being used nationwide.

First, though, to fully comprehend the criminal justice's response to domestic violence, one must begin with an understanding of this system. In fact, many argue that our criminal justice system is really a "nonsystem," comprised of three separate but interrelated components: the police, courts, and corrections (where probationers and parolees fall under community supervision). Changes to one component of the criminal justice system in an attempt to improve it not atypically lead to unintended consequences in other parts of this system. Students of criminal justice have long studied this "system effect."

In studying the criminal justice system's handling of domestic violence, one also sees this system effect. Practitioners, policy makers, and researchers, realizing that any change in one part of the system cannot be sustained without coordination with the other parts of the system, have only recently begun to call for a "coordinated community approach" when implementing new programs or policies. Therefore, to better understand probation's response to domestic violence, we begin with a quick overview of how each part of the system has approached domestic violence and what the research tells us about these various responses.

A Recent History of IPV and the Criminal Justice System

Though wife beating has long been considered a crime, historically our criminal justice system has been reluctant to officially handle these cases (Buzawa & Buzawa, 1985; Feder, 1999; Friedman & Shulman, 1990). Starting in the 1960s, the women's movement identified domestic violence as a major issue and demanded that police respond more vigorously (Greenblat, 1985). Additionally, research results from a large-scale police observation study conducted during this period found that police were underenforcing the law when responding to these calls (Black, 1978), thereby providing additional legitimacy to critics' calls for change. Since the 1980s, courts began holding police departments liable for the injuries sustained by battered women when officers failed to rigorously respond to these calls (see *Thurman v. City of Torrington Police Department*, 1984). Finally, results from a widely publicized study, the Minneapolis Domestic Violence Experiment, indicated that an arrest response was more effective at reducing recidivism among domestic violence offenders (Sherman & Berk, 1984). While the results were controversial and polarizing, the study provided policy makers and others with the hope that criminal justice policies could effectively reduce the frequency and severity of intimate partner violence incidents.

Due to the changes described above, among others, state legislatures began to directly address the problem of domestic violence by writing statutes limiting police discretion when responding to domestic violence calls for service. Some jurisdictions specified that an arrest was the presumptive response to a misdemeanor domestic violence incident, while others went even further and mandated that police were to arrest when answering to all domestic violence calls (Lerman, Livingston, & Jackson, 1983). The magnitude and speed of the change that occurred in police department policies nationwide can be seen in the fact that in 1984 only 10% of all large police departments indicated that they made an arrest when responding to misdemeanor domestic violence calls. Yet, in only two years, the proportion was 43% (Sherman & Cohn, 1989), and today most jurisdictions nationwide presume or mandate an arrest response when police attend to a domestic violence call for service (Healey, Smith, & O'Sullivan, 1998).

In the ensuing years, the Minneapolis Experiment has been replicated and the conclusions from these sites have led to heated debates regarding whether an arrest actually increases or decreases the likelihood of subsequent reabuse (Berk, Campbell, Klap, & Western, 1992; Dunford, Huizinga, & Elliot, 1990; Maxwell, Garner, & Fagan, 2001). Sherman, Smith, Schmidt, and Rogan (1992), in reviewing the findings across these arrest studies, concluded that arrest means different things to different offenders. They hypothesized that where an individual has a high stake in conformity (e.g., was employed, married, had high residential stability, etc.), an arrest deterred future abusive acts. However, where the offender was low in stake in conformity, the arrest led to an increase in the likelihood of reabuse.

In spite of this ongoing debate about what the results from Minneapolis and its replication studies mean, jurisdictions continued to write pro-arrest laws and researchers followed this by investigating whether police behavior was in compliance with these statutes (Bell, 1984; Buzawa & Buzawa, 1985; Lawrenz, Lembo, & Schade, 1988). Results from many of these studies point to police not fulfilling the legislature's mandate (Blount, Yegidis, & Maheux, 1992; Feder, 1997; Mignon & Holmes, 1995) though one study found that there may be cause to question the premise upon which these studies were based (Feder, 1998b). In an effort to better understand these findings, researchers then turned to looking at specific factors—offender, offense, and police characteristics—associated with the likelihood of an arrest response (Berk, Fenstermaker, & Newton, 1988; Feder, 1996; Worden & Pollitz, 1984).

While the arrest decision continues to receive a great deal of interest, other components in the criminal justice system have received far less attention in their handling of domestic violence cases (Cramer, 1999). For example, the court response to IPV seemed to lag behind that of the police (Buzawa & Buzawa, 1985; Dutton, 1988; Friedman & Shulman, 1990; Ford & Regoli, 1993). This was probably due in large part to there being less litigation and research on the court's handling of domestic violence cases (Buzawa & Buzawa, 1985; Dutton, 1988). However, with pro-arrest statutes gaining popularity nationwide, the number of batterers entering the court system increased, which led to alternative ways to more effectively handle these offenders (Feder, 1997; Hotaling & Sugarman, 1986; Johnson & Kanzler, 1993).

One alternative has been the recent and significant increase in the numbers of specialized domestic violence courts. Indeed, this is very much in line with the move to court specialization occurring throughout the American court system (Lapham, C'deBaca, Lapidus, & McMillan, 2007). Domestic violence courts were established to exclusively handle cases of intimate partner violence because they offered several advantages, including (1) judges who are specifically trained about domestic violence and are therefore more knowledgeable and sympathetic to the victims, (2) a more coordinated courtroom work group allowing for better management of these cases as well as greater consistency when dealing with batterers, and (3) an ability to provide more comprehensive services (and do it more quickly) for the victims. Many times they also offer greater judicial monitoring of domestic violence offenders (Rempel, Labriola, & Davis, 2008). A recent survey estimated that there were over 300 domestic violence courts nationwide (Keilitz, 2001), with the number growing yearly (Visher, Harrell, & Newmark, 2007).

Although enthusiasm for these courts builds and their numbers continue to grow, there is a lack of rigorous research studying their effectiveness in deterring IPV offenders or increasing victim safety. In essence, we really do not know whether this recent trend is beneficial or harmful. One quasi-experimental study investigated the effectiveness of one critical component of a domestic violence court. Rempel and his associates (2008) studied the specific effects of judicial monitoring on domestic violence offenders' rate of recidivism. They found that judicial monitoring, whether done on a regular or graduated basis, made no difference in terms of the probationers' recidivism rates (for neither domestic nor non-domestic offenses) (Rempel et al., 2008). Alternately, the Judicial Oversight Demonstration (JOD) project, looked at judicial oversight set within a coordinated community response to intimate partner violence. In addition to a specialized domestic violence court, the project also coordinated with a family violence unit within the police department, a specialized domestic violence prosecution unit within the district attorney's office, and an intensive community supervision program for high-risk batterers within probation. Harrell and her colleagues found that domestic violence recidivism (as measured by IPV rearrests) significantly decreased. However, their evaluation indicated that this was not due to judicial monitoring but rather the increased likelihood of probation revocation from the special probation unit. That is, intensive supervision of these offenders led to a greater likelihood that they would be removed from the community, thereby decreasing their ability to reoffend (Harrell, Schaffer, DeStefano, & Castro, 2006). In essence, these results speak to the effectiveness of incapacitation (incarceration) rather than deterrence (monitoring) when working with batterers.

New programs are also being tried within the prosecutors' offices. In line with the establishment of domestic violence courts, some prosecutors have created specialized domestic violence units, while others have implemented no-drop prosecution policies designed to remove the responsibility for litigation from the victims of intimate partner violence (Archer, 1989; Lerman, 1981; Waits, 1985). A recent survey of prosecutors found that, in large cities, half the prosecutors' offices said they had implemented a special domestic violence prosecution unit, and fully 66% said that they had a no-drop prosecution protocol for domestic violence cases (Rebovich, 1996). And again, with few exceptions (see Ford & Regoli, 1992), there has been very little research conducted to test the value of these new methods. We therefore cannot say whether these programs are effective in decreasing the likelihood of batterer's reabuse or increasing victim's safety.

However, there is one area concerning prosecutorial decision making that has been the focus of a good deal of recent research. Just as police received pressure to use a law enforcement response when answering to intimate partner violence, prosecutors have been the recipients of pressure to ensure similar sentencing to domestic violence offenders relative to non-domestic violence cases (Olson & Stalans, 2001). Researchers have responded by studying the effect that court disposition has on domestic violence offenders' rates of reabuse and recidivism. As each study uses different populations (misdemeanor vs. felony domestic violence offenders), studies their adjustment in the community for varying lengths of time (6 months, 12 months, 18 months, and 24 months), and uses methodologies that vary in their rigor (preexperimental, quasi-experimental, experimental), results have been inconsistent. In looking at the effects that sentence severity has had on misdemeanor domestic violence offenders, some researcher failed to find court disposition having any significant effect on later recidivism (Davis, Smith, & Nickles, 1998; Gross, Cramer, Gordon, Kunkel, & Moriarty, 2000;Kingsnorth, 2006). Alternately, Wooldredge and Thistlethwaite (2005) found that sanction severity did impact on an offender's likelihood of committing future IPV offenses, but that this was only for misdemeanor domestic violence offenders, and furthermore, it was mediated by their particular characteristics. As an example, they found that a lenient court disposition among more socially advantaged domestic violence offenders increased the likelihood of recidivism. Conversely, increased sanctioning of high stakes in conformity offenders decreased their likelihood of recidivism.

Probation and Intimate Partner Violence

Comparatively, decisions made by the courts and prosecutors have, until recently, received less attention than that given to police's decision to arrest. Probationary practices have received an even smaller amount of attention (Canales-Portalatin, 2000). The consequence of this largess is that we have less information on probation's handling of domestic violence offenders. With that said, there are four programs that can be discussed in terms of what the research tells us about probation's handling of domestic violence offenders.

Batterer Intervention Programs

Batterer intervention programs (BIPs) provide the exception to the above rule, as they have been extensively evaluated. Though BIPs are not run by probation, they are typically ordered as part of a convicted batterer's sentence, and it is then left to probation to monitor their compliance with this mandated treatment. Not surprisingly, BIPs came to the forefront in the late 1980s as courts were experiencing a large influx of domestic violence offenders due to the pro-arrest policies being implemented nationwide. As this was occurring during a time of jail overcrowding, it placed increased pressure on court personnel to think of alternative ways to handle this problem (Feder, 1998b, 1999).

At about this time, a new method for dealing with batterers was gaining attention. Its focus was on making batterers accountable while reeducating them about the negative effects of battering. Though there was variation from one program to the next, typically these BIPs encouraged men to confront their sexist beliefs and accept responsibility for their past abuse. The most popular of these programs is the Domestic Abuse Intervention Project (DAIP) out of Duluth, Minnesota. Referred to simply as the Duluth model, this program relies on a feminist cognitive psychoeducational approach that teaches men that battering is part of a range of behaviors they use to control women. The curriculum is taught in group sessions that emphasize the modification and development of alternative techniques batterers can use to avoid conflict (e.g., anger management, assertiveness training, relaxation techniques, and communication skills).

Soon after BIPs began appearing, studies evaluating their efficacy surfaced. In this first wave of evaluation research, the results indicated suspiciously high rates of success in reducing the frequency and severity of subsequent violence among those completing batterer intervention programs (Deschner & McNeil, 1986; Neidig, Friedman, & Collins, 1985). While researchers recognized the many methodological shortcomings inherent in these studies, leading to questions about their actual effectiveness (Chen, Bersani, Myers, & Denton, 1989; Ford & Regoli, 1993), court personnel, victim advocates, and policy makers thought they had found a program for reducing violence in the family.

The only drawback was the fact that batterers were proving to be a difficult population to work with as evidenced by their high rates of attrition from these programs (Pirog-Good & Stets-Kealey, 1985; Roberts, 1982). Batterers' high rate of attrition was therefore viewed as an opportunity for court involvement. By mandating a batterer to attend a BIP (typically run for 26 weeks, though sites show tremendous variation nationwide), judges thought they could ensure treatment compliance while providing an alternative to incarceration. Given overloaded court dockets, mandated counseling in a batterer intervention program also offered the promise of shortening court proceedings while simultaneously adding to the deterrent effects of arrest (Dutton, 1987). And all of this could be accomplished while holding out the hope of changing the behavior of domestic violence offenders, and in that way ending the cycle of violence.

With their popularity growing, BIPs continued to attract the attention of researchers interested in their effectiveness. This second wave of research typically used more rigorous evaluation tools, including quasi-experimental and experimental designs (instead of the preexperimental designs used previously) and larger sample sizes. Unlike the earlier studies, these evaluations produced mixed findings regarding the effectiveness of these court-mandated programs. For instance, a multisite evaluation using a quasi-experimental design compared men who completed the BIP with those who rejected treatment (as indicated by not showing or dropping out) and found the former significantly less likely to reabuse (Jones & Gondolf, 2002). Alternately, another quasi-experimental study compared men who were mandated into counseling with those who were not so mandated and found indications that BIP treatment was not only ineffective, but actually led to higher rates of reabuse (Harrell, 1991).

There have also been several experiments that have looked at the effectiveness of BIPs in deterring future abuse. One study used a small sample (N = 56) of men convicted of domestic violence (Palmer, Brown, & Barrera, 1992) and found a large and significant effect for the added benefits of treatment. Another experiment used a larger (N = 376) population of convicted batterers. Though Davis and his colleagues first reported significant effects for assignment into a BIP (Taylor, Davis, & Maxwell, 2001), they later reanalyzed their data and reported that BIP treatment did not add to a reduction in recidivism beyond that provided by criminal justice processing (Davis, Maxwell, & Taylor, 2003).

Dunford's study (2000a), probably one of the most rigorous, used a large (N = 861) Navy-based population of batterers and concluded that there were no differences in rates of recidivism between those assigned into batterer treatment and those not so assigned. Feder and Dugan's (2004) experimental study used all men convicted of misdemeanor domestic violence in one jurisdiction (N = 404). Though victim attrition was high (affecting their survey response), the rates of reabuse reported by victims was consistent with those found by official reports. And both measures indicated a lack of effectiveness for BIP treatment above and beyond the deterrent effects of criminal justice processing (e.g., arrest, sanction, and community supervision on probation). Finally, a recent study conducted by Labriola, Rempel, and Davis (2008) randomly assigned men convicted of misdemeanor domestic violence to (1) batterer program plus monthly judicial monitoring, (2) batterer program plus graduated judicial monitoring, (3) monthly monitoring only, and (4) graduated monitoring only. Based on their sample of 420 offenders, they found no differences in terms of official rates of rearrest for any offense, for domestic violence offenses, or for domestic violence against the same victim. Since then, others have found that neither batterer treatment length (Cissner & Puffett, 2006) nor treatment type, including use of the Duluth model (Cissner & Puffett, 2006; Davis & Taylor, 1997; Dutton & Sonkin, 2001), predicts treatment completion or future reoffending.

Given that there has been some conflict in the findings, researchers have turned to meta-analysis to aid in drawing conclusions across these various studies. Recently, two meta-analyses have been completed and both have come to similar conclusions about the effectiveness of BIPs. While both meta-analyses use the original findings from Davis's Brooklyn study (thereby increasing the likelihood of finding treatment effectiveness), they still raise serious doubts about the effectiveness of this treatment program. For instance, Babcock, Green, and Robie's (2004) meta-analysis concluded that "the effect size due to group battering intervention on recidivism of domestic violence is in the 'small' range.... The practical importance of an effect size of this magnitude is that with treatment ... there is a 5% increase in the success rate attributable to treatment" (p. 1052).

Like the Babcock study, Feder and Wilson's (2005) meta-analysis analyzed BIP effectiveness separately for studies using an experimental versus quasi-experimental design. However, unlike Babcock and her colleagues, Feder and Wilson then separately analyzed those quasi-experimental studies that used a no-treatment control group (considered a stronger quasi-experimental design) and those studies using treatment dropouts as their comparison group (considered a weaker quasi-experimental design). While they found some support for the modest benefits of batterer programs based on official reports in the experimental studies, this effect was reduced when including studies that only used a general batterer population. Additionally, there was no effect when using victim reports of repeated reabuse. The quasi-experimental studies using a no-treatment comparison group also failed to find any evidence of treatment effectiveness. Interestingly, quasi-experimental studies using men who were rejected from treatment or who rejected treatment (the treatment dropouts) showed a large, positive, and significant effect on reducing reoffending. As a number of studies have recently found an inverse relationship between design rigor and likelihood of finding program effectiveness (Feder & Forde, 2000; Weisburd, Lum, & Petrosino, 2001), this raised suspicion about the validity of the results from quasi-experimental studies that compare treatment completers with treatment dropouts as a way of assessing BIP effectiveness.

One final point requires mention. Recently, some practitioners and researchers have suggested that batterer programs might not lead to changes in the batterer, but that their purpose may instead lie in providing increased monitoring for these individuals when they are released into the community (Ames & Dunham, 2002; Murphy, Musser, & Maton, 1998; Stalans, Yarnold, Seng, Olson, & Repp, 2004; Cissner & Puffett, 2006). That is, where an offender does not fulfill the judicial mandate to participate in a BIP, it serves as a signal that he or she is probably not complying with the other parts of his or her sentence. The assumption is that probation officers would then use the failure to comply as grounds to revoke probation. Though this may indeed be a service that BIPs provide, they were never originally intended to serve this purpose. As such, there is presently no research investigating whether they are successful in providing increased monitoring and whether this is keeping victims safer. However, such an evaluation could be easily implemented if funding agencies viewed this as a worthwhile research opportunity.

For now, though, the weight of research results raises serious concerns about the effectiveness of court-mandated BIPs to reduce the likelihood of future reabuse. Despite this, requiring convicted misdemeanor domestic violence offenders to participate in a BIP as a condition of their probation has become one of the most widely used responses to intimate partner violence in jurisdictions nationwide (Healey et al., 1998; Bennett & Williams, 2001).

Electronic Monitoring

Electronic monitoring of offenders has been around since the 1980s (Lilly, Ball, Curry, & McMullen, 1993). While the exact number of offenders in communities nationwide under electronic supervision is unknown, its use has grown rapidly, with one researcher estimating a 10-fold increase in its use since the early 1990s (Gainey, Payne, & O'Toole, 2000), with possibly 100,000 or more offenders presently under electronic monitoring in the United States alone. A 1995 National Institute of Corrections survey of state and local parole and probation departments found that more than 88% of these agencies said that they currently used electronic monitoring (Finn & Muirhead-Steves, 2002).

Electronic monitoring can be used for pretrial offenders being released into the community to ensure that they do not abscond. More typically, though, it is used postconviction to provide a method to supervise, control, and punish offenders being released into the community while simultaneously keeping the public safe (Payne & Gainey, 2004). There is no doubt that one of the primary catalysts to its use was that it increased public comfort even as it provided a way to divert offenders from the more costly jail or prison stay (Lily et al., 1993). Renzema and Mayo-Wilson (2005), who conducted a Campbell review of electronic monitoring, note that a wide range of individuals have been placed under electronic monitoring, including children, those refusing to pay child support, tax cheaters, child molesters, those who have been convicted of driving while intoxicated, and even paroled killers.

Despite the fact that electronic monitoring has been around for more than 20 years and that it has experienced a rapid growth, there really is very little evidence on its effectiveness as either a deterrent or a safe diversion. There has only been one experimental evaluation using electronic monitoring. Lapham and her colleagues looked at several interventions for individuals convicted of driving under the influence (Lapham et al., 2007). Unfortunately, their study used different combinations of multiple interventions in each of the various groups that individuals were randomly assigned to, making it impossible to definitively decipher the impact that electronic monitoring alone had. The researchers concluded that the groups using electronic monitoring (in addition to other interventions) initially demonstrated lower rates of recidivism than the other groups. However, these effects decreased once the intervention stopped, with the result that all groups showed comparable reoffending rates three years postsentencing. If these results could be replicated, it would speak to electronic monitoring having an incapacitative effect while in use.

Two other studies used a quasi-experimental design to test the effectiveness of electronic monitoring. Though neither test is without limitations, it is interesting to note that both resulted in a similar conclusion that electronic monitoring alone may not demonstrate any positive effect. However, when it is paired with other interventions, at least for some offender types, it may force greater treatment completion, which then leads to lower rates of recidivism. In Bonta, Wallace-Capretta, and Rooney's (2000) quasi-experimental study, offenders released to the community were either placed in a cognitive-behavioral treatment program with electronic monitoring or, alternately, released in the community without the treatment or the electronic monitoring. To compensate for the lack of random assignment, statistical controls were used to equate the two offender groups. A comparison of recidivism rates between the groups initially indicated no significant differences. However, closer inspection indicated that treatment/monitoring had a different effect depending on the type of offender. For those who were high risk, this experimental intervention had a large and significant effect in decreasing their likelihood of recidivating. Alternately, lower-risk offenders in the treatment/monitoring group showed significantly higher rates of recidivism than their no-treatment counterparts.

Finn and Muirhead-Steves (2002) also conducted a quasi-experimental study looking at the effectiveness of electronic monitoring for high-risk violent offenders being released into the community. Using statistical controls to make the groups equivalent, individuals mandated into electronic monitoring were compared to individuals released into the community without electronic monitoring. Finn and Muirhead-Steves found that electronic monitoring seemed to have no independent effect when measured in terms of either the likelihood of prison recommitments or time until failure overall. However, they found electronic monitoring to have a significant and positive effect (in terms of lowering recidivism) for one particular type of offender. For sex offenders who were released into the community with electronic monitoring, their rates of recidivism were lower than for sex offenders released without electronic monitoring. Like the above-mentioned study, the researchers speculated that electronic monitoring may have had indirect and positive effects in increasing the likelihood of offenders complying with treatment mandates, which then might lower their likelihood of recidivating. And again, like Bonta and his colleagues' study, the research by Finn and Muirhead-Steves could only speculate, as they had not monitored treatment compliance and therefore could not directly test this hypothesis.

The state of the research has led Renzema and Mayo-Wilson to conclude, "All studies of EM … have serious limitations…. Governments that choose to use EM in the future ought to use it to enhance other services that have a known effect on crime reduction. Those governments must test the marginal effects of EM, publish the results, and discontinue use of EM if it fails to provide quantifiable public benefits. Money spent on EM could be spent on empirically tested programs that demonstrably protect our communities" (Renzema & Mayo-Wilson, 2005, p. 233).

Despite the fact that studies on the effectiveness of electronic monitoring have not demonstrated consistent support for this method when used on the general population, it has begun to be used on domestic violence offenders. Erez and Ibarra (2007) conducted interviews with 30 women whose violent estranged partners were given bilateral electronic monitoring. Unlike the other studies where electronic monitoring was used to only track the offender, bilateral electronic monitoring (BEM) tracks the offender vis-à-vis his victim and in this way attempts to increase victim safety. As their study did not use a control group, it relied only on victim perceptions, which may or may not be accurate. According to these victims, they felt that BEM kept them safer (though some were still menaced during the time that they used BEM), leading to their feeling more positively toward the criminal justice system (Erez & Ibarra, 2007; Erez, Ibarra, & Lurie, 2004; Ibarra & Erez, 2005). Though the women's accounts were interesting to read, an experiment is clearly called for whereby individuals would be randomly assigned to either a control condition (treatment as usual) or electronic monitoring. This is especially critical as many of these women reported that electronic monitoring made them feel safer. If they really are not safer, then this method may be creating a false sense of security, which may lull them to let down their guard.

Special Domestic Violence Probation Units

Like domestic violence courts, similar rationales have been used for establishing special domestic violence probation units. Some of the reasons given include the idea that probation officers (POs) who are specifically trained on the dynamics of intimate partner violence and handle only caseloads with intimate partner violence offenders will be better able to provide enhanced supervision to these batterers (through increased contact) while better meeting the needs of their victims (Bureau of Justice Assistance, 1993; Tatum, Lee, & Kunselman, 2008). Typically, probation officers in these units have smaller caseloads so that they can more closely monitor the probationers on their caseload. This is supposed to be done by having more offender contact as well as reaching out to the victims (Ames & Dunham, 2002). The first special domestic violence probation units occurred in Quincy, Massachusetts, in the late 1980s. However, their numbers have been increasing with the advent of pro-arrest statutes and its consequent rise in batterers entering into the system (Klein & Crowe, 2008).

Despite the rise in popularity of these specialized units, there is little research available on their effectiveness. The one exception comes from a series of research publications by Klein and his colleagues conducted out of the Rhode Island Domestic Violence Probation Unit (DVU). Based on a quasi-experimental design, these researchers studied the effect of this special domestic violence unit (which reduced POs' caseload size in order to increase their monitoring of the domestic violent probationers) in comparison to similar domestic violence offenders who were not placed in these special units (due only to geographical differences). They found that probationers assigned to the DVU reoffended 56% of the time in comparison to their domestic violent counterparts not assigned to these specialized units, who reoffended 64% of the time. In studying these differences more closely, they found that the DVU decreased recidivism, but only for low-risk domestic violent probationers (Klein & Crowe, 2008). Alternately, for high-risk domestic violent probationers, the DVU's increased monitoring seemed to lead to higher rates of recidivism (Klein & Tobin, 2008). Finally, they also found that the DVU succeeded in increasing victim satisfaction with probation (Klein, Wilson, Crowe, & DeMichele, 2008).

This gives us cautious optimism that specialized domestic violence probation units may be effective in reducing subsequent violence while increasing victim satisfaction for at least some IPV offenders. However, the results from this quasi-experimental design need to be replicated using an experimental design where probationers are randomly assigned to either regular probation or these specialized units. Such a replication would go a long way in telling us whether these specialized units should continue to be pursued. In the interim, though, jurisdictions nationwide are implementing specialized domestic violence probation units based on less than rigorous evidence.

Intensive Supervision on Probation (ISP)

Another alternative that has been tried within the field for domestic violence offenders either pre- or postconviction is intensive supervision probation (ISP). ISP programs began to be used in the late 1980s with various offender groups, including drug, juvenile, and high-risk offenders. The original reason for ISP was to provide an intermediate sanction between probation and incarceration, which would, first and foremost, protect the public and deter offenders even while keeping them in the community (Petersilia, Turner, & Deschenes, 1992). However, research consistently found that this program increased the numbers of arrests (via an upsurge in the number of revocations for technical violations), thereby increasing incarceration rates due to the intensive nature of the monitoring (Turner, Petersilia, & Deschenes, 1992). Whether ISP could be labeled a success was hotly debated at the time. However, what was not debated was the fact that ISP cost more (due to incarceration costs) despite the fact that the two offender groups (ISP probationers and non-ISP probationers) did not differ in terms of new criminal arrests.

Intensive supervision probation has more recently been applied to domestic violence offenders (Tolman, 1996). Unfortunately, most publications on its use have been preexperimental (see Johnson, 2001; Duffy, Nolan,

& Scruggs, 2003) and therefore largely descriptive. There are, however, three quasi-experimental studies that can better inform this discussion. The first, conducted by Krmpotich (2000), evaluated the implementation of an ISP program in one county and found that it succeeded in reducing recidivism (as defined by new convictions) among ISP probationers with higher stakes in conformity. Another quasi-experimental study conducted by Harrell and her colleagues (2006) looked specifically at intensive supervision probation as part of a larger community coordinated response to domestic violence. In their Judicial Oversight Demonstration (JOD) project (previously discussed in terms of judicial monitoring), the researchers found that ISP did in fact reduce the rate of rearrests among probationers. However, in line with past ISP results, they found that this reduced rearrest rate was largely attributable to the very high rate at which these offenders had their probation revoked, thereby decreasing their time in the community and lessening their ability to reoffend. Finally, the last study, conducted by Klein and his colleagues (2008), has already been noted, when specialized domestic violence units were discussed. The Rhode Island Domestic Violence Probation Unit also included an intensive probation supervision program for high-risk offenders on probation. Unlike Harrell et al. (2006), Klein and Crowe (2008) did not find that ISP lowered recidivism among this high-risk domestic violence offender group.

Coming Full Circle

In providing this cursory overview of the criminal justice system's handling of domestic violence (especially in terms of the response from probation) two points emerge. First, given the predominant use of a sentence to probation upon conviction for misdemeanor domestic violence, one might have expected a greater variety of programs to have been developed and experimentally implemented. Unfortunately, this has not been the case.

This leads to the second point. Whether it is domestic violence courts, special domestic violence probation units, intensive supervision probation, electronic monitoring, or court-mandated batterer treatment, ideology seems to continuously outweigh research. It is as Eckhardt and his colleagues (2006) recently noted:

> The limited research on batterer intervention program effectiveness and the lack of suitable application of sophisticated research design strategies that have so clearly benefited research on psychotherapy and behavior change are not because of a lack of awareness that these issues exist; rather, any careful examination of the general batterer intervention program literature suggests that it is an area where theoretical/ideological concerns have

largely outstripped the importance of empirical evidence. For example, some have argued that state standards governing batterer intervention program content appear to have been formulated largely on the basis of loyalty to a particular explanatory model rather than on a careful examination of the research evidence on abuse perpetrators or evidence for a particular intervention model's empirical support. (Eckhardt, Murphy, Black, & Suhr, 2006, p. 378)

Just at a time when researchers should be building on the foundation of these previous quasi-experimental and experimental studies to develop improved tests on the effectiveness of these different programs, rigorous research seems to have halted. This is occurring even while there is continued growth of BIPs, specialized probation units, electronic monitoring, and intensive supervision probation. Presently the United States leads the industrialized world in developing and implementing these treatment programs (Rees & Rivett, 2005). In terms of BIPs, current estimates are that 80% of all individuals attending them are court mandated (Bennett & Williams, 2001). But if these programs are not reducing the likelihood of future rearrests or increasing victim safety, then the government is mandating that individuals participate (and typically pay for) services that provide no benefit. This is instead of possibly finding interventions that might prove more effective. Making things even more illogical, in terms of batterer intervention programs, many jurisdictions have now written statutes mandating that upon conviction for misdemeanor domestic violence, judges must place batterers into these programs (Healy et al., 1998). The effect of this is that we cannot even conduct further research on whether these programs are beneficial. It is as if no amount of additional information will allow for a reexamination, let alone a reconsideration, of this earlier decision.

One recent example will suffice. The author was asked by a domestic violence judge to come into his jurisdiction and conduct an experiment testing the effectiveness of the county's certified BIP in his jurisdiction. He thought his jurisdiction would be a perfect site, as they were a rather small and tight-knit community where all the officials had worked together to create a truly coordinated community response to domestic violence. The researcher worked with the judge, looking at the numbers of misdemeanor domestic violence offenders that come through the court and ensuring that other key officials were on board with this proposed study. However, in the end, no study could be implemented, as this state had a statute mandating that upon conviction for misdemeanor domestic violence, individuals had to be placed in a BIP for two years. Without the ability to randomly assign some batterers to a control (probation only) condition, a valid test of the BIP's effectiveness in decreasing recidivism above and beyond that provided by criminal justice processing could not be conducted. The only way around this statute would have been to lobby the legislature, a process that would have been too time-consuming and costly. Therefore, this study was never done. And yet, this type of study is exactly what is needed now—an experimental test in a community with a coordinated response where all the key players are interested in seeing that this research be completed.

Adding to the difficulty in conducting research to determine what programs work with which types of offenders, many jurisdictions are now writing standards for these BIPs. Presently, all but three states have, or are in the process of establishing, mandatory standards for these programs, including the type of modality to be used, the content permitted, the qualifications of those providing the intervention, and the duration of treatment (Austin & Dankwort, 1999). In these standards, the most widely adopted BIP intervention is the Duluth model. In fact, in some states' standards treatment programs cannot receive funding unless they use the Duluth model (Eckhardt et al., 2006; Healey et al., 1998). And yet, the research indicates that this specific treatment intervention is no more effective than any other treatment modality, and possibly no more effective than just criminal justice processing (Cissner & Puffett, 2006; Dutton & Sonkin, 2003; Jones & Gondolf, 2002).

While standards typically are used to ensure a level of quality control, they are premature in this case given the many conflicting research findings regarding the effectiveness of BIPs. Additionally, as these standards specify which treatments are appropriate, they will impede the development of new and alternative interventions that might prove more effective in lessening the likelihood of reabuse among batterers or increasing victim safety. In fact, a number of researchers have called for caution in establishing any standards, noting that much is still unknown about what types of treatment work with which types of batterers (Gelles, 2001; Maiuro, Hagar, Lin, & Olson, 2001; Holtzworth-Munroe, 2001; Rees & Rivett, 2005). It is as Saunders (2001) has noted, "Without being closely tied to research knowledge, however, standards run the risk of creating rigid paradigms.... Standards may also instill a false sense of confidence in the effectiveness of programs" (Saunders, 2001, p. 236).

The results from studies, along with warnings from researchers to avoid setting standards, seem to have had very little impact on changing policy. State legislatures are continuing to write statutes mandating these treatment programs for batterers, while officials are continuing to look at establishing standards for these programs in their localities. As with other areas of domestic violence research, it seems that philosophy on what should work continues to trump research demonstrating what does and does not work. It may be, as Klein says, "Batterer treatment was adopted not because there was any evidence it worked, but because police, prosecutors, and judges refused to proceed against batterers unless there was some place to put them after arrest, prosecution and sentencing" (Klein, 1997: 1). This, in fact, may be the real reason for all domestic violence interventions. That is, they provide a way for criminal justice agencies to dispose of these cases regardless of their effectiveness.

Summary and Conclusion

Undoubtedly, when the problem of intimate partner violence first emerged from behind closed doors, "there [was] a tremendous sense of urgency and alarm in the treatment of domestic violence—and rightly so. After all, protecting the physical and emotional safety of women and their children is the first priority. Consequently, clinicians [felt] a primary obligation to 'do something' immediately and decisively to halt and prevent violence" (Jennings, 1987, p. 204). Originally, the quick rise in the popularity and growth of many of these programs and policies made sense. Policy makers and practitioners had little or no research to guide them, and yet decisions had to be made about what to do with batterers and their victims. But in the intervening years, a large amount of research has been conducted that could be used to inform public policy and direct further areas of study. Unfortunately, researchers whose findings challenge the prevailing views have many times found themselves vilified and cut out of domestic violence circles (Dutton, 2008; Feder, 1998a; Feder, Jolin, & Feyerherm, 2000; Straus, 2008).

We may all unconsciously shop for facts that support our attitudes and beliefs. However, if we want to move the field ahead we need to approach domestic violence using the scientific method. This approach holds all assertions as tentative until there is observable evidence that has been collected in a disciplined manner, with each step in the process being explicit and transparent. In other words, the scientific approach demands empirical support from rigorous research. And in the process of discovering these scientific truths, it would help greatly if we did so in an atmosphere where we allow divergent viewpoints. We need to constantly remember that we are all working toward the same goal—the development of ways to effectively lessen family violence and its consequences.

A social scientist who developed and implemented an extensive program to help children who were at high risk due to their impoverished circumstances returned to these subjects many years later and found that, whether measuring criminal behavior, death, disease, occupational status, suicides, marital happiness, job satisfaction, mental health, or alcohol or drug abuse, subjects who were in the program fared worse than those who had not received the intervention (McCord, 1978, 2003). She then made it her mission to ensure that social scientists and policy makers understand that "unless social programs are evaluated for potential harm as well as benefit, safety as well as efficacy, the choice of which social programs to use will remain a dangerous guess" (McCord, 2003, p. 16). The lesson is that even our best intentions can have harmful unintended consequences (Dishion et al., 2003). As such, we cannot continue to assume that programs are beneficial. Programs and poli-cies need to be tested, and this needs to be done using rigorous experimental evaluations.

As researchers we need to continue to be skeptical about any program that is provided (let alone mandated) to individuals. If we truly want to assist toward solving this social ill, we must remember that we are not here to prove or disprove that certain programs or policies work. Rather, we are here to help take the field just a bit further so that future social scientists can con-tinue this work. It is this slow and gradual process that will build this field's knowledge base so that we get increasingly effective programs to deal with intimate partner violence. But first we must demand greater scientific rigor. Recently, Dutton and Corvo (2006) noted:

> Against a national movement toward evidence-based and best-practice criteria for assessing program continuance, interventions with perpetrators of domes-tic violence remain immune to those evaluative criteria.... There is no rational reason for domestic violence to be viewed outside of the broad theoretical and professional frameworks used to analyze and respond to most contemporary behavioral and psychological problems. On the contrary, this isolation of domestic violence has resulted in a backwater of tautological pseudo-theory and failed intervention programs. (Dutton & Corvo, 2006, p. 478)

Almost 40 years ago, Donald Campbell (1969) called for an experimen-tal approach to social reform. This social policy experimentation would be facilitated by implementing pilot programs, which would then be rigorously evaluated. Or as Berk and his colleagues noted, "Thus a social policy experi-ment is an effort to introduce some social change in a way that allows one to effectively discern the net effect of the change on important social outcomes" (Berk, Boruch, Chambers, Rossi, & Witte, 1985, p. 388). This approach, there-fore, does not make us wait until we have conducted research and have all the results before we can implement a policy and program. Rather, and in opposition to what we are currently doing, these programs should be experi-mentally implemented in a few carefully chosen sites. The evaluations should then be rigorous and thorough. If the program or policy shows positive results, we can implement it more widely. However, if the program fails to be beneficial, we can modify it or scrap it. It is akin to Franklin Roosevelt's approach during the Great Depression. He did not know what would get the country out of its economic woes. But he was willing to be cautiously experi-mental in trying different approaches until he found those that worked. Such an approach applied to the social sciences would allow society to be innova-tive and experimental while also being careful and deliberate.

Jeffrey Fagan noted a dozen years ago, "Without meaningful change in the structure of research and evaluation in domestic violence, a reviewer five or ten years from now will likely reach the same conclusions reached in this review: 'We just don't know, the evaluation data aren't very good.' We could have said all this five years ago and actually did say it ten years ago. Let's not be embarrassed or embarrass ourselves by continuing on this frustrating path of fad-driven and nonsystematic policies with weak after-the-fact evaluations" (Fagan, 1996, p. 48). Sadly, his words are as true today as they were more than 10 years ago. After years of doing what we have always done (and then being surprised when we get what we have always gotten), it would be nice to try a different approach—perhaps a scientific one this time.

References

Ames, L., & Dunham, K. (2002). Aysymptotic justice: Probation as a criminal justice response to intimate partner violence. *Violence Against Women, 8,* 6–34.

Archer, N. H. (1989). Battered women and the legal system: Past, present and future. *Law and Psychology Review, 13,* 145–163.

Austin, J., & Dankwort, J. (1999). Standards for batterer programs: A review and analysis. *Journal of Interpersonal Violence, 14,* 152–168.

Babcock, J. C., Green, C. E., & Robie, C. (2004). Does batterers' treatment work? A meta-analytic review of domestic violence treatment. *Clinical Psychology Review, 23,* 1023–1053.

Bell, D. (1984). The police response to domestic violence: An exploratory study. *Police Studies, 7,* 23–30.

Bennett, L., & Williams, O. (2001, August). Controversies and recent studies of batterer intervention program effectiveness. *Applied Research Forum,* pp. 1–13.

Berk, R., Boruch, R., Chambers, D., Rossi, P., & Witte, A. (1985). Social policy experimentation: A position paper. *Evaluation Review, 9,* 387–429.

Berk, R., Campbell, A., Klap, R., & Western, B. (1992). The deterrent effect of arrest in incidents of domestic violence: A Bayesian analysis of four field experiments. *American Sociological Review, 57,* 698–708.

Berk, R., Fenstermaker, S., & Newton, P. (1988). An empirical analysis of police responses to incidents of wife battering. In G. Hotaling, D. Finkelhor, J. Kirkpatrick, & M. Straus (Eds.), *Coping with family violence: Research and policy perspectives* (pp. 158–168). Newbury Park, CA: Sage Publications.

Black, D. (1978). Production of crime rates. In L. Savitz & N. Johnston (Eds), *Crime and society.* New York: Wiley, 45–60.

Blount, W., Yegidis, B., & Maheux, R. (1992). Police attitudes toward preferred arrest: Influences of rank and productivity. *American Journal of Police, 11,* 35–52.

Bonta, J., Wallace-Capretta, S., & Rooney, J. (2000). A quasi-experimental evaluation of an intensive rehabilitation supervision program. *Criminal Justice and Behavior, 27,* 312–329.

Bureau of Justice Assistance. (1993). *Family violence: Interventions for the justice system.* Washington, DC: Author.

Buzawa, E., & Buzawa, C. (1985). Legislative trends in the criminal justice response to domestic violence. In A. Lincoln & M. Straus (Eds.), *Crime in the family* (pp. 134–147). Springfield, IL: Charles C. Thomas.

Campbell, D. (1969). Reforms as experiments. *American Psychologist, 24,* 409–429.

Campbell, J. C., Webster, D., Koziol-McLain, J., Block, C. R., Campbell, D. W., Curry, M. A., et al. (2003). Assessing risk factors for intimate partner homicide. *National Institute of Justice Journal, 250,* 14–19.

Canales-Portalatin, D. (2000). Intimate partner assailants: Comparison of cases referred to a probation department. *Journal of Interpersonal Violence, 15,* 843–854.

Centers for Disease Control and Prevention. (2006). *Understanding intimate partner violence.* Washington, DC: Author.

Centers for Disease Control and Prevention. (2008). *Understanding teen dating violence.* Washington, DC: Author.

Chen, H., Bersani, C., Myers, S., & Denton, R. (1989). Evaluating the effectiveness of a court sponsored treatment program. *Journal of Family Violence, 4,* 309–322.

Cissner, A., & Puffett, N. (2006). *Do batterer program length or approach affect completion or re-arrest rates? A comparison of outcomes between defendants sentenced to two batterer programs in Brooklyn.* New York: Center for Court Innovation.

Cramer, E. (1999). Variables that predict verdicts in domestic violence cases. *Journal of Interpersonal Violence, 14,* 1137–1151.

Davis, R., Maxwell, C., & Taylor, B. (2003). The Brooklyn experiment. In S. Jackson, L. Feder, D. Forde, R. Davis, B. Taylor, & C. Maxwell (Eds.), *Batterer intervention programs: Where do we go from here?* Washington, DC: National Institute of Justice Research Report. Also available at http://www.ncjrs.org/txtfiles1/nij/195079.txt

Davis, R., Smith, B., & Nickles, L. (1998). The deterrent effect of prosecuting domestic violence misdemeanors. *Crime and Delinquency, 44,* 434–442.

Davis, R., & Taylor, B. (1997). *A randomized experiment of the effects of batterer treatment: Summary of preliminary research findings.* Paper presented at the International Family Violence Conference, New Hampshire.

Deschner, J., & McNeil, J. (1986). Results of anger control training for battering couples. *Journal of Family Violence, 1,* 111–120.

Dishion, T., McCord, J., & Poulin, F. (1999). When interventions harm: Peer groups and problem behavior. *American Psychologist, 54,* 755–764.

Duffy, M., Nolan, A., & Scruggs, D. (2003, February). Addressing issues of domestic violence through community supervision of offenders. *Corrections Today,* pp. 50–53.

Dunford, F. (2000a). The San Diego Navy experiment: An assessment of interventions for men who assault their wives. *Journal of Consulting and Clinical Psychology, 68,* 468–476.

Dunford, F. (2000b). Determining program success: The importance of employing experimental research designs. *Crime and Delinquency, 46,* 425–434.

Dunford, F., Huizinga, D., & Elliot, D. (1990). The role of arrest in domestic assault: The Omaha police experiment. *Criminology, 28,* 183–206.

Dutton, D. (1987). The criminal justice response to wife assault. *Law and Human Behavior, 11,* 189–206.

Dutton, D. (1988). Research advances in the study of wife assault: Etiology and prevention. *Law and Mental Health, 4,* 161–220.

Dutton, D. (2008). My back pages. Reflections on thirty years of domestic violence research. *Trauma, Violence and Abuse, 9,* 131–143.

Dutton, D., & Corvo, K. (2006). Transforming a flawed policy: A call to revive psychology and science in domestic violence research and practice. *Aggression and Violent Behavior, 11*, 457–483.

Dutton, D., & Sonkin, D. (2001). Introduction: Perspectives on the treatment of intimate violence. *Journal of Aggression, Maltreatment and Trauma, 5*, 1–6.

Eckhardt, C., Murphy, C., Black, D., & Suhr, L. (2006). Intervention programs for perpetrators of intimate partner violence: Conclusions from a clinical research perspective. *Public Health Reports, 121*, 369–381.

Erez, E., & Ibarra, P. (2007). Making your home a shelter: Electronic monitoring and victim re-entry in domestic violence cases. *British Journal of Criminology, 47*, 100–120.

Erez, E., Ibarra, P., & Lurie, N. (2004). Electronic monitoring of domestic violence cases: A study of two bilateral programs. *Federal Probation, 68*, 5–20.

Fagan, J. (1996). *The criminalization of domestic violence: Promises and limits.* Washington, DC: National Institute of Justice.

Feder, L. (1996). Police handling of domestic calls: The importance of offender's presence in the arrest decision. *Journal of Criminal Justice, 24*, 1–10.

Feder, L. (1997). Domestic violence and police response in a pro-arrest jurisdiction. *Women and Criminal Justice, 8*, 79–98.

Feder, L. (1998a). Using random assignment in social science settings. *Professional Ethics Report, 11*, 1–7.

Feder, L. (1998b). Police handling of domestic and non-domestic violence calls: Is there a case for discrimination? *Crime and Delinquency, 44*, 139–153.

Feder, L. (1999). Police handling of domestic violence calls: An overview and further investigation. *Women & Criminal Justice, 10*, 49–68.

Feder, L., & Dugan, L. (2002). A test of the efficacy of court-mandated counseling for domestic violence offenders: The Broward experiment. *Justice Quarterly, 19*, 343–375.

Feder, L., & Forde, D. (2000). *A test of the efficacy of court-mandated counseling for domestic violence offenders: The Broward experiment.* National Institute of Justice Final Report (Grant NIJ-96-WT-NX-0008).

Feder, L., Jolin, A., & Feyerherm, W. (2000). Lessons from two randomized experiments in criminal justice settings. *Crime and Delinquency, 46*, 380–400.

Feder, L., & Wilson, D. (2005). A meta-analytic review of court-mandated batterer intervention programs: Can courts affect abusers' behavior? *Experimental Criminology, 1*, 239–262.

Finn, M., & Muirhead-Steves, S. (2002). The effectiveness of electronic monitoring with violent male parolees. *Justice Quarterly, 19*, 294–314.

Ford, D., & Regoli, M. (1992). The preventive impacts of policies for prosecuting wife batterers. In E. Buzawa & C. Buzawa (Eds.), *Domestic violence: The changing criminal justice response* (pp. 181–208). Dover, MA: Auburn House.

Ford, D., & Regoli, M. (1993). The criminal prosecution of wife assaulters. In Z. Hilton (Ed.), *Legal responses to wife assault: Current trends and evaluation* (pp. 127–164). Newbury Park, CA: Sage Publications.

Friedman, L., & Shulman, M. (1990). Domestic violence: The criminal justice response. In A. Lurigio, W. Skogan, & R. Davis (Eds.), *Victims of crime: Problems, policies, and programs* (pp. 87–103). Newbury Park, CA: Sage Publications.

Gainey, R., Payne, B., & O'Toole, M. (2000). The relationships between time in jail, time on electronic monitoring, and recidivism: An event history analysis of a jail-based program. *Justice Quarterly, 17,* 739–752.

Gelles, R. (2001). Standards for men who batter? Not yet. *Journal of Aggression, Maltreatment and Trauma, 5,* 11–20.

Glass, N. E., Campbell, J. C., Kub, J., Sharps, P. W., Fredland, N., & Yonas, M. (2003). Adolescent dating violence: Prevalence, risk factors, health outcomes and implications for clinical practice. *JOGNN, 32,* 2–12.

Greenblat, C. (1985). "Don't hit your wife … unless …": Preliminary findings on normative support for the use of physical force by husbands. *Victimology: An International Journal, 10,* 221–241.

Gross, M., Cramer, E., Gordon, J., Kunkel, T., & Moriarty, L. (2000). The impact of sentencing options on recidivism among domestic violence offenders: A case study. *American Journal of Criminal Justice, 24,* 301–312.

Harrell, A. (1991). *Evaluation of court-ordered treatment for domestic violence offenders: Final report.* Washington, DC: Institute for Social Analysis.

Harrell, A., Schaffer, M., DeStefano, C., & Castro, J. (2006). *The evaluation of Milwaukee's judicial oversight demonstration.* Washington, DC: Urban Institute Justice Policy Center.

Healey, K., Smith, C., & O'Sullivan, C. (1998). *Batterer intervention: Program approaches and criminal justice strategies.* Washington, DC: U.S. Department of Justice.

Holtzworth-Munroe, A. (2001). Standards for batterer treatment programs: How can research inform our decisions? *Journal of Aggression, Maltreatment and Trauma, 5,* 165–180.

Hotaling, G., & Sugarman, D. (1986). An analysis of risk markers in husband to wife violence: The current state of knowledge. *Violence and Victims, 1,* 101–124.

Ibarra, P., & Erez, E. (2005). Victim-centric diversion? The electronic monitoring of domestic violence cases. *Behavioral Sciences and the Law, 23,* 259–276.

Jennings, J. (1987). History and issues in the treatment of battering men: A case for unstructured group therapy. *Journal of Family Violence, 2,* 193–213.

Johnson, J., & Kanzler, D. (1993). Treating domestic violence: Evaluating the effectiveness of a domestic violence diversion program. *Studies in Symbolic Interaction, 15,* 271–289.

Johnson, R. (2001). Intensive probation for domestic violence offenders. *Federal Probation, 65,* 36–39.

Jones, A., & Gondolf, E. (2002). Assessing the effect of batterer program completion on reassault: An instrumental variables analysis. *Journal of Quantitative Criminology, 18,* 71–98.

Keilitz, S. (2001). *Specialization of domestic violence case management in the courts: A national survey.* National Institute of Justice Final Report (Grant NIJ-98-WT-VX-0002).

Kingsnorth, R. (2006). Intimate partner violence: Predictors of recidivism in a sample of arrestees. *Violence Against Women, 12,* 917–935.

Klein, A. (1997). Batterers' treatment. *National Bulletin on Domestic Violence Prevention, 3,* 1–3.

Klein, A., & Crowe, A. (2008). Findings from an outcome examination of Rhode Island's specialized domestic violence probation supervision: Do specialized supervision programs of batterers reduce reabuse? *Violence Against Women, 14,* 226–246.

Klein, A., & Tobin, T. (2008). A longitudinal study of arrested batterers, 1995–2005. *Violence Against Women, 14,* 136–157.

Klein, A., Wilson, D., Crowe, A., & DeMichele, M. (2008). *Evaluation of the Rhode Island Probation Specialized Domestic Violence Supervision Unit.* National Institute of Justice Final Report (Grant NIJ-2002-WG-BX-0011).

Krmpotich, S. (2000). *Domestic Assault Program evaluation: Final (2-year) results.* Hennepin County Department of Corrections Final Report.

Labriola, M., Rempel, M., & Davis, R. (2008). Do batterer programs reduce recidivism? Results from a randomized trial in the Bronx. *Justice Quarterly, 25,* 252–282.

Langan, P., & Innes, C. (1986). *Preventing domestic violence against women.* Washington, DC: U.S. Department of Justice, National Institute of Justice.

Lapham, S., C'de Baca, J., Lapidus, J., & McMillan, G. (2007). Randomized sanctions to reduce re-offense among repeat impaired-driving offenders. *Addiction, 102,* 1618–1625.

Lawrenz, F., Lembo, J., & Schade, T. (1988). Time series analysis of the effect of a domestic violence directive on the number of arrests per day. *Journal of Criminal Justice, 16,* 493–498.

Lerman, L. (1981). Criminal prosecution of wife beaters. *Response to Violence in the Family and Sexual Assault, 4,* 1–19.

Lerman, L., Livingston, F., & Jackson, V. (1983). State legislation on domestic violence. *Response to Violence in the Family and Sexual Assault, 6,* 1–27.

Lilly, J., Ball, R., Curry, G., & McMullen, J. (1993). Electronic monitoring of the drunk driver: A seven year study of the home confinement alternative. *Crime and Delinquency, 39,* 462–484.

Maiuro, R., Hagar, T., Lin, H., & Olson, N. (2001). Are current state standards for domestic violence perpetrator treatment adequately informed by research? A question of questions. *Journal of Aggression, Maltreatment and Trauma, 5,* 21–44.

Maxwell, C., Garner, J., & Fagan, J. (2001). *The effects of arrest on intimate partner violence: New evidence from the Spouse Assault Replication Program* (NCJ-188199). Washington, DC: U.S. Department of Justice.

McCord, J. (1978). A thirty-year follow-up of treatment effects. *American Psychologist, 33,* 284–289.

McCord, J. (2003). Cures that harm: Unanticipated outcomes of crime prevention programs. *Annals of the American Academy of Political and Social Science, 587,* 16–30.

Mignon, S., & Holmes, W. (1995). Police response to mandatory arrest laws. *Crime and Delinquency, 41,* 430–443.

Miller, T., Cohen, M., & Wiersema, B. (1996). *Victim costs and consequences: A new look.* Washington, DC: National Institute of Justice.

Murphy, C., Musser, P., & Maton, K. (1998). Coordinated community intervention for domestic abusers: Intervention system involvement and criminal recidivism. *Journal of Family Violence, 13,* 263–284.

Neidig, P., Friedman, D., & Collins, B. (1985, April). Domestic conflict containment: A spouse abuse treatment program. *Social Casework: The Journal of Contemporary Social Work*, pp. 195–204.

Olson, D., & Stalans, L. (2001). Violent offenders on probation: Profile, sentence and outcome differences among domestic violence and other violent probationers. *Violence Against Women, 7*, 1164–1185.

Palmer, S., Brown, R., & Barrera, M. (1992). Group treatment program for abusive husbands: Long-term evaluation. *American Journal of Orthopsychiatry, 62*, 276–283.

Payne, B., & Gainey, R. (2004). The electronic monitoring of offenders released from jail or prison: Safety, control, and comparisons to the incarceration experience. *The Prison Journal, 84*, 413–435.

Petersilia, J., Turner, S., & Deschenes, E. (1992). The costs and effects of intensive supervision for drug offenders. *Federal Probation, 56*, 12–17.

Pirog-Good, M., & Stets-Kealey, J. (1985). Male batterers and battering prevention programs: A national survey. *Response, 8*, 8–12.

Plichta S., & Falik M. (2001). Prevalence of violence and its implications for women's health. *Women's Health Issues, 11*, 244–258.

Rebovich, D. (1996). Prosecution response to domestic violence: Results of a survey of large jurisdictions. In E. Buzawa & C. Buazawa (Eds.), *Do arrests and restraining orders work?* (pp. 176–191). Thousand Oaks, CA: Sage.

Rees, A., & Rivett, M. (2005). Let a hundred flowers bloom, let a hundred schools of thought contend? Towards a variety in programmes for perpetrators of domestic violence. *Probation Journal, 52*, 277–288.

Rempel, M., Labriola, M., & Davis, R. (2008). Does judicial monitoring deter domestic violence recidivism? Results of a quasi-experimental comparison in the Bronx. *Violence Against Women, 14*, 185–207.

Renzema, M., & Mayo-Wilson, E. (2005). Can electronic monitoring reduce crime for moderate to high-risk offenders? *Journal of Experimental Criminology, 1*, 215–237.

Roberts, A. (1982). A national survey of services for batterers. In M. Roy (Ed.), *The abusive partner: An analysis of domestic battering* (pp. 230–243). New York: Van Nostrand Reinhold Company.

Saunders, D. (2001). Developing guidelines for domestic violence offender programs: What can we learn from related fields and current research? *Journal of Aggression, Maltreatment and Trauma, 5*, 235–248.

Sherman, L., & Berk, R. (1984). The specific deterrent effects of arrest for domestic assault. *American Sociological Review, 49*, 261–272.

Sherman, L., & Cohn, E. (1989). The impact of research on legal policy: The Minneapolis Domestic Violence Experiment. *Law & Society Review, 23*, 117–144.

Sherman, L., Schmidt, J., Rogan, D., Gartin, P., Cohn, E., Collins, D., et al. (1991). From initial deterrence to long-term escalation: Short-custody arrest for poverty ghetto domestic violence. *Criminology, 29*, 821–850.

Sherman, L., Smith, D., Schmidt, J., & Rogan, D. (1992). Crime, punishment, and stake in conformity: Legal and informal control of domestic violence. *American Sociological Review, 57*, 680–690.

Socolar, R. R. S. (2000). Domestic violence and children: A review. *NCMJ, 61*, 279–283.

Stalans, L., Yarnold, P., Seng, M., Olson, D., & Repp, M. (2004). Identifying three types of violent offenders and predicting violent recidivism while on probation: A classification tree analysis. *Law and Human Behavior, 28*, 253–271.

Straus, M. (2008). Bucking the tide in family violence research. *Trauma, Violence and Abuse, 9*, 191–213.

Tatum, K., Lee, A., & Kunselman, J. (2008). A pre-trial domestic violence intensive supervision unit: Exploring case seriousness and successful disposition. *American Journal of Criminal Justice, 33*, 32–43.

Taylor, B., Davis, R., & Maxwell, C. (2001). The effects of a group batterer treatment program: A randomized experiment in Brooklyn. *Justice Quarterly, 18*, 171–201.

Tjaden, P., & Thoennes, N., (2000). *Extent, nature and consequences of intimate partner violence: Findings from the National Violence Against Women Survey* (NCJ 181867). Washington, DC: U.S. Department of Justice.

Tolman, R. (1996). Expanding sanctions for batterers: What can we do besides jailing and counseling them? In J. Edleson & Z. Eisikovits (Eds.), *Future interventions with battered women and their families* (pp. 170–185). Thousand Oaks, CA: Sage.

Turner, S., Petersilia, J., & Deschenes, E. (1992). Evaluating intensive supervision probation/parole (ISP) for drug offenders. *Crime and Delinquency, 38*, 539–556.

Visher, C., Harrell, A., & Newmark, L. (2007). *Pretrial innovations for domestic violence offenders and victims.* Washington, DC: National Institute of Justice.

Waits, K. (1985). The criminal justice system's response to battering: Understanding the problem, forging the solution. *Washington Law Review, 60*, 267–329.

Weisburd, D., Lum, C., & Petrosino, A. (2001). Does research design affect study outcomes in criminal justice? *Annals of the American Academy of Political and Social Science, 578*, 50–70.

Wisner, C. L., Gilmer, T. P., Saltzman, L. E., & Zink, T. (1999). Intimate partner violence against women: Do victims cost health plans more? *Journal of Family Practice, 4*, 439–443.

Wooldredge, J., & Thistlethwaite, A. (2005). Court dispositions and rearrest for intimate assault. *Crime and Delinquency, 51*, 75–100.

Worden, R., & Pollitz, A. (1984). Police arrests in domestic disturbances: A further look. *Law and Society Review, 18*, 105–119.

Restorative Approaches to Domestic Violence
The Cornerposts in Action

18

DEBRA HEATH-THORNTON

Contents

Introduction

Abuse between intimate partners has reached epidemic proportions. Primarily, partner violence is viewed as violence precipitated by men against women. Generally, the data suggest that in situations of domestic abuse, men are significantly more abusive toward women than the reverse, male abuse results in more damage than that of female, and male victims generally experience less emotional fear than female victims. Moreover, women's violence against men often involves actions initiated in self-defense (Mattaini, 1999). With that said, it should be recognized that violence can and does occur in intimate relationships of various characteristics.

This chapter identifies behavior that constitutes domestic violence with a specific focus on the patterned acts that constitute these events. Forms of domestic violence and historical influences are discussed. The restorative justice perspective is presented as a theoretical framework for offering effective approaches to reducing violence among intimates. Issues of spirituality are addressed, and the restorative justice perspective is applied through the discussion on restorative approaches.

Domestic Violence

Domestic violence constitutes a criminal justice concern that annually affects hundreds of thousands of people in the United States. The resulting negative social, psychological, and economic impacts have implications not only for victims, offenders, and communities, but also for the nation as a whole (Fulkerson, 2001; Saltzman, Fanslow, McMahon, & Shelley, 2002). Because of the numerous variables that affect this phenomenon, domestic violence is one of the concepts that most people would have general knowledge of but to which many would have difficulty applying a specific definition. Accordingly, this chapter adopts the definition established by Roslyn Muraskin (2007, 274):

> A pattern of acts committed by a person against his or her intimate partner with the expressed or implied intent of exerting power and control over that person. This abuse may result in physical, sexual, emotional or financial harm.

The chapter includes the caveat proposed by Buzawa and Buzawa (2003) that the violence addressed here has occurred between partners who may or may not be living together. The Centers for Disease Control and Prevention recognizes domestic violence as a serious, preventable public health problem (Saltzman et al., 2002). The phenomenon, as addressed here, is arguably gender-neutral since violence occurs among and between both genders, and it's primarily the oppressive behavior that gains our focus here more so than the gender of the parties involved.

It is important to note that domestic violence can occur between intimates of any configurations: single, married, separated, divorced, heterosexual, gay or lesbian (Muraskin, 2007). For those external to the relationship, domestic violence is often difficult to detect because of the coercive and controlling nature of the abuse. For example, the victim is often isolated from family, friends, and other supporters as abusers attempt to control as many aspects of their victims' lives as possible, particularly those that would undermine their control (Muraskin, 2007; Ferraro, 2001; Mattaini, 1999). However, victims who remain connected with family and friends stand a greater likelihood of eventually separating themselves from abusive relationships. Informal support networks can mitigate the effects of these relationships as appropriate positive peer relationships are important throughout the life course (Mattaini, 1999). In addition and depending on their nature, many informal networks can serve to insulate an individual inside the relationship. One area where this is commonly found is in relationships that are strongly influenced by religion.

Forms of Domestic Violence

One problem with identifying and measuring domestic violence is that it encompasses a wide range of behaviors. Some actions are explicitly violent in nature while others are much more subtle. Yet, both can yield similarly oppressive and manipulative results. While individual incidents are of importance and worthy of being addressed, it is the pattern of continued violent, oppressive, and manipulative behavior that usually reaches the attention of authorities (Buzawa & Buzawa, 2003). The Centers for Disease Control and Prevention divides behavior that constitutes domestic violence into five significant categories: physical, sexual, threats of physical and sexual, psychological/emotional, and stalking (Saltzman et al., 2002):

> *Physical violence*: Intentional use of physical force that could result in death, injury, harm, or disability. Examples include but are not limited to pushing or shoving, throwing or grabbing, choking or shaking, slapping, threatened and actual use of a weapon, and use of restraints or one's body, size, or strength against another person.
>
> *Sexual violence*: Physical force used to coerce a person to engage in a sexual act against his or her will. This includes attempted or completed acts against a person who is unable to understand the nature or condition of the act, to decline participation, or to communicate unwillingness to engage in the sexual act (because of disability, illness, incapacitation due to alcohol or other drugs, or because of intimidation or pressure by the perpetrator or his or her proxy), and abusive sexual violence.
>
> *Threats of physical or sexual violence*: Words, deeds, or weapons that communicate the intent to cause death, disability, injury, or physical harm if the victim doesn't comply.
>
> *Psychological/emotional violence*: Trauma sustained by the victim resulting from acts, threats, or coercive tactics. These acts are generally considered psychological or emotional violence when prior incidents or threats of physical or sexual violence have occurred.
>
> *Stalking*: Repeated threatening or harassing actions such as making harassing phone calls, following a person, appearing at a person's home or place of business, leaving written messages, objects, or unwelcome gifts, or vandalizing a person's property (Tjaden & Thoennes, 1998).

History and Religious Influence

For centuries legal traditions, including the English common law upon which American jurisprudence is based, considered women the property of their husbands, thereby denying them equal protection under the law while granting husbands what amounted to nonintervention protection in instances of their abusive treatment toward their wives (Karmen, 2007; Pollock, 2009). The crime was largely considered a private matter as opposed to a social problem, with both legal traditions and social institutions supporting the hands-off approach (Muraskin, 2007). In addition, many societal principles hindered the belief, even by battered women, that they themselves were actual victims of abuse (Karmen, 2007). This reality received attention in 1979 through Dr. Lenore Walker's work on battered women's syndrome. Walker established the notion of learned helplessness, a phenomenon whereby women who are severely battered believe they are somehow responsible and that they have no control over the situation (Presser & Gaarder, 2000; Kemp, 1998).

The 1970s revealed a rediscovery of violence between intimates, spearheaded by social science research and feminist groups such as the National Organization of Women. The attention in the 1970s focused on victim-support services, wife beating as oppression against women, and the criminal justice system's unwillingness or inability to adequately address these matters (Karmen, 2007). One key difference between the 1970s and previous eras was the professional interest in "spousal abuse," a term first recognized in the social science literature in the early 1970s and prior to which very little professional literature existed on the subject. This emergence is believed to have led to the appearance of the first wave of shelters for battered women across the United States (Kemp, 1998).

No discussion on the ability to redeem domestic violence in the United States is complete without reference to the influence of religion. Religious beliefs have governed political and social attitudes throughout history and have had a significant impact on how domestic violence is viewed. For example, Western religions have supported a husband's right to maintain control over his wife, and the biblical text has been used selectively to justify such practices. Over the past two decades, however, many denominations have endeavored to address influences that espouse male domination over women in marital relationships (Buzawa & Buzawa, 2003).

The Restorative Justice Perspective

The most immediate need for victims of crime is safety (Van Ness & Strong, 2006; Mattaini, 1999). A fact not yet fully recognized is that victims of domestic violence are also victims of crime. Understanding this principle is paramount in addressing the plight of both victims of domestic violence and the offenders responsible for their victimization. One way to guarantee the safety of domestic violence victims is to ensure a reduced likelihood of the continued violence that occurs at the hands of perpetrators. A restorative justice approach provides one potential framework for achieving this result.

What Is Restorative Justice?

The restorative justice perspective seeks to address and balance the needs of crime victims, criminal offenders, and the communities from which they come. This justice perspective provides a unique paradigm for understanding and responding to crime and victimization and is unique in that it respects victims, traditionally a forgotten constituent in the criminal justice system. In the process, a restorative justice framework holds offenders accountable to their victims, and often allows the community and other supporters to take an active role in the justice process.

Albert Eglash is credited for coining the phrase *restorative justice* in his 1977 article "Beyond Restitution: Creative Restitution," where he identifies three types of justice. The first, retributive justice, is a foundation for punishment and a perspective that views crime as simply the violation of the law. The second, rehabilitative justice, also views the state as the victim (because its laws were broken), but is based on the therapeutic treatment of offenders. In this view the emphasis is on accountability through punishment. The third, restorative justice, is an alternative to both retributive justice and rehabilitative justice. Restorative justice, rooted in biblical principles, differs from the previous two paradigms in that crime is viewed not only as a violation of law, but also as a violation of people and relationships. This perspective concentrates on the harmful outcomes of an offender's actions and actively engages both victims and offenders in a process of justice, where the main objectives are to restore, repair, and promote healing (Heath-Thornton, 2002, 2009a). However, it is also essential to recognize that restorative justice provides distinct values that can and should be used in conjunction with prevailing criminal justice system operations, thereby ensuring that the needs of victims, offenders, and communities are addressed. In other words, restorative justice does not constitute a specific program (Presser & Garder, 2000) or suggest that the criminal justice system as we know it be disbanded. Instead, it represents a set of unique principles and ideals that address the needs of all stakeholders—victims, offenders, and communities.

The number of countries giving consideration to restorative justice is on the rise. This has resulted in many governments supporting the development of new initiatives, expanding the role of existing ones, and modifying legislation to provide for new interventions. For example, in the early 1990s, the U.S. Department of Justice promoted a number of restorative justice initiatives, and in the late 1990s the National Institute of Corrections engaged in restorative justice training for criminal justice practitioners. Several African nations and European countries have implemented restorative principles and practices for handling adult and juvenile offenders. In New Zealand, restorative justice legislation has been expanded to include procedures for addressing adult offenders. Some former Soviet bloc countries have included restorative justice in their postcommunist criminal codes. Most importantly, in 2002 the United Nations Economic and Social Council (ECOSOC) encouraged the global use of restorative justice by promoting its approaches in ways that preserve the human rights of victims and offenders (Van Ness & Strong, 2006). Since domestic violence is believed to permeate most societies, neither its global nor spiritual implications should be ignored.

Spirituality

Although spirituality as a concept has proven difficult to define, it is well documented as an important part of the human experience. Armstrong and Crowther (2002) contend that spirituality is a relationship with a (the) transcendent power that brings meaning and purpose to life and affects the way we operate in the world. Over the past half century, researchers have established that more than 90% of Americans admit to a belief in God (Simpson, Newman, & Fuqua, 2007). Social scientists and others have endeavored to conceptualize and define *spirituality* across various disciplines. Still, consensus on the exact definition of *spirituality has not been achieved*. What is known and commonly agreed upon is that spirituality is a complex construct comprised of beliefs and attitudes, behaviors and rituals, personal experiences, and varying levels of consciousness and awareness, each encompassing both public and private characteristics. Researchers do agree, however, that spirituality constitutes foremost human experiences that help create meaning in the world. Accordingly, the term *spirituality* is generally used in reference to meaning and purpose in one's life, a search for wholeness, and a relationship with a transcendent being. One's spirituality may be expressed in a multitude of ways, including through religious beliefs and religious involvement (King & Boyatzis, 2004; Fukuyama & Sevig, 1999).

King and Boyatzis (2004) argue that spirituality involves a developmental process whereby people acquire the intrinsic human capacity to embed the self in something greater than oneself. In doing so, they agree with Benson et al. that spirituality entails the awareness of self in relation to other humans and the divine. In other words, spirituality includes a respect for life that connects us to one another, aids us in embracing life's demands (Bender &

Armour, 2007), and allows positive and creative connection between our-selves and others in the world around us. Spirituality, then, affects our ability to make choices, take responsibility for our lives, and shape our ability to relate to others (Kus, 1995).

The relationship between spirituality and restorative justice has only recently received attention in the literature. In 2007, for example, Bender and Armour attempted to establish relationships that may exist between the two.

Restorative Societal Responses

The tenets of restorative justice have surfaced in diverse cultures and loca-tions across the globe and have led to the development of numerous asso-ciations and organizations driven to advance restorative justice experiences, innovations, and outcomes both within and outside of the criminal justice system. In numerous jurisdictions across the United States restorative poli-cies serve a reparative and supplemental role within existing justice practices. The restorative process seeks to right the wrong while repairing the damages endured by both victims and offenders.

A review of the literature on the effects of restorative justice on domestic violence reveals what could be regarded as a template for effective program-ming. Moreover, this template contains certain characteristics that have been shown to have a positive impact. Yet, these are a set of characteristics or tra-ditions, not specific program guidelines. This rubric supports well the struc-ture established by Van Ness and Strong's (2006) work that identifies four "cornerposts" of restorative justice: encounter, amends, reintegration, and inclusion. These are depicted in Table 18.1, and each is described below.

Encounter involves structured opportunities for the victims and offend-ers to meet one another—outside the courtroom—in a personalized approach called narrative. In this process each party tells his or her story from his or her own vantage point. Listening and understanding the perspective of the other is just as important as telling one's own story. Genuine emotion is often displayed as the parties tell how the incident has impacted their lives. It is important that the parties understand that, in encounter, the goal is not to reverse the past but to repair the damage that resulted from the circum-stances of the past.

Table 18.1 also illustrates the cornerposts of restorative justice and depicts Coward-Yaskiw's (2002) rubric fit, primarily the five phases that are paramount to restorative initiatives that address domestic violence. Two of them, full participation and agreement and full and direct accountability, fall along the guidelines of encounter. Presser and Gaarder (2000) also identify with elements of encounter, namely, "restoring a victim's well-being."

Table 18.1   Cornerposts of Restorative Justice

Van Ness & Strong (2006) Focus on Issues of Healing *The Cornerposts*	Coward-Yaskiw (2002) and Sharpe (1998) *Focus on Issues of Healing*	Presser and Gaarder (2000) *Focus on Community*
Encounter • Structured opportunities for parties to encounter one another outside the courtroom • *Examples:* Victim-offender reconciliation programs (VORPs), conferences, victim impact panels	• Full participation and agreement • Full and direct accountability	• Encounter (Part I) • Restores victim's well-being
Amends • Four elements of amends: apology, changed behavior, restitution, and generosity • *Examples of generosity:* Doing more than the community requires you to do (i.e., additional hours of community service once the minimum requirement is completed)	• Healing	• Outcomes • Apologies to the victim
Reintegration • Components of reintegration: safety, respect, help, and spiritual guidance and care • *Outcome:* Transform an offender's self-image in terms of how he or she sees himself or herself in relation to the rest of society	• Strengthened communities	• Encounter (Part II) • Reintegrating victim and offender into communitites of concern

—continued

Table 18.1   Cornerposts of Restorative Justice

Van Ness & Strong (2006) Focus on Issues of Healing *The Cornerposts*	Coward-Yaskiw (2002) and Sharpe (1998) *Focus on Issues of Healing*	Presser and Gaarder (2000) *Focus on Community*

Inclusion
 • Critical pieces of integration: invitation, recognition, acceptance, and willingness to consider alternative approaches; involves opportunities for the full and direct involvement of each party in all procedures that follow a crime
 Examples: Inviting all stakeholders to the process, openness to diverse interests, willingness to consider diverse approaches
 • Inclusion generally occurs through four mechanisms:
   • Information
   • Observing proceedings
   • Formal presentation (i.e., victim impact statements)
   • Pursuit of restitution or reparation
	• Reunite
	   • Bridge "us" and "them"
		• Agreements
		   • Reinstitution or other services by offenders to victims or communities in an attempt to restore

The second cornerpost is amends. According to Van Ness and Strong (2006), amends incorporates an apology, changed behavior, restitution, and generosity. Each of these components plays an important role in the healing process.

The cornerpost of apology has three parts. The first is acknowledgment by offenders that a wrong was committed, that they (themselves) are responsible and accountable for the harm. Changed behavior must accompany the apology affect, and vulnerability. The second part is affect. Here, the offender expresses regret or shame in words or disposition. This often represents the validating experience for victims from which the healing process can begin. The last part is vulnerability. According to Van Ness and Strong, this represents an "exchange of shame and power between the offender and the offended" (Van Ness & Strong, 2006).

The second cornerpost of restorative justice is changed behavior, generally considered a second way to make amends. Simply put, this means to stop the law-violating behavior, in this case, the abusive conduct. This includes changed values that are displayed through the changed behavior, and the transformation of the new values into actions. Coward-Yaskiw (2000) identifies healing and Presser and Gaarder (2000) identify an aspect of outcomes, apologies to the victim, as elements of making amends.

The third cornerpost is reintegration, which includes the safety of the parties involved, respect or their human dignity and self-worth, practical and material assistance, and moral and spiritual guidance and care. This often involves working with offenders to help them develop a positive self-image and garner faith that positive change is possible (Van Ness & Strong, 2006). Coward-Yaskiw (2000) points to strengthened communities, while Presser and Gaarder (2000) identify reintegrating victims and offenders into communities of concern to address this component.

The fourth cornerpost of restorative justice is inclusion. According to Van Ness and Strong (2006), this cornerpost incorporates the victims, offenders, and communities impacted by the criminal conduct. This includes wholly engaging each stakeholder in the steps and processes that follow the crime. Coward-Yaskiw (2000) highlights reuniting the parties (bridging "us" and "them"), and Presser and Gaarder (2000) emphasize agreements, restitution, and other services for which offenders are responsible, in an effort to restore and promote healing.

Contemporary Restorative Approaches

Victim-offender reconciliation programs (VORPs) are celebrated as the longest-standing restorative approach to victim-offender dialogue in North America and are regarded as the prevailing form of restorative justice practice currently in operation in the United States. VORPs are believed to have begun in Canada in 1974 after a vandalism crime spree by two young men in Ontario. Representatives from probation and the community arranged a meeting with the victims for offenders to accept responsibility for their actions, apologize, and arrange restitution. The result was so positive that the parties developed a project called Victim-Offender Reconciliation Program to continue the efforts (Dorne, 2008; Johnstone & Van Ness, 2007).

Victim-offender reconciliation programs are often confused with victim-offender mediation (VOM) programs. While these two endeavors are similar, there are distinct differences. While, like VOM programs, VORPs utilize a preparatory process, they emphasize movement that takes the objective beyond simply problem solving and more toward reconciliation (i.e., settlement and understanding). Reconciliation, defined as understanding past experiences, holding offenders accountable, and seeking reparations for victims, is the desired outcome since it allows the healing process to begin

(Schreiter, 1998). Foundational to VORPs is the restorative justice perspective that the crime not only violated a relationship between two or more people, but has also violated the law. Accordingly, it encompasses the key features of encounter and understanding that many believe initiate the healing process for not only the victims and community members, but also the offenders (Heath-Thornton, 2009b; Dorne, 2008).

A little less than half of the VORPs in the United States are run by religious organizations, with the majority run by nonprofit organizations. Participating offenders generally have pled or been found guilty in court and are awaiting sentence when the reconciliation meeting takes place. In these settings, offenders listen to victims, and sometimes their supporters, tell of how the victimization experience disrupted and negatively impacted the victim's life and the lives of those around them. Offenders are usually afforded an opportunity to respond, which often includes taking responsibility for the criminal incident, apologizing, and asking for forgiveness, which can include dialogue around issues of restitution or reparations (Dorne, 2008).

A second common restorative initiative is victim impact panels (VIPs), viewed by some as a modification of VORPs and first popularized by Mothers Against Drunk Driving (MADD), whose experience in organizing and implementing these panels has been effective in drunk-driving cases. This initiative has proven effective with domestic violence offenders as well (Fulkerson, 2001). With VIPs, a group of offenders hears presentations by a panel of victims in a nonadversarial manner, where victims explain the effects that have resulted for themselves and their supporters as a result of their victimization through domestic violence. The purpose of these sessions is to allow a forum for victims to be heard and express their feelings while simultaneously providing offenders with the opportunity to understand the consequences of their abusive behavior on the lives of others. While the results of a recent study suggest that victims who participated on the panel experienced an enhanced psychological well-being and experienced less long-term emotional trauma than victims that did not participate on such panels, a small number reported that they did not find their participation helpful. This study did conclude that because of the balanced approach restorative justice provides, VIPs benefit victims as much as they do offenders (Fulkerson, 2001; Mercer, Lorden, & Lord, 1994).

Conclusion

The restorative justice perspective offers tremendous opportunities to impact victims, offenders, and communities, particularly domestic violence, in ways that have heretofore been unmatched by other justice initiatives. This holds true because restorative justice premises the potential to bring all stakeholders into the process, whether in person or by proxy (as with the case of victim impact panels), and provides a forum for the spiritual connection necessary for genuine transformation to take place.

Restorative initiatives also significantly impact domestic violence because they build on community support by acknowledging the genuineness of the victim's plight and offering practical and concrete steps toward positive change for the future. Informal networks in the community can also serve to regulate the behavior of domestic violence offenders. Not only is the offender expected to cease the abusive behavior, but community support exists to see that this occurs (Presser & Gaarder, 2000). Informal communities often provide an atmosphere capable of addressing the unique needs of specific nonplace communities, such as those based on social class, race and ethnicity, or other cultural attributes (Crenshaw, 1997).

The restorative justice model is directed toward a preestablished outcome, primarily reconciliation, which often precedes healing. With restorative justice, an encounter is established to allow the healing process to begin for all stakeholders involved. It is essential for victims to engage in an arena that fully validates their plight and acknowledges that they have been hurt without justification and due to no fault of their own (Presser & Gaarder, 2000). Other preestablished outcomes are giving victims voice and elevating their role in the criminal process and offering offenders a mechanism from which they can learn of the long-term negative effects of their abusive criminal conduct. The whole community benefits when the needs of both victims and offenders are met, often resulting in the level of reintegration necessary for both parties to return to full participation and acceptance within their communities (Fulkerson, 2001).

Effective screening mechanisms should be exercised whenever restorative initiatives are employed. Care should be taken to ensure that victims are emotionally ready to confront the abuse and the abuser. Equally important is that offenders must possess cognitive, psychological, and social skills necessary for their full participation in ways that are not coercive or manipulative, thereby hindering the victim's journey toward healing.

In situations where it is neither safe or healthy to bring together victims and offenders, restorative initiatives can still be employed through proxy. A common example of this is the nature of the victim impact panels discussed earlier. In these instances, care must be used to ensure that proper screening and preparation takes place.

Although restorative justice lends itself effectively to addressing situations of domestic violence, much care should be used with these approaches. For example, safety must be the most immediate need addressed for victims of this and any other crime (Van Ness & Strong, 2006; Mattaini, 1999). Reconciliation in terms of "preserving the relationship" should not be the goal. Instead, the goal should be reconciliation in terms of discerning the past victimization experiences, holding offenders accountable to victims and communities, and seeking reparations for victims whenever possible (Presser & Gaarder, 2000).

References

Armstrong, T., & Crowther, M. (2002). Spirituality among older African Americans. *Journal of Adult Development, 9*, 3–12.

Bender, K., & Armour, M. (2007). The spiritual components of restorative justice. *Victims & Offenders, 2*, 251–267.

Buzawa, E., & Buzawa, C. (2003). *Domestic violence: The criminal justice response.* Thousand Oaks, CA: SAGE Publications.

Clear, T. (1994). *Harm in American penology: Offenders, victims and their communities* (SUNY Series in New Directions in Crime and Justice Studies). Albany: State University of New York Press.

Clear, T. (1998). *Abuse in the family: An introduction.* Belmont, CA: Wadsworth Publishing.

Coward-Yaskiw, S. (2002). Restorative justice. *Herizons, 15*, 22–26.

Crenshaw, K. (1997). *Mapping the margins: Intersectionality, identity politics and violence against women of color.*

Dorne, C. (2008). *Restorative justice in the United States.* Upper Saddle River, NJ: Prentice Hall.

Eglash, A. (1958). Creative restitution: A broader meaning for an old term. *Journal of Criminal Law, Criminology, and Police Sciences, 48*, 619–622.

Fukuyama, M., & Sevig, T. (1999). *Integrating spirituality into multicultural counseling.* Thousand Oaks, CA: Sage Publications.

Fulkerson, A. (2001). The use of victim impact panels in domestic violence cases: A restorative justice approach. *Contemporary Justice Review, 4*, 355–368.

Heath-Thornton, D. (2002). Restorative Justice. In D. Levinson (Ed.), *Encyclopedia of crime and punishment* (pp. 1388–1393). Thousand Oaks, CA: Sage Publications.

Heath-Thornton, D. (2009a). Restorative justice. In *Praeger handbook of victimology.* 227–229. Westport, CT: Greenwood Publishing.

Heath-Thornton, D. (2009b). Victim-Offender Reconciliation Program (VORP). In *Praeger handbook of victimology.* 296–298. Westport, CT: Greenwood Publishing.

Herman, J. (1997). *Trauma and recovery.* New York: Basic Books.

Johnstone, G., & Van Ness, D. (2006). *Handbook of restorative justice.* Portland, OR: Willan.

Karmen, A. (2006). *Crime victims: An introduction to victimology* (Wadsworth Contemporary Issues in Crime and Justice). Belmont, CA: Wadsworth Publishing.

Kemp, A. (1998). *Abuse in the family: An introduction.* Belmont, CA: Wadsworth Publishing.

King, P., & Boyatzis, C. (2004). Exploring adolescent spiritual and religious development: Current and future theological and empirical perspectives. *Applied Developmental Science, 8*, 2–6.

Kus, R. J. (1995). *Spirituality and chemical dependency.* New York: Harrington Park Press.

Mattaini, M. (1999). *Clinical intervention with families.* Baltimore: NASW Press.

Mercer, D., Lorden, R., & Lord, J. (1994). Sharing their stories: What are the benefits? Who is helped? *National Institute for Health, XX,* XX.

Muraskin, R. (2007). *It's a crime women and justice custom edition.* Upper Saddle River, NJ: Prentice Hall.

Presser, L., & Gaarder, E. (2000). Can restorative justice reduce battering? Some preliminary considerations. *Social Justice, 27,* 175–197.

Saltzman, L. E., Fanslow, J. L., McMahon, P. M., & Shelley, G. A. (2002). *Intimate partner violence surveillance: Uniform definitions and recommended data elements,*(Version 1.0). Atlanta, GA: Centers for Disease Control and Prevention, National Center for Injury Prevention and Control.

Schreither, R. (1998). *The ministry of reconciliation: Spirituality and strategies.* New York: Orbis Books.

Sharpe, S. (1998). *Restorative justice: A vision for healing and change.* Edmonton: Edmonton Victim Offender Mediation Society.

Simpson, D., Newman, J., & Fuqua, D. (2007). Spirituality and personality. *Journal of Psychology and Christianity, 26,* 33–44.

Tjaden, P., & Thoennes N. (1998). *Stalking in America: Findings from the National Violence Against Women Survey.* Washington, DC: U.S. Department of Justice.

Van Ness, D., & Strong, K. (2006). *Restoring justice: An introduction to restorative justice.* Cincinnati, OH: Anderson Publishing Company.

Creating and Executing an Applied Interdisciplinary Campaign for Domestic Violence Prevention

19

SARAH N. KELLER
A. J. OTJEN

Contents

Introduction

This chapter describes an interdisciplinary, experiential learning project that combined marketing and communications courses in a domestic violence education campaign. Two professors from different colleges partnered with a local domestic violence service center to enable students to create a community-based social marketing campaign to raise awareness and combat common myths surrounding partner violence. Student assessments indicated success in achieving educational objectives and practical knowledge. The resulting multimedia campaign was well received throughout the state and illustrates opportunities for developing interdisciplinary knowledge and teaching in business and communication studies.

Creating and Executing an Applied Interdisciplinary Campaign for Domestic Violence Prevention

Despite an emerging consensus on the importance of interdisciplinary, applied education, few scholars have attempted to apply this technique to important public health topics, such as domestic violence. The significance of cooperative experiential learning has received a remarkable amount of attention in the marketing education literature (Kolb, 1984; Titus & Petroshius, 1993; Petkus, 2000), but relatively few applied educational efforts are bridging the disciplinary gaps that so often befall universities and public health endeavors (Athaide & Desai, 2005; Crittenden & Wilson, 2006; Locker, 1998). The emergence of integrated marketing communication in the world of business has not been paralleled by a comparable effort to marry business and communication skills in local health programs and community service. As Bobbitt, Inks, Kemp, and Mayo (2000) note, students too frequently isolate concepts and skills learned in different classes without learning how to integrate them. Students pursuing careers in public health or communication may leave academia without a good understanding of the interrelationships that exist among subject areas professionally.

While cross-functional teaching and learning does take place in the marketing classroom, it is clearly not widespread across academia, and what is done tends to be accomplished within traditional pedagogical formats (Crittenden & Wilson, 2006).

The experiential learning project described here was unique insofar as it brought together the marketing and communications classes from two different colleges at a state university. This intermarriage was not without its difficulties, given the differences in models and theories, media selection, segmentation approaches, and curriculum, difficulties further pronounced by the few examples in the literature that exist to guide team teaching approaches to interdisciplinary education (Athaide & Desai, 2005). However, the resulting domestic violence educational project that the classes produced benefitted from its interdisciplinary origins in many ways.

Background

Interdisciplinary Learning as a Process

Bobbitt et al. (2000) discuss how applied learning can create a unique opportunity for integrating disciplines. There are a few examples of projects that have integrated different subject areas in the marketing and communication literatures. Cooper, Carlisle, Gibbs, and Watkins (2001) found that most applied interdisciplinary projects are limited to health care fields, although there are a few examples that combine different types of business courses or science courses together. O'Hara and Shaffer (1995) developed an experiential learning project that combined personal selling and purchasing to teach the roles of buying and selling, while Lunsford and Henshaw (1992) combined research and engineering courses in product development. By integrating across disciplinary boundaries, students may become aware of the relationships that exist among functional units within society and between organizations.

Cause Marketing

The selection of a nonprofit client and social issue as the objective of the marketing campaign enriched the learning process in many ways. The communication studies professor had traditionally addressed social issues so the collaboration necessitated that the marketing professor move in the direction of cause marketing. From a vocational perspective, the choice of a cause marketing objective is supported by recent trends in industry. "Issues of breast cancer awareness, the environment, special needs education, and feeding the hungry have caught the fancy of corporate marketers, with an estimated $6 to $8 billion being transferred from for-profits to non-profits in the United States in 2000" (Gourville & Rangan, 2004, p. 39).

Segmentation research also shows that marketing professionals are using cause marketing increasingly in their business plans. "The 2002 Corporate Citizenship poll conducted by Cone Communications finds that 84% of Americans say they would be likely to switch brands to one associated with a good *cause*, if price and quality are similar" (Bhattacharya & Sen, 2004, p. 10). In a nationwide telephone study of adults 18 years and older by Smith and Alcorn (1991), 45% were likely to switch brands to support a company that donates to charitable causes. Thus, the choice of a nonprofit client and a social cause seemed only to enhance the students' future career opportunities.

Social Issue

Domestic violence was selected as a cause marketing topic because of its prevalence, both locally and nationwide, as well as its association with audience denial. The costs of domestic violence in the United States are enormous. For example, one out of three U.S. women will be beaten, coerced into sex, or otherwise abused during her lifetime; nearly 25% of American women report being raped or physically assaulted by a current or former spouse, cohabiting partner, or date; partner violence results in nearly 2 million injuries and 1,200 deaths nationwide every year; and the financial costs of intimate partner violence in 2003 were estimated at $5.8 billion, including nearly $4.1 billion in the direct costs of medical and mental health care and nearly $1.8 billion in the indirect costs of lost productivity (Finklestein, Corso, & Miller, 2006; Commonwealth Fund Survey, 1998; Tjaden & Thoennes, 1998).

The complexity and sensitivity of domestic violence provided an interesting—and worthy—challenge upon which to apply this interdisciplinary approach to student learning and community education (The Commonwealth Fund, 1998).

Methodology

In summer 2005, two professors initiated a partnership between two colleges at a state university to produce a social marketing campaign for a local domestic violence service center. This was an interdisciplinary effort integrating three classes over two semesters with the goal of providing experiential learning for students with a real outcome for a nonprofit client.

Preclass Planning

Work was allocated by the professors ahead of time among the three classes—social marketing communication (SMC), a spring course offered in the college of arts and sciences' communication department; integrated marketing communication (IMC), a fall course offered in the college of business; and applied marketing communication (AMC), a spring course offered in the college of business. IMC students would synthesize research findings to develop a brand statement and strategy for the client; students from SMC in the spring would research audience reactions to message concepts; and AMC students would concurrently develop and execute message concepts for dissemination in live media. It was agreed that students would work in teams largely within each class and only come together across disciplines for interaction with clients and professionals, and brainstorming sessions.

This project attempted to achieve several educational objectives:

- Highlight the overlap and differences between the fields of mass communication and marketing in their approaches to campaign work
- Teach students how to simultaneously take advantage of expertise from different fields and resolve differences professionally
- Teach students how to operate in a real-world setting and to inspire them by disseminating the fruits of their labor
- Heighten students' awareness of the nonprofit sector, and their ability to apply their skills to an important community service topic
- Improve the domestic violence education and prevention in the community

Professors conducted several key steps of the campaign prior to the start of class. They identified professional colleagues, found a client, planned fundraising, and networked with media partners. Some initial funding was solicited by professors, prior to the semester's start, to pay for anticipated costs of research and creative artwork or advertising. A mini university grant supplied funding for research, and various community organizations donated funds for media. Partnerships with producers, graphic artists, domestic violence experts, and the client (a domestic and sexual violence service organization) were also negotiated by professors to lay the groundwork for the campaign. Students were engaged in the key steps that followed: baseline research, setting objectives, formative research, crafting creative messages, pretesting messages, production, and dissemination.

Fall Course Activities

Baseline Research

Grant funding was used to hire a professional research agency to conduct a randomized mail survey with 2,500 adults to assess baseline levels of attitudes and beliefs about domestic violence in the fall. These data would provide a quantitative benchmark against which to measure the campaign's impact. While the data were collected by professionals, students in both spring classes would design the instrument and analyze and interpret the results. Findings showed that while awareness of domestic violence was high, perceived levels of personal risk for domestic violence were low (Witte, Meyer, & Martell, 2000). Changing these perceived levels of severity and risk—as well as correcting some common myths about domestic violence—would ultimately serve as objectives for campaign messages.

Identifying Target Audience

Since the baseline data collection was still under way, IMC students used 2004 census data and secondary literature on domestic violence awareness to define the campaign targets. They broke the audience down into two very broad segments: (1) reproductive-age women ages 18 to 50, all income levels, most of whom are living in family households, and (2) all men, all ages and income levels, in the two counties. All men were included based on research indicating that more than 90% of perpetrators of abuse are male, and that the tendency is not greater among any particular educational, ethnic, or economic group.

To narrow their focus to more specific targets, IMC students developed a plan to segment the male audience based on their potential response to messages about domestic violence awareness and prevention. Men would fall into three groups: (1) those whose attitudes were sympathetic to the message and needed to be reinforced, (2) those who were resistant to the message and needed to be changed, and (3) those who were well meaning but neutral to the message and needed to be informed. These groups coincidentally fit neatly with the public health stages of change model that the communication professor would use in the spring (Prochaska, DiClemente, & Norcross, 1992) (Table 19.1).

The IMC class also segmented audience members by levels of involvement, an approach that (again, coincidentally) fit with the elaboration likelihood model (Petty, Cacioppo, & Schumann, 1983), another model used by the communications professor in teaching students to design health messages (see Table 19.1). Involved audience members included potential or current victims of abuse, and those who are not directly involved in abuse but might have friends or relatives who are victims. This audience included all women and bystanders (male and female) that were in need of the services. It also included resistant men with attitudes that students deemed necessary to change, such as those who might say, "Who are you to tell me what to do? Mind your own business!" and "She deserves it!"

Uninvolved audience members included those who were not directly involved in abuse, were unaware of anyone experiencing it, and who had not thought about the issue or didn't perceive it as significant. This group needed to change attitudes and increase awareness. The uninvolved audience included men with attitudes students deemed as well meaning but neutral, who might say, "I never really thought about it" or "That does not happen here!" or deemed necessary to reinforce, such as those who might say, "Yes, I feel guilty, help me!" or "I agree, men like that are horrible!"

Setting Objectives

IMC students utilized secondary research to determine that many in the community did not consider domestic violence to be a serious risk for themselves

Table 19.1   Summary of Marketing Concepts and Models

Model	How Used	Significance	Author
Perceptual map	Plotting message vs. competition	Determines playing field on which to win	Perreault & McCarthy (2006)
Elaboration likelihood model	Tailoring message to fit audience level of involvement	Audience segmentation	Petty, Cacioppo, & Schumann (1983)
Means end chain conceptual advertising strategy (MECCAS)	Establishing value of message in consumer's mind	Translates into message strategy	Peter & Olson (2005)
Awareness, interest, desire, and action (AIDA)	Establishing strategy for influencing target	Affects media strategy	Perreault & McCarthy (2006)
Stages of behavior change model	Tailoring to fit audience stage of awareness or intended action	Identifies key message(s)	Prochaska, DiClemente, & Norcross (1992)
Decision-making process	Cognitive vs. affective reasoning	Translates into opportunities	Peter & Olson (2005)

or their families, and were uninvolved in the issue. (This was later confirmed and verified by the baseline findings.) Given this low level of involvement, students in IMC planned an affective path for the message, or feel, think, do (Belch & Belch, 2006, p. 200). Using the communications effects pyramid, the students set communications objectives to reach 80% of the target with a media budget, hoping half of them would "feel," or respond with the affective message, and half of them would respond to the "think" or cognitive objectives. Thus, the marketing objectives were to (1) reach 80% of our target audience, (2) make 40% of them *feel* that family violence is a serious issue and crime, (3) make 20% of targeted males *think* that family violence is not acceptable and 20% of targeted women *think* there is hope and security because of the services offered by the client, and (4) increase levels (*do*) of agreement that domestic violence is a serious issue and in 10% see some change in behavior.

IMC students continued to follow a process of marketing concepts and models to develop a brand position to enable the spring classes to create messages. It was a challenge to apply the subject of domestic violence to a typical marketing model. Models for product marketing are about how to position one's brand versus the competition, but it was not clear what the competition would be in this context. A student solved the problem by suggesting the campaign treat the subject or the message as a product in competition

Table 19.2   Means End Chain Conceptual Advertising Strategy

Levels of Means End Chain	The Message	Elements of the Advertising Strategy
Values	Anger, violated, hard to turn your back, still pretending it isn't real, want to close your eyes	Driving force
Psychosocial consequences	Shame, pain, cycle of violence, pity, "It's better than the alternative"	Leverage point or "hook"
Physical consequences	Jail, injuries, child is displaced and loss of family	Consumer benefits
Attributes	The issue is personal, private, painful, sexist, involves helpless children and innocent bystanders	Message elements

with other messages that are just as painful or difficult, such as Hurricane Katrina, Sri Lanka, Iraq, or Sudan. The first model the students used in the brainstorming process was means end chain conceptual advertising strategy (MECCAS) (Peter & Olson, 2005, p. 448) (Table 19.2).

The students determined the audience's values or myths related to the topic of domestic violence and used these values to plan attitude and awareness change strategy. Attributes of the message were identified as painful as well as private and sexist. The physical consequences of the message involved going to jail or breaking up families and children being uprooted from their family. Despite the many negative associations with domestic violence, the students realized there were also social values that fostered tacit acceptance, insofar as many considered it to be better to accept a violent situation in the home than to face the alternative of breaking up a family. The perceptual map compares the client's message with the competition in terms of the values determined by the students (Perreault & McCarthy, 2006, p. 74) (Table 19.3). In order to compete more effectively with other cause-related messages, the students attempted to make the issue more personal and to address audience denial, or the tendency to want to close one's eyes to the problem in one's own community or in one's own life. And thus, the brand positioning statement became: *Open your eyes.*

Spring Course Activities

Formative Research

Equipped with the baseline research results and the IMC students' brand statement, SMC students were well positioned to further probe audience

Table 19.3 Perceptual Map

Denial Genocide in Sudan Iraq War	Domestic violence HIV testing
Far away Hurricane Katrina Indonesian Tsunami Overexposed	Personal Montana Methamphetamine Campaign Mothers Against Drunk Driving

Note: The value scales on the grid range from messages that are very personal to messages that are perceived as distant, and from messages that are often denied by audiences to messages with which audiences are frequently confronted. The students considered the message of domestic violence prevention to be a product that had to compete with other nonprofit messages. This competitive climate is shown in the perceptual map using examples of competing social causes. This map is intended to make it easier to develop a brand positioning statement that is competitive by ensuring that it is personal and not easily denied.

attitudes and beliefs in relationship to the issue in order to develop effective media strategies. They began the spring semester by reviewing the baseline data and secondary literature on domestic violence to familiarize them with the issue. Once a general understanding had been attained, they recruited focus groups to assess audience levels of perceived severity, risk, and common myths around domestic violence. Five focus groups were conducted with men and women from the community at various business and campus locations. Expert interviews with domestic violence prevention workers and survivors also informed the campaign.

Given their background in communication research, a slightly different, but related, model was used for analysis. Using the extended parallel process model, communication students noted low levels of perceived risk for domestic violence (affecting oneself personally) among the target audience (Witte, Meyer, & Martell, 2000; Rosenstock, Strecher, & Becker, 1988). The model states that an audience must perceive a threat to be both significant (severe) and personal in order to be open to behavior change. The common myths about domestic violence identified by the baseline survey (that victims typically deserve it, or that they can leave any time) were considered to be the perceived barriers to change that needed to be addressed. SMC students identified campaign objectives that fit with the objectives that the IMC students had chosen: (1) to increase perceived risk of domestic violence affecting oneself or one's family, and (2) to decrease the belief that victims can easily leave a violent situation at any time, and that victims typically deserve to be hit. The identification of these myths was buttressed by recent research conducted in New York with 1,200 residents in six communities, measuring the perceptions of the causes of domestic violence (Worden & Carlson, 2005).

In this study, two-thirds of the sample agreed that women could exit violent relationships if they really wanted to, and almost half said that women provoke men. In terms of perceived risks, this study put childhood exposure to violence as "least interpretable." The students had found through secondary research (the statistic is used in the creative) that childhood exposure for boys was a very high risk. Hence, the students agreed that the effort to change myths and increase perceived risk would fit neatly with the "feel" and "think" objectives identified in the fall.

Crafting Messages

Both the social marketing and applied marketing students were charged with drafting creative television messages. The AMC students followed the awareness, interest, desire, and action (AIDA) model (Perreault & McCarthy, 2006, p. 324) with a specific plan for the involved and uninvolved audiences. Because of their preexisting high levels of interest in the topic, involved audiences were expected to be interested in getting more information or take other action. The majority of the community, however, was shown by baseline research to be uninvolved and would therefore only take an affective path in response to the message. The students deduced that uninvolved audiences would be emotionally affected by the attention-getting messages, such as messages mentioning the negative consequences of domestic violence (e.g., injuries, jail, and child displacement), but would not become interested in the details or taking immediate action. Messages tailored to the uninvolved would therefore attempt to change attitudes only and plant a seed for action later (see Tables 19.4 to 19.7).

Print Development

AMC students developed concepts for three newspaper ads, a billboard, and a poster. The poster concept, called "Morgue," showed a photo of two feet and a toe tag with a headline that read, "Mommy, wake up." The client was concerned that the ad would potentially be victim blaming by indicating the woman was a bad mother for not being there for her children. After much deliberation, this concern was resolved by adding the following statistic: "47% of women killed in Montana last year were murdered by their husbands or boyfriends" (Figure 19.1). The billboard was based on the focus group data showing that consequences of jail could be a deterrent to abuse. A photo found on the Internet by a student of a young man behind bars was used, with a headline that reads, "Welcome home, tough guy. Domestic violence is a crime." The original version, "Don't think you can get away with it," had to be changed due to client concerns that it would be laughed at by the target audience, since not many men actually do go to jail for abuse (Figure 19.2).

Table 19.4   "Brain Injury" Television Script

Video	S/F	Audio
Shot comes into the kitchen.	Phone ringing.	"Hello? Hey man, what's going on?"
A man is on the phone, drinking a jug of milk.		"You wont believe what she just did. She just pushes my buttons."
He talks to his buddy.		"What do you mean? Is she okay?"
He starts to get frustrated with person on phone and clenches fists.		"She should just do what I say."
Shot pans to woman on floor. She is lying there, lifeless.		Voice-over: Domestic violence is the leading cause of brain injuries in women.
Close-up of face of woman— eyes wide open, obvious brain injury.		
Tag: Domestic and Sexual Violence Services 425-2222		"I don't know man. She's not moving."
OPEN YOUR EYES		(Sirens)

Pretesting Messages

SMC students were responsible for pretesting messages drafted by both spring classes. Message concepts were first pretested and refined by peers before being formally tested with members of the target audience in focus groups. Four pretest focus groups were organized, two with men, two with women, to assess the effectiveness and reaction of the messages among audience members, and the messages were revised according to the input received. Pretest comments resulted in changing the beer to milk in one ad, in order to disassociate the problem from alcohol, which reviewers said was mistakenly considered a cause of abuse. The ad was also edited to give the perpetrator more emotion—fear or regret—to highlight the consequences of his actions (Table 19.4). Family spots tested well; the best one told the story of a family barbecue that evolved into the man hitting his wife in front of their children for "burning" the food. It was combined with an ending that showed the man eating in jail to illustrate that domestic violence is a crime, punishable by jail (Table 19.6). Another spot addressed the child exposure risk, meaning that abuse is handed down across generations, by showing a little boy punching his teddy bear after observing his father hitting his mother (Table 19.7).

The creative process was chaotic and personal feelings were involved. In the end, staying consistent and meeting objectives won the day. Research was utilized to make the campaign as response oriented as possible. Both

Table 19.5   "MP3 Player" Television Script

Video	Audio
Woman in her 30s is dressed in athletic apparel. She is standing by the front door with an MP3 player in her hands.	Male voice sounds like a motivational speaker, soft music in the background.
She turns on the player. She places the headphones on and begins her morning jog.	"I prepared this tape for you to enjoy on your morning run."
She continues to jog around the neighborhood. As the time passes, she starts to look worn down and her pace gets slower. The effects of the words start to show. Two neighbors, also jogging, pass her, unaware, as she slows down.	"You're ugly, you are worthless, don't even think of leaving, where would you go, who would believe you, you can leave but the children are mine, it's all your fault, why do you make me do this," etc.
As the woman nears her house, you see a once beautiful woman, now beaten down by words. Her whole posture has crippled and her pace has slowed down to a walk.	Continue with insults. Drifts off.
She gets home and the doormat to her house says "Welcome to Paradise"	Voice-over, young female: One in three women in the U.S. will experience domestic violence at some point in her lifetime—with or without broken bones.
Tag: Domestic and Sexual Violence Services 425-2222 OPEN YOUR EYES (graphic)	

professors worked very hard to make sure their students understood the purpose of the exercise, to put the objectives above personal needs.

Production

AMC students took over the execution of the messages, working with partner producers and graphic artists from the community, recruiting acting talent and locations for production of the television public service announcements (Table 19.5). The students worked on publicity and promotion of the campaign, revised script wording where necessary, and wrote about the process and perceived results of their work.

Discussion

Student Outcomes

Students who participated in the campaign achieved higher scores in their overall final marketing discipline assessments, and communication students reported remarkable life-changing experiences as a result of the class.

Table 19.6   "Barbecue" Television Script

Client:	DSVS
Project:	BBQ
Length:	30 seconds

Video	Audio
Middle-class family outdoors cooking BBQ dinner—Mom, Dad, two children ages 7 and 10, boy and girl.	(Piano music, sounds of laughter)
Close-up of Mom cooking the hot dogs on the grill.	Woman's voice: "Food's ready! Come and get it!"
Father walks over to grill with plate in hand. Looks at food. Frowns.	Man's voice: "Why don't you ever learn?! You burned the food again, you idiot! Now what am I going to eat."
Man picks up the grill and dumps food on the ground.	
Children cower under picnic table.	(Sound effect: sizzling, big slam sound)
Man picks up spatula and strikes woman's head. Woman falls to ground.	(Sound effect: Loud cracking)
	Children's voices: Mommy! Mommy?
He slowly turns around, and instead of being with his family, he is in a different place.	
The table is now one of those long tables in a prison cafeteria, and the family has been replaced by fellow prisoners eating from trays.	Voice-over: The state of Montana feeds hundreds of perpetrators of domestic violence every year.
Tag: Domestic and Sexual Violence Services 425-2222	
OPEN YOUR EYES	Open your eyes.

Student outcomes are shown by qualitative data from the communication students and quantitative data in marketing. Ninety percent of the marketing students who participated in this campaign achieved an A in the marketing senior's capstone course compared to 45% of the marketing students overall. Based on assessment tools, students in the applied courses learned theoretical concepts and models better than others, lending further support for the premise that students learn better through hands-on work than through lectures and reading alone.

Communication student outcomes were assessed by comments written in their final papers. Most pertinent to this paper were their self-reported lessons in (1) the importance of cause marketing, (2) strategies of campaign design, (3) research methods, and (4) empowerment and confidence in their ability to affect change through application of their communication skills. In expressing his struggle to appreciate the cause

Table 19.7   "Teddy Bear" Television Script

Video	Audio
Little boy plays with teddy bear in hs bedroom and hears parents argue.	
Boy moves into the inside of the house in the living room.	Husband and wife arguing very loudly about money.
Show little boy peeking out of his bedroom door.	
The husband pushes his wife down.	Husband yells: "Shut up, just shut up!"
The little boy is playing on the floor with his teddy bear. He starts shaking the bear violently.	Boy's voice: "Shut up! Shut up!"
Tag: Domestic and Sexual Violence Services 425-2222	Boys who experience domestic violence in the home are twice as likely to become abusers themselves.
OPEN YOUR EYES	Open your eyes.

selected, the only male in the class writes about the value he perceives of the class project:

> This class was a great experience. At first I was a little bit nervous but, to be honest, I learned a lot and loved the topic of domestic and sexual violence. Before this class I was one of those people who were truly unaware that this was such a major problem in today's society. (Reese Davis, personal communication, April 30, 2006)

Another student wrote about both the importance of cause marketing and her resulting personal empowerment:

> I can honestly say this is one of the best and more insightful courses I have taken in my college career. Not only is it helpful for a future in social marketing/nonprofit marketing, but we have worked hard and collaborated for a greater good.... I now leave this semester an educated female, and wholeheartedly plan to continue to journey on my own against domestic violence. (Tara Osbourne, personal communication, April 30, 2006)

A health promotion student from the communications class wrote about campaign strategies. She echoed lessons from Andreasen (1995) about the importance of audience involvement in campaign design:

> I have learned so much from this campaign. I have learned not only about domestic violence but also about human behavior. In creating any campaign, I have learned that it is important to put yourself in the shoes of the audience. In addressing an issue such as domestic violence, or any other social issue, it is

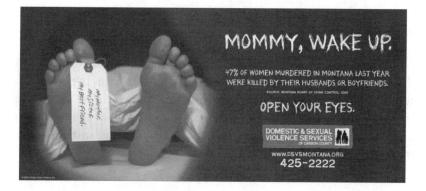

Figure 19.1 "Morgue" newspaper ad.

Figure 19.2 Billboard advertisement.

important to realize that the public may not have ever thought about the issue that you, as a social marketer, may be very passionate about. (Jennifer Arnold, personal communication, April 30, 2006)

Another student called for a broader media mix than had been utilized, such as radio, bench ads, speaking engagements, and involving survivors as peer educators, indicating her marketing savvy for improving campaign effectiveness through multiple channels.

Many students wrote about their personal dedication to continue community service as a result of the campaign. One example of a student being empowered by the campaign follows:

I will continue standing up for my younger sisters when I see and hear of abuse in their life as I have in many cases in [this county]. But now I have numbers to give to them and tell them of different agencies that are out there for their benefit. Because of this class I will also be able to advertise by word of mouth in the different groups that I am among about the upcoming

PSAs that will be broadcast. (Holly Barnhart, personal communication, April 30, 2006)

Although these results have questionable reliability and are difficult to replicate in any quantifiable way, the tone of the students is powerful and thought provoking. While many students made suggestions for strategies that would improve the campaign's effectiveness, or the course design, not a single student expressed regret for having participated in the course or doubted that he or she had done a good job.

Community Outcomes

Feedback from the community included ADDY awards and the Montana Broadcaster Public Service Award for 2007. Comments in general were widely positive reactions, and perceived effectiveness of the messages showed target variances anecdotally. Older, more affluent women were moved by the "not able to exit" myth message and not moved by the "woman provoked him" myth message. Younger, less affluent audiences were moved in just the opposite way. This agrees with the social segmentation results found by the Worden and Carlson study in 2005.

Outcomes of the campaign in terms of affecting attitude and behavior change in the community were measured by a follow-up survey administered in 2007. This survey was nearly identical to the one in 2006 (using all mailable addresses as the sample frame) of 2,500 men and women in two Montana counties both before and after the campaign.

The overall response rate for usable responses to the baseline survey was 17%, and 15% for the follow-up (or posttest) survey, well above the anticipated response rates. A total of 21% (n = 78) of respondents said yes in response to the question, "Do you recall having seen any TV or print advertisements from the 'Open Your Eyes' campaign to prevent domestic violence?" Self-reported exposure was equal for men and women. Twenty-one percent (n = 42) of women reported having seen the ads, as did 21% (n = 36) of men.

The most common channel for exposure was television. When asked where the ad was seen (TV, billboards, newspaper, or posters), 15% (n = 55) marked television, 7% (n = 25) marked billboards, and the remaining categories were unmarked.

Six percent of the respondents reported taking action, and our objective for taking action or *doing* was 10%, as stated above. Of these respondents 5% (n = 4) said they tried to help others, 2.5% (n = 2) said they left a relationship, 6.4% (n = 5) recommended someone else leave a relationship, 3.8% (n = 3) intervened in an abusive situation, 2.5% (n = 2) said they called the police, and 10% (n = 10) said they took some kind of action as a result of seeing the ads.

Significant differences emerged in nearly all attitudinal items after the campaign took place—although women appeared much more receptive to the campaign than men, a result that is discussed at length in another article (Keller, Wilkinson, Otjen, 2009). Women were much more likely to increase their perceived severity of and susceptibility to domestic violence, while men were more likely to decrease their perceived threat. Awareness of domestic violence services increased significantly for both genders, and logistical regression analysis showed that this awareness was 3.2 times greater among respondents exposed to the campaign.

This augers well for public health campaigners as the mass media strategy here has proven effective at reaching its target audience(s). This degree of audience reach is particularly impressive given the nonprofit nature of the project, and the fact that most of the media funding was obtained through donations, pro bono rates, or public service announcements. The degree of audience recall is also impressive given the fact that the advertisements were all creatively and strategically designed by undergraduate marketing and communication students (albeit with professional help in production).

References

Andreasen, A. (1995). *Marketing social change: Changing behavior to promote health, social development and the environment*. New York: Jossey-Bass.

Athaide, G. A., & Desai, H. B. (2005). Design and implementation of an interdisciplinary marketing/management course on technology and innovation management. *Journal of Marketing Education, 27*, 239–249.

Belch, G. E., & Belch, M. A. (2006). *Advertising and promotion*. New York: McGraw Hill.

Bhattacharya, C. B., & Sen, S. (2004). Doing better at doing good: When, why, and how consumers respond to corporate social responsibility initiatives. *California Management Review, 47*, 9–24.

Bobbitt, M. L., Inks, S. A., Kemp, K. J., & Mayo, D. T. (2000). Integrating marketing courses to enhance team-based experiential learning. *Journal of Marketing Education, 22*, 15–24.

The Commonwealth Fund (1998). *1998 Survey of Women's Health*. New York: Louis Harris & Associates, Inc.

Cooper, H., Carlisle, C., Gibbs, T., & Watkins, L. (Eds.). (2001). Developing an evidence base for interdisciplinary learning: A systematic review. *Journal of Advanced Nursing, 35*, 228–237.

Crittenden, V. L., & Wilson, E. J. (2006). An exploratory study of cross-functional education in the undergraduate marketing curriculum. *Journal of Marketing Education, 28*, 81–86.

Dommeyer, C. J. (1986). A comparison of the individual proposal and team project in the marketing research course. *Journal of Marketing Education, 8*, 30–38.

Finklestein, E, A., Corso, P. S. & Miller, T. R. (2006). *Incidence and economic burden of injuries in the United States*. London: Oxford University Press.

Gourville, J., & Rangan, K. (2004). Valuing the cause of marketing relationship. *California Management Review, 47*, 38–57.

Kellers, S., Wilkinson, T., & Otjen, A. (2009). Gender-Specific Reactions to a Domestic Violence Campaign. Unintended Effects of Social Marketing. Presented at the Association for Marketing and Healthcare Research, March 3–4, Jackson Hole, Wyoming.

Kolb, D. A. (1984). *Experiential learning: Experience as the source of learning and development.* Englewood Cliffs, NJ: Prentice Hall.

Locker, K. O. (1998). The role of association in business communication in shaping business communication as an academic discipline challenge. *Journal of Business Communication, 35*, 14–49.

Lunsford, D. A., & Henshaw, J. M. (1992). Integrating courses in marketing research and engineering design. *Journal of Marketing Education, 14*, 10–19.

O'hara, B. S., & Shaffer, T. R. (1995). Details and student perceptions of an experiential program for personal selling and purchasing classes. *Journal of Marketing Education, 17*, 41–49.

Perreault, W. D., & McCarthy, J. (2006). *Essentials of marketing: A global marketing approach.* New York: McGraw Hill.

Peter, P. J., & Olson, J. C. (2005). *Consumer behavior and marketing strategy.* New York: McGraw Hill.

Petkus, E. (2000). A theoretical and practical framework for service-learning in marketing; Kolb's experiential learning cycle. *Journal of Marketing Education, 229*, 64–70.

Petty, R. E., Cacioppo, J. T., & Schumann, D. (1983). Central and peripheral routes to advertising effectiveness: The moderating role of involvement. *Journal of Consumer Research, 15*, 379–385.

Prochaska, J. O., DiClemente, C. C., & Norcross, J. C. (1992). In search of how people change: Applications to addictive behaviors. *American Psychologist, 47*, 1102–1114.

Rosenstock, I. M., Strecher, V. J., & Becker, M. H. (1988). Social learning theory and the health belief model. *Health Education Quarterly, 15*, 183–197.

Smith, S. M., & Alcorn, D. S. (1991). Cause marketing: A new direction in the marketing of corporate responsibility. *Journal of Services Marketing, 5*, 21–38.

Titus, P. A., & Petroshius, S. M. (1993). Bringing consumer behavior to the workbench: An experiential approach. *Journal of Marketing Education, 15*, 20–41.

Tjaden, P., & Thoennes, N. (1998, November). *Prevalence, incidence, and consequences of violence against women: Findings from the National Violence Against Women Survey research in brief.* Washington, DC: U.S. Department of Justice.

Witte, K., Meyer, G., & Martell, D. (2000). *Effective health risk messages: A step-by-step guide.* Thousand Oaks, CA: Sage Publications.

Worden, A., & Carlson, B. (2005). Attitudes and beliefs about domestic violence: Results of a public opinion survey II. *Journal of Interpersonal Violence, 20*, 1219–1243.

Index